THE
REALM
of
GLORY

THE EXPANDED EDITION

A DIVINE REVELATION OF HOW TO TAP INTO HIGHER REALMS, GREATER DEPTHS AND DEEPER TERRITORIES OF THE GLORY REALM

D1359803

APOSTLE FREQUENCY REVELATOR

GLOBAL DESTINY
PUBLISHING HOUSE

ISBN: 978-1-5217066-5-7 (e-book)

The author has made every effort to trace and acknowledge sources, resources and individuals. In the event that any images or information has been incorrectly attributed or credited, the author will be pleased to rectify these omissions at the earliest opportunity.

Scripture quotations are all taken from the Holy Bible, the New King James Version (Authorized Version). First published in 1611. Quoted from the KJV Classic Reference Bible, Copyright © 1983 by The Zondervan Corporation

Published by the Author © Global Destiny Publishing House,

No. 128 Peter Road, Greystone Office Park, Sandton, 2031, South Africa

Website: www.globaldestinypublishers.co.za

Email: frequency.revelator@gmail.com

Phone: 0027622436745 * 0027785416006 * 0027797921646

Book layout and cover designed by Godwin T. Mupakairi for Global Destiny Publishing House.

*****Propagating Deeper Revelations of God's Prophetic Word,*

Divine Presence and Resurrection Power

From The United Kingdom (UK)

*To The Extreme Ends of The Word*****

DEDICATION

In retrospect to the previous version of the catalogue of revelations on the Glory Realm titled, "The Realm of Glory," which has tremendously impacted the masses across the globe, this publication remains an exclusive property of Heaven, as it has been given birth to by the Holy Ghost in the Throne Room of Heaven. As a product of the effulgence of the glory of God birthed in the deepest territories of the Glory Realm, it is geared at propagating deeper revelations of God's Word, Divine presence and Glory from the Throne Room to the extreme ends of the World. Therefore, this book is dedicated to millions of believers, whom through the abundance of these revelations, shall be positioned to move and function in higher realms of God's glory and propagate it to the extreme quarters of the earth.

Metaphorically speaking, Heavens are pregnant with the possibilities of God and the womb of the Spirit is rumbling, ready to unleash the glory of God over the masses. The waters are breaking forth and the flood of the river of glory is gushing out. Clouds have been cloud-seeded by the power of the Holy Ghost and now saturated to the brim of full spiritual capacity. The glory cloud is now hovering over the earth, heralding its readiness to pour out of the Heavens and precipitate its contents over the masses. The waves are shifting and the skies are vibrating with a whirl of extraordinary divine aura invading the natural realm, culminating in a Heaven-on-earth landscape. The atmosphere is reverberating with the sound of the Wind of the Spirit, billowing in the

v

direction of the earth, in what Elijah described in prophetic language as the sound of the abundance of rain.

In tandem with this move of the Spirit, is the rise of a rare breed of believers to which this book is dedicated, who are surfacing over the horizon and rising beyond the confines and dictates of the realm of senses, to unlock the Heavens and precipitate the glory of God to the extreme ends of the earth. The masses are about to be dazzled to the last degree as you step out of the convictions of ordinary life of mediocrity and complacency into the realm of the undefinable, uncharted and unrecorded miracles, signs and wonders, to launch the world into an arena of divine exploits. God is about to use you to explode in the demonstration of His glory such that the masses will witness a factory of mind-blowing signs and wonders, coupled with a warehouse of jaw-dropping miracles, that will culminate in an inventory of breathtaking testimonies, across the globe.

As the viscosity of the Glory cloud unreservedly precipitates supernatural rains over the earth in this critical season, the supernatural realm is no longer a secret as Heavens's contents are unfolded to a heightened degree. The Throne Room is now our living room as we are catapulted to the Third Heaven, to unresevedly partake of what Paul described as, "something inexpressible for man to tell". The glory cloud is no longer a mystery as it is visibly seen manifesting its density in the natural realm. Supernatural rains are tangibly precipitating on the earth and the wealth of Heaven manifested through the Golden Rain (Gold dust and other precious stones) is increasingly littering the surface of the earth. Angels are no longer strangers as they are seen walking visibly in the natural realm just like fellow human beings. Therefore, welcome to the world in which it is naturally supernatural to live, move and operate in the Glory Realm.

FOREWORD BY APOSTLE GABRIEL COKE

This publication is a quintessential model of how believers can ignite a spark of the glory invasion that will culminate in the prolonged prevalence of an atmosphere of Heaven on earth. It explores the hidden mysteries of God's glory and thus, ushers a rebirth of new manifestations of glory that humanity has never seen before. As a custodian of divine truth, Apostle Frequency Revelator has endeavoured to unveil, unpack and uncover the divine revelation of these new realms of glory so as to awaken an insatiable appetite, perennial hunger and unquenchable thirst for the global demonstration of the glory of God in this final chapter of human history. He has made a conscientious effort to download Throne Room revelations and decode the divinely coded mysteries of the Glory realm that will catapult you to the highest realms of glory never experienced before. This insightful, refreshing, profound and biblically sound revelation gives you a penetrating look behind the curtain of how the glory of God is administered from the Throne Room of Heaven and how humanity in the extreme quarters of the world can splash into the rain of glory which Heaven is precipitating on planet earth at this time. The central theme of this publication is to uncover the knowledge gap in the body of Christ through the exegesis of divine truths and mysteries of the new waves of glory encapsulated in the Word of God, so that multitudes of believers can take a revolutionary leap into the fullness of the glory. Through a hermeneutical exposition of biblical truths, in this book, Apostle Frequency Revelator has removed the veil of mystery from the dynamic tandem of God's glory, paving a way for millions across the globe to delve into the greater depths of the miraculous. Therefore, if you are hungry to take the glory of God to the next level in your life, then get ready to have your life transformed as you take a quantum leap into the Glory Realm.

The Realm of Glory

This book is jam-packed with revelations that will blow your mind.! It takes you on a journey through the looking glass into the unlimited possibilities of the Glory Realm, debunking the myths and misconceptions which for ages have been ingrained in the minds of the masses. This publication is a foretaste of what it means to live in the realities of the Glory Realm, unearthing the hidden mysteries which the Apostle Paul penned as, *"something inexpressible for man to tell "*. Therefore, if you are tired of being a sailor or existing on the shores of tradition and religion, this book is the right recipe for you. It will blow up your mind and awaken you to an arena of divine consciousness in which living in the Glory Realm is a norm and visitations to the Throne Room of Heaven is a normal occurrence. Therefore, prepare your world to be turned upside down and your traditions, religion and theology to be messed up. The whistle is blowing and it's time to sail into the great adventure of this unknown dimension. Congratulations and welcome to the journey into the Glory Realm!

- Apostle Gabriel Coke

ACKNOWLEDGEMENTS

This provocative publication is primarily dedicated to the Holy Ghost who is the Author and the Finisher of the deep mysteries and Throne Room revelations encapsulated in it. It is the Holy Ghost who trained me in matters of moving in the higher realms of God's glory and awakened my consciousness to a rapsody of revelations on the new realms of glory so as to align humanity in the extreme quarters of the world with the blueprints of Heaven in this final chapter of human history. Hence, without Him, I would have nothing to talk about! He has made the Glory Realm more real to me than the reality we are living in the natural realm such that everywhere I go, I am more conscious of the tangibility of the Glory Cloud in the Glory Realm in which my spirit operate than the natural realm in which my body is resident. It is this visible Glory Cloud that has opened an atmosphere of "Heaven on Earth" over my life as it constantly releases a rain of revelations, culminating in the volumes of publications I have written. I'm humbled by His demonstrative love for dispatching Angels who work in the Department of Revelation in Heaven, to collaborate with me in accentuating avenues in the realm of the spirit to awaken my spirit to a flood of revelations and deeper mysteries of the Glory Realm, never known since the history of mankind. To God be the glory!

I would like to express my deep and unparalleled gratitude to our frontline generals in the *Glory Realm*: Apostle Guillermo Maldonado of King Jesus International Ministries (USA), Apostle Dr Renny G. McLean of Global Glory International Ministries and Prophet David Herzog of David Herzog Ministries, for their deeper insights into the realities of the Glory Realm and for enlightening me in the integral matters of operating in God's glory. It is through their tutelage that I was awakened into the reality of living in the Glory Realm and the need to propagate the *creative miracles of glory* to the furthest extremes of the world. Scientifically speaking, if you mix different gases, you create a bomb. By the same token, securing an optimum combination of different insights from these great men of God has sparked an explosion of revelations on the Glory Realm. Like highly skilled sailors, hand-picked for a treacherous expedition, each of these authors has masterfully conveyed their personal insights in the Glory Realm which has culminated in this beautiful collage of unfolding wisdom titled *"The Realm of Glory"*.

Special thanks goes to Apostle - Prophet Maphosa the President of the Manifest Sons of God Movement (MSG), Apostle Chris Lord Hills of the Supernatural Church, Bishop D.J Comfort of Favours Cathedral Church and Pastor Chris the President of Christ Embassy. Words fail to capture or contain the gratitude I have for my own staff who have typified a new type of man coming forth on the earth, rising beyond the confines and dictates of the realm of time, to access higher realms of glory: Pastor Moses Vhikey my Director for Christ Resurrection Movement, Nicole Campher my Marketing Director for Kingdom Millionaires Global Investments (KMGI) (Pty) Ltd, Pastor Gabriel Coky, Pastor Patson May, Pastor Victor Ekwunife, Prophet Ron and Dr. Franklin, for demonstrating an unquestionable thirst, perennial hunger and an insatiable appetite to pursue the glory of God. I would like to extend a hand of appreciation to Prophetess Emelda and Maryna De Canha, my manager, for her relentless inspiration. Further thanks goes to my siblings namely, Kaizer, Target, Keeper, Colleter and Presence Nkomo for their love and support in every way. Thanks to my best college students who have now become part of my family namely, Precious Akapelwa, Clarissa Strachan, Chantel Dickson, Shaheena Sherif, Lana Holmes, Phylicia Green, Felicia Roopram, Jessica Venter, Monique Depolt, Poshee-Lee Ross, Trace-Lee Botha, Roxanne Osborn and many others. To Author House (UK), I recognize that this project would not have been possible without your assistance. Thanks for heeding God's call to have these revelations propagated from the United Kingdom (UK) to the furthest extremes of the world. To God be the glory!

- Apostle Frequency Revelator

CONTENT

PREFACE

Are you experiencing the effulgence of God's glory in every sphere of human endeavour in this end time season? Have you ever thought of taping into higher realms, greater depths, deeper territories and immeasurable dimensions of God's glory to unlock *Heaven on earth* in this Kairos moment? Have you ever envisaged being catapulted into the highest realms of glory and thus, unreservedly used by God as a divine instrument to propagate, disseminate and proliferate the newly unfolding blueprints of the glory of God to the furthest extremes of the world? Whatever the case might be, you need to be awakened to a divine revelation of the *Glory Realm* so that you can be ignited by spiritual passion to experience the reality of its invasion, either in your personal life, ministry, business and every facet of human existence. Therefore, don't you dare stay in the same place; there is more for you in God in terms of deeper territories, newer realities and higher realms of glory than what you might be currently experiencing. Hence, you need to take your foot off the brakes of religion and tradition so that you can accelerate into the new realms of glory which God is unfolding from the Heavenly realm. In this end time season, you will have to stop clinging on the shoreline and delve into the river of glory as God is calling men and women to step out of the convictions of ordinary life of mediocrity and complacency into a realm of overflowing, explosive and electrifying glory. It is worth exploring the divine truth that a plethora of revelations on the glory realm are unreservedly available for exploration and discovery especially in this season of *glory invasion*, hence it is imperative that you become so infused, mingled and enraptured in the glory realm in order to explore the mysteries of this unknown dimension. As you decode the divinely coded mysteries on the glory realm encapsulated in this publication, you will begn to explode in the demonstration of creative miracles, signs and wonders that will dazzle the minds of religious charlatans and ruffle the feathers of those comfortable with the status quo.

It is of paramount significance to unveil the divine truth that there are realms of God's personality being revealed now that were not known five minutes ago. The angels are parading around the throne, revealing the new realms of glory that they haven't seen before. The glory of God at the *Throne Room* is constantly evolving, with each change reflected through the radiation of different colours. Like birth pangs signalling the time of delivery, things are being released from the Heaven's *Throne Room* that have been preserved through the ages for this particular hour. The *glory realm* is becoming more real than the reality we are living in the natural realm. Therefore, the time has come for us to align ourselves with the blueprints of Heaven as the glory of God is unreservedly radiating upon the masses in the furthest extremes of the world. In this final chapter of human history, God's dream for you is to be catapulted to the highest realms of glory in the *Throne Room*, to see the unseen, hear the unheard and know the unknowable, such that you no longer return to the natural realm of reasoning, ever again!.

Prophetically speaking, a new day in the spirit is dawning. There is a new dimension of glory surfacing on the horizon. The skies are changing and the waves are shifting. Tremendous manifestations of new realms of glory are surfacing on the horizon as the Body of Christ is catapulted right to the ultimate climax of God's glory on earth. The Lord is echoing the same words which He spoke through the voice of Isaiah and He is saying, *"I'm doing a new thing! They are created now, and not so long ago, you have not heard of them before today, so you cannot say, "Yes, I knew them"* (Isaiah 48:7). God is about to explode in the demonstration of signs and wonders by doing something so brand new that we don't yet have the language to describe it, neither do we have any vocabulary to speak about it. It would be like what Paul described as, *"Something inexpressible for man to tell"* because there won't be any vernacular, jargon or vocabulary good enough to define it. The reason why God calls it a *"new thing"* it's because it doesn't have a name as yet. It's a brand new phenomenon unfolding from the *Throne Room* of Heaven such that even the angels are still trying to comprehend it. It doesn't exist in our dictionary nor does it have a reference point. Hence, we will not call it by the name we used in the past because then, we would need a new vocabulary to describe it. God said, *"Down through the ages, I have given every man and woman a foretaste of my glory but what is coming now, it's never been seen"*. There is a rebirth of new manifestations in these end times such that humanity will not be able to look at it or recognise it because it will be completely fresh and brand new just like when *manna,* the food of angels was rained down on earth for the first time from Heaven. Therefore, in this season of the *glory invasion,* you need to break loose from the old and step into the new realms of glory so that you can impact the nations with the fresh spark of God's glory.

My solemn intent in this publication therefore is to act as a custodian of divine truth in the capacity of an apostle, to unveil, unpack and uncover the divine revelation of these *new realms of glory* so as to awaken an insatiable appetite, perennial hunger and unquenchable thirst for the global demonstration of the glory of God in this season. This insightful, refreshing, profound and biblically sound writing gives you a penetrating look behind the curtain of how the glory of God is administered from the *Throne Room* of Heaven. Therefore, the sole purpose of this writing is to uncover the knowledge gap in the body of Christ through the exegesis of divine truths and mysteries of the glory encapsulated in the Word of God, so that many believers can tap into the fullness of the glory. Through a hermeneutical presentation of biblical truths, in this book, Apostle Frequency Revelator has removed the veil of mystery from the dynamic tandem of God's glory, paving a way for millions across the globe to delve into the greater depths of the miraculous.

To cement this divine revelation of glory with reference to prophetic evidence, God said,

> *"Son, declare in the hearing of all nations that a season of the invasion of end time glory has just begun. There are realms of My Glory that have not been revealed yet. I have created deeper realms in the Heavens that have not yet been known. There is a reservoir of the effulgence of My glory that has remained largely untapped in the Heavens and have yet to be manifested on the earth. The angels have not seen all the Glory in Me. The living creatures, the Cherubim and Seraphim have not seen all the Glory in Me. As the angelic hosts have to go from Glory to Glory, so must you must go from Glory to Glory too. Therefore, everywhere you go, elevate My people into an atmosphere of worship and enter the glory zone. When they worship, the door of Heaven opens, and they will see another side of My Glory and power that has never been seen in the days gone by."*

Prophetically speaking, we are living in the days of the outpouring of unimaginable waves of glory as prophesied through the voice of Prophet Habakkuk that,

> *In the last days, knowledge shall increase and the earth shall be filled with the knowledge of the glory of God* (Habakkuk 2:14).

This implies that we are living right on the brink of an age when natural knowledge has increased exponentially as science is making newer discoveries and tremendous innovative technologies are being developed. The medical world has opened up new ways of diagnosing patients such that cures for many illnesses have been found and new ideas and phenomenal inventions in the business world and many other facets of human existence are springing up. At the same time, God is also unsealing areas of His knowledge in the arena of glory. He has never wanted to be a mystery to His people, and throughout the ages, He has manifested His nature, character and power in divergent ways. In this new age of His end time plan for humanity, God has begun to reveal tremendous manifestations of new realms of His glory to the present generation, igniting His final move on the planet earth, to bring multitudes to faith in Him. While humanity has been riddled by many best-kept mysteries and secrets embedded in our universe since time immemorial, paradigms are shifting and lids are being lifted off the pots as knowledge (*secular, scientific and biblical*) is increasing at an astronomical and unbelievable speed right now. This is the time of knowledge and *revelation explosion* and truly an end time biblical sensation! We must therefore be ready to shift with the Lord's movements in order to flow in the fullness of what He is doing in this final chapter of human history.

It is a greater truth that the supreme calling of every Christian is to walk in the realm of God's glory since we were born into that realm. God never designed man to be a casual visitor in the realm of the spirit but to be a permanent residence of the supernatural realm. The Glory realm is the realm of our birth; it's where we were born into the glory. That's were our true identity and origin is. We were created in the realm of glory. We are from there; our origin is in the glory. The reality is that when we are born again, God places His glory in our spirit so that we receive the divine *"breath of life"* and His spiritual DNA. As custodians of God's glory, it is therefore part of our genetic make-up and nature to ignite a spark of the glory invasion that will culminate in an atmosphere of *Heaven on earth*. Did you know that the original atmosphere of the earth was the glory of God and not the excruciatingly high temperatures and ice cold freezing wheather that we experience today? As the ocean is to a fish, so was the environment of Eden to Adam. While the modern man inhales oxygen to live, God would exhale His glory so that the original man could inhale the glory of God to sustain him. This unveils the truth that man was created to abundantly live and bask in the atmosphere of God's glory since he had the distinction to possess the DNA of God as a God-breathed, God-inspired and God-being on earth.

The greater truth is that it's only after the fall in the Garden of Eden that man had to reciprocate with strenuous spiritual sacrifices in order to connect back to the realm of glory which originally used to be his playground. What the modern day man call a *"prayer"* was originally a casual talk with God and what he calls a *"fast"* was not even part of the vocabulary of Heaven because the body of the original man only needed the glory to sustain it and not food. The appetite for food was activated the minute they ate from the tree of knowledge of good and evil. The greater truth is that man was originally not required to undertake any rigorous spiritual exercises such as *praying and fasting* in order to qualify to operate in the realm of glory because living, functioning and operating in the glory realm is part of his nature and DNA as a God-being. However, it is a typical scenario in today's church that many cling on to the short-sighted veiw that if only we just fasted and prayed more, somehow our lives would be an ambassadorship of God's glory, only to realize later that all we have done is fasted, prayed and aligned our spiritual position in the realm of the spirit but still have not provoked the glory of God into manifestation. Those spiritual exercises are good in some respects as they enable us to move swiftly in the dimension of the spirit, but they may not necessarily trigger an outbreak of the glory of God in its full measure. It is only through the sovereignty of God's grace, coupled with *faith* and *revelation* that can get us beyond this limited dimension into the supernatural realm.

It is worth exploring the divine truth that there are new waves of glory that have not yet manifested on the earth and *revelation knowledge* is the master key to unlocking these hidden mysteries of God's glory and pressing into the new realms of glory. It is an indispensable necessity to accessing the gates of the supernatural and unlocking the flood of glory that can precipitate over the masses in the furthest extremes of the world. The truth is that God will not go beyond the level of revelation that you have about Him, hence the concept of *"knowledge of the glory"* is critical in sparking off the *glory invasion* in this end time season. However, it is one thing to, *"know about the glory"*, and yet another thing to have, *"the knowledge of the glory."* The greatest challenge facing multitudes of believers across a broad spectrum of Christian faith is that many people *"know about the glory".* In other words they have a *theological* and *theoretical* understanding of this divine phenomenon based on research and intellectualism. However, very few have, *"the knowledge of the Glory".* To *"know the glory "*, means to be elevated into a birthing position in the spirit whereby one has an undeniably deep, profound and personal encounter with God in the *Glory Realm*, such that you have an acute understanding of what to do, when and how to channel the glory in a specific direction. In a view to uncover the deeper realities of the *Glory realm* and its antici-pated invasion on the natural realm, let's closely consider our opening scripture:

The Realm of Glory

"The earth will be filled, not only with the glory of the Lord, but with the knowledge of the glory of the LORD, as the waters cover the sea" (Habakkuk 2:14).

As aforementioned, God is unsealing new realms of revelation and this new flood of knowledge is unlocking hidden realms of glory ever known since the existence of mankind. The phrase, *"Knowledge of the Glory,"* as unpacked in the above scripture implies having an optimum mix of both *theoretical* (theological) and *practical* (experiential) knowledge of the glory realm. The Greek word for *"knowledge"* is *epignosis,* which means *a deep spiritual knowledge that surpasses all knowledge.* The truth is that the level of knowledge you have about the glory is what would determine the dimension of glory you can be catapulted into the supernatural realm. Through *revelation knowledge,* the time has come whereby operating in the glory realm and demonstrating the new realms of glory through miracles, signs and wonders shall become a common experience to God's children and an order of the day in the Body of Christ. This shall culminate in a scenario whereby millions of souls are pouring and streaming into the Kingdom of God. Metaphorically speaking, the glory of God among us is like a cloud that we see and sense, but we need to know how to get the cloud to manifest rain. It is not enough to say that the spirit of revival or glory is near or on the horizon as popularly preached in many conferences, for this is not an expression of faith but hope. Instead, we need the knowledge of the glory to see the heavens opened and the mysteries of the glory unveiled, now.

Spiritually speaking, the manifestation of glory is originally designed to be a progressive spiritual transition from *glory to glory.* However, even though there is a continuous progression into deeper realities of God's unlimited glory, there is also a considerable challenge faced by multitudes of believers of being potentially stuck in the outer court mentality. It is a typical scenario in some Christian charismatic cycles that many have inadvertently restricted themselves from accessing higher realms of glory by relegating the glory and majesty of the King to sight and the realm of senses (Luke 17:20), as opposed to the foresight of the Holy place, and the insight of the Most Holy place. It is disheartening to note that multitudes of believers across a broad spectrum of Christian faith sing about wanting God's glory to come to them, and other songs of a similar nature when in actuality they have no idea what they are asking for. To truly want to be in God's glory, you need to realize that it has nothing to do with you. Instead, it has more to do with the revelation of who God is, what He wants to do and How He wants it done in a particular season as well as developing an insatiable appetite, perennial hunger and unquenchable thirst to be so absorbed, infused and mingled in His presence such that dwelling in the glory becomes our second nature.

> *As a matter of fact, the level of revelation a man has about God is directly proportional to the level or dimension of glory he can be elevated into.*

Moses is a quintessential model of how we can provoke the glory of God into manifestation as he sincerely wanted to behold the Lord's glory, hence he desperately asked God to allow him to see Him because he had a better understanding of what that meant than most ordinary people today do. To demonstrate the gravity of how significant the glory of God is as a central theme in the Kingdom in this final chapter of human history, the Lord adjudicated as recorded in Numbers 14: 21 that,

> *As truly as I live, all the earth shall be filled with the glory of the LORD.*

This speaks of the unprecedented *explosion* and *invasion* of the glory that shall engulf the extreme geographical territories of the earth. To bring full clarity of this divine revelation, lets cross reference to a related scripture in Isaiah 40:5:

> *"The glory of the Lord shall be revealed and all the earth shall see it".*

This gives an idea that the glory is no longer a mystical vapour of God's power as some have erroneously presumed it to be, but a tangible spiritual reality that is visibly seen in the natural realm. That means according to God's original master plan and purpose concerning humanity, walking in the glory is the primary agenda of Heaven and a central theme in God's end time plan and purpose. This implies that we have been catapulted right into the very special divine moments in the calendar of God, whereby the Heavens are pregnant with the glory of God and the womb of the Spirit is ready to unleash the realities of the glory to flood even the extreme quarters of the world.

To bring more clarity to this divine revelation of glory, Apostle Peter attests to the divine truth that, *"God has called us to glory and virtue."* (2 Peter 1:3), It is therefore of paramount importance to highlight as an introductory perspective to the subject of glory that according to God's original master plan concerning humanity, man was created for God's glory and meant to live a life of glory. God intended men and women to live and walk in glory and be carriers of His glory, hence as far as God is concerned, the glory is our birth right and an irrevocable inheritance of every believer.

The greater truth is that the glory was never created for angels but for man. That is why upon creating humanity, God imparted His breath of life which represents His glory on man and he became a living being (Genesis 2:7). In other words, the glory is what brings life to a man, hence in the absence of glory, there is no life.

As far as God is concerned, life is defined as a progressive movement or migration in the glory realm from one level, realm or dimension to another.

The greater truth is that we are the supreme beings of His creation because we have been crowned with His glory. Spiritually speaking, man is an extension of God's glory and an exact representation of His image, hence living, functioning and operating in the glory is our divine nature. David caught this revelation, hence he declared in Psalms 8:5 that *what man are you mind full of him that you have made him a little lower than angels and you have crowned him with glory and honour.* However, man chose to live outside the parameters of glory so, they had to be exiled from that atmosphere of gory. Owing to ignorance of the divine truth that Christ has now restored us to a level above our original position of glory, multitudes of Christians are not living in the reality of this glory.

The overarching divine truth is that we were created as vessels to propagate the glory of God to the furthest extremes of the world. However, when God says He made us for His glory, He does not mean that He made us so that He could become more glorious in Himself. Instead, what Isaiah 43:7 means is that He created us to display His glory, so that His glory might be known and publicly manifested just like the experience of the disciples in the Upper Room who burst forth into the marketplace, filled with the power and glory of God and impacted the nations. The Bible even makes it clear that *we have been called to display the virtues and perfections of God* and the glory is one of the virtues of God that we have to publicly display across the globe. This is the ultimate agenda of Heaven, to manifest the glory of God in a global arena. This means that you are the effulgence of God's glory as He wants to perambulate in your body. When the Bible says that *we have treasures in earthen vessels*, it alludes to the divine truth that we have the glory of God resident in the extreme quarters of our spirit. However, the father's purpose is not just to have the glory dwell in us. Instead, He wants the glory to so much soak us to the extent that we are completely inundated by it, until we become inseparable with the glory, until we become the glory. Moses got so infused and mingled with the glory of God to the extent that his face shone and sent forth beams of blazing glory that ruffled the feathers of the masses. Moses begged to see the glory of God and when he did see it, it changed his life for ever. Now, that very glory resides in us through the Holy Spirit. The good news is that we are no longer beggars of the glory like Moses but carriers of the glory. We have become a live demonstration of the glory as we have it in the inside, perambulating in the extreme quarters of our spirit. In other words, the glory has been internalised. What a Heavenly privilege God has granted us in these critical times!

To provide a historical background on the phenomenon of the glory, in the days of the Old Testament, the glory of God was temporary as it was only manifested when the Spirit descended on someone and caused him to prophesy or do something but once he finished what he had been led to do, the Spirit would leave. This is contrary to how we operate in the glory in the New Testament dispensation. In this end time season, the glory now permanently resides in our spirit, hence we are the ark of God's glory because we carry it whenever we go. Therefore, the purpose of the glory is for believers to have a continuous experience with His presence in order that we may be transformed into the image of Christ as we await His second coming. Secondly, the purpose of the glory is to enable us to move in the spirit realm and function in a dimension where we can display God's glory through miracles, signs and wonders so as to impact the nations. Thirdly, the purpose of the glory is to manifest the sovereignty of God in the light of His creation and to enforce His divine plans and purposes on earth in this present time; to launch the church into the greater depths of the miraculous as a mark of the end times so that we can witness an unprecedented avalanche of millions of souls across the globe into the kingdom.

Prophetically speaking, there is a changing in the spiritual atmosphere. God is making a sudden appearance in our lives today so He calls us to be ready for His glory in season and out of season. Therefore, we must know the art of how to walk in the glory. Sadly, many folks have lived so much in the anointing of God but you will never be satisfied until you see the glory. The substance of the anointing is so much commoditised and advertised within church walls and broadcasted on the pulpit at the expense of the glory. That is why there ought to be a paradigm shift and drastic transition from the *realm of the anointing* into *the realm of glory*. Therefore, this book points to the coming invasion of God's glory which believers can freely and unreservedly tap into. The purpose of this book is to fuel your fire for a full blown invasion of Glory and to awaken an insatiable appetite for a live demonstration of glory in this generation.

The Realm of Glory

Smith Wigglesworth, the great Apostle of Faith, a man who ushered an unquestionable heavy weight of God's glory in his generation, to the extent of being mightily used in the ministry of raising the dead, said when he was in New Zealand many years ago, a young man came to him and said,

"Isn't it wonderful what God had done and God is doing through your life and through many others."

In response to the compliment, Smith Wigglesworth looked straight at the young man and said,

" Son, what you have seen is great, is wonderful, its powerful, but there is a revival coming that will be even greater and more powerful than what we have seen. It will be a worldwide thrust of God's glory". He then continued, *"I will not live to see those days. But young man, you will live to see those days."*

If a man who led to a break out of a global resurrection revival that saw many being raised from the dead, says that more is coming, it means that deeper and greater dimensions of God's glory shall break out that shall culminate in mass resurrection of people from the dead in the end times. That means the end time revival that shall consume all the nations of the world has just broke out and shall spread like veld fire to engulf territories in all quarters of life. This shall be characterised by the rise of a unique breed of believers whom God is raising who shall step into spiritual maturity as they encounter new realms of glory and to manifest that glorious expression of the Heavenly Father from within the *third dimension.* This is to tell you that there is a new type of man coming forth on the earth rising beyond the confines and dictates of the realm of time, to access the glory. The question is: *Are you that type of man?*

This book is a call for radical revivalists and revolutionaries to rise up on this epic transition and take their rightful place on earth by manifesting the glory of God to the furthest extremes of the world. It is jam-packed with revelations that will blow your mind. It takes you on a journey through the looking glass into the possibilities and realities of the Glory Realm, debunking the myths and misconceptions which for ages have been ingrained in the minds of the masses. This publication is a foretaste of what it means to live in the realities of the Glory Realm, unearthing the hidden mysteries which the Apostle Paul penned as, *"something inexpressible for man to tell".* Therefore, if you are hungry to take the glory of God to the next level in your life, then get ready to have your life transformed and blessed as you take a quantum leap into the *Glory Realm*. If you are a God-chaser and fire-starter who is eager to spark off the mighty wave of God's glory, continue to inundate your spirit with a flood of revelations encapsulated in this publication. If you are tired of being a sailor or existing on the shores of tradition and religion, this book is the right recipe for you. It will blow up your mind and awaken you to an arena of divine consciousness in which living in the Glory Realm is a norm and visitations to the Throne Room of Heaven is a normal occurrence. Therefore, prepare your world to be turned upside down and your traditions, religion and theology to be messed up! The whistle is blowing and it's time to sail through the great adventure of this unknown dimension. Congratulations and welcome to the journey in the Glory Realm!

CHAPTER ONE

A DIVINE PROPHETIC REVELATION OF THE GLORY REALM

Unveiling The Prophetic Revelation of the End Time Glory Invasion.

In an endeavour to accurately convey a prophetic insight into the mysteries of the glory of the end time season, it is of paramount significance to unveil right from the onset the divine revelation that there is a heightened degree of acceleration in the Glory of God in this end time season. As the body of Christ, we are standing at the threshold of a critical era and the brink of a new age where the *"Kairos "* (times) and *"Chronos"* (seasons) of God are coming together. The power for acceleration is in the timeless realm of God's glory. The realm of God's glory is not limited by time, space and matter. When the glory of God moves into the realm of the natural, there comes a great acceleration for miracles, healings, signs and wonders and the tremendous release of God's creative power, marking the greatest end-time glory invasion on planet earth. There are waves of glory approaching the earth that have never been seen before and their current is changing and these waves are breaking forth on the surface of the earth, causing a flood of God's glory streaming to the furthest extremes of the world. The end time church is nearer to the Throne than ever before. Prophetically speaking, the Lord showed me recently in a divine encounter how time is running out and eternity is rushing in. In this experience of glory, I began to understand how, in the Book of Amos, the ploughman could overtake the reaper. In

1

other words, the eternal realm was literally overtaking time in the natural and these are the very sacred, special and delicate moments into which we have been ushered in the calendar of God.

Spiritually speaking, seeds of destiny are ready for reaping. In accordance with God's times and seasons, we are in a critical time of acceleration. We have stepped into Amos 9:13, where *the ploughman shall overtake the reaper.* In other words, all of eternity is pouring into the present causing acceleration in the realm of the natural. Seeds that have been sown in the past, seeds of destiny, both good and evil, are full-grown and ready for reaping. We are living in the period when the prophecies declared over the past 6 000 years are being fulfilled in a short span of remaining time. For many years, the church has prayed and anxiously awaited another wave of Heavenly glory that would catapult us out of spiritual lethargy into the greater depths of the miraculous never demonstrated in past revivals. However, the prayers you have prayed for years will be answered in minutes. You will begin to see an acceleration beyond belief. As the realm of eternity is meshed with the present, we are witnessing a culmination of events as loose ends are being tied up before the return of Christ. In that realm of glory, things that would normally take ten years to happen will only take ten months and what could have taken the whole year to figure out will materialise in few seconds. There is a rapid maturity taking place in the body of Christ as the cloud of His glory descends and blankets us corporately. This is not a time for business as usual. We don't have much time left as the lease God has granted to the earth is about to expire. We are living at a unique juncture in history – the period just prior to the glorious return of the Lord Jesus Christ and the final summation of the ages. A day when the Lord will bring to conclusion all He began in the Garden of Eden. Therefore, in this season, the Lord shall propel you into the future, catapult you to the higher realms of His glory and elevate you to deeper dimensions of His presence where you shall bask in the glory like never before.

The greater truth is that we are feeling the first sprinkles of the greatest revival of miracles, signs and wonders ever recorded since the Book of Acts. But we are beginning to see little trickles, maybe even streams of the power of the Holy Spirit, breaking out in places around the globe as all nations are being overtaken by the glory of God. This is the result of the glory of God being manifested upon the earth in its intensity. Philosophically speaking, taking into account the character of the times and seasons in which we have been ushered as per calendar of God, we are not in the book of Numbers but we are operating in the Book of acts. Even the Book of

Acts itself is not yet complete because miracles of a greater magnitude and higher dimension as Jesus proclaimed are increasingly being performed in the glory and documented on a daily basis in this present era. With this increase in signs and wonders has come new revelation and a great harvest of souls, since every great move of God naturally brings with it a new harvest. In this new move of God, there is not only an increase in signs and wonders, but there are unusual manifestation of creative miracles including resurrections of people from the dead, angelic visitations, and the restoration of key revelations, mysteries and divine truths that have been lost through the centuries. Great mysteries are being rediscovered that will unleash the greatest outpouring of God's glory and harvest since the early Church, even since the beginning of time. Philosophically speaking, God's golden glory will bring in a golden harvest!

In this current season, through the glory, God is releasing mandates, mantles, and miracles; the spirits of might and multiplication are being poured out on the body of Christ all over the world, for the purpose of attaining a global harvest. Therefore, in this season, we shall witness unparalleled demonstrations of Kingdom Power and Glory more than ever before. Moreover, in this time, the Lord is demanding that believers be set apart for His plans and purpose hence, extreme obedience and passionate purity are essential. Furthermore, lifestyles of radical worship and faith are the fuels that will ignite revival fires among this generation, a people wholly consumed with, and consecrated in the fiery presence of the living Christ.

Prophetically speaking, tremendous manifestations of new realms of glory are surfacing on the horizon as the Body of Christ is catapulted right to the ultimate climax of God's glory on earth. The clouds of revival glory are constantly changing, and new glory cloud formations are on the horizon. As aforementioned, God is echoing the same words which He declared through Prophet Isaiah for these end times but this time, it's louder than ever before: *"Behold, I'm doing a new thing! They are created now, and not so long ago, you have not heard of them before today, so you cannot say, "Yes, I knew them"* (Isaiah 48:7). There are glories coming into meetings such that we won't know how to contain it. If ever there is an hour when God is going to pour out a new wave of His glory, it is now. Therefore, those who seek the new will find it, while those who are content with their anointing will not see the next move of God. For a move to be a move, it has to keep moving, hence we must keep moving with it. This is undeniably a season of new manifestations of God's glory!

Just like a cloud as small as a man's hand which Elijah build up in prayer, the movement of the glory of God shall begin as small as a current of water; the current will increase until it becomes a brook; the brook will grow into a great river, which will overflow and become a sea and that sea will transform into a powerful ocean. Then the glory of God will cover the earth as the waters cover the sea and Jesus will come for his church.

The greater truth is that there is a mighty stir brewing in the most Holy place, as the very essence and pure nature of the manifested Son Jesus Christ in throne ship and dominion, executive power is pouring out his life-giving nature to all humanity, and particularly the church; bringing a powerful release from bondage, corruption, futility, and captivity (Hebrews 12:2; Revelation 4:2; Daniel 7:14; 1 Corinthians 15:24- 26). To the eye of the Spirit, there is radiant life and light flooding our whole man, as we not only desire to walk in the rest of God, but to manifest and to become that glorious expression of the Heavenly Father from within *the third dimension.*

These are the days when the Glory of God is being revealed in, and through, the Body of Christ in its intensity as prophesised beforehand through the voice of Prophet Haggai that,

The Glory of this latter house will truly be greater than the former (Haggai 2:9).

At the same time, there is a corporate remnant, an overcoming body of believers, a rising glory generation that will rise to new levels of kingly authority, and administrate the dominion of the Kingdom of God with great power, as it steps into the fullness of the measure of the stature of Christ. This remnant is the new man coming forth in the earth, hence we are about to see the full manifestation of the resurrection power of Jesus, as this body rises to maturity. We are living in a miraculous era, a time when we can't live without the amazing, life-giving release of God's glory. In this regard, we are seeing the restoration of the spirit of Elijah upon the Church, as was prophesied:

"Behold, I am going to send you Elijah the prophet before the coming of the great and terrible day of the LORD" (Malachi 4:5).

This speaks of the rise of apostles and prophets that will speak to head of nations with prophetic signs and wonders that government leaders will be unable to deny what God is declaring to them. As the spirit of Elijah is increasingly being poured out from the Heavens, so will speaking His glory into governments increase at an accelerated pace and they will be released in unprecedented ways. This wave of revival will be greater than any other because we are entering the culmination of time, when we will experience the *former rains* and the *latter rains* of revival glory combined. Some of the things we are experiencing are familiar, but many things are brand new, straight from the throne room. We are therefore experiencing the last wave of revival of miracles, signs and wonders which shall culminate in an unprecedented avalanche of millions of souls into the kingdom. Prophetically speaking, in these end times, we shall experience greater manifestations of glory than ever before and this shall culminate in greater dimensions of signs and wonders such as raising of the dead, physical shaking of geographical territories, people falling under the power of God miles away from church, as the glory of God invades the streets, market places and the public arena. Moreover, greater healings, deliverances and breakthroughs shall take place in the streets even without an usher, Church song or religious gathering, as God unreservedly unveils the fullness of His glory to humanity.

Prophetically speaking, we are now entering into a dimension of glory that is to become common place to the children of God and walking in the supernatural, a normal mode of operation. The days have come whereby the glory of God shall manifest intensely such that an average believer will walk into a hospital and all the people shall be healed and an ordinary Christian shall step into a mortuary and command the dead to rise back to life. This shall culminate in mass resurrection of people from the dead, where mortuaries shall be empty as the dead are raised in multitudes. We are entering into a season of heightened signs and wonders, evidenced by deep *creative miracles of glory* such as germination of hair on bold heads, growth of new body parts, supernatural increase in height, change in complexion, instantaneous weight loss or weight gain, supernatural pregnancy, levitation, walking on water, as well as natural substances getting altered in the glory.

I believe beyond any shadow of doubt that the coming move of God will be greater than what we read about in the book of Acts. The Bible clearly states that, *"The glory of the latter house shall be greater than that of the former"* (Haggai 2:9). In this coming move, multiplied millions will stream into the kingdom as an unusual wave of miracles sweep across the body of Christ in an unprecedented manner. The blessings of God will overflow in the body of Christ, so much that, as the psalmist David exclaimed, *"My cup runneth over"* (Psalm 23:5). Many believers will be catapulted into the realm of Kingdom millionaires to finance the work of the gospel. In the same way the glory of the Lord filled the temple to such an extent that the priest could not enter (2

Chronicles 7:1- 2), the glory of these days shall fill the masses with such awesome power such that no one would even stand in His presence. Prophetically speaking, the very glory of God is going to descend upon His church as never before. That time is quickly approaching and we are on the verge of the most awesome move of God in history, a move so great that *"No eye has seen, nor ear heard, neither has it entered into the heart of man, the things which God has prepared for them that love Him"* (1 Corinthians 2:9).

Prophetically speaking, there is a new type of man coming forth on the earth rising beyond the confines and dictates of the realm of time, to access the glory of God. God is raising a new generation of men and women who will know the art of how to respond to His glory. A distinct breed of people who shall thirst for His glory to manifest on earth and shall release a glory invasion to accelerate God's purpose on earth. Many of these will be emerging from obscure and isolated places but shall bring an unusual anointing and illuminating glory to calm the troubled waters presently in the Church and will carry authority to speak into people's hearts. This is not merely an exercise of spiritual gifts but a token of the end- time scenario when God takes up residence in a body of people to do the greater works. The darkness on the world will become denser each day and wickedness will multiply but the manifestation of God's glory on earth will also become more powerful and weighty with each passing moment (Isaiah 60:3). This is a glorious generation that will impact the world and gather the greatest harvest of souls ever seen. Entire cities and nations will be shaken by His glory and will constitutionally endorse Jesus Christ as the Lord and saviour as He declared that,

> *Once more and in a little while, I will shake the Heavens, I will shake the earth,*
> *I will shake the seas and all fleshshall come to the desires of nations (Jesus)*
> (Hagai 2:8).

This implies that the movement of the glory will culminate in a mighty stir brewing, agitating and shaking in the Heavens, as the very essence and pure nature of the manifested Son, Jesus Christ in throne ship, dominion and executive power is pouring out the abundance of His glory to all humanity, bringing a powerful release from the futility, captivity and bondage of death. Funeral processions shall be turned into revival sessions, Burial societies into Church committees and mortuaries into Worship centres, as the cloud of God's *resurrection glory* invades the earthly realm. This means that the most remarkable manifestations of His presence through miracles, signs and wonders will take place before millions around the world, in an instant and this shall culminate in an avalanche of billions of souls into the kingdom.

The Realm of Glory

It is a divine truth that we are at the very door of entrance into God's next intervention in the affairs of humanity. We are on the verge of an awakening as well as a massive global transformation. In other words, we are about to witness the most incredible act of not only this century, but of all time since the resurrection of Jesus from the dead. Jesus is about to return in the clouds of the air to receive His bride to Himself. Every prophecy which must be fulfilled in order for His return to take place has occurred with the exception of the propagation of the gospel to all nations. And we are nearing that milestone as well. Moreover, as the activity of heaven increases in preparation for this great event, signs and wonders, miracles and spiritual manifestations are increasing, as God is moving mightily in the earth. We are therefore witnessing in renewal, with unexplainable manifestations, the direct result of the Holy Spirit touching, healing, preparing God's people to complete the task of reaching the entire planet with the message of salvation through the blood of Jesus. Such is the magnitude of the current awakening. As God has begun to sweep through His church with His glory, those elements of Christian religion which have been created by man and not by God are being challenged and consumed. Elements of worship which have held sacred position but which were man-made and not God-ordained are being replaced by the components of *the glory* A more *"authentic"* Christianity is appearing among more and more churches around the world. In this hour of great spiritual awakening, believers are divorcing, every vestige of dead tradition and empty religion to pursue the glory of God like never before.

Conclusively, there is much more coming, hence we need to begin a new quest, seeking newer and greater realms of glory. God is therefore looking for those who will dare to say that there is yet another wave of greater glory in the midst of the current glory. As John the Baptist preached repentance and prepared the way for Jesus' ministry which included miracles, signs and wonders, so the current move has greatly helped and continues to prepare the way for this exciting new move of God. Therefore, in order for us to step into the new realms of glory, it is essential that we first learn how to cultivate an atmosphere of God's presence in our individual lives through devotion, prayer, holiness, and humility. Priorities are shifting, sometimes evaporating, to make room for the chief priority of life, which is to bring glory to the Father and His Son, Jesus. Secondly, we must learn how to corporately usher in the cloud of glory through high praise, worship, and faith. And thirdly, for us to step into maturity, we must learn how to operate in, and from, the realm of glory. This means receiving revelation by faith, through vision and imagination while in the glory, and also speaking and declaring the word of God from the glory realm.

THE ESSENCE OF GOD'S GLORY

What exactly is the accurate measure of the refection of God's glory?

It is worth exploring the truth that *"Glory"* as a term used in scripture is a somewhat elusive term to describe succinctly. Although it is a buzz word that is trending in our streamline Christian programmes, it is never fully understood by multitudes of believers. It suffices to assert that the most overworked terminology or Christian vocabulary across a broad spectrum of Christian charismatic cycles is the word *"glory"*, yet it is one of the subjects that have not been fully comprehended by dozens of believers. Multitudes of books have been written and countless messages preached behind the pulpit on the subject of the *'glory'* yet for all the attention the subject is given, it is one of the least understood and least experienced gifts which God has freely made available to every believer in Christ. Owing to a lack of revelation, many believers consider the term *glory* as a rather vague, ethereal concept that they struggle to comprehend clearly. The daunting task of defining glory is exacerbated by the fact that it is used in a variety of ways to mean different things in the scripture. Some people erroneously presume the glory to be the anointing; others think it's God's power; others perceive it to be a spiritual substance while others just can't see any difference between these concepts. Therefore, in order for us to have an in-depth understanding of the divine phenomenon of *glory*, it is imperative that we define the concept in its original context with reference to both *Greek* and *Hebrew* terminology.

> *The Greek word for glory is "DOXA", which means brilliance, splendour, brightness, glittering appearance, radiance, flamboyance, magnificence, excellence or pre-eminence. The Hebrew word for glory is "KABOWD", which alludes figuratively to honour, abundance, dignity, abundance, majesty, admiration, tribute, heavy, weighty or rich. It speaks of the essence, nature, attributes and infinite perfection of God, His personality and character or what He is in Himself.*

It is worth exploring the divine truth that there are two key areas in which the word, *"glory"* is used in the Bible.

In one context, it is used to refer to the attributes, nature, character and virtues of God. In a different context, it is used to refer to the tangible and visible manifestation of the Shekinah presence in the natural realm.

To cement this revelation with reference to scriptural evidence, let us look at Exodus 34, where God unreservedly showed Moses His Glory. In analysis of this scripture, you must bear in mind that Exodus 34:5 was the answer to Exodus 33:18 when Moses said to the Lord, *"Please, show me Your glory."* He was so hungry and craving for the glory of God that he pleaded, *"God please show me your glory."* Then God answered him in Chapter 34:5. Let's closely look at what exactly transpired:

Now the Lord descended in the cloud and stood with him there and proclaimed the name of the Lord. And the Lord passed before him and proclaimed, "The Lord God, merciful and gracious, longsuffering, and abounding in goodness and truth, keeping mercy for thousands, forgiving iniquity and transgression and sin, by no means clearing the guilty, visiting the iniquity of the fathers upon the children and the children's children to the third and the fourth generation."

Now, when God came down with a response to Moses's request, what exactly did He show Moses? He showed Him His infinite values of mercy, longsuffering, goodness, graciousness and truth. Bear in mind that what God was doing was showing His glory as requested by Moses. After all, Moses had asked God in his petition, *"Please, show me Your glory."* And God said, *"I will show you the back part of My glory."* and now God was showing him exactly what he had requested to see.

In view of the above, when God came down the mountain, His glory was manifested and He proclaimed the name of the Lord, saying, *"The Lord, God, merciful, gracious, longsuffering, and abounding in goodness and truth."* This tells us that the glory of God that came down consists of five ingredients, that is, *the Lord is No. 1 merciful, No. 2 gracious, No. 3 longsuffering, No. 4 goodness and No. 5 truth.* So, God outlined His glory. These five attributes make up God's glory, hence if ever we want to grow in God's glory and be in a place and position for God's glory to grow strong in our lives, we need to grow in all these five attributes of God. And this is what Moses meant in his request, that God would reveal Himself to his mind so that he would know Him and have a clear and powerful apprehension of those things which constitute God's glory. This unveils the revelation that there is a direct correlation between the *glory of God* and the *attributes of God.* To move in the glory of God is to move in love, mercy, grace, longsuffering, goodness and truth. Anyone who desires to manifest in God's glory fully must develop these attributes of God in his life. We therefore need to grow in glory and in order to do so, we need to understand what the glory consists of. We must grow in these five above-mentioned elements of God's glory in order to mature in the glory. They are an impartation of God's very nature and being into us. In fact, all these 5 attributes have relevance to God's nature but each has its special aspect.

FIRST DEFINITION:

Firstly, the glory of God is therefore His totality or state of perfection and completeness manifested and expressed through the attributes of mercy, grace, longsuffering, goodness and truth. In other words, it is the visible splendour and moral beauty of God's manifold perfections. Put differently, it is the total sum of God's attributes, character, and intrinsic virtues, the brilliance of His presence, and the splendour of His majesty. It is the intrinsic essence of who God is manifested by His nature, character, attributes or virtues.

Owing to lack of revelation, some people erroneously perceive the glory to be an otherworldly form or a divine energy force that floats in the atmosphere, something ethereal or mystical but the greater truth is that the glory of God goes beyond these things. In essence, the glory of God is His character and His divine nature; it is the very essence of His presence. And because the glory is the essence of who God is, everything is complete in Him. This implies that the glory is the nature of God and an exact representation or extension of His being. In other words, it proceeds from Him. It is part of His being. The glory is the essence of all that God is. It is the realm of eternity, infinite, boundless, with no restrictions; it is beyond human imagination. It is God's unforgettable mark, seen and heard in the natural.

SECOND DEFINITION:

Secondly, the word "glory" could also refer to the substance of glory or Shekinah which is the visible, tangible, and feel-able manifestation of His presence to mankind in the natural realm. In this context, the glory of God is perceived as a spiritual substance that emanates from the Throne Room of God in Heaven and is then manifested in the natural realm as a visible and tangible substance.

This occurs when God's glory transcends the spiritual realm to impact the natural realm. Although the glory of God is a spiritual substance, it can transmute itself into a form that can be seen, felt and touched when it infiltrates down into the natural realm. The most popular forms of manifestation of the substance of glory in the Bible are *clouds, thunder and lightning, tempest, earthquake and fire.* To cement this revelation with reference to scriptural evidence, the Bible records in Exodus 19:16 that,

It came to pass on the third day in the morning that there were thunderings and lightning and a thick cloud on the mountain and the sound of the trumpet was very loud, so that all the people who were in the camp trembled.

The question you are probably asking yourself is: Where did the thunder and lightning and the thick cloud come from? Was it part of the natural weather conditions? Definitely not! This was the glory of God emanating from His Throne in Heaven that had now spilled over to the earth in such a way that it was now visibly and tangibly manifesting as thunder, lightning and clouds. For clarity of this divine truth, lets closely refer to another separate event in Exodus 40:35, where the Bible narrates that,

Moses was not able to enter into the tent of the congregation, because the cloud abode on it, and the glory of the LORD filled the tabernacle.

This tells me that the glory of God is a tangible and visible spiritual substance. Why? Because it is said to have *filled* the terbanalce. The act of the glory *filing* the terbanacle unveils the key properties or attributes of a *substance* because only a substance can *fill* a place. From a scientific point of view, the word *substance* means anything that carries the physical properties of weight, density and mass such that it can be measured, weighed and substantiated. The truth is that as much as there are natural substances there are also *spiritual substances.* By the same token, the glory is a tangible spiritual substance just like the *anointing.* That means the glory can be touched, seen, felt, received, experienced and imparted. That is why we perceive the glory of God as a *spiritual substance.* During impartation, the glory is actually *transacted* as a tangible spiritual substance into our spirit from God. In the Old Testament, whenever the glory of God manifested, physical phenomena took place such as fire or clouds. His glory was always tangible to the senses. The glory of God was unequivocally seen as the visible, tangible and feel-able manifestation of the presence of God. When God manifested Himself in the form of a pillar of cloud by day and a pillar of fire by night, that visible and tangible substance which dwelt amongst men and was beheld by all, was actually a manifestation of the glory of God in the natural realm.

Holistically, the glory of God could therefore be described as a tangible and visible supernatural manifestation of the fullness or totality of God from the realm of the spirit into the realm of the physical. It could also be best described as the divine impartation and revelation of the substance, heaviness, imminence and supremacy of the transcending presence of God in the affairs of humanity.

This implies that the glory is the impartation of the nature and the life of God upon a human vessel. Moreover, it is the highest dimension, depth, realm or level of concentration of God's supreme power or sovereignty manifested in the realm of the physical, which transcends all natural laws, principles and processes. Philosophically speaking, the glory is the spiritual atmosphere of Heaven just like air is the physical atmosphere of the earth.

THE NATURE AND OPERATION OF THE GLORY

How does the glory of God operate?

It is of paramount importance to advance the divine truth that the glory is the source of all manifestations. The power, anointing and mantle are all products of the glory. In other words, their manifestation alludes to God's glory. The glory is what brings the presence because the presence is a radiation or refection of His glory. The presence is what brings the anointing because the anointing is an impartation of His ability when He rests upon a vessel. The anointing is what brings about the power because power is an end product that is manifested when one is anointed. Philosophically speaking, the glory is the source, the anointing is an intermediate product and power is an end product.

It is worth mentioning at this stage that each one of us carries a measure of God's glory and presence. It is sufficient to see from a study of Hebrew and Greek words that the glory of God has form, shape and materiality. In other words, it has substance. Paul speaks of *the eternal weight of glory* (2 Corinthians 4:17). If that glory is increased in our lives we are more enabled to move in higher realms of power than ever before. The truth is that we all receive a proportional measure of glory but our zeal, level of expectation, revelation, faith and hunger for more is what distinguishes us from the rest. Just like Moses, although he had known God just for a short time period, he came to a stage whereby he asked God show him His glory. And when God showed him, there was a profound difference in the relationship of God in his life. The glory of God is the manifest presence of God (Exodus 40:34; 2 Chronicles 5:13-14). With a greater presence, there is always a greater demonstration of the anointing and power (Luke 5:17; Acts 10:38; Mark 16:20). If the glory of God increases in our lives, the anointing will increase proportionately. It is a greater truth that God relates to you at the point of glory, hence it is imperative for us to rigorously seek after the glory and the presence of God in our lives more than anything else. All of us know what God's presence is but we need to develop an insatiable appetite, perennial hunger and unquenchable thirst for God's glory. We need to desire for more of His glory because it is through His glory that the anointing, presence and power comes.

Tactically speaking, what makes the glory so spectacular as compared to other spiritual substances is that when one finally departs for Heaven, he doesn't leave with the anointing and mantle but with the Glory as it will determine which plane of glory to live in Heaven.

It is worth exploring the truth that at the death of a human vessel, the anointing and mantle remains on earth to fall upon the next generation but the glory goes with the person to heaven because it is the level of glory that would determine in which realm or plane of Glory the person will live in heaven. In actual fact, the anointing was never designed for inhabitants of Heaven but was given to earthly vessels in order for them to operate with heavenly efficiency. This explains why Elisha did not go with his anointing and mantle to Heaven such that even after hundreds of years, his bones still retained the anointing to the extent that when a man who was being hastily buried came into contact with the bones of Elisha, long after he had died, he was raised back to life (2 Kings 13:20-21). This tells me that in Heaven, we don't go with the substance of the anointing. Instead, we go with the glory because it is the glory upon us that will determine the plane of Heavenly glory we shall reside in. Spiritually speaking, the glory is the only spiritual substance that is permitted to enter Heaven. Hence, in this end time dispensation, there is a progressive transition from the realm of the anointing to the realm of glory. The truth of the matter is that many people know the anointing but they don't know the glory. This is because the anointing has been so much advertised and broadcasted behind the pulpit yet very few believers have been able to fully tap into the fullness of the realm of glory.

A Divine Prophetic Revelation of The Realm of Glory

There are spiritual truths that we need to put into correct perspective pertaining to the nature and operation of the glory. As much as there is a *Greater light* and a *Lesser light* as unveiled in the scriptures (Genesis 1:16), in the realm of God, there are also *greater truths* and *lesser truths*. The greater truth is that the glory of God is not an external force as some have erroneously presumed. Instead, it is already resident in your spirit in measures and degrees. That is why the word of God affirms in Colossians 1:27, that *Christ in you, the Hope of glory*. This implies that the glory of God is resident in our spirit through Christ our Lord. Therefore, it is our duty is to learn how to draw the glory of God from within the depths of our spirit by yielding more to God and praying in the Holy Ghost to trigger or provoke the power of God to flow. The Bible proclaims in John 7:38 that *out of your belly shall flow rivers of living waters*. While this scripture could be interpreted to mean the anointing flowing out of us, it actually refers to the outflow of glory from our spirit because it is the river of Glory that is resident in your spirit and flows out to touch those in your sphere of contact, as power is displayed. Hence, when we move in the power of God, we actually exhibit and display that glory which comes from within us. Contrary to what multitudes of people presume, the glory is not an external force. Instead, it operates from within a person. In other words, it perambulates from within the extreme quarters of your spirit. Upon receiving Christ into our hearts, God imparts His glory into our spirit and the glory would then flow out of our spirit to touch others in our sphere of contact. That is how we make an impact in our world as believers filled to the brink of full spiritual capacity with the glory of God.

Moreover, another divine truth to be unveiled is that we can constantly receive the anointing, the mantle and the presence but what makes the glory so special and sacred is that we don't receive it but we walk into it. There is a difference between *receiving the glory* and *walking in the glory*. Walking in the glory means manifesting the glory in a global arena to impact the lives of people in our generation and the world. Sadly, multitudes of people erroneously cling onto the old belief that when they come together in corporate worship, the glory of God is going to fall down from heaven like apples falling from a tree. While this view has been engrained in many believers' minds, it is a lesser truth. The greater truth is that the glory does not fall down upon us but it flows out of us. It is more of an upward movement from our spirit to God or others than it is a downward movement of power from God to us. Therefore, our duty is to learn how to walk in the glory, meaning to manifest the glory of God from within the depths of our spirit in a global arena through practically demonstrating the power of God in miracles, signs and wonders.

A DIVINE REVELATION OF THE GLORY ZONE

The Glory Zone is a region of high concentration of God's glory in a specific territory in the natural realm. It is a supernatural atmospheric sphere in which the glory of God is highly concentrated, contracted and crystallised such that heavenly beings, blessings and subjects (angels) visibly and tangibly manifests in the natural realm at the same level, dimension and degree as in Heaven. It denotes the climax of manifestation of the atmosphere of "Heaven on earth" in a particular territory. In that zone, death is rendered illegal, sickness is declared illegitimate and demons are not permitted to enter. It is a territory that has been demarcated, designated and earmarked to host or incubate the move of God and radiate the effulgence of His glory in the natural realm. It projects the spiritual direction in which the spirit of God is moving in the natural realm.

The glory zone operates just like a magnetic sphere of a magnet. Scientifically speaking, every magnet has a magnetic sphere or region within which it attracts or repels substances. In that region or sphere, there is a high concentration of either attractive power or repulsive energy such that metallic substances are instantaneously attracted or repelled. By the same token, the Glory zone is a region of high concentration of God's glory such that in that region, there is nether death, sickness, poverty nor decay as these are classed as negative spiritual gravity, hence they are subject to repulsion. In a similar fashion in which a magnet attracts and repels substances, in the Glory Zone, there is a higher concentration of God's glory producing a supernatural influence that attracts blessings, favour, anointing, breakthrough and angelic presence while at the same time repelling curses, sicknesses, death or any other debilitating circumstance or calamity that might befall humanity. The Glory zone is an arena of divine exploits. In that territory, the dead arises by themselves without anybody praying for them, the sick are healed without anybody laying hands on them and souls are saved in the absence of a church song. It marks an invasion of Heaven on earth. Did you know that the Garden of Eden was a Glory zone? This is because it had the highest concentration of God's glory on earth. It was the centre of Heaven on earth and a revelatory realm or geographical portal that directly linked the earth with the Heavens. It was where the headquarters of God's glory on earth were located, so to speak.

Do you know that the *Throne Room* of Heaven is an extreme degree of the Glory zone as the Headquarters of the Universe? That is why few subjects are qualified to thrive under such an extremely high degree of glory. The reason why some believers are not catapulted into the Throne Room is not because God doesn't want them in Heaven but it's simply because the quality of their spirit is not so much developed that they can qualify to enter such an excessively high degree of glory. Paul even testifies that when he was caught up to the third heaven, *he heard things which are inexpressible for man to tell*. Why? It's because of the extreme degree of glory in that atmosphere. Paul was so overwhelmed by the glory of God such that although his spiritual ears were unlocked to hear the mysteries of Heaven, his speech was locked such that he could not utter them. At the entrance into this extreme degree of glory, Paul, the man who was so highly educated under the tutelage of the greatest scholar, Gamaliel, suddenly lacked the vocabulary to describe what he saw in the Glory Realm. This is to tell you that even your language of expression in the Glory Realm changes. It cannot be punctuated by the vocabulary of the ordinary man. That is why in the Glory Zone, your language changes such that you don't pray for the sick to be healed. Instead, they are healed automatically because sickness is rendered illegal. You don't even pray for deliverance because demons are not permitted to enter; just by stepping on the Glory Zone, they leave instantly. Even prophecy ceases to operate because the glory realm is a realm beyond the gifts, where everything is revealed and known. In the Glory Zone, the past, present and future are all in past tense; everything is compete and finished. In the Glory Zone, you are therefore not allowed to talk about the future because everything (*the past, present and future*) is in the now. The only tense in the language of spiritual communication that is permitted is the *present tense*. Even the way you prophesy changes, from the dimension of *futuristic prophecy* to the dimension of *now prophecy*. In the glory zone, you cannot be prophesying about people receiving their breakthrough after five years into the future when their breakthrough can be brought forth into manifestation in the now. In the Glory zone, the eternal realm invades the natural realm, hence there is no time. The clock does not tick in the Glory zone. That is why things that would normally take years to happen are accomplished within few seconds.

The Glory zone is a zone of creative miracles; outside that zone, life is business as usual. Inside the zone, it is naturally supernatural to perform signs and wonders. Have you ever wondered why God warned Moses to take off His sandals when he came near the burning bush? It's because that territory was demarcated by God as a Glory zone. When you enter into that territory, anything that is not consistent with the will of God has to be dilapidated. Some churches are Glory zones while in some extremes of the world, even cities and towns or territorial regions can actually be Glory zones. There are certain territories in the natural realm that when you step into them, you feel a change in the atmosphere. When a sick person enters, suddenly he is healed and when the demon possessed tread on that territory, suddenly demons flee from them. Even the devil can't tread on the Glory zone. In the Glory zone, there is no room for fear because the devil is absent.

The truth is that God's dream is for the world to be turned into a Glory Zone. As a career of God's glory, you carry God everywhere you go, hence you have the prerogative to demarcate every territory you tread on as a Glory zone. Once you are in a Glory zone, anything is possible. Even the dead arises on their own accord without being commanded to because in the glory zone, death is rendered illegal and not permitted to reign. In the Glory Zone, every miracle, blessing, breakthrough and body parts are available although in an expanded form, hence you can command the original blue print of body parts to appear in bodily territories where they previously did not exist and they will instantaneously reappear. You can command short people to become taller, hair to appear on bold heads, money to appear miraculously in people's wallets, and whatever you want to see and it shall be established. In the Glory Zone, angels manifest visibly in the natural realm; they are no longer in an expanded form but they are visibly seen in a human bodily form. In the Glory zone, it's normal to see angels, have conversation with them and walk with them as if you are dealing with human beings. In the Glory Zone, spiritual substances available for impartation such as the anointing, the power and the glory are in a tangible, solid form; they are no longer a vapour of God's power or an ethereal spiritual sensation. That is why in the Glory Zone, you can literally cut a slice of God's power, put it in a handbag and take it home to the sick and demon possessed and they will be healed. That is why aprons and handkerchiefs were taken from the body of Paul and laid on the sick and demon possessed and they were healed. This is akin to how the sick and demon possessed laid on the streets received their healing as Peter passed by because the shadow of Peter was a Glory Zone that anybody who stepped into its sphere got healed. The sick were not healed by the shadow per se but by the glory of God reflected from his spirit. You see, when you read this portion of scripture with the eyes of flesh, you see Peter's shadow healing the sick but when you read it with the eyes of the Spirit, you see the glory of God being radiated from Peter's shadow, falling upon the sick and healing them. The Glory zone is a point of entry and exit into the spirit realm. That is why someday Jacob woke up in a Glory Zone and declared, *"This is the gate of*

Heaven". The Glory zone is a geographical portal that connects the earth directly with Heaven. In the glory Zone, there is a high angelic traffic, with angels ascending and descending to Heaven.

Do you remember that God declared in Hagai 2:8 that, *"Once more, in a little while, I will shake the heavens, I will shake the earth and I will shake the sea. I will shake all the nations and the desire of all nations shall come, and I will fill this house with glory"*. Do you realise that God is shaking the Heavens, earth and seas with His glory? Why do you think God is shaking these three realms of existence? It's because He is demarcating every territory in the universe as a Glory zone, as part of His end time glory invasion. Prophetically speaking, we are about to enter the eternal zone whereby time is loosing its grip on earth as eternity is invading time. The whole earth is turning into a Glory zone as Heaven is coming closer to the earth since we are adjourning quickly towards the second coming of Christ. We are at the consummation of time, early in the morning on the third day when Heaven's atmosphere is invading the earth. This Heavenly atmosphere brings with it the eternal realm of glory, transforming every extreme end of the world into a Glory zone. Do you remember that God vowed saying, *"As long as I live, the earth will be filled, not only with the glory of the Lord, but with the knowledge of the glory of the LORD, as the waters cover the sea"* (Habakkuk 2:14). This is to tell you that God's idea is to turn the whole earth into a Glory zone and the only way to achieve that is to fill it with His glory. This is because as a heavenly substance, the glory carries a supernatural mass or weight that can transform the universe. In this end time season, the glory of God is going to manifest so intensely on earth such that you will not have to pray with your eyes closed anymore because the glory of God will be manifesting visibly in the natural realm. God is going to unreservedly precipitate the rain of His golden glory in the form of gold dust, diamonds, silver stones, miracle money and other precious stones. In tandem with this new move, creative miracles shall become a norm and angels shall manifest visibly in the natural realm so much that it becomes naturally supernatural to live in the natural realm.

A DIVINE REVELATION OF THE GLORY INVASION

The glory invasion is a situation in which the glory of God invades, engulfs or subjugate a territory in the natural realm, culminating in a manifestation of "Heaven on earth". It is a drastic and phenomenal change in the properties of the natural atmosphere, resulting from the perpetration of the spiritual atmosphere of glory in a specific locality. When the atmosphere of the natural realm comes into contact with the atmosphere of the glory, an explosion called a glory invasion takes place. The glory invasion is therefore a product of collision between the atmospheric pressures of the two realms of existence. It is when the glory of God transmutes itself from the spirit realm such that it manifests in the natural realm as a tangible and visible substance impacting every sphere of life. In a practical sense, the glory invasion is therefore an explosion and outpouring of the substance of God's glory in the extreme quarters of life such as the streets, market place and the public arena. It happens when the glory of God bursts off, escapes and spills over from within the church walls to engulf geographical territories in the natural realm in such a way that the masses, cities, and nations of the world are transformed.

It is worth exploring the divine truth that the glory invasion in the New Testament dispensation, began with the advent of the Holy Ghost in Acts 2: 1, which culminated in a scenario in which the disciples vacated the Upper Room and burst forth into the marketplace, filled with the power and glory of God and impacted the nations. The sound of a rushing mighty wind and the divided tongues of fire which separated and rested upon each and very disciple in the Upper Room were actually divergent manifestations of the glory of God which ignited the spark of the *glory invasion* in the natural realm. The notion of the mighty wind *filling* the whole room speaks of the invasion of the physical atmosphere by the glory of the Spirit of God. In other words, the atmosphere of the glory engulfed and enveloped the natural atmosphere in that territory such that the disciples could literally breathe and inhale the glory instead of the normal oxygen.

This wave of glory invasion was further sparked off by the disciples when they prayed in Acts 4:29-30, saying, *"Now, Lord, grant to your bond servants to declare your message fearlessly, and stretch out your hand to heal and to perform signs and wonders in the name of thy servant Jesus Christ." And when they had prayed, the place where they met was shaken"*. The reality is that when they prayed in this way, the grip of fear vanquished and they saw the dawn of a greater glory operate— as in the signs and wonders which tangibly and visibly shook the geographical teritories on the face of the earth. Have you ever wondered what exactly shook the building or what triggered the supernatural earthquake? It was the heaviness of the glory of God in that territory. The shaking was a product of the glory invasion. It was a sign that the glory of God had started invading the territories of that region. When the glory of God is released and transmitted through the natural landscape, it culminates in a *supernatural earthquake.* In other words, a third-day wave of God's glory was released from the *Heavens Power House,* transmitted through the airwaves, and infiltrated right into the natural landscape such that it was tangibly manifesting itself as a supernatural earthquake, wreaking havoc in the natural realm. Unfortunately, most of the church today is missing this fullness of the glory. Most of us are potentially stuck living in Acts 2 — when the Holy Spirit fell, that's why multitudes still consider falling under the power as the greatest demonstration of power. Many of us get caught up in a cloud of celebration and wave of contentment when we speak in tongues, lay hands on the sick, and often see people added to the church but what we need to bring about a *Glory Invasion* is an Acts 4 outpouring to reap Acts 4 results. The Pentecost outpouring is fine, but a new level of glory and power came after the Acts 2 outpouring. Many want the results of Acts 4 power and glory without moving beyond Acts 2. You need an Acts 4 visitation to have an Acts 4 manifestation of revival and glory.

This is the same degree of glory invasion that had earlier split the rocks and ripped the graves apart such that many bodies of saints who had died were raised and came out of their graves because in the glory zone death is not permitted to reign (Mathew 27:50-53). Something strikingly spectacular happened in the spirit world at the point of release of the *resurrection glory.* The ever-coursing torrent of the rain of glory shot right through the atmosphere like an ethereal voltage – running solvent through the airwaves such that the veil of the temple which separated the Holy place from the Holy of Holies was torn apart from top to bottom, heralding the invasion of every extreme quarter of the world by God's glory. In an instant, everything had changed. The limp frustration of mortality was swallowed up in immortality. Death was turned into destiny. Sorrow was eclipsed by ecstasy. A holocaust became a holiday. A fast turned into a festival, wailing into dancing, and spiritual recession into resurrection. This is what happens when the glory of God invades geographical territories in the natural realm.

Another quintessential example of a *glory invasion* took place during the dedication of the temple (2 Chronicles 5:14; 1 Kings 8:10). It is recorded that during the dedication of Solomon's temple, the glory of God was so strongly manifested such that even priests could not enter the temple to perform their usual duties. In other words, the advent of the glory in its heightened degree tampered with their religious programmes and messed up their spiritual agenda such that nothing was business as usual.). In a similar vein, when the glory of God invaded the terbanacle, Moses was not able to enter into the tent of the congregation, because the cloud abode thereon, and the glory of the Lord filled the tabernacle (Exodus 40:35). The heaviness of the glory filled the whole atmosphere, such that only the atmosphere of the glory prevailed. In other words, oxygen seemed to cease and humans could only breathe the atmosphere of the glory, that's why they could not continue with business as usual. This is akin to the experience of Smith Wigglesworth, a man who ushered an unquestionable heavy weight of God's glory, to the extent of being mightily used by God to raise the dead. It is said that one day he invited several pastors to pray with him and the instant they began to worship God, the glory was manifested to a greater magnitude and intensity such that the atmosphere began to feel heavy and one by one, the pastors began to leave because they could not withstand that atmosphere of glory. The glory of God invaded that place such that pastors felt like they were going to explode, hence they never dared to invite Smith Wigglesworth again.

Another glory invasion in the New Testament dispensation was experienced in Acts 10 at Cornelius's house when the Gentiles received the infilling of the Holy Ghost for the first time. It is said that *as Peter began to speak, the Holy Ghost fell upon all them that heard the word.* The notion of the *Holy Ghost falling* describes the character of manifestation of the rain of God's glory as it precipitated upon all those who were connected to the heavenly air waves through the word of God. When you speak over the airwaves, you are invading and taking back the space of, *"the prince of the power of the air"*, and displacing the enemy so that God can rule over the airwaves and bring His purposes to pass. The truth is that every creation responds to sound waves spoken within the glory realm and Spirit of God, hence sound waves created by speech are so powerful that when you speak words of faith in the glory realm, everything responds to your words. When you declare God's word in the glory realm, the words you speak are released into the air which then joins with the breath of the Holy Ghost, causing an explosion in the realm of the spirit, scattering demonic powers, healing the sick and raising the dead. Upon ministration in the natural realm, the glory of God travels through the waves of the air before it could land on its recipients. This is Akin to the experience of John G. Lake who ignited a glory invasion in South Africa during the 1950s. It is said that the man ushered an explosive heavy weight of God's glory such that two weeks after the conference had ended, the glory of God was still falling upon the masses in the streets as they were seen falling under the power in the absence of a religious song or church gathering. The glory of God had infiltrated through the corridors of the air, engulfed the surrounding atmosphere and lingered on the clouds, buildings and streets that's why multitudes of people were falling under the power in the streets two weeks after the man of God had left the country. That is a quintessential example of an end time glory invasion. This is to tell you that the glory of God has its own atmosphere or climate that changes the atmosphere of the natural environment, culminating in what we call *heaven on earth*. Upon ministration in a given territory, the atmosphere of the glory gets to be infused in the natural atmosphere. In other words, it gets to be conditioned in the atmosphere of the territory in which it has been administered such that it creates its own spiritual environment or atmosphere which is different from the one that is naturally prevailing in that place.

Having you ever wondered what exactly happens to the substance of glory once it has been administered in a specific territory in the natural realm? Does it wear off or revert back to heaven? No! Upon administration in the natural realm, the glory of God lingers or hovers over the natural atmosphere upon buildings, trees, human bodies, cars, electric gargets, on the streets and the surrounding places or on any other natural substance that can retain the substance of glory. Through this way, that's how the *mantles* are able to fall on the next generation. Do you remember that the bones of Elisha, the Prophet retained the substance of glory for more than four hundred years after his death to the extent of raising a man from the dead? Does it sound quizzical to you that the substance of glory was even present in the grave? This is to tell you how profound, impactful and sustainable the glory is as a spiritual substance.

A DIVINE REVELATION OF AN OPEN HEAVEN

Have you ever noticed that the natural atmosphere in some geographical territories in the natural realm is not purely natural? It's because it has been impregnated by the substance of God's glory, which is why stepping into such territories culminates in the release of an unusual presence of God. Jerusalem and Bethel are quintessential examples of such places whose physical atmosphere has been permanently altered by the glory of God, hence they are operating as geographical portals to heaven. This is the reason why Heavens are opened over some territories while in some places they are closed. Have you ever wondered why it's like that? It's because the spiritual atmosphere of the glory would have been infused into the natural atmosphere of that particular territory.

When the atmosphere of the natural realm comes into contact with the atmosphere of the glory, it results in an Open Heaven in that territory.

That means territories where Heavens are closed require above all else the invasion of the substance of glory for them to open up and release the rain of Heaven. The glory of God is what opens the Heavens over geographical territories in the natural realm. Have you ever heard of *cloud seeding*, a process whereby a chemical is sprayed into the atmosphere in order to increase its humidity and provoke rain to fall? The administration of the glory operates in a like manner. It's like a spiritual substance that gets sprayed into the atmosphere, changing the weather conditions of that territory. That is why I have proved that the glory has it's own spiritual atmosphere, climate and even weather conditions.

An Open Heaven is a product of the precipitation of an atmospheric glory in a given territory in the natural realm.

Many people are accustomed to the internal dimension of glory which flows from the spirit of human vessels to touch the sick and cast out devils in their sphere of contact. However, there is another external dimension of glory called the *atmospheric glory*, which operates outside of human bodies, in the air. It occurs when the Holy Ghost impregnates the natural atmosphere with God's glory causing an explosion in the spirit realm. Did you know that it's not only human beings or objects which get anointed; even the atmosphere itself gets to be anointed, and when the atmosphere is anointed, its properties change such that it is enabled to operate with heavenly efficiency. It starts to operate just like the atmosphere of Heaven, radiating God's glory on earth and precipitating the rain of creative miracles. When the natural atmosphere is anointed with the substance of glory, we get the results of what we call an *open heaven*. That is why in some territories, it is always raining while others are in a dry period, spiritually speaking.

Prophetically speaking, we are about to enter a new season in church history— a phase that goes beyond the initial Pentecost experience of being filled with the Spirit. We are entering a phase that will cause us to challenge the very powers holding back the advance of the church. When this glory invasion is fully realized, it will usher in a supernatural acceleration of the things of God. The key to unlocking these new realms of glory is *faith* and *revelation*. When these elements are mixed together in a ministry or at a meeting, there will be a major glory explosion leading to visistations from Heaven's *Throne Room*, unimaginable signs and wonders and an unprecedented avalanche of souls into the Kingdom, glory to God!.

A DIVINE REVELATION OF "HEAVEN ON EARTH"

It is of paramount importance to unveil from the onset the divine reality that when God created Heavens and earth, His idea was not for these realms to function as two separate entities, completely alien to each other. He has always wanted an atmosphere of Heaven to overlay the earth so that it could function according to the original blueprint of Heaven. To substantiate this divine revelation with reference to scriptural evidence, Deuteronomy 11:21 (NKJV) reads, *"That your days may be multiplied and the days of your children and the days of **Heaven upon the earth."*** We see from this that God has intended for man to walk in Heaven's atmosphere right here on this planet. That is why the original atmosphere of earth in the Garden of Eden was the glory of God. Did you know that Adam used to live in *Heaven on earth*? In other words, he used to move freely across both realms of existence and to him moving from earth to Heaven was tantamount to moving from his living room into his bedroom. Figuratively speaking, the Garden of Eden was his *"little bed room"* where he rested after engaging animals while Heaven was his *"large living room"* where he operated and conversed with God in the coolness of the day. This was the case with Jesus who also easily shifted between these two realms to the extent that at one point He declared that *no one has ever been to Heaven except the son of man who lives in Heaven.* While the unveiling of this revelation became controversial as it ruffled the feathers of the critics, Jesus provided a quintessential example of how we should operate between Heaven and earth. That is why His life was a life of torrential miracles because He lived on earth as if it is Heaven.

When Jesus taught His disciples to pray *"Your Kingdom come and your will be done on earth as it is in Heaven"* this was not a beggarly request but He was sharing a revelation of how His disciples could bring down Heaven to earth (Mathew 6:10). He provided a quintessential model of how to rain down God's glory, anointing, blessings required by the inhabitants of the earth. In the context of the above scripture, the phrase, *"As it is in Heaven"* speaks of a conformance to the original design and blueprint of how things operate in Heaven. In Heaven there is neither sickness, death nor decay. So, when we usher the atmosphere of Heaven on earth, death becomes a stranger on the earth and sickness ceases to be a part of our vocabulary anymore. Therefore when Jesus taught His disciples to say, *"Your will be done on earth as it is in heaven* (Matthew 6:10), He was actually alluding to the manifestation of the glory. Why do I say so? It's because the will of God is for His glory to manifests intensely on earth. If God's will is to be done on earth as it is in Heaven, then one ingredient missing from earth as it is in heaven is the glory. When that glory appears on earth, then we can say with confidence that His will be done rapidly on earth as it would be in Heaven. The greater truth is that when Heaven invades the earth, things come into divine alignment and function according to the original blueprint God designed for humanity. How then do I live in the reality of Heaven on earth? By subduing the power of death, sickness, corruption as it is in Heaven as well as enforcing God's plan and purpose by moulding the destinies of multitudes in line with God's will.

The Bible begins with the creation of Heaven and earth and concludes its narrative with a beautiful picture of a new Heaven on earth. If you read these accounts together, it's almost as if the first book of the Bible and the last one are in conversation with each other. The New Testament is jam-packed with *Heaven on earth collisions.* Since Jesus's arrival on earth, Heaven has been colliding with the earthly realm. That is why the Bible says *ever since the time of John the Baptist the kingdom of Heaven has suffered violence and the violent shall take it by force.* The word, *"violence"* highlighted in this scripture does not speak of physical violence but a friction of collision between the Heavens and the earth as Heavens invades the natural realm. When Heaven collides with the earth, in what I call a *'Convergence of realms'*, that's when humanity experiences alarming breakthroughs, untold miracles and torrential flow of blessings in proportions never seen before. This collision culminates in streams of miracles, signs and wonders whereby it becomes naturally supernatural for one to converse with angels like a man talking to his friends and to parade on the streets of Heaven like a man marching over his own yard. At that level, walking in the supernatural or miraculous realm becomes your second nature and seeing the dead raised, cripples walk and the blind see becomes your normal mode of operation.

The other notion held by dozens of believers across the world which needs to be given divine correction is that Heaven is some kind of eutrophic atmosphere somewhere high up in the galaxies. Owing to a lack of revelation, some believers erroneously presume that when they come together in worship, the glory of God falls upon the congregation like apples falling from a tree. This creates a scenario in which believers are staring up in the atmosphere in search for a manifestation instead of drawing the Heavenly glory from within the inner corridors of their being. The greater truth is that the glory does not fall down upon you, instead, it flows out of you because Heaven is in you. It is more of an upward movement of glory from your spirit to God than it is a downward movement of glory from God to you. Therefore, your duty is to learn the art of drawing the glory of God from the Heaven within the depths of your spirit to bless your world. The truth is that Heaven is right in you. God's kingdom within you is waiting to be released against anything that is seeking to subvert His will in your life. As the Body of Christ, we are not meant to be at mercy of any negative influences of death, sickness, poverty or wickedness that grossly manifests in this word. In this season of glory, you don't have to wait for eternity or for you to die so that you can go to Heaven, instead, Heaven is coming down to you. It is imperative that you begin to live in *"Heaven"*, now while you are still on *'earth'* such that the day you finally depart to Heaven, you will not be a stranger in that realm.

The truth is that whether you like it or not, whether you are aware of it or not and whether you are ready for it or not, it is an inevitable reality that the glory of God is going to inundate planet earth as God is irrevocably determined to saturate the entire earth with a river of His glory in this end time season. We are stepping into God's original perfect design for the earth as the distance between Heaven and earth is being shortened. It Has further been scientifically discovered that the speed of lighting is slowing down and while the human mind can't comprehend this phenomena, it paints a prophetic picture of God's plan before He closes the curtain at the end of this age. That is why the purpose of this revelation is to fuel your fire for a full-blown no-holds-barren invasion of glory in this generation.

A DIVINE REVELATION OF THE GLORY OF GOD IN THE THRONE ROOM OF HEAVEN

What is a Throne Room?

It worth exploring the divine truth that God the Father, the Lord Jesus and Holy Spirit do not have a mansion or a place to stay unlike the saints in heaven who have mansions to live in. The Throne Room is God's house. This is where He lives. God's Throne Room is actually His house. We know all of heaven is His habitation, but the Throne Room is where He lives. In John 14: 1, Jesus said, *"In my Father's house are many mansions"*. Heaven is God's house. You never read anywhere in the Bible where it says that Jesus has a mansion or the Father has a special place where He goes in to retire from time to time or do whatever things He wants. The Throne Room is actually where He resides. It is His living room, bedroom and working place, where He permanently dwells. Everything in Heaven revolves around the Throne Room, the creatures with eyes at the front and back serve at the Throne Room; the 24 elders lie prostate before God at the throne Room and the angles move around the glory of God in the Throne Room.

How is the glory of God administered from the heavenly realm in the Throne Room?

In the throne room, God is the source of all light in the whole heavens. In reality, *there is no sun in heaven for the glory of God lights up all of heaven.* We read in the Word that angels radiate light and their presence has shininess about them. In heaven, angels have different degrees of brightness of the glory of God. At the throne room the life of God is in everything. It is because of the constant pulsating river of life that keeps flowing out from the throne of God that light up every life in Heaven. Glory and life are one in heaven. To have life is to have the glory and on the other side of the coin, to have the glory is to have life. In the throne room, angels do not have the same garments but garments are constantly changing for different purposes and there are different types of clothing that are won and these are a reflection of God's glory. In the throne room, the past, present and the future disappear. It is a realm where you entered into whereby everything in the past and everything in the future is just like the present, everything is already done, completed and finished. There is no time. You do not feel it. And everything that God has spoken from the Throne through the prophets that spoke and what Jesus said while He was on the earth will come to pass and Jesus and the Father need not to lift one finger to make the word of God come to pass. The power and impact of the spoken word of God even if it was spoken ages ago is so powerful. It is like looking into infinity. You cannot see the end.

Then within Heaven itself, there were different planes or realms of glory. Within each place is a manifestation of God. It is not like having different planes or degrees of glory and there is a throne of God for each plane. There is only one plane where the throne of God is but if you were on the lower plane and you approached God from that lower plane, you would still see God's Throne but the Throne of God you would see and experience would be from that lower plane. It is the same Throne but reflected through, for example, seven degrees of glory and you see the Throne of God differently from the way I see it. Believers could reach to the Throne of God and see different parts of the Throne. Heaven is a bee-hive of activities. Different things are coming to the Throne of God and things are also being issued forth. The Throne Room of God is not static. It does not stay the same where you imagine you see only the glory of God and the shininess of it all the time. Different things take place at the Throne at different times. Sometimes the manifestation of the glory of God is so powerful in the Throne Room that it feels like one is in a furnace and could not even see the face of God. This is what it means to experience the glory of God in fullness.

A DIVINE REVELATION OF THE RESURRECTION GLORY

*Firstly, the resurrection glory is the dynamic ability or transfusion of the incorruptible life of God imparted upon a human vessel, that causes him to raise the dead or resuscitate a person from death after his spirit has departed or been relinquished from the body. Contextually, it implies reinstatement, recuperation and resuscitation of lost life of humanity due to the spirit of death in operation. It is the ultimate in the school of power as it depicts the highest dimension of power in the realm of God which humanity in all extreme quarters of life can tap into. It is the fullness of God's power exhibited in a particular locality as it denotes the highest level of concentration of God's power in a given territory. It is the power of God in its visible, tangible and solidly demonstrative form.

It must be expressly understood in this context that in the realm of God's glory, there is neither sickness, death nor decay nor any form of corruption. In Heaven, death is rendered non-existent, sickness is declared illegitimate and corruption is not even a part of the vocabulary of Heaven. That is why when operating in the glory realm, the instant a believer steps on the death scene and the glory of God upon him comes into contact with the dead body, even without saying a word, the dead arises instantaneously. Once commanded in the glory realm, the spirit of the dead person comes back into the dead body within the twinkling of an eye because nothing can resist the compelling, alluring and attractive magnetic force that comes through the glory of God. This is the essence of *Resurrection glory*. Therefore, when you step on any death scene, you need to have the audacity to release Heaven in you into the atmosphere of any death-infested territory you step on. Since there is neither death, sickness nor decay in Heaven, the dead are compelled to rise up when you confront them with an atmosphere of Heaven in you. That is why when you command the dead to arise, they respond instantaneously because the word in your mouth is actually God talking from the Throne room of Heaven in you. Therefore all spiritual beings even angels respond as if it's God actually instructing them to move.

> **Secondly, the resurrection glory is a third day wave of ever-coursing torrent of electrifying divine power that was released from the cross as a result of the resurrection of the Lord Jesus Christ from the dead and serves as an acid test, infallible proof and incontestable evidence that He indeed rose from the dead. It is the earth-quaking, grave-opening, dead-raising and death-busting power of Christ that was legitimately given birth to in the spirit realm through the cross at Calvary and divinely transacted following the resurrection of the Lord Jesus Christ from the dead. It is the very same power that shook the earth, split the rocks, opened the grave and tore apart the curtain in the Holy of Holies after Jesus yielded His last breath on the cross.*

The truth is that as long as death, in the form of either tumour, cancer or any kind of sickness can still express itself in your body or on anybody in your sphere of contact, it's against your reign as an ambassador of Heaven. Sadly, not knowing how to rightly apply the Word has made some not to see the reality of God's Word, and as a result, live in the realm of promises. It's the reason some are still subject to the elements of this world, battling with headaches, sicknesses or death, instead of living the life of dominion through the Spirit. Faith is the response of the human spirit to the word of God. In response to the scripture: Romans 8:11, "*...if the Spirit of him that raised up Jesus from the dead dwell in me, he that raised up Christ from the dead shall also quicken my mortal body,*" begin to declare,

> *"The same Spirit that raised Jesus from the dead has taken up His abode in me, and has vitalized my mortal body; He has made my body come alive with the life of God! Now I have the life and nature of God in me. I'm therefore programmed to raise the dead, glory to God!"*

This is a present-hour reality. This was what the Apostle Paul knew, that's why he didn't panic when facing the dead body of Eutycus. Instead, he confronted it, imparted the *resurrection anointing* and then publicly announced that the boy was alive. Neither did he panic when a venomous viper fastened itself around his arm. Instead, he merely shook the beast into the fire and continued what he was doing. Being born again and filled with the Holy Spirit, you no longer live by blood but by the power of the Spirit. The same Spirit that raised Jesus Christ from the dead has given life to your physical body, making you indestructible, glory to God! Therefore, it is now your turn to impart that immortal life upon the dead, mortal bodies of man and raise them up. That's why you need to reject any infestation of death and just like what Smith Wigglesworth did, decree that no one is going to die in your locality without your permission and it will be established. That's what Jesus was when He walked the earth; He was the unveiling of the Word: "*And the Word was made flesh, and dwelt among us*" (John 1:14). He was the manifestation of God; the express image of His person hence He never allowed death to reign. Now that you're in Christ, you're the express image of Christ and the quintessence or embodiment of everything that Jesus was while on earth. Through you, the world should be able to see Jesus walking amongst them. His presence is evident in your words and actions. You're Christ alive in your world today hence you are a point of contact with Heaven. You're a God-carrying vessel; you make manifest the His *resurrection glory* in every territory of the world (2 Corinthians 2:14). That is why when you step on any death scene, God has arrived because you carry Him in your spirit. Carry this consciousness with you every day, that Christ is alive in you and you shall have the tenacity to raise multitudes form the dead as if you are waking them up from a slumber.

> *Thirdly, the resurrection glory is a Supernatural manifestation of a special grace granted by the Holy Spirit to vitalise or quicken a mortally wounded body of a man and bring it back to life after it would have been separated from its eternal spirit. It is the same degree and measure of power which the Holy Ghost exerted upon Jesus when He raised Him up from the dead.*

Prophetically speaking, we are now entering into a dimension of glory that is to become common place to the children of God and walking in the supernatural and raising the dead shall become a daily experience just like healing a headache. It is worth exploring in this regard the divine truth that contrary to what multitudes of believers presume, the pulpit is not the only platform or setting for the explosive acts of God to be played out on. For too long has the power of God been confined on the artificial stage within church bars and premises but the time has come that the power of God will be demonstrated live in the streets, market place and the public arena. The days have come whereby the glory of God shall manifest intensely on earth such that an ordinary Christian will walk into a hospital and get all the sick healed and an average believer will just step into a mortuary and command all the dead bodies to rise up and walk and it shall be established. This shall curtail the rampage instigated by the devil through alarming deaths and de-programme his operations, while installing the agenda of heaven.

To cement this revelation with reference to further experiential evidence, let me officially introduce you to a man called Smith Wigglesworth, who lived in England during the 19th century and unequivocally set a standard of *resurrection power* for his generation such that he was called the Great Apostle of Faith,. This man was mightily used by God in raising the dead to the extent that no one died in his neighbourhood without his permission. To him, that was unacceptable and if anybody happened to die in his town or city, he would go and raise him from the dead. To him, raising the dead was a common phenomenon just like healing the sick. What's so striking about him is that when he raised the dead, he would not beg that anybody rise up from the dead. Instead, he would use his royal prerogative as a son of God to drag them out of their coffins, thrust them against the walls, point at their faces and command them to walk, and in some cases to start running. He had such unquenchable thirst, insatiable appetite and perennial hunger for resurrection and basing his unwavering faith on the divine truth that *as the father raises the dead, so does the son give life to whoever he wills,* he believed that no one in his locality should die without his permission. It is for this reason that he had such unusual tenacity to confront the dead in any situation and results were remarkable. Even when his wife died, Smith took the authority over death that he had wielded very successfully on many occasions and He boldly commanded her spirit to return to her body. He would not give up until God responded to His anointed servant and she revived. However, she sat up and said to him, "*Smith Wigglesworth, what are you doing, let me go. I'm with the Lord*", and he finally released her.

If God used a man like him to that extent, then he can use you too. You too can walk in the footsteps of Smith Wigglesworth and make up your mind that no one is going to die in your community without your permission and it shall be established in heaven. As a matter of fact, in your capacity as a son of God, you form part of the *Board of Heaven*, hence you have an exclusive right and power to use your royal prerogative to decide who should depart from earth and who shouldn't. This is because the Bible unveils the spiritual reality in John 5:21, that *as the Father raises the dead and gives life to man, so does the son gives life to whosoever he wishes.* That means you have the exclusive birth right as a son of God to declare that no one should die in your community without your permission just like what Smith Wigglesworth did and heaven will endorse it with a stamp of God's approval.

Another thrilling and spectacular display of resurrection power, which boggles the mind, was exhibited by Saint Patrick, the Apostle of Ireland, whom God used mightily to raise a man from the dead two weeks after he had died, a case almost similar to the resurrection of Lazarus by the Lord Jesus Christ. One striking reality is that the man had already been buried but upon arrival at the grave, Saint Patrick signed the grave with his staff and then commanded the people to dig up the grave and take out the coffin. He then commanded the dead man to rise up from the dead and instantly, the man whose body was now rotting in the grave, stood up from the coffin and began to talk. As if that was not enough, Saint Patrick also raised an unbeliever who had died and suffered torments in hell and after raising him up, he led him to Christ and then sent him, this time to heaven. On another occasion, a band of man who hated Saint Patrick, falsely accused him of stealing and then sentenced him to death. Saint Patrick needed someone to witness for him in court, so, he raised a man from a nearby tomb and commanded him to testify for him and the man who had been dead for years, came forth from the tomb and testified for him. Seeing this spectacular demonstration of resurrection power, all his accusers repented and became his converts, glory to God. Although it boggles the mind, this is a deeper realm and dimension of resurrection which the world is about to witness in this end time season.

In a similar vein, God mightily used Saint Francis Xavier who performed a spectacular act of resurrection after a woman cried to him to raise her daughter from the dead after she was already buried. He knelt down and prayed shortly, after that he said to the woman, *"Go to the grave and check, for your daughter lives"* and when they hurriedly went to the grave, they removed the tomb and her daughter came out alive. If you think this is the worst case scenario of resurrection you have ever heard of, wait until I unveil one more recent testimony of the resurrection of a Ghananian man from the dead after one year of his death. It is said that the man was buried for the whole year but came back to life, having seen Michael Jackson and the Pope in hell fire. This is to tell you that the grave is not a point of no return since it is possible for a man to be raised from the dead even long after he is buried. The excruciating truth is that whether Lazarus was buried for four days (John 11:39) and this man for a year makes no difference because time is not of essence in resurrection since God lives in the realm of eternity which is outside our time dimension. The above scenarios are some of the mind-blowing divine resurrection encounters which believers are about to experience as a worldwide global sensation in this very hour. And you too are part of *God's League of Revolutionaries* to spearhead the *Global Resurrection Revolution* in this end time season.

Prophetically speaking, as I'm birthing forth this revelation from the spirit realm, I'm seeing in the spirit, a rise of multitudes of people whom God is going to use mightily in the ministry of raising the dead. I see them rise up from small beginning, casting off their old clocks and declaring that enough is enough! Never again shall we watch the devil wreak havoc in our communities and the time has come to break the rod of wickedness centred on the phenomenon of death! And as they boldly utter these words, I see multitudes rise from the dead, to the glory of God. Therefore, raising the dead in this end time season shall be as common in the Body of Christ as the phenomenon of people falling under the power. God will use you mightily to such an extent that raising the dead becomes a second nature to you. A phenomenon that gets the whole world trembling on its knees will be to you like a walk through a park. If you view all things from God's perspective, you will then realise that it is a small thing to raise the dead. While you thought this was an unfathomable impossibility prior to this revelation, your mind is now opened into the new realities of resurrection and the dimension of understanding the purpose of God in your life. Now, you will begin to feel what God feels, see the way God sees and ultimately act the way God acts. This is the extent to which God will use you in this end time season, to provoke an insatiable appetite for resurrection that will cause you to raise the dead as if you are waking up man from a slumber! For a deeper revelation on this subject, I would like to refer you to one of my anointed books tilted, *"The Realm of Power to Raise the Dead"*, By Apostle Frequency Revelator.

CHAPTER TWO

TRANSITION FROM THE REALM OF THE ANOINTING TO THE REALM OF GLORY

A Divine Revelation of the Distinction between the Dimension of the Anointing and the Dimension Glory

What Is The Difference Between The Glory And The Anointing?

It is a fact that in the current scenario across a broad spectrum of Christian faith, multitudes of believers are familiar with the manifestation of the anointing but know little about the manifestation of the glory. This is because in the recent times, more emphasis has been placed on believers walking in the anointing as opposed to the glory hence, few of them have managed to tap into the realm of God's glory. The consequence or result of this trend has been the spiritual production of believers who are full of the substance of the anointing but devoid of the glory which sustains that anointing. Therefore, we should learn to move in the realm of God's glory just as we learn to move in the anointing. We should learn to develop in glory as we develop in the anointing. Contrary to what multitudes of Christians across a broad spectrum of Christian faith presume, having an anointing is not as same thing as moving in God's glory, which alludes to His attributes. The anointing is a part of God, operating through us. Basically, the anointing of God is a manifestation of the power of God while the glory of God is a manifestation of His attributes. It is only one aspect of His power because there are many divergent aspects of God's power. In view of the above, carefully consider the following divine truth:

Holistically speaking, God's power demonstrated in the arena of spiritual warfare is called MIGHT, God's power manifested in the arena of finances is called WEALTH, God's power demonstrated in the arena of territorial governance is called is DOMINION, God's power manifested in the arena of ministry is called the ANOINTING, but God's power demonstrated in the arena of sovereignty is called THE GLORY, which is the highest dimension of power in the realm of God.

The anointing of God is the tangible manifestation of God's power while the glory of God is the manifestation of God's person and attributes. Both are manifestations. Both are touchable. Both have degrees or levels of manifestation. Both are of a heavenly materiality. Both are manifested together inseparably, just as God's attributes and power are inseparable parts of His being. The manifestation of the anointing of God is in direct proportion to the manifestation of the glory of God. Although the anointing and the glory can be attributable or traced to the same source, the glory supersedes the anointing in divergent spheres. The following are therefore aspects of distinction between operating in the anointing and operating in the glory:

It is of paramount significance to unveil right from the onset the divine truth that in the context of this revelation, there are two ways through which God administers His power on earth, which is through qualified agent *(anointing)* or by Himself *(glory)*. No matter the various ways God has shown His power, they can be summed up in two categorical words, that is the *anointing* (manifestation), and the *glory* (revelation). These two stages equate to direct versus indirect engagement or involvement of the person of God, which ushers in His power. The application of the power of God is designed to achieve or materialize God's purpose. Whether channelled through alternative source or direct application, the result must be the same. Remember that the person of the Godhead must be involved to experience the power of God. The power of God cannot be imitated or manufactured because it is part of God's special personal qualities and qualifications.

You get to see the glory of God through the anointing because the anointing is what connects you to the glory of God.

It is worth exploring the divine truth that the anointing lays a groundwork or preparation platform for the glory to be revealed or manifested. God's presence and power are resident in the anointing, hence any man of God who taps into the realm of the anointing and manifests miracles, signs and wonders, ushers the glory of God on the scene. In this case, the anointing reveals or manifests the glory of God. In Acts 10:38, the Bible speaks of *how God anointed Jesus of Nazareth with the Holy Ghost and with power, who went about doing good, and healing all those oppressed of the devil, for God was with Him.* In other words, what qualified Him to usher such an immeasurable glory of God manifested through signs and wonders is the anointing. This implies that the anointing is what certifies and authenticates God's unwavering supremacy, divine plans and purpose in the light of His creation. In the absence of the anointing, the glory is not revealed because the anointing is what prepares us for the glory. Faith calls the anointing and the anointing calls the glory but both are key dimensions of the supernatural.

It is a typical scenario in some charismatic cycles that some people presume that the anointing and the glory is one and the same thing hence they are devoid of revelation knowledge to press from the realm of the anointing into that of glory. On the other extreme, some are just so obsessed about the anointing and in the process neglects the glory that brings that anointing. That is why in this end time dispensation there is an emphasis in the supernatural for a progressive transition from the realm of the anointing to the realm of God's glory and this is what forms the central theme and agenda of Heaven in these current times. Philosophically speaking, the anointing is like the light. The light is what manifests the glory of the sun. Without the sun, there is no light and by the same token without the glory, there is no anointing. However, it is the light which makes manifest the glory of the sun and in a similar vein, it is the anointing that manifest the glory of God.

It is worth mentioning that elevation into higher realms of the anointing is largely dependent on the persistent and progressive application of spiritual laws and principles while migration into higher realms of glory is dependent on the sovereign will of God.

The anointing operates by human discretion, prerogative or initiative while the glory works by divine initiative

This implies that you operate by faith in the realm of the anointing but in the realm of glory, you operate by God's initiative and divine sovereignty since it is an unknown dimension. However, only if the glory does not manifest, can you tap into the realm of gifts, faith and the anointing. When operating in the realm of glory, God demands a greater degree of humility and dependence on Him. This is because elevation into higher realms of glory demands pure motives and boldness in the spirit.

We operate in the anointing to make things happen but in the realm of glory, everything has already happened

---

It is worth exploring the truth that when you operate in the glory realm, it's not necessarily the level of faith that brings about a miracle when your faith brings you to the realm where things have already happened. It is not your faith that is trying to make something happen because you are in a realm where it already exists. Therefore, when operating in the realm of glory, don't allow your mind to be programmed to think according to earthly time because you have dominion over time. Heavens are perfect, there is nothing you lack or need, while the earth is in a prophetic drama, Heaven is a realm where it has already happened. It is not going to happen. It has already happened, yet in the earth it has not happened yet. To shade clarity and more light on this revelation, it is of paramount importance to highlight the divine truth that there are two dimensions of time, the *earthly time* measured in hours and seconds and *eternity or Heaven's time* which is infinite. But the truth is that God operates according to the eternal time which falls outside our time dimension in the natural realm and has given us the ability to have dominion over time in the natural realm by superimposing eternal time on the earthly time. So, with regard to possessing your possessions, you have to decide whether you are going to wait for the earthly time for them to mature so that you can possess them or you are going to shift to the eternal realm, which is Heavens' time to possess your blessings before time.

The greater truth is that while modern day believers are so much conscious about the issue of timing, you need to understand that when operating in the glory realm, things happen before the time they are scheduled to happen. Do you know that when Jesus changed water into wine at a wedding in Galilee, that miracle happened before its time? Why do I say so? Because even Jesus said it himself that, *"Woman why do you bother me before My time?"* The miracle was not supposed to happen at that time but it happened because Mary placed a demand on the anointing upon Jesus, thereby provoking Him to usher in the miracle before its time. That is the same principle by which Jesus ushered an atmosphere of glory such that the Syrophonician woman who insisted that *even dogs eat the crumbs from the children's table,* received her healing way before her time. She became an exception because in time, the cross had not occurred yet and salvation had not yet been made available to the gentiles. But she received her salvation and healing before its scheduled time according to God's calendar. Smith Wigglesworth, the man of God who raised the greatest number of people from the dead, understood this divine principle, hence he declared *"If the Holy Ghost does not move, I move the Holy Ghost"*, meaning if the Spirit of God does not do certain divine tasks because it's not yet time for them to be released, I place a demand on Heavens for them to be released, whether it's time or not.

That is why the man who understand how to operate in the glory realm does not wait for the next six months the doctor has prescribed as time for him to receive his healing in the future, but he reaches up to the glory realm and possess his healing whether it's time or not. That is why when a healthy, bouncing baby boy is given birth within 3 months, humanity don't accept it but consider the baby to be premature because they don't understand the operation of the glory realm in which things happen way before their scheduled time. It might not be my earthly time for me to receive my breakthrough but my Heaven's time to receive. Hence, if I can't get what I want because the earthly time does not permit me to, I shift to the eternal realm, which is Heavens' time, and get it way before my earthy time. Do you want to become a millionaire and the world's richest? Don't wait until you are sixty to become one. Do you want move in miracles, signs and wonders manifested in raising the dead, opening the eyes of the blind and raising cripples form wheel chairs? Don't wait until you are ordained as a Bishop for you to start moving in power. Just tap into the glory ream and reach out to your miracle whether it's your time or not.

In view of this divine truth, the Bible also attests to the divine truth that *the lamb was slain before the foundation of time.* (Revelation 13:8). But how can Jesus be said to be crucified before even coming into the world? It's because long before Jesus came down to earth, in the realm of God, it was deemed as already completed. Although the inhabitants of the earth were waiting for the time for Jesus to enact the scenes by coming down to earth, and go through the cross, die and rise from the dead, in the realm of God, it was already a done deal because in God, the past, present and future are all in past tense. In other words, Jesus just went back in time into the foundations of the world where the stripes were already laid and enacted the scenes. This is to tell you that eternity breaks the law of time, gives you dominion over earthly time and ushers you into a dimension where you are able to touch the past, present and future as if they have already happened. That is why in the glory realm there is neither waiting, procrastination, postponement nor delays of any nature for things happen before their time.

In the absence of God's glory, the anointing is such a powerful way to minister to the congregation

---

The reality is that when you minister under the anointing, the Holy Spirit uses your physical body to minister to the congregation such that when that anointing lifts off, the body is usually exhausted although you might not feel that physical drain or sudden experience of fatigue while the anointing is flowing. On the contrary, when you minister in the atmosphere of glory, you do it so effortlessly such that there are times when you just have to step aside and wait on the Lord because you cannot do anything under the weight of His presence. It is at that level of operation that you become a witness to the power of God as you watch and see the King of glory Himslef in action. During ministerial sessions, when the glory of God is moving powerfully, I have often stepped aside and relinquished my place to God and simply said, *"Holy Spirit, here I am. If you want me to do anything, just let me know"*. This is a realm where people receive instantaneous healing and deliverance all over the congregation even without anybody praying for them.

The reality is that some people taste the spectacular experience of moving in the glory but then still want to crash back and minister under the anointing. Once you taste the glory, you may never want to go back to minister in the anointing again. However, this is not meant to dishonour the anointing in any way since it is such a great treasure of Heaven. What it simply means is that in the absence of God's glory, the anointing is such a powerful way to minister to the congregation but when the glory shows up in a meeting, the anointing gives way. When operating in the anointing, at times you can burn out. This is because the anointing of God is the outpouring for work. It's power for service. But operating in the glory of God is not the display of any gift. In the glory of God, you rest because energy is not being used. In the glory realm, it is all Him. Therefore, when we learn to live in the glory of God, our work becomes easy; from the outpouring to the glory, our lives are renewed.

The anointing can be measured in realms and dimensions but the glory is immeasurable and inexhaustible

In the realm of the spirit, our levels of achievement are metered by the measure of the grace of God which is either the anointing or the dimension of the glory. However, it must be understood that the glory is not measured like the anointing. The anointing is a substitute substance for the glory. This means that you can substitute the glory for the anointing but you can never substitute the anointing for the glory because the operation of the glory is not subject to human control. It is therefore advisable that you operate under the anointing only when the glory of God does not show up but when it does, you can give way to God's sovereignty.

The truth is that the anointing could be measured. In 2 Kings 2, the Bible tells the story of the great prophet, Elijah, and how he was transported via a chariot of fire to Heaven. But before that time, Elisha, one of the prophets that served him entreated *"I pray thee, let a double portion of thy spirit be upon me"* (2 Kings 2:9). So, Elisha received a *double portion* of Elijah's spirit (2 Kings 2:9), which simply refers to a *double measure* of the anointing. As a result of that double measure of the anointing, the miracles recorded of his ministry exactly doubled those of Elijah. In essence, Elijah performed eight miracles while Elisha performed sixteen, which is exactly the *double measure* of what Elijah had accomplished in his life time. This record of an exact double portion of miracles in Elisha's life shows us that Elisha functioned in twice the power that Elijah had. This is the same principle by which God took the same Spirit that was upon Moses and imparted it upon the seventy elders (Numbers 11:17). In fact, it was said of Jesus by John that He had the Spirit upon Him without measure (John 3:34). The word *'measure'* being used here implies that the anointing had been previously given in measures to people in the Old Testament dispensation but now was given without measure to our Lord Jesus Christ.

Therefore, the term *double portion* refers to a mega or double dose of the anointing released for a massive supernatural harvest. It is a magnified or multiplied anointing given to individuals to accomplish tasks to greater or unimaginable proportions as compared to others. The term *double portion* does not mean something multiplied by itself; instead, it implies a measure of anointing that has been greatly enlarged, multiplied, increased exorbitantly in superfluous and measureless proportions. In essence, the *double portion* of the anointing is actually the mantle because a mantle is an anointing that has thickened as one graduate in a particular office. What Elisha called a *"double portion"*, we could term a *"double measure"* of the anointing to stand in the same office. The thing that was special about this anointing was the added dimension. It's the same anointing, except a different measure. What Elisha meant by requesting for a double portion was that he wanted a *double measure* of that anointing of God to stand in the office of prophet. That is why he did twice as many miracles as Elijah.

However, precaution must be taken regarding how we interpret the phrase, *"Double portion"* of one's spirit. This is because today, there are Christians who take a cue from Elisha and pray that the Lord would grant them *"a double portion"* of the anointing. That's a wrong prayer. The new creation doesn't require any double portion of the anointing because He's got all of it! When you were born again and the Holy Spirit came into your life, He didn't come in bits and fragments; He came to dwell in you in His fullness. What Elisha meant by *"double portion"* is understood from Moses' instruction to the Israelites about the rights of the firstborn in Deuteronomy 21:17: *"he shall acknowledge the son of the hated for the firstborn, by giving him a double portion of all that he hath: for he is the beginning of his strength; the right of the firstborn is his."* What this means is that, if for example, a man had six sons, he'd have to divide his entire inheritance into seven places, such that the firstborn gets a double share, as the right of the firstborn, while the remaining five sons get one each.

This was what Elisha requested for; the right of the firstborn. He wanted to assume the position of leadership amongst the other prophets in Israel, who at that time were under the tutelage of the prophet Elijah. And because of his spiritual perception, he got it and became the leading prophet over them (2 Kings 2:1-25). It's a misapprehension to say that Elisha wanted twice what Elijah had; there's no way that could have happened because it would mean Elisha asking Elijah for what he (Elijah) didn't have. Therefore, you don't have to ask God for a double portion of the Spirit, because the Bible says *"And of his fulness have all we received, and grace for grace"* (John 1:16). *For he whom God has sent speaks the words of God: for God gives not the Spirit by measure unto him* (John 3:34). Just as the Lord Jesus had the Spirit without measure, because He was sent of the Father, you also have the Spirit without measure (John 3:34) because Jesus said, *"As my Father hath sent me, even so send I you"* (John 20:21). So, all you need do is to continually get yourself filled with the glory to overflowing as the Apostle Paul admonished in Ephesians 5:18-19.

While we prophesy into the future when operating in the anointing, in the realm of glory, things happen the instant they are declared in the natural realm.

It is worth exploring the divine truth that contrary to operating in the realm of gifts and the anointing, in the glory, things happen the instant they are declared. You don't have to wait forver in order for something to be delivered to you. In view of this divine truth, let me explain the difference between *confession* and *declaration*. The word *confession* is originally derived from the Greek word, *"Homologous",* which means to say exactly the same things as God says; If God says something should happen next year, it doesn't change, it remains next year; if He says you are going to receive a blessing after 10 years, it doesn't change, it remains 10 years according to earthly time. On the other hand, the word, *declare* comes from a Greek word *edere,* which means to bring something forward by either announcing, predicting or proclaiming it. That means you don't have to wait for it to happen. Instead, you make it happen within whichever time frame you decide to. You reach out into the future and bring it forth into the present such that it manifests now.

Therefore, in this *kairos* moment which marks the summation of ages and God's conclusion of His eternal plan for the earth, we need to move beyond the realm of *confession* to the realm of *prophetic declaration* so that we can secure things before their earthly time. The good news is that when operating in the glory realm, you don't have to wait for December to come. Why? Because when you declare a thing, you are bringing something forward that should occur in its natural time. In the Glory realm, there is no time. Time does not exist because the cloak is not ticking. Therefore, when operating in the realm of the Spirit, we must discern that time is virtually at an end, hence you don't have to wait until the end to believe God for the fulfilment of great things. That is why in Isaiah 46:10, God talks about, *"Declaring the end from the beginning, and from ancient times the things that are not yet done, saying, My counsel shall stand, and I will do all my pleasure."* This is to tell you that while the human mind is programmed to start something from the beginning and finish it at the end, God starts from the end and then comes back to the beginning to announce to us what He has already accomplished in the end. What an interestingly amazing God! And He does that for fun, for pleasure!

Therefore, when you begin flowing in the Glory of God, your level of faith begins to change. You learn that it is not necessarily the level of faith that brings the miracle when your faith brings you to the realm where things have already happened. It is not your faith that is trying to make something happen because you are in a realm where it already exits. Since we are still programmed to think according to time, we can miss something that truly is for now. I am not talking about a confession or how much faith you have because confession is simply agreeing with what God has said but declaration is altering that which God has determined to happen at a specific earthly time so that it can happen earlier according to Heaven's time. Do you know that there are times whereby you have to place a demand on the Heavens to release what you want and Heavens will not be left with any other choice except to release it? This is what Jesus meant when He said *whatever you release on earth shall be released in heaven*, meaning if you release something in Heaven, even way before its earthly time, it will be released. That is why when operating in the glory realm, we have to believe that no word that comes from the Throne is "next year". Because the Heaven is the realm where it has already happened, it's not going to happen. Instead, it has already happened although in the earth it has not happened as yet. That is why you need to go beyond the realm of *confession* to the realm of *declaration* to bring forward that which is supposed to happen in the future, according to earthly time.

Philosophically speaking, the presence says God is here, the anointing says God has something in His hands but the Glory says IAM

The presence is the multifaceted way that God shows up to meet us where we are. The presence is God with us. It is God inhabiting our praises (Psalms 22:3). The anointing is when God shows up in the presence and has something in His hands to give us. The anointing is associated with the hand of God but it is the presence that brings the anointing. It is not the other way around. The glory of God is His manifest presence, when God makes Himself visible to His people. When the men on the street can see God, they stand in awe of God for they have seen the glory. Things happen in the glory without us asking. That is why in this end time season, many people will be healed, delivered and even raised from the dead without a congregation, a song or an usher as the power of God invades the streets, market places and the public arena.

There is a new prophetic dimension surfacing in the glory realm whereby things are coming to pass as they are being said. In the glory realm, there is no procrastination, or delays because time is inconsequential. When God declared in an atmosphere of glory, *let there be light*, light came forth instantly. He didnt have to wait. Results came as words were declared. In the glory zone, there is no waiting because waiting is a process in time, of which we have dominion over time, we operate outside the time dimension because we were given birth to in the eternal realm which falls outside our time dimension. The reason why some believers experience delays in their lives is because of the absence of glory. The less you are filled with the glory, the longer it takes for you to cast out darkness and experience victory in your life. Real spiritual warfare takes place in the glory because there, the Lord fights for your battles. Outside the glory, you fight your own battles but inside the glory, God fights for you.

Notable is the realisation that even deliverance happens so fast in the glory zone because demons are not permitted to enter, death is rendered illegitimate and sickness is not permitted to reign. Because we have dominion over time, in the glory realm, you can declare a thing and use your royal prerogative to stipulate the time frame when that thing must come to pass, whether in a day, week or few hours. When the Bible says *you shall declare a thing and it shall be established for you*, it doesn't talk about flippantly declaring empty words in any direction but it talks about declaring things while in the glory realm or in an atmosphere of glory. That's when things happen. That is why those who function in higher reallms of glory don't wait for things to happen, instead, they make things happen.

It is much quicker to accomplish tasks under the glory than with the anointing

---

It is worth exploring the divine truth that when the glory of God is fully realised, it ushers in a supernatural acceleration of the things of God. With this heightened degree of acceleration, comes a greater accomplishment of divine tasks, something that would not have been possible when solely operating under the anointing. The greater truth is that there is a heightened degree of acceleration in the realm of God's glory. Prophetically speaking, we are about to enter the eternal zone where time is loosing its grip on earth as eternity is invading time in the natural realm and the dominant realm, eternity, displaces time as the two worlds collide. As aforementioned, we are at the consummation of time when Heaven's atmosphere of glory is invading the earthly realm. This Heavenly atmosphere of bliss brings with it the eternal realm of glory, culminating in the manifestation of *Heaven on earth* and the rendering of the time dimension in the earthly realm inconsequential. In other words, we have entered *the rush hour* of God, a critical moment in God's calendar in which things are moving so fast in the realm of the spirit as we are adjourning quickly towards the second coming of the Lord, Jesus Christ.

In this critical *"Kairos"* moment, alarming breakthroughs in the realm of the spirit will be encountered in all extreme quarters of life. In other words, things which man never thought possible will be accomplished with the speed of lightning in this very hour. It has been scientifically proven that even the speed of light is slowing down as we are nearing the end of age. The Lord showed me recently in a divine encounter how time is running out and eternity is rushing in. It appears that we are encroaching towards a season when even time is even coming to a point of halt. Paul concurs that even *tongues are going to cease* (I Corinthians 13). Likewise, prophecy will also cease because everything is in the glory where there is no time. We are nearing the end of time, hence the time for prophecy to be fulfilled is narrowing. What would normally take 6 months is going to take a month. What would take a month is going to take a week. What would take a week is going to take a day. In just one week, God will allow you to do what would have taken fifty years to accomplish. This is to tell you how fast tasks are accomplished in the glory as opposed to operating in the anointing.

To cement this revelation with reference to scriptural evidence, the Bible records an incident in Luke 5:1-11, whereby Peter spent the whole night fishing but could not catch anything despite the fact that he was an experienced fisherman. Peter had previously received an impartation of the anointing from Jesus by virtue of his association with Him. However, he needed to be catapulted to the realm of glory to expedite or accelerate the process. That means the anointing to get the job done was present but the glory to perfect that anointing and speed up the process is what was lacking because in the glory, things are accomplished within the twinkling of an eye. However, when Peter received a divine instruction from Jesus to shift his position and cast into the deep and let down the nets for a catch, he exited the dimension of the anointing where he was operating using his own strength and stepped into the glory realm and instantaneously, he caught a multitude of fish within a split of a moment. This is because when the glory of God manifests, everything accelerates.

With the gifts of the spirit, we can reach individuals and with the anointing we can reach the multitudes but with the glory we can reach the whole world in a spilt of a moment

The realm of glory is a higher dimension beyond the realm of gifts and the anointing, hence we need to tap into the realm of glory if ever we want to make a global impact. Prophetically speaking, that means millions of souls can be reached within a short period of time when operating under the glory than under the anointing. As a matter of fact, divine tasks which could have taken years to complete are accomplished within a flip of a moment in the glory. This is the reason why three thousand people were converted to Christ in one day when the Greater glory of God was extensively manifested during the days of the early church (Acts 2:41). The reality is that what could have taken a decade to build, with the anointing can be accomplished within a year or less when we consistently dwell in the glory. This is because time does not exist in the dimension of God's glory. That is why we can stand in the presence of God for hours and it seems like we were only there for thirty minutes.

The greater truth is that when the church operates in the dimension of glory, a spiritual acceleration takes place both in *quantity* and *quality*. In other words, there is a transformation that takes place evidenced by change in people's characters, drastic growth in ministry, alarming increase in finances, increased visitations to the Throne Room as well as an outburst of creative miracles. This tells me that when operating in the glory, everything accelerates and waiting time decreases. This is what happens when God is at work from a dimension that lacks the variables of time, space and matter. That means what used to take us a year to accomplish in the anointing will now take a day when operating in the glory. For example, if it normally takes a pastor five years under the anointing to build a two hundred member congregation, under the glory, it can take him one day to reach a thousand members. When operating in the atmosphere of glory, it is possible on the same day you start a ministry that you attain thousands of members. This happened at Pentecost whereby three thousand believers were added to the church as a result of the intense manifestation of the glory of God's spirit. With the glory of God, we can reach the whole world within a short space of time and witness and unprecedented avalanche of billions of souls into the Kingdom of God.

While the anointing is given to an individual for service to complete a specific task or assignment, the glory is given for elevation or promotion in the spirit

---

Did you know that the glory is your divine credentials that qualify you to operate in the realm of the spirit? The glory comes as a result of one having successfully completed the delegated divine tasks and graduated to enter a higher spiritual realm. Hence, the anointing is what breeds the glory because the anointing causes one to execute tasks and brings them to perfect completion, which would then entitle one to be in a position to qualify to receive the glory. In other words, the anointing lays a ground or accentuates an avenue for the glory of God to be revealed. Remember that faith is the *first dimension* of the supernatural, the anointing is the *second dimension* and the glory is the *third dimension*. This implies that in order for one to operate and walk in the fullness of the glory, he should successfully operate in the anointing and foster a progressive application of the anointing so that he can graduate or be catapulted from the realm of the anointing into the realm of glory.

It is a greater truth that the anointing is given to bring the glory of God into manifestation. This is the ultimate purpose of the anointing in the kingdom. On the other hand, the glory is what establishes you in the realm of the spirit. The glory is your divine credentials that qualifies you to ascend to greater heights in the realm of God. When someone talks about being promoted to a higher position in the spirit realm, it's because they would have been elevated to a higher plane or realm of glory. This might not be the case in the realm of the anointing because the ministration of the anointing is still dependent on other factors, such as the character of the minister, the level of expectation of the recipients and the degree of consecration of the minister.

The anointing is the ability given to man by God to do whatever He has called him to do but the glory is God doing His work and operating according to His sovereignty and initiative

---

It is worth unveiling the divine truth that the anointing operates according to human ability but the glory operates according to God's ability. God does everything by

His glory and man does the work of God by His anointing. It is therefore stricter to operate in the glory than in the anointing because God demands that we move at the same pace, in the same direction and with the same perspective as Him when operating in the glory.

Mistakes for operating in the anointing can be overlooked but God demands accountability and judgement for any misconduct exhibited during the display of His glory.

That is why it is very painful for man to be left behind when the cloud of God's glory has moved forward. The glory of God has moved to another location, leaving you clinging to the residue of His last visitation. It is therefore spiritually dangerous to stay behind where the glory or presence of God no longer manifests. Therefore, we need to keep pace with the glory of God and move at the same pace and in the same direction as the Spirit so that we stay relevant.

While the anointing is temporary as it comes and takes off depending on the nature of service, the glory takes a permanent abode or spiritual residence in humanity

---

The major difference between the anointing and the glory is in longevity. The anointing comes upon a minister to enable him to perform certain ministerial tasks but once the glory of God comes, it takes a permanent abode in your spirit. Once an atmosphere of glory is present, it ushers a supernatural influence and divine arrangement of circumstances in the realm of the spirit that begins to attract favour, blessings, promotion, divine health, prosperity as it perambulates in the extreme quarters of your spirit. That is why the Bible declares in Philippians 4:19 that *the Lord supplies all our needs according to the riches in Christ glory*. That means all our needs, demands, prosperity and increase is regulated by the pre-eminence of glory. The glory is therefore the ultimate key to every prosperity, success, promotion and increase. It is a prerequisite for all dimensions of prosperity to be manifested. Hence, there is such a thing called *prosperity by the glory*.

What makes the glory permanent is that it's a supernatural substance that carries weight and has a long lasting effect in a human body.

The Realm of Glory

Did you know that the glory of God is the heaviest *substance* in the universe in terms of weight and mass? That is why we talk of the heavy weight of God's glory. If energy is equal to matter or mass, then that means the glory of God, which is the supernatural power and energy is also matter and has weight, even though you can't see it. For instance, when you saturate a piece of cloth with the glory, substance and weight of God, it will be heavier than before it was saturated. In other words, it will have a greater weight that it did not have before. The object simply holds the same glory and then releases and transfers it when placed on someone by faith. That is why aprons and handkerchiefs were taken from the body of Paul and laid on the sick such that they were healed. Why? Because the glory of God carries weight and natural substances were used as a medium to carry that weight. This is also the reason why people fall under the power when they come into contact with the heavy weight of the glory of God.

The anointing and faith are governed by spiritual laws and principles but there is no law that governs the glory.

While we have the law of faith and the law of the anointing that prescribes specific principles to be followed or applied for these to manifest, there is no such thing as the law of glory. The glory is not governed by any law since it is administered directly by God himself. God created the laws for the universe and not for Himself, hence He is not accountable to any law. He did not create the law for Himself but for the purposes of governing the universe, hence His glory transcends all His laws. Operating in the dimension of glory therefore guarantees one success, greater power and greater manifestations because it is regulated directly from the Throne room of Heaven.

In the faith realm, the gifts never come to their maximum because the faith realm is the realm of susbstance. It is the realm of the beginning. That is why it is called *the first dimension*. However, in the glory, you see the maxcimum of the manifestation of the gifts of the Spirit. It is the higest level of operating in the realm of God. That is why it is called *the third dimension*. In the glory, it doesn't take two gifts to bring forth a manifestation. While in the faith realm it might take some time for gifts to reach full maturity, in the glory realm, there is no time period for growth. That's why when you get into the glory, miracles are instantaneous.

> *As believers, we can operate in the gifts of the spirit by faith and the anointing if we know the principles that activate them to operate. However the glory of God is the manifest presence which testifies of Heaven and the powers of the age to come*

It is worth exploring the divine truth that while in the past, more emphasis was placed on believers operating in the gifts of the spirit, there is a drastic transition from the realm of gifts (faith) to the realm of glory as God demands every believer to operate in the realm of glory in this end time season. While in the early days of revival, it was *"Just believe"*, now its *"Just enter in"*. That bypasses your struggle and the glory of God does the rest. Notable is the realisation that the glory of God operates according to God's sovereignty and initiative, not of man. He does whatever He wants, whenever He wants and in whichever manner He wants without depending on our faith, gifts or anointing. It is God doing His works without bringing in the participation of human beings. That is why the last move of God upon the earth will not come through a man or a woman but directly from God. Therefore, on the basis of the above revelation, a man knows he is in the dimension of glory when he does not operate in his personal measure of faith and the anointing. When one operates in the anointing, there is a tendency to feel physically exhausted because people place a demand on the anointing. However, operating in the glory automatically generates or produces more strength and power because of a direct divine connection with heaven hence, power flows directly from a perennial source of supply.

The truth is that the glory realm is a realm beyond the gifts and talents. Sadly, many believers today are majoring in the prophetic gift but not in the glory. Prophecy like any other gift, operates in the absence of glory but when the glory shows up, prophecy ceases as it is no longer needed as everything is revealed. That is why the best way to operate in the prophetic is in the presence of God's glory. This is what we call the *prophetic glory*. The prophetic glory is the Prophetic gifts intertwined with the glory. This is to tell you that although your prophecy may be accurate, the weight of the effect of your prophecy will depend on the level of glory of God in your life. A prophecy given in the glory has immediate and drastic life changing results. Jesus prophetically declared to a fig tree that it would die and at that moment it started to die. (Mark 11:12-14; 20-24). Prophecy is the means by which time is created. Revelation is the means by which time is known. Too many prophets today are putting into the future what God has already done and is available now. But the time has come that prophecy will no longer be about a future event waiting to come to pass. Instead, as the prophetic words are coming out of the mouths, that which we say will already be created and in motion before we finish speaking. Why? Because in the glory realm, there is no time for the clock is not ticking.

The glory of God's presence supersedes all gifts, anointing, faith or ministerial function although all these things come from Him.

It is a divine truth that God can heal, deliver and transform people during a service without the use of our faith or anointing but takes the initiative and works according to His will, hence the glory of God cannot be manufactured or faked. However, His glory can be attracted through worship. This means that you can never manufacture or produce the glory but you can attract, magnetise it and provoke it into manifestation. That is why we don't have to work very hard in order to bring the glory into manifestation. The reality is that many believers work hard to polish and perfect their gifts and anointing but in the glory there is not even an inch of hard work. Men work hard to graduate and perfect their gifts and anointing and that is what Paul advised in Philippians 2:12 when he said *that you must work out your own salvation with fear and trembling.* However, in the glory there is not even a kilojoule of energy required.

Let me illustrate this with a quintessential example. In Exodus 19:8, the glory of God descended on Mount Sinai without the Israelites having to do anything. This is because the glory is not about you but God, while the anointing has everything to do with you. If the glory of God came as a result of us having to do something, then every day would be a revival because people are always fasting and praying. That is why man does not initiate revivals but every revival is initiated by God and driven by human beings. Therefore, the popular Christian cliché that men and women of God start revivals is a lesser truth. The greater truth is that God uses His sovereignty to initiate the greatest revivals on earth as stipulated in His calendar of times and seasons and then ignites the fire of passion in a man to bring it to accomplishment. In other words, human beings are just used as instruments to drive, spearhead and channel or direct the power of God is a particular direction in such a way that lives are changed and impacted.

On the basis of ample scriptural references, it is therefore evident that the experiences in the glory are profoundly different from those of operating under the anointing. By nature of operation, the anointing is the multiplying power of God. There is an anointing in every assignment God gives. For us to fulfil the divine destiny He has for us, it requires divine power. The Glory is the manifest presence of God releasing the power of God through the faith of God. The anointing is God's divine release while the glory is God's divine residence. In the anointing, Moses stretched forth the rod across the Red sea and it divided it but in the Glory, the shoes and clothes of the children of Israel did not wear out. In the anointing, David grabbed a lion and tore it apart with his bare hands but in the glory the appetite or metabolic system of the lion was altered when Daniel was thrown in a lion's den. In the anointing, Elijah earnestly prayed for rain to fall after three and a half years of drought but in the glory, water supernaturally appeared in a desert even without a sign of a cloud. The anointing is what God does through someone but the Glory is what God does without anybody. It is the Sovereign will of God moving in our midst. The atmosphere itself is charged by heaven. Through the blood of Jesus, we all have divine access to the throne of God. We can go there. But the gory is different. The Glory is when eternity comes to earth. It's when God chooses to arrive and appear to His people.

When operating in the realm of the anointing, you feel power coming out of you but in the glory you swim in the pool of God's power

---

To illustrate this revelation with reference to a quintessential example from the word of God, when the woman with the flow of blood touched the hem of Jesus's garment, in response Jesus said *"Who touched me; for I perceive that power* (Dunamis) *has gone out of Me"* (Like 8:45-46). In other words, she made a withdrawal of the anointing upon Jesus. This is because it was God's power working through Jesus and people could place a demand and make a withdrawal of the anointing upon Him. Therefore, when the anointing is in operation, you feel virtue and power coming out of you as Christ did because there is a spiritual transaction that is effected by faith. According to the law of impartation, as people place a demand on the anointing or mantle of a man of God, they can receive whatever they desire. However, when we experience the glory, in His sovereignty, God chooses to work alone because the realm of glory is the realm of rest. Hence, we do not do anything, instead we just worship and bask in His presence. The glory of God works independently and is not influenced by any human action. We work under the anointing but we rest in God's glory.

> *God will anoint you for everything He wants you to do but in the cloud of His glory, He will do His own works.*

As aforementioned, the anointing is correspondingly to man, what the glory is to God. While we move, function and operate in the anointing, in the glory, God does His own work. However, in view of the above revelation, does it then mean that we should sit idle by with nothing to do and let the glory of God do everything? No! You mustn't sit and do nothing in hope that everything will automatically fall on your lap from the blue sky. At the same time, you must not haste and do everything by yourself. In a ministerial context, the secret is waiting on God to see if He chooses to manifest His glory and if He doesn't, then we can operate according to the anointing and spiritual gifts He has given us. We therefore need to strike a balance between *operating under the anointing* and *operating in the glory* since both of them are crucial in fulfilling God's plans and purpose in this end time season. In reality, there are certain things God has told us to do and anointed us to do hence, we should move forward in them if He doesn't take the initiative .

How then do I know whether I am moving in the anointing or in the glory?

People know that they are moving in the dimension of glory where they no longer need to use their faith or anointing. As long as you are still using your faith, you are still operating in the *first dimension* of the supernatural and as long as you are still operating in the anointing, you are still in the *second dimension*. You need to migrate or progress a step further to operate in the realm of glory, which is the *third dimension* of the supernatural. When you get to a point when you exhaust all your gifts and they cease to operate, it's an indication that you have entered into the realm of glory.

> *The anointing was given to heal the sick, but in the glory, we are covered with a supernatural immunity to sickness*

Did you know that in the atmosphere of glory, neither death, sickness nor any form of calamity or danger is permitted to prevail? This is because the same glory that operates on earth carries the same properties as that which originates in Heaven where there is no death or decay. Figuratively speaking, the anointing would shut the mouth of a lion but the glory changes the appetite and genetic make-up of a lion. Unknown to many people, it is actually the glory of God that changed the appetite of the lions when Daniel was thrown in a den of lion in (Daniel 6:16-24). It's not that the lions were not hungry that they could not devour him per se. Instead, it's the glory of God which filled the den that changed the whole metabolic or digestive system of lions.

The anointing can stop a lion from advancing in your direction but the glory changes the appetite and metabolism of a lion.

That is the reason why Adam could call or play with lions without them hurting him, because in the life of glory, there is neither danger nor calamity. The hunger pangs of a lion were activated the instant Adam sinned and lost the glory of God such that when they looked at Adam, they no longer saw their Master but a piece of meat that should be devoured. This is because in the atmosphere of glory, lions are herbivores but in the absence of glory, they are carnivorous. Likewise, the anointing was given to cut the head off of giants, but in the glory, giants don't even enter a territory at all.

The anointing operates in levels or measures but the glory operates in dimensions and degrees

The glory enables us to reach nations, continents or the whole world because it is no longer faith, gifting or measure of anointing of man in operation. Instead, it is God himself doing the work. It is because the glory operates in dimensions. A spiritual dimension has greater coverage, as it consists of the width, length, depth and height. The Bible says in Ephesians 3:18 that *you being rooted and grounded in love, may be able to comprehend with all saints what is the width, length and depth and height of God's presence.* This speaks of the divergent realms and dimensions of operating in the glory. That means in the glory, we can explore deeper realms, depths and dimensions of God. That means the one who operates in the glory has a deeper experience of God than the one who operates in faith or anointing.

In Ezekiel 47:1-9, Ezekiel uses the physical phenomenon of water to demonstrate the various levels and degrees of the anointing. By so doing, Ezekiel's prophecy gives believers a clear picture of how the level of God's presence and power can increase in the lives of His people. In the context of this revelation, *water, streams and rivers* often refer to the presence and flow of God's Spirit. The highest attainable level of God's anointing is represented by the waters which flow from God's throne to individuals, groups or nations, and is often referred to as *the sea of the anointing*. Wherever these waters go, they bring healing and life to the needy. This implies that Spirit-filled believers have rivers of living water continuously flowing from their innermost being. Ezekiel gives a clear description of *a four-fold level of the anointing* upon every Spirit-filled believer, which is *the ankle deep anointing, knee deep anointing, waist deep anointing, overflow anointing or measureless anointing*. On the contrary, as much as there are different degrees of the glory of the sun, which is the *glory of sunrise, glory of sunshine and the glory of sunset*, there are also different degrees of the glory of God. There is the *first degree glory* which is an entry level, then there is a *second degree* which is a continuous progression into the realities of the glory realm and then there is the *third degree glory* which is highest realm of glory, which Paul described as a *far exceeding weight of glory*. However, the levels of the anointing cannot be equated to the *first, second and third* dimensions of glory, which is a higher plane of existence.

The realm of glory is timeless and holds greater creative power than the realm of the anointing

---

In the anointing, when God speaks, we become impregnated with His word and as time passes, that word grows and develops, eventually causing us to give birth to that specific promise. However, when God's word is spoken in the realm of glory, the time it takes for the word to grow and mature is reduced to only a few moments; we see the promise instantly. This happens because the realm of glory is the timeless, eternal realm where God is. When God created Adam, he was timeless, ageless, eternal, and set into a timeless environment, which is God's glory. Man was not designed to be sick or to die, but to live in the glory of God, the realm of timelessness. Healings performed under the anointing might gradually happen over a period of time. However, miracles performed under the glory are instantaneous. That is why in the realm of glory, God causes our hair, teeth and fingernails to grow and our bodies to go through the natural progression of replenishing and replacing cells and this happens daily. An injury that would normally take weeks or months to be healed will be restored instantly when touched by God's glory. Time is actually made to serve those who know and understand their rights as citizens of heaven. When we experience the glory realm, we are experiencing timelessness.

The realm of glory holds the highest concentration of God's creative power than the anointing

It is a divine truth that the glory carries the highest level of concentration of God's power. The Greek word to describe this spiritual phenomenon is, *"Epicaizo"*. When coming into contact with God's glory, creative power can be released for creative miracles to take place. A creative miracle is not something broke being fixed, healed, or revived. A creative miracle is when something new is actually created in the place of the old. We've seen many creative miracles take place when the glory cloud manifests: new eyeballs, new eardrums, hearts recreated, legs grown out, and so forth. God wants to take you from glory to glory. If you are missing an organ, bone, flesh, or hair in any place on your body, God's glory is coming upon you now. If you have a limb shorter than the other, receive your miracle now. Any mental problems in your life or in your kids' lives, right now it is fixed in the name of Jesus. If you have lost your loved one and is lying on a death bed, in a coffin or at the mortuary, in the atmosphere of glory (*highest concentration of God's power*), command the dead to rise up and you will be thrilled at how the glory will quicken their spirit just like when Jesus commanded Lazarus to come forth.

Faith places a demand on the anointing of man but the glory places a demand on God Himself

Where faith is exercised, it attracts anointing and pulls from the mantle; faith and anointing work together. When you go to a service, you pull from the mantle of the man of God. However, in the Glory, you make a pulling from God Himself. In other words, God introduces you to the glory Himself. In the realm of glory you are moving with the cloud, not the crowd. In the anointing, the man is seen. Unfortunately people look at the man as the one with the great anointing but when God uses humanity, people become mistaken and begin to idolize the man. In the glory, God demands to be seen Himself. Many people know how to stretch their hand to the mantle but don't know how to receive directly from God. We speak of *the cloud of glory* and the *rain of the Anointing*. The glory is like a cloud and the anointing is rain coming out of the cloud. The glory releases, produces or breeds the anointing. This means that the operation of the anointing is dependent on the glory.

The anointing was given to us to heal the sick, but in the glory of God, sickness is illegal

---

There is a supernatural immunity that is given in the glory of God. The current church scenario is that multitudes are addicted to the anointing of man. Yes, the anointing is from God but you can come out of there and go directly to Him. In the anointing, Christ is our Healer. In the glory, He is our Creator. However, we need Him as both. In the anointing, we work. In the glory, we rest. In the anointing healings occur, but it's more on an individual level. For example, the minister may pray for someone and they're healed, then moving to the next, he prays, they're healed, and so on. The minster is operating in the healing anointing which covers him, and he releases it to the people. The cloud of glory however, is like a covering or a canopy that blankets the people and they all get touched at the same time. When the cloud of glory is present, there is direct contact with heaven hence revelation increases, the seer realm is opened, gifts are activated, and miracles happen all over the show.

Conclusively, it is therefore evident that the realm of glory is a higher dimension that operates on different spiritual principles as compared to that of the anointing. Hence, we should seek more of the glory than the anointing if ever we want to impact the world for Christ in this end time season. However, it must be expressly understood that although the glory supersedes the dimension of the anointing, that does not mean that the anointing is irrelevant. Both of them are required since they serve a specific purpose in the kingdom. The above revelation is given to help you migrate or graduate to a higher level which is the realm of glory. Both the anointing and the glory reveals, materializes and actualizes God's provisions and promises. They are the keys to integrating the spiritual kingdom of God with the natural life. There is no other way to materialize and actualize spiritual blessing outside the confinement or protocol of manifestation and revelation, which define how the anointing and the glory works.

HOW TO TRANSITION FROM THE REALM OF THE ANOINTING TO THE REALM OF GLORY

How do we step into the New Realms of Glory?

It is a typical scenario across a broad spectrum of Christian faith that many believers have had spiritual encounters and experiences in the anointing but a few have experienced the tangibility of God's glory. Due to reasons attributable to a lack of revelation, in some instances, many Biblical teachings in the church are centred around matters of faith, gifting and the anointing, but very little is said about the glory. The consequence of this divine phenomenon is that there is so much emphasis placed on faith and the anointing and less on the glory. This is a biased representation of spiritual truths, taking into account the reality that the Body of Christ is living on the edge as we have been ushered right into the very special moments of glory in the calendar of God.

However, it suffices to highlight that in this end time dispensation there is an alarming outcry and emphasis in the supernatural for a progressive transition from the realm of the anointing to the realm of God's glory. There is a paradigm shift and global migration from the substance of the anointing into the transcending higher realms of Glory. In essence, there is a drastic and profound transformation in the governance and administration of the anointing to the release of the glory in unfathomable ways never imagined before. While in the past decades there have been an emphasis for a transition from the realm of senses into the realm of faith and from the realm of faith into the realm of the anointing, now Heavens demands a further migration from the realm of the anointing into higher realms of glory. This is a major characteristic feature of the end time dispensation which shall see the masses being catapulted into higher realms of glory to experience what they have never seen, heard, conceived or experienced before. God wants to take us to newer, deeper and higher realms of glory we have never experienced before. In an endeavour to awaken this present generation to the reality of permanently moving, operating and functioning in the revelation of glory, God is raising a unique breed of ministers who shall actively drive, spearhead, rigorously participate or partake in the final move of God's glory and He is leading them on the path of transition from the anointing into the glory so that they can enter into the river of God's Shekinah.

58

In the current season across the body of Christ, there is a progression from the realm of the anointing and presence to the realm of Glory. In other words, more emphasis is placed on believers operating and tapping into higher realms of the glory than the anointing because the glory is a higher dimension of God's power as compared to the of the anointing. As a matter of fact, when Moses said to God, *"Please, show me your glory,"* he was actually implying that thank you for your anointing but I now want your glory. In other words, he had operated in the realm of anointing for quite some time and now he was expressing his readiness and wiliness to delve into a higher realm, which is that of glory. The statement which Moses uttered above shows a transition from the realm of anointing to glory by placing a demand in the spirit. Moreover, when Moses said to the Lord in Exodus 33:15, *"If you don't come with us, I'm not going"*, he was so acclimatised to God's glory to such an extent that he could not do anything without the glory. That is why in the absence of God's glory, we can't do anything because the glory is the key and secret behind any dimension of miracles, signs and wonders which any believer can perform in this dispensation. It must therefore be expressly understood that life revolves around the glory as the source of all manifestations and this is the principal reason why I define life as *a constant migration, movement and operation in the dimension of glory.*

The reality is that there is a major transition occurring among us in this end time season as a result of an extraordinary move of God. Perhaps many people might sense it, perceive it or even feel the impact of its change. In some instances, you can't define it or label it but you sense the atmosphere is in transition. It is a Supernatural transition which marks the perfect timing in the calendar of God. It is a multiplying power within us, among us, and upon us. The church is transitioning to a different level, a deeper level of divine presence and power from one degree of radiant glory to another. We are moving from anointing to Glory, we are expecting a mighty wave of Glory to move us or plunge us deeper into His throne room in this season. In a practical sense, Moses moved from anointing to glory. Moses trekked up Mt. Sinai to commune with the Glory of the Lord. He'd seen the Glory at the burning bush but this was different. He'd moved in an Anointing when he confronted Pharoah and delivered the Prophetic word to him but this was different. He'd moved in the anointing when He stretched out his rod and divided the Red Sea but this was different. It was an intense time in the glory of Jehovah. There, Moses received the divine norms for establishing the new nation of Israel.

In terms of efficiency, frequency and impact, this transition from the anointing to glory is like a person who moves from driving a car into driving an aeroplane. While both a car and a plane are means of transportation but the frequency, efficiency and speed with which they operate is totally different. By the same token while both the anointing and glory are aspects of God's power, the frequency of the glory, the level, depth, dimension and area of operation is much higher and greater as compared to the anointing. This revelation must propel your faith to move and tap into higher realms of awaiting glory. A car would stop at the robots, be intercepted by the road blocks, at times be hindered or delayed by the speed of other cars on the road. Contrary to how the anointing operates, the glory cannot be stopped; it does not operate on spiritual laws, hence cannot be hindered or delayed since it is the highest concentration of God's power.

This dispensation therefore marks the beginning of the season of divine exploration and discovery, to discover things in the supernatural that have never been experienced before. Increased visitations to the *throne room* shall therefore become a common experience as people are launched into the depths of God's presence to explore and unleash the fullness of His glory. The opening of the heavens to connect man with the release of the rain of glory shall consequentially result in many being elevated to greater heights in the supernatural. Therefore, in order for the body of Christ to access all these realms, it is highly imperative that we be sensitive to the transition that is taking place in the realm of the spirit.

THE SECRET TO TAPING INTO HIGHER REALMS OF GLORY

How do We Progressively Migrate into the Higher Realms of Glory?

A migration into any dimension or realm in the supernatural is always governed by revelation and a change in the application of spiritual laws and principles

The Bible makes it clear that as far as operating in the glory is concerned, we are designed to move progressively from one realm of glory to a higher realm of glory

(2 Corinthians 3:18). However, a migration into the dimension or realm of glory is always governed by the revelation and a change in the application of spiritual laws and principles. In view of the above, it is of paramount importance to highlight the fact that any migration or elevation from one level of the anointing to the other requires paying a price through undertaking intense sacrifices and strenuous spiritual exercises such as intense meditation on the word of God, persistent fasting as well as relentless prayer and practising the presence. And it happens that after advancing through various levels and dimensions of the anointing in the supernatural, one reaches a *breakthrough or ceiling point* beyond which he can no longer proceed further under reasonable circumstances. When this happens, this serves as an indication of one's readiness to make a transition from the anointing to the realm of glory. In other words, when you get to a level where you have operated so much in the anointing, to the extent that you have reached a ceiling point, then you are ready to break forth into a new realm of glory.

If a believer reaches a level of faith in the anointing in which nothing new is happening, then this is an indication that he is ready to enter the dimension of glory

---

If an individual has reached a level of faith in the anointing whereby he has done everything in the Word but nothing new is happening, then this is a sign that one is ready to enter a new dimension of glory. Christianity is a life of progressive movement or migration from one level to the other hence believers are not supposed to operate at the same level of anointing or power for a long time. However, if you have managed to move in the power of God and tested all divergent depths and dimensions of the anointing but then nothing new seem to be coming your way, then that means the next level is to enter the realm of glory. I'm not talking about just siting and doing nothing and then waiting to enter the dimension of glory, but I'm talking about having exhausted all the dimensions of the anointing and stretched your faith to the limit of a breakthrough in the spirit. The Bible records an incident whereby Peter spent the whole night fishing but could not catch anything until Jesus stepped on the scene and ushered the glory of God and commanded him *to cast into the deep and let down the nets for a cash* (Luke 5:4). Peter was then convinced that it was time to change his career from that of fishing fish to that of fishing souls. It is important to note that one requires the right timing to migrate into higher realms of Glory. Prophetically speaking, you might have been labouring hard or migrating from one church to the other pursuing men of God or seeking after the anointing but when it's time to migrate to a higher realm of glory, Jesus will show up on the scene and you will be instantly catapulted into a higher realm of glory.

Transition into the realm of glory requires revelation knowledge for one cannot move into what has not been revealed to him

---

Contrary to the unanimous view held by dozens of believers across a broad spectrum of Christian faith that a transition from one level of the anointing to the other requires undertaking certain spiritual exercises, transition into the realm of glory requires revelation knowledge for one cannot move into what has not been revealed to him. Without revelation, we can never see beyond the natural senses. The key that grants us access to the manifestation of glory in the natural realm is revelation since it can trigger or provoke a supernatural experience.

The level of revelation one has is directly proportional to the dimension of Glory one can be elevated into

The greater truth is that God's glory must be revealed by the Spirit; it cannot be discovered by research or understood by reason. That is the reason why the church has been for long seeking the manifestation of glory without any success because they lacked the required revelation knowledge to manifest that glory. Hence, for the glory of God to manifest, it must be captured, received and recognised by our spirits through the revelation of the Spirit. Revelation is nothing more than the logics of God revealed to man for him to be able to think and operate out of eternity. Revelation elevates you above matter. You will never fully understand the present age until you understand the eternal age. Unless revelation comes, you have no access to the eternal. That is why we can't explain why there are some things that haven't happened yet unless God puts that faith in your spirit according to the revelation. Revelation precedes an impartation of faith. That is why faith comes by hearing the word of God. It's smooth sailing when the revelation comes and then faith abides. Revelation provides access to the highest realm of substance: the invisible. The name of the matter we cannot see is the substance from which God formulates things. This is what He has put resident in you. It is a five-letter word called *faith*. Faith is not a confession; it's what you have. It's a substance, matter and supernatural mass. The problem with us today is that we have diluted what the Bible calls faith and turned it into a cheap commodity. We have substituted alternatives for faith.

There are certain deep things of God that will never be known until they are revealed. This is the reality which Paul unveiled in 1 Corinthians 2:7 when he asserted that there are mysteries of God that are spoken in codes: *but we speak the wisdom of God in a mystery, even the hidden wisdom which God ordained before the world unto our glory.* Let me paraphrase it another way. If there is ever an hour the divine code are being decoded and revealed, it's now. I'm talking about the things of the spirit that are divinely coded and hidden to the natural man. There are manifestations of the spirit that are divinely coded. They don't happen for the sake of happening. In order for you to unlock these codes, you need to be catapulted into the higher realms of glory to access the secret pin and decode them in the natural realm.

A perennial hunger, unquenchable thirst and an insatiable appetite can catapult a believer into higher, deeper or newer realms of God's glory

---

One key indication that portrays the church's readiness to migrate into higher realms of glory is a hunger, thirst and an insatiable appetite for the new revelation of God's glory. This forms the basis for *the law of desire*. It is a greater truth that in the realm of the spirit, things work according to people's desires. Your desire, passion and willingness to walk with God is what would provoke or trigger catapult-action into higher realms of glory. When Moses said to God, *"Please show me your glory"*, he was not just saying a general statement but he was expressing his deep desire for the supernatural glory and God unreservedly unveiled it to Him. Moreover, the Bible makes it clear that *the Lord shall grant the desires of your heart* (Psalms 47:4) but if you don't have any desires or hunger for the glory, what do you expect God to work with? A desire is like a flame of fire that ignites the glory of God in your spirit and set you ablaze, ready to move in signs and wonders. Therefore, a desire and hunger for the supernatural and to function in the heightened realm of the supernatural in signs and wonders is another indication that one is ready to embrace the realm of glory.

Spiritual readiness or preparedness is a prerequisite for one to enter into a higher dimension of glory

Spiritual readiness or preparedness is another pre- requisite to taking a quantum leap into higher realms of glory. Whenever the glory of God shows up, it brings forth new spiritual encounters and experiences, unusual manifestations, creative miracles, signs and wonders, some of which might be peculiar or complex to understand. We must therefore be ready to deal with any manifestation lest we grieve the Spirit. There must not be any mistakes for operating in the glory to avoid side effects like Uzzah who mistakenly touched the ark of God and died (2 Samuel 6:7). A multitude of people have been restricted from entering a higher dimension of glory because they are not well prepared for that dimension. Preparedness for the glory entails rubbing thyself in His presence, fostering a heightened degree of intimacy with the Holy Ghost, provoking and building a glorious cloud of His presence by praying in other tongues as well as fervently and relentlessly staying in the Word of God. This is the essence of the law of preparation. If only you could do that, you can easily break into a new realm of glory. The Bible makes it clear that we grow from faith to faith, from glory to glory, and from one level of the anointing to the other. In other words, the life of a Christian is designed to progressively move in one direction – upward and forward only.

Openness and willingness for the progressive graduation from one dimension of the supernatural to the next

It is the openness and willingness for the graduation and progressive migration from one level of faith to the other, from one level of anointing to another and from one level of glory to another that will catapult you to higher realms of glory. This entails a progressive – upwards and forward movement from the first dimension of the supernatural (*faith*) though the second dimension (*anointing*) until we reach the third dimension (*glory*). Lack of momentum and prowess can restrict or limit a man from operating in the realm of glory. This is because the dimension of glory requires a complete dependence on God. Therefore, anyone who is not willing to submit under the supremacy or pre-eminence or sovereignty of God is not ready for the realm of glory. It is bad theology, humanism and carnality that will prevent one from reaching higher dimensions of glory. Therefore, in your quest to attain higher realms of glory, you have to make an effort to align your attitude, character and mentality, to the will of God.

A progressive and exhaustive migration through the realms or the depths of the supernatural such as realm of faith, anointing, power, mantle and presence could also serve as an acid test and evidence that one is ready for the dimension of glory. Successfully rising up the ladder across these dimensions of the universe is also evidence that one is ready for the dimension of glory. The ability to pay a greater price to see the manifestation of Glory is therefore incontestable evidence that indicates one's readiness for higher realms of glory (Psalms 63:1- 2). The truth is that *faith* and the *anointing* works together. A person can exercise faith that puts a demand on the anointing of another believer. Faith attracts the anointing in that one places a demand of the anointing by faith. That is why there is such a thing as *faith in the anointing*. Likewise, faith also opens a doorway or passage for one to be catapulted into the realm of operating in the glory. That is why there is such a thing as *faith in the glory,* meaning *operating in the glory through faith.*

Progressive migration and development from one level of faith to the other

---

There is an intricate connection between faith and the glory of God. Faith is the believer's spiritual antenna to hear beyond the natural dimension. Jesus said to Martha, in John 11:40, *"Did I not say to you that if you would believe you would see the glory of God?".* This implies that faith is a prerequisite for seeing the glory because having faith means you believe in what God can do. There is a difference between believing God for something using the measure of faith He has given you and God exercising His own God kind of faith. The realm of glory is the latter- God Himself in faith in action, what He believes and does on his own compared to what we believe based on our faith and anointing. While multitudes of believers attempt to operate directly in the glory, without the foundation of faith, it is highly advisable that believers first understand the dynamic operation of faith as a stepping stone to catapult you to higher realms of glory.

Faith's measure of rule is not the seen but the unseen. Faith openes to us the world, the realm and the zone that was before time. Faith affirms the invisible as its reality. Faith does not affirm the seen. Faith transcends the seen because it knows the seen is temporary. It supersedes reason. It supersedes your head and intellectualism. It supersedes the counterfeit because the counterfeit knows it isn't real. Do you remember that the Bible describes faith as *the substance of things hoped for and the evidence of things not seen?* Unknown to many believers, this is the basic, ordinary entry level of operating in the realm of faith. But when operating in the glory realm, even your level of faith changes. Faith stands on what has been predetermined by God, hence it imposes eternity into time. That is why time lines up with what God says you are and have now! It's not what time says, it's what God says. Therefore, when operating in the glory realm, hope is converted into evidence and evidence is converted into the substance and when it is converted into substance, it becomes time in the now. In a similar fashion in which deep calls unto deep, hope calls unto evidence; evidence calls unto substance and substance calls unto now. That is why in a deeper sense, faith is described as an invisible hand that reaches into the future to grab something and bring it into the present. Hope calls the beyond to here and now. Hope calls unto faith for its reality because it depends on faith for its structure, its embodiment. Hope is calling out for reality, coexistence and actuality. That's why when operating in the glory realm, you must have expectancy and act as if you know something is about to happen. Dance about it, shout about it and publicly declare it to the whole world and by so doing, you will be pulling it from its location in the future and bringing it into the present.

Transition from one realm of the anointing to the other

There is an intricate connection between the anointing and the glory. If one continues to apply the anointing relentlessly, it is possible for him to be elevated or catapulted straight from the realm of the anointing into that of glory. The realm of the anointing is a lower place hence, moving into the realm of glory of like migrating from high school straight into tertiary. In the Old Testament, the glory of God fell on the terbanacle after the priests, the later and utensils had been anointed (Exodus 40). So, the anointing is the power of God working through us to do what He wants done on earth (glory). There are various degrees, levels and dimensions in the realm of the anointing. One level is equivalent to a step that must be taken or ascended as we progress in our ability to move in that anointing and grow spiritually in relation to it. No step can be skipped because each step represents essential aspect of maturity in spiritual matters. We must therefore go from step to step and from level to level without missing one until we reach a level at which we have fully developed the measure of the anointing we have received. When we reach the last level whereby we can do nothing further in terms of our anointing, then we have reached the fullness of that measure and stretched ourselves to the maximum limit. At this point, the only available option is to enter the realm of glory. However, many people have been taught that they can only move from faith to faith, glory to glory but they have not been exposed to the revelation that not only do we move within these dimensions of the supernatural but we can also move right across divergent realms of the supernatural, for instance from faith to the anointing and from anointing to the glory.

Ezekiel uses the physical phenomenon of water to demonstrate the various levels and degrees of the anointing. By so doing, Ezekiel's prophecy gives believers a clear picture of how the level of God's presence and power can increase in the lives of His people. Ezekiel gives a clear description of a five-fold level of the anointing upon every Spirit-filled believer. To cement this revelation with reference to a scriptural evidence Ezekiel gives us a narrative in which he says ,

> *"Afterward he (the man with a measuring line) brought me again unto the door of the house; and, behold, waters issued out from under the threshold of the house eastward: for the forefront of the house stood toward the east, and the waters came down from under from the right side of the house, at the south side of the altar. Then brought he me out of the way of the gate northward, and led me about the way without unto the utter gate by the way that looked eastward; and, behold, there ran out waters on the right side. And when the man that had the line in his hand went forth eastward, he measured a thousand cubits, and he brought me through the waters; the waters were to his ankles. Again he measured a thousand, and brought me through the waters; the waters were to the knees. Again the measured a thousand, and brought me through; the waters were to the loins. Afterward he measured a thousand; and it was a river that i could not pass over: for the waters were raised, waters to swim in, a river that could not be passed over* (Ezekiel 47:1-9).

In the description of the anointing presented in the above mentioned scripture, Ezekiel reveals the **FOUR LEVELS** of spiritual maturity in the anointing. These are *ankle deep level, knee deep level, waste deep level and the overflow level.* By description, an ankle is the lowest part of a human body which can only take you to a certain point. By the same token, the *Ankle Deep level anointing* speaks of the first or initial level of the anointing that is released within a believer at the beginning of the Christian Life. In other words, at new birth as an individual receives Jesus Christ into his spirit, there is a measure of the anointing that is planted or deposited within him as he begins the Christian journey or walk. By the same token, the *Knee Deep level* of the anointing is not much greater than the ankle deep experience. However, it does indicate a deeper experience with God. The knee is slightly higher than the ankle and has the ability to bend and allow the body to perform diverse tasks. The knee is connected to prayer, hence this level represents entering into this second dimension of the anointing whereby Christians are learning to pray and develop a prayer life and dependence upon the power of God. The *Waist level* anointing often refers to influence, hence at this level, the believer is beginning to use the anointing to influence those who are in his sphere of contact. By description, the waist is a central part of the body which has the ability to influence or determine the direction of other parts of the body. At this level, a believer is active in the things of God and interacts with others around them. At *Overflow anointing*, the believer starts to produce the results of what the words of God talks about. In the same way a body is fully immersed at this level, believers operating at this level of anointing are fully immersed or deeper into the Spirit such that they are led by the Spirit. Therefore, this is a level of deeper miracles, deeper revelations, deeper faith and everything which believers do in executed in greater depth.

Moreover, this level of the *overflow anointing* is also a realm of supernatural manifestations and practical demonstrations of the Spirit and Power. This speaks of a *measureless anointing*. This is the level of the anointing at which Jesus operated or functioned under during His earthly ministry. The greater truth is that at this level of anointing, believers will do *greater works* than what Jesus did (John 14:12) because the Holy Spirit has now been sent without measure. It is at this level that the dead are raised, as there are mass resurrections experienced right across the body of Christ. Believers have developed a significant level of maturity in the anointing such that they are able to channel it in the right direction to impact the whole world. Therefore, the next level to break into after the measureless anointing is *the realm of glory*. The measureless anointing ushers you into the realm of glory in the same way a river in flood ushers water into the sea.

Ability to create an atmosphere of glory as evidenced by a cloud of His presence

It is a divine truth that we are able to make a pull on the glory of God by staying long enough in His presence. The glory of God is given birth to in His presence. From a natural perspective rain does not come without the accumulation of clouds. Clouds represent the glory and rain represents His presence. Unless and until we have learnt how to build up an atmosphere of glory, we might not be able to make a pulling or withdrawal from it. It is therefore, highly recommended that believers build up an atmosphere of God's glory so that they can function in a realm of God's superabundance of glory. Building an atmosphere of God's glory is therefore such an imperative action if ever we have want to see the glory of God manifested like never before.

The question you are probably asking is: *How to we build an atmosphere of the glory cloud?* It's through prophetic declarations in the now. One of the principles of the spirit realm is that we must understand that the believer is God's agent on the earth who is authorised by God to declare the things of Heaven to earth. Heavens stands behind our words and agrees with it coming to pass (Mathew 16:19). To *declare* means to bring something forth. When you declare a thing, you are bringing something forward that should occur in its natural time. Just seeing it is not enough, declaring it and framing it causes it to stay framed. God wants us to declare in the realm of the spirit what we see in the Heavens. Faith believes and speaks it ahead of time. Time is not a determining factor anymore because in the realm of God, it doesn't exist. Until you speak, nothing is manufactured from the world beyond. One of the laws of mass that we were taught in science is that not all mass is visible. Faith is the invisible mass from which God creates the seen dimension. That is why it is the substance of things hoped for. Therefore until we speak, nothing is allowed to come from the world beyond without a revealed spoken word. Declaration gives permission or a license for things to be legally transacted from Heaven down to earth. It puts a stamp of Gods approval on any breakthrough or blessing to be released by the Heavens on earth.

Deepening of the realm of the miraculous or progressive demonstration of miracles, signs and wonders

It is a divine truth that a progressive and consistent demonstration or practical display of God's supernatural power through miracles, signs and wonders can delve one into a higher realm of glory. This is because as we demonstrate the power of God, we trigger or provoke the flow of the glory of God from within our spirits. This implies that the realm of the miraculous is the realm of glory because it is thorough the miraculous that the glory of God is revealed more and more. In some cases, it might happen that the glory of God is hidden or unknown to the masses. However, if a miracle such as raising one from the dead, is publicly performed, God's glory is revealed. That means the main purpose of miracles is to reveal the glory.

HOW TO ENTER THE NEXT LEVEL AND TAKE GLORY OF GOD TO THE EXTREME

How do we practically enter Deeper and Unexplored Territories of the Glory Realm?

PROPHETIC DECLARATION:

Prophetically declaring the new thing God has shown us is the first step. Without taking this initial step of obedience, the other steps are in vain. Elijah prophesied during a time of famine that the rains would come. (1 Kings 18: 1-2,41) Once God had spoken, the prophecy and declaration alone caused it to come forth. When we declare something under the direction of the Holy Spirit, that thing is being formed as we declare it. When you are in the glory zone and speak out what God is telling or showing you, things will start to be created at that very moment. Just as when God declared in Genesis 1:3, *"Let there be light"*, a sound greater than a sonic boom ripping across time and space echoed through the universe such that light came forth instantaneously. When God tells you something while in the Glory zone, prophetically declare it and as you do this, God will send angels, people and circumstances to make the arrangements. Lack of prophetic declaration hinders the creation and birthing forth of those things into existence. We must mature to the stage where we declare what we see I the glory realm. Unknown to many believers, there are some things in the realm of the Spirit for which man declares the time frame, not God. To "*declare*" means to bring something forward. You don't have to wait for it to happen. Instead, you have to make it happen. You can bring it forth and it will manifest now. We lack the understanding of how to grasp these mysteries and bring them into our experience now. Prophetically speaking, there is a deposit, much like a bank account, in the Glory with your name on it. It is laid up for you in the Heavens. Accessing it is much easier than you would ever imagine. If we are trapped in this earth's time zone, then in one manner it is so. If we access the eternal realm, and begin to declare things, then we would be speaking from "up" to "down". If we have laid up treasure in Heaven, where our heart is, and where we have originated from, then why do you think it impossible to access the account you have there? God has already given us the compound interest rates of Heaven. They are up to one-hundred-fold return on our investment. Only when we tap into the glory realm are we be able to access these manifold blessings of heaven.

PROPHETIC PROCESS AND INTERCESSION:

Between prophetic *declaration* and *manifestation*, you need to put yourself into a "*prophetic process*" called *intercession*, which is a birthing position in which you align your spirit to give birth to the prophetic word in the realm of the spirit. Intercession aligns our spirit and causes us to be rightly positioned in the spirit dimension so as to swiftly move, function and operate in the realm of the spirit. After declaring the word, we must enter into prayer or intercession so as to birth forth a manifestation in the physical realm. This was exemplified by Elijah who got down and put himself into a birthing position and prayed until it came (1 Kings 18:42). The prophecy is what gave life to it but the intercession is what caused it to grow until it was birthed forth. I'm reminded of what John Wesley, the great man of God once said, *"I pray for two hours every morning, that is if I don't have a lot to do. If I have a lot to do that day, I pray for three hours"*. However, there are few things that need to be given divine correction pertaining to the ministry of intercession. Intercessory prayer is not a laundry list of requests. Intercession is not about making faithless, beggarly prayers as Heaven does not understand that kind of language. Intercession is not about pleading a cause and getting answers. We don't just get answers to our prayers - we become the answers because the world requires Heavens' solutions and not google answers. In other words, we gain knowledge and insight into solutions, hence we become a solution to the cries of millions across the globe.

PROPHETIC PERCEPTION:

Since it is a divine truth that in the realm of the spirit things are taken hold of through vision, imagination is such an integral aspect of possessing our possessions. Once you have interceded long enough to give birth to a manifestation in the spirit realm, the next step is to see those things that we have decreed in the spirit realm. This is what we call *Prophetic perception*. This is a spiritual sight necessary to see what God is doing in the invisible arena and in tandem with Him, you do exactly the same in the visible realm. It incorporates the ability to see the unseen, hear the unheard and then speak the unspeakable. This means that your imagination was intended by God to be the lens through which you apprehend the realms of spiritual realities. After intercessory prayer, Elijah started to look for the prophecy. He told his servant to look until he saw something – a cloud as small as a man's hand. And the minute he saw it, he got hold of the answer. This is because in the realm of the spirit, things are procured through vision. The instant you see, you take a hold of it.

PROPHETIC ACTION:

Everything is perfected in the realm of the spirit when we demonstrate our actions of faith. According to the law of manifestation, in every action, there is a reaction. Actions of faith causes manifestations to be birthed forth in the natural realm as they send signals in the realm of the spirit alerting spiritual subjects of the legality of power being exercised. Therefore, the final step in tapping into the glory realm is prophetic action. Immediately after making a prophetic declaration, Elijah demonstrated his actions of faith when he began to run so as not to miss the next move of God. Strikingly, he girded up his loins and outran Ahab's chariot (1 Kings 18:43-46). Running was a prophetic action of faith that validated his declaration. Now, it's time to run, as the first signs have already appeared heralding the new outpouring. As Elijah did, gird up your lions and so as not to miss the next agenda of Heaven.

CHAPTER THREE

DIVERGENT REALMS OF GOD'S GLORY

In an endeavour to holistically and comprehensively present an in-depth under-standing of the divine phenomenon of glory, it is highly imperative that we examine it from all perspectives or angles by looking at its *dimensions, realms and levels*. As much as there are different levels of the anointing, faith, power and other dimensions of the supernatural realm, there are also divergent realms, dimensions and degrees of the glory. These are intensively manifested when we provoke the glory of God into manifestation by cultivating a conducive atmosphere and spiritual climate that manoeuvres the hand of God and compels heaven to move on behalf of the earth. However, even though man plays such a pivotal role in terms of spearheading these realms of glory to fulfil God's purpose on earth, the nature and magnitude of the manifestation of the glory is executed within the framework of God's sovereign initiative.

It is of paramount significance to unveil right from the onset the divine truth that in many instances across a broad spectrum of Christian faith, whenever people talk about the realms of God's glory there is a tendency to confine their categorisation to only two realms, that is the *former glory* and the *latter glory*. These two realms have popularly dominated the theme of sermons in many churches, yet there is another special type of Glory at creation called *prime glory*. This is the glory which initially prevailed during the creation of the earth and regulated the life of man before the fall. From my observation, it appears that since time immemorial, the prime glory is the highest concentration of God's glory. However the latter glory is expected to supersedes all past dimensions of glory that is both the *prime glory* and the *Shekinah glory.* Therefore, throughout the ages, there are three stages at which the glory of God is revealed or manifested in its intensity, that is *No. 1 Prime glory, No. 2 Shekinah glory and 3. Latter or end time glory.*

THE PRIME GLORY

"This is also known as the glory of God at creation"

It is a typical scenario in some Christian charismatic cycles across the globe that many at times Christians are only exposed to the former glory and the latter glory and they hardly touch on this critical subject of the prime glory, which is the foundation of all dimensions of glory which ever manifested on this earth. A divine revelation of the state of man in the Garden of Eden before the fall will help you to clearly understand the original life of glory which God prepared for us. Tactically speaking, the Garden of Eden was a perfect demonstration of God's plan for this earth and an exact proto-type of what He wanted the earth to look like in the glory. The prime glory is the ini-tial glory which God revealed to man at creation. This is the glory of God which He imparted upon Adam in the Garden of Eden before the fall. This glory represents God's original intention concerning humanity. It is original, pure, unfaked, undiluted, uncompromised and crude in its manifestation. It depicts the highest level of concen-tration of God's power on earth at that time. The Bible records in Genesis 2:7 that *God breathed His breath on Adam and he became a living being.* This speaks of an imparta-tion of God's glory and the life of God (*God Kind of Life*)upon humanity.

Prime glory represents the highest concentration or intensity or manifestation of glory God has ever imparted upon humanity.

This was the highest level of glory operating on the earth at the time of creation. It is the most special type of glory because it portrays God's original master plan, intension and purpose about mankind. In that dimension of Glory, there was neither death, sickness nor decay but everything was in perfect harmony and synchronisation with each other.

It is a greater truth that God did not originally want man to access the supernatural through faith and gifts. Instead, He wanted man to operate freely in the realm of the spirit by His glory. For example in the Garden of Eden, Adam did not have to prophesy or speak in a tongue or operate in the word of knowledge in order to contact the realm of God. Instead, he permanently functioned and moved in both realms of existence without any difficulty. It was like living in an open vision. Adam effortlessly moved in both realms of existence. For example, he moved into the realm of the spirit to communicate with God and then moved back into the realm of the natural to interact with animals. His movement in both realms of existence was like moving from his bed room into the living room. This is the dimension of glory which God wants us to experience especially in these end times and we are already witnessing the first sprinkles of this glory.

For example, I once heard a testimony of a man whom God instructed to go and preach in another country but the man did not have money for transportation. However, God told him to pack his belongings and head off to catch a plane at the airport. In obedience, he did exactly as he was told and when he got to the airport, God told him to enter a certain room and suddenly he appeared in another country where he was supposed to go and preach. In that country, he hold a massive crusade where he made a tremendous impact in the lives of the people. When he was done, God told him to go back to the airport and enter the same room which he had entered before and all of a sudden he appeared in his living room, together with his luggage. That means His body was enabled to take up a different level of quality where he was divinely transported in the spirit across both realms. This is a manifestation of life in the prime glory, similar to how Adam used to move from the natural realm into the spirit realm and from the spirit realm back into the natural again.

In the prime glory, there was neither danger nor harm of any nature but only harmony and synchronisation of all things in accordance with God's will.

Have you ever wondered how Adam used to communicate with animals in the Garden of Eden? It was because of the atmosphere of the prime glory. Did you know that it was Adam who named a lion, *"Lion"* and a snake, *"Snake"* and commanded all animals to do anything he wanted just like a man commanding his pets? In the atmosphere of revelation glory, Adam intrinsically knew what was expected of him. How else would he know the animals were to be named and how they would respond. In the glory realm, Adam could freely interact with the wild animals and they would not dare harm him. Imagine Adam could reach out his had to touch the head of the tiger, the scales of the crocodile and soft down on the skin of the cobra without any harm.

In the prime glory, animals are pets but in the absence of glory, they are wild.

This is the reason why lions could not devour Daniel when he was thrown in a den of lions (Daniel 6:16). Daniel was instantly catapulted into the same realm of glory which Adam operated under in the Garden of Eden before the fall. The explanation is that in the glory realm, the hunger pangs of a lion which makes it dangerous were disabled. In the glory, there are no carnivores, instead, there are herbivores only. However, it was after the glory was lifted up in the Garden of Eden that all of a sudden a lion developed hunger pains and when it looked at a human being, it no longer saw its master but a prey or a piece of meat that could be devoured and cannibalism became a normal mode of survival in the animal world.

In the realm of prime glory there is nether sickness, nor decay, nor death of any kind.

The glory of God is like oxygen in the natural realm, it is the life blood of all things. Anything that comes into contact with the glory of God receives an impartation of the life of God. That is why in the dimension of Glory the dead are raised because of an impartation of the eternal life of God. In the glory are healings, creative miracles and deliverance. When human beings were first created, they did not know sickness, poverty, or death because in the prime glory, there is no death, sickness or poverty. It was after the fall that they started experiencing these things. Since that time, all human beings have undergone a process of birth, growth and eventual death. When Adam and even fell, the essence of who they were as human beings made in the image of God, die (Genesis 3). They also began to die physically even though it took more than 930 years for Adam's body to stop functioning. The residual of glory that remained in his body kept him physically alive for that long. This shows how powerful it was to live in the dimension of prime glory.

In the realm of prime glory, everything is complete and perfect in itself.

Adam was never an infant, child or teenager; therefore he did not have to undergo the growth process we experience. There we created and formed as adults because in the beginning God created all things in their finished form, while placing a seed in every kind of species so that it could reproduce (Genesis 1:12). The greater truth is that Adam was born in a life of prime glory and he never had to wait for the earth to produce fruits. By virtue of the life in the prime glory, Adam was exempted from going through the normal stages of plant conception, growth and maturity and just by sowing a seed, he was instantaneously catapulted right into the season of harvesting. This implies that plants and trees grew as each seed hit the ground. In other words, Adam did not have to wait to gather the harvest because waiting implies a space in time but the glory is eternity where everything is in the now.

In the dimension of prime glory, the law of faith had broken the law of time, hence everything produced fruits instantaneously. With the prime glory, everything in the natural accelerates and manifest at a higher speed as is the case in the supernatural. In other words, the glory brings the supernatural and natural realms into harmony and function together for our good. The Bible records in Amos 9:13, that, *"Behold the days are coming says the Lord, when the ploughman shall overtake the reaper and the treader of grapes him who sows seed"*. This speaks of the season of the *overtaking anointing* into which we have been ushered in this end time dispensation. Prophetically speaking, by reason of the overtaking anointing, we have been accelerated into the realm of the supernatural, propelled by the law of faith in antagonistic with the limitations of time and catapulted into higher realms of glory. We are therefore living in a season and operating in a dimension whereby immediately after we sow a seed we see a harvest. In other words planting and harvesting are taking place concurrently or at the same time. Where then is the law of waiting? In a practical sense, our debts can be cancelled instantaneously as God launches us into the greater depths of glory in a split of a second by reason of the overtaking anointing.

Moreover, in the atmosphere of prime glory in the Garden of Eden, man did not even have to sow a seed in order to reap a harvest as is the case today. In the dimension of glory, the earth was completely fertile, fruitful and productive. Its times and seasons were different from what the situation is today. As a matter of fact, its order was harvesting first then seed time later. But after the fall, man got disconnected from the glory of God as God inhaled back his glory from Adam's body and at that moment man exited the dimension of glory and started experiencing drastic changes. When Adam was thrown out of the garden, he fell short of the glory. In other words, he lost his position in the glory realm. That is why the Bible records in Romans 3:23, *that for all have sinned and fallen short of the glory of God*. One of the changes which Adam experienced was in the order of *sowing* and *harvesting*. For example, the process of provision was no longer harvesting first and seed time later as it was in the beginning. Instead, the order was changed such that now seed time comes first then harvesting later, of which it takes time to wait for the harvest after sowing. That is why it is recorded in Genesis 8:22 that, *"while the earth remains, seed time and harvest, cold and heat, winter and summer and day and night shall not cease"*. This came as a result of the curse.

The current set up of things is that in order to harvest, one has to sow first and without a seed there is no harvesting but it was not like that during the former days of prime glory. Immediately after the fall, God demanded that man gives something and that is why Abel and Cain were instructed to give a sacrifice of which before the fall, God never demanded Adam to give him anything. Even now God demands that one must not come into His presence empty handed (Deuteronomy 16:16). In other words, in order to receive something from God, you must give something and this could be in any form, whether it's time, effort, money or any material possession. All these changes came as a result of the loss of prime glory. This is to show you how powerful the prime glory was as it laid a concrete foundation for the manifestation of other realms of glory, which manifested thereafter.

THE SHEKINAH GLORY

"This is also known as the former glory"

It is of paramount importance to unveil the divine truth that immediately after the fall of man, man was disconnected from the prime glory hence, he needed faith and the gifts to operate and function in the supernatural. It is for this reason that the *Shekinah glory* was introduced by Heaven in order for God to dwell and walk with man side by side in a visible and tangible manner. That is why at this level of glory, we see the rise of prophets like Elijah, Elisha, Isaiah and Jeremiah with prophetic gifts which enabled them to see in the spirit and foretell the future.

The word, *"Shekinah"* does not appear in the Bible, but the concept clearly does. The Jewish rabbis coined this extra biblical expression, a form of a Hebrew word that literally means *"he caused to dwell,"* signifying that it was a divine visitation of the presence or dwelling of Jehovah on this earth. The Shekinah glory was first evident when the Israelites set out from Succoth in their escape from Egypt. There it appeared as a cloudy pillar during the day and a fiery pillar by night. Let's carefully examine the following scripture that clearly depicts how the word, *Shekinah* was derived.

" And Moses was not able to enter into the tent of the congregation, because the cloud abode thereon, and the glory of the Lord filled the tabernacle." (Exodus 40:35).

The Hebrew word used in the above- scripture for "abode" is "shaw-kan´," hence, "Shekinah Glory." It is derived from the Hebrew verb "shakan,", which literally means to settle, inhabit, or dwell or take up residence with long continuity in a neighbourhood. It also means royalty or royal residence. That's what we call the "Shekinah Glory." Therefore in Biblical Hebrew language, the word "Shekinah" means the dwelling or settling, and is used to denote the dwelling or settling presence of God amongst His people, especially in the Temple in Jerusalem.

The distinction between this word and *"yashav"* which is also translated "dwell" is just this: You can use the latter to mean an individual doing the dwelling without reference to others or to duration while *"Shakan"* means a protracted dwelling in the midst of a neighbourhood or a group of people or might be limited to one other person but only by extension. The primary meaning is to reside and continue as a member of the community. This is a common word used for all classes to convey this idea. However, when it refers to God, it takes on an added mysticism which is obvious upon small consideration

Let's closely look at what exactly transpired as the children of Israel journeyed from Succoth:

After leaving Succoth, they camped at Etham on the edge of the desert. By day the Lord went ahead of them in a pillar of cloud to guide them on their way and by night in a pillar of fire to give them light, so that they could travel by day or night. Neither the pillar of cloud by day nor the pillar of fire by night left its place in front of the people" (Exodus 13:20-22).

That visible and tangible cloud and pillar of fire which dwelt amongst men and was beheld by all is the *Shekinah glory*, which means the dwelling, settling, abiding, residing, and habituating presence of God. In essence, the Shekinah glory refers to the visible and tangible manifestation of the glory of God amongst His people. In a related scripture in Exodus 14:19 the Bible says,

And the angel of God, which went before the camp of Israel, removed and went behind them; and the pillar of the cloud went from before their face, and stood behind them. And it came between the camp of the Egyptians and the camp of Israel; and it was a cloud and darkness to them, but it gave light by night to these: so that the one came not near the other all the night.
(Exodus 40:38).

Divergent Realms of Glory

From an arm chair view, it is difficult to imagine a pillar of cloud bright enough to lighten the desert at night so that 2,500,000 people, with all their belongings and animals, could see where they were going. How would one describe such a light? In that day they probably used the term *"fire"*. Today, we might describe it as similar to the light of an atomic bomb blast. Whatever it was, it was a tremendous light.

The greater truth is that God's dream has always been to dwell amongst His people and to manifest Himself visibly to humanity. In the Old Testament, whenever the glory of God manifested, physical phenomena took place such as fire, smoke or clouds. His presence was always tangible to the senses. The glory of God was unequivocally seen as the visible and tangible manifestation of the presence of God. *Shekinah* describes the place where God rests, the eminent presence of God that transcends the spiritual realm and manifests in the physical world. It is the immediate and intimate activity of God, the splendour of the Lord while He is present in the now, in action. This is the same glory that covered the face of Moses on Mount Sinai to such an extent that it was glittering and shining and the children of Israel could not dare look at his him (Exodus 34:29). The glory of God had so much mingled and permeated the core of his being such that he literally became a career of God's glory.

The Bible talks about the former glory and the latter glory. In Hagai 2:9, God Himself declared that *the glory of the latter house shall be greater than the former.* It is called the *former glory* because it incorporates all the events and supernatural acts that took place from the law of the prophets in the Old Testament right up to the time of John the Baptist in the New Testament. Jesus said in Luke 16:16, *the law and the prophets were until John. Since that time, the kingdom of God has been preached and everyone is pressing into it.* The *former glory* therefore incorporates miracles performed by the Old Testament folks who functioned in the realm of the miraculous and demonstrated the power of God through miracles signs and wonders   .

> *Some spectacular manifestations of the former glory were; the experience of Moses with the burning bush, Aaron's road tuning into a serpent, and eating pharaoh's snakes, ten plagues of Egypt, deliverance of Israelites from Egypt and instant wealth transfer, the crossing of the Red sea by Israelites, on dry ground, bitter waters of Mariah made sweet, the raining down of manna from heaven, Moses drawing water from the rock, the manifestation of a pillar of fire by night and pillar of cloud by day.*

Practical examples of manifestations of Shekinah Glory in the Old Testament:

We have already established that the glory of the Lord and the Shekinah cloud are synonymous terms. Moses experienced God's glory and witnessed it's tangible presence. The Lord said to Moses, *"I am going to come to you in a dense cloud, so that the people will hear me speaking with you and will always put their trust in you"*. On the morning of the third day there was thunder and lightning, with a thick cloud over the mountain, and a very loud trumpet blast. (Exodus 19:9,16). This means the glory of God is not a mystical phenomenon but a visible and tangible substance manifesting in the natural realm.

The Bible records in Exodus 16:10 that *it came to pass, as Aaron spoke to the whole congregation of the children of Israel, that they looked toward the wilderness, and, behold, the glory of the Lord appeared in the cloud.* This shows that the brightness of the cloud was associated with the glory, or presence of the Lord, and that this was the place where He dwelt among them. To cement this revelation with reference to further scriptural evidence, the Bible further records in Exodus 40:34 that *a cloud covered the tent of the congregation, and the glory of the Lord filled the tabernacle.* The idea of the glory of God filling the terbanacle reinforces the divine truth that the glory is a tangible divine substance that can manifest in degrees and measures.

The Bible further records in Exodus 19:16 *that it came to pass on the third day in the morning, that there were thunders and lightings, and a thick cloud upon the mountain, and the voice of the trumpet thundered, so that all the people who were in the camp trembled. And Mount Sinai was altogether on a smoke, because the Lord descended upon it in fire and the smoke ascended as the smoke of a furnace, and the whole mount quaked greatly.* In affirmation, Exodus 24:16 states quite clearly that this was the glory of God: *"And the glory of the Lord abode upon Mount Sinai, and the cloud covered it six days: and the seventh day he called unto Moses out of the midst of the cloud." This cloud guided the people until later in their wanderings when the Lord told Moses to build him a tabernacle* (Exodus 25:8).

The Bible records an event during the dedication of a temple in 2 Chronicles 7:1,

Now when Solomon had finished praying, fire came down from heaven and consumed the burnt offering and the sacrifices, and the glory of the Lord filled the house. The priests could not enter into the house of the Lord because the glory of the Lord filled the Lord's house. It happened that all the sons of Israel, seeing the fire come down and the glory of the Lord upon the house, bowed down on the pavement with their faces to the ground, and they worshiped and gave praise to the Lord, saying, "Truly He is good, truly His loving kindness is everlasting."

This was a quintessential example of the glory of God manifesting visibly in the natural realm. The act of the fire coming down and consuming the sacrifice denotes the *glory invasion*. The act of the glory *filling* the house describes the phenomenal experience of the glory of God engulfing the natural atmosphere and altering its natural properties.

In a related incident in 1Kings 8:10 the Bible says that,

It came to pass, when the priests were come out of the holy place, that the cloud filled the house of the Lord, So that the priests could not stand to minister because of the cloud: for the glory of the Lord had filled the house of the Lord. Then Solomon said, The Lord said that he would dwell in the thick darkness. I have surely built thee a house to dwell in, a settled place for thee to abide in for ever.

There are moments whereby the glory of God is so strong such that our bodies are not able to take the weight of God's presence. Moreover, God also manifested His Shekinah glory to Moses in the form of a burning bush and the experience was so spectacular such that he beheld the glory of God in action. Unknown to Moses, this was the same pillar of fire that would lead him and the children of Israel through the wilderness on their way to Canaan. The Bible records in Numbers 9:15 that,

On the day that the tabernacle was reared up the cloud covered the tabernacle, namely, the tent of the testimony: and at even there was upon the tabernacle as it were the appearance of fire, until the morning.

Note that God did not just reveal His glory to Moses but he also spoke to him from that atmosphere of glory. It is therefore important to note that if a manifestation of God occurs and we don't hear His voice, we are only spectators and not participators. But if God speaks to you and you receive what He says, it becomes established in you. Furthermore, in Exodus 29:43-46 God said,

"There, I will meet with the children of Israel, and the tabernacle shall be sanctified by My glory. And I will sanctify the tabernacle of the congregation, and the altar: I will sanctify also both Aaron and his sons, to minister to me in the priest's office. And I will dwell among the children of Israel, and will be their God. And they shall know that I am the Lord their God, that brought them forth out of Egypt, that I may dwell among them. I am the Lord their God."

82

Practical examples of manifestations of Shekinah Glory in the New Testament:

It must be expressly understood that although the magnitude of manifestation of the Shekinah glory was intensified in the Old Testament, it continued to manifest even on the New Testament dispensation. The dominant idea of the Shekinah as a dwelling for the Lord is actually more than an indwelling. This is shown by several scriptures in the New Testament. In Luke 2:9, what the angel told the shepherds shows the approval of God by the presence of the Shekinah glory cloud. *"And, lo, the angel of the Lord came upon them, and the glory of the Lord shone round about them: and they were sore afraid."* In Acts 1:9, Jesus ascended to the Father through the glory cloud: *"And when he had spoken these things, while they beheld, he was taken up; and a cloud received him out of their sight."* Jesus was taken up in the Shekinah glory, or cloud, and he will return in the glory of the Father, or in the Shekinah cloud, in which he left.

Paul also saw the Shekinah glory cloud of God. Saul, a dedicated and knowledgeable Hebrew, knew that the Shekinah cloud indicated not only authenticity, but also the authority of The God. Acts 9:3-5 described the event:

"And as he journeyed, he came near Damascus: and suddenly there shined round about him a light from heaven: And he fell to the earth, and heard a voice saying unto him, Saul, Saul, why persecutest thou me? And he said, Who art thou, Lord? And the Lord said, I am Jesus whom thou persecutest: it is hard for thee to kick against the pricks."

Paul addressed his question to the Lord. He knew this cloud indicated great authority, but he asked the question to find out specifically which authority spoke to him. After this Saul was blind for several days. In Acts 22:11, he said, *"And when I could not see for the glory of that light."*

When Stephen was stoned, he was allowed to see the glory of God in heaven. Acts 7:55 says,

"But he, being full of the Holy Ghost, looked up steadfastly into heaven, and saw the glory of God, and Jesus standing on the right hand of God."

Letting him see this great cloud of glory may have been to keep his mind on God and not on his pain. Another instance of the light, or cloud, of the glory of the Lord is related in Acts 12:7. Peter had been thrown in prison by Herod. While Peter was languishing in prison, the scriptures say,

"And, behold, the angel of the Lord came upon him, and the glory of God shined in the prison: and he smote Peter on the side, and raised him up, saying, Arise up quickly. And his chains fell off from his hands."

Peter was not certain if this had really happened or if he had seen a vision. The reality of his release, however, proved that this actually happened. This is to show you how powerful it is to dwell in the glory cloud.

Apostle Maldonado says that while he was preaching in one of his churches, people physically saw a Shekinah cloud of glory, as it was moving in a certain section of the audience. And instantly people in that section started being healed from cancer, developing new body parts and delivered without anybody laying hands on them or doing anything.

1. THE END TIME GLORY

"This is also known as the latter glory"

The latter or end time glory represents the final move of God as He unleashes the abundance and fullness of His might, power and saving grace to conclude His eternal plan on earth shortly before the second coming of the Lord Jesus Christ. The Bible declares in Joel 2:23, that,

"Be glad then, You children of Zion, and rejoice in the Lord your God: for He has given you the former rain moderately, and He will cause to come down for you the rain, the former rain, and the latter rain in the first month."

On the basis of the above scriptural evidence, the end time glory is the joint manifestation of the *latter glory* and *former glory*. This means it is a total sum or combination of all the dimensions of glory which have ever manifested on earth right from the time of creation till the end time dispensation. It is a sum of all the miracles performed by Old Testament folks, plus all which Jesus and the apostle did plus all performed in this end time season. Therefore, mathematically speaking:

Mathematically speaking, the Latter Glory = The prime glory manifested in the Garden of Eden + Shekinah glory manifested by prophets in the Old Testament + The glory manifested in the New Testament dispensation until the second coming of the Lord Jesus Christ.

However, although both dimensions of glory are crucial to fulfilling God's plan and purpose on earth, the Bible unveils the divine truth that in comparison, *the glory of the latter house shall by far exceed that of the former.* This means that the magnitude and intensity of manifestation of the end time glory shall by far supersedes the glory which has been manifested in the former days, which is the Old Testament era. This implies that if the former glory was intensely manifested to the extent that Moses's face shone brightly that people could not dare stare at his face, then in this end times, your whole body must be dazzling with the glory such that devils cannot dare withstand your presence. If in the former glory, Moses saw the back of God, then it means you must be catapulted right into the throne room of heaven to behold the fullness of God - His face, hands, legs, and all that represents His Majesty. In other words, you must have 100% access into the throne room. That is why in these end times there is a heightened degree of translation and visitation into the throne room on study tours.

In the Old Testament, the glory was manifested on a part time basis but in these end time days, it is an order of the day and a common experience amongst God's children as believers are launched right into the greater depths of God's presence. This means we have the capacity to move in greater measure of Glory as compared to Old Testament folks. For instance, in Old Testament, the glory was an outside experience but now the glory has been internalised in us. We are careers of God's glory hence wherever we go, the glory of God is manifested. That means you can transfer and impact the glory of God wherever you go. That is why the glory of the *latter house* shall exceed that of the *former*. The new creation believer can do more than what Old Testament folks accomplished in the glory because they have the glory resident in their spirits. In the New Testament, God is no longer with us only but He is both *with us* and *within us*. The Old Testament folks caught a revelation of Emanuel that means God with us but our revelation for this end time is: *Christ in me the hope of glory*, meaning *"God in us"*. The Bible further declares in Hosea 6:3 that,

"Then shall we know, if we follow on to know the Lord: his going forth is prepared as the morning; and he shall come unto us as the rain, as the latter and former rain unto the earth."

It is of paramount significance in this regard to unveil the greater truth that the major difference between the former and the later glory is that the former glory was manifested over a long period of time as God revealed His glory one at a time but the latter glory shall be manifested in an instant. In the latter glory, time is not of essence, hence as believers are catapulted into a realm that is beyond the time dimension and limitation of time, distance, space and matter. In other words, they have been capacitated to manifest the highest degree of miracles, signs and wonders in an instant. This means that what could have taken years to be accomplished shall be done within a short period of time. Therefore, in the latter glory, the revelation of God manifesting in times and seasons does not apply anymore as God manifests anywhere, anytime and in any measure at one goal. Therefore, there are no more delays, no more waiting and no more timing as the law of time has been broken to give way or accentuate an avenue for the overarching law of grace to take precedence.

It is important to unveil the truth that Jesus was the bridge between the former glory and the latter glory. In other words, He participated in the former glory since He lived under the law and fulfilled it while He was on earth. (Mathew 5:17). Then he ushered in the latter glory after His resurrection. So the latter glory refers to joint manifestation of all the miracles which Jesus performed in His participation in the former glory and the miracles which Jesus predicted will occur in the church in the last dispensation. More specifically, it refers to greater works which Jesus commanded in John 14:12 when He pronounced that,

Whoever shall believe in my name shall do all the things which I have done (Former glory)
And that greater things than these shall you do (Latter Glory

In the context of this scripture, it is called *greater works* in the sense that it is a combination of both the miracles of Old Testament and New Testament that will invade the world in the last days. In the analysis of the above statement which Jesus uttered, it is evident that the latter glory shall by far exceed the former because Jesus said *greater things than these shall you do*, meaning that what is coming is more powerful than what has already been done. Therefore the scriptural phrase *"greater things"* refer to the portion of heightened degree of miracles, signs and wonders which shall characterise this end time dispensation. The phrase *"these things"* refers to the miracles of the former glory of which Jesus participated. Unknown to many people, in this statement, Jesus was actually making a comparison of the former glory and the latter glory and emphatically emphasising that the latter glory shall be administered on a higher level, dimension and intensity than the former, hence believers should have an expectation to tap into deeper and higher realms of glory in this end time dispensation.Moreover, the Bible declares in Zechariah 10:1 that,

"Ask the Lord for rain in the time of the latter rain; so the Lord shall make bright clouds, and give you showers of rain, to every one grass in the field."

From the analysis of the above scripture the phrase, *"time of the latter rain"*, speaks of the end time season and from a spiritual point of view, *"clouds"* speak of the glory of God and *"rain"* speaks of the anointing. Hence, in the context of this scripture, this speaks of a heightened degree of manifestation of God's glory coupled with measureless anointing which God shall shower, propagate and proliferate upon the masses. This implies that latter glory points to the deeper realm of the miraculous manifested in creative miracles, signs and wonders that shall characterise this end time dispensation as man operate in the realm of the miraculous in measures never witnessed before. It represents the final move of God and a final display of God's power in ways never been imagined before in the history of humanity. For example, as people minister unto the Lord, physical fire shall visibly descend from heaven and fall in the auditoriums, culminating in the creative miracles such as the creation of new body organs where they previously did not exist, short legs growing taller, development of hair on bald heads, emergence of pregnancy without sexual intercourse. Moreover, one notable manifestation of end time glory shall be the raising of the dead which shall become a normal occurrence as mortuaries are displaced and undertakers taken out of business.

Prophetically speaking, while there shall be a rebirth of new manifestations and increase dimensions into the miraculous in this end time season, part of the package will be a return or migration back into the prime glory. This is because the prime glory or the glory of man before the fall has not yet been widely manifested for the past dispensations despite the restoration of man to His former or original position of glory as a result of Jesus Christ's resurrection from the dead. Therefore, the latter glory shall culminate in the rise of a unique breed of people who shall reinstate the glory that was lost in the Garden of Eden. God is therefore raising a generation of people who shall be custodians of His divine glory and ignite a spiritual invasion of the devil's key territories such as hospitals, prisons, mortuaries, thereby fling heaven and emptying hell through the salvation of billions of souls across the globe.

Moreover, the latter glory also represents the prophetic move of the Holy spirit predicted by the Prophet Joel in Joel 2:28, whose manifestation was initially ignited during the Pentecostal experience in Acts 2:1, and spread to engulf the territories of the world throughout the ages and shall continue to flow right until the time of Jesus' second coming. It speaks of the unprecedented move and avalanche of the Holy Ghost in the last days. More specifically, it speaks of a divine outpouring of the Spirit of God which shall culminate in the emergence of a unique breed of prophets and vision bearers as proclaimed by Joel when he prophesied that,

"It shall come to pass that in the last days, says the Lord, I shall pour out my spirit upon all flesh. Your sons and daughters shall prophesy and old man shall see visions".

Therefore, the restoration of the latter day glory is neither the idea of a prophet nor the opinion of a man, but the Holy Spirit. The glory of the Pentecostal outpouring and the Tabernacles outpouring will be as John G. Lake expressed:

"As a drop of water in a bucket full of water in comparison" A double portion."

In view of the above scriptural reference, it is therefore undeniably evident that the latter glory is the union of the two glories; it magnifies the power that is released and the wonders for which we testify. The manifestation of this new glory is already taking place in this season and we shall see them in their fullness in the future. It also incorporates new, peculiar manifestations, spiritual encounters and experiences of the end time dispensation which have not been witnessed before. This shall be a fulfilment of Isaiah 43:19 where God says,

"Behold I'm doing a new thing, something that you have not seen or known yesterday. Can't you perceive it as it spring forth?"

Therefore, this is the time to experience or witness the greatest manifestations ever seen in the history of humanity as the bible confirms in 1 Corinthians 2:9 that, *"No eye has seen nor ear heard no mind conceived what God has prepared for those who love him".* This speaks of the new manifestations and spiritual experiences which God has prepared for the end times.Therefore, believers must be alerted because some of the miracles that shall take place in this end time dispensation are not recorded anywhere, not even in the Bible but are a raw, fresh and new manifestations streaming forth directly from the throne room in heaven. However, the fact that a miracle manifested is not recorded in the bible doesn't mean that it is not from God because God operates in times and seasons, which means He does something specific in a certain point in time. Eternity is already laid bare before Him hence He unfolds the reality of new things as we approach the second coming of Christ. Therefore, new miracles or manifestations previously not recorded in the bible are accommodated in this scripture in Isaiah 43:19, where God says *He shall do new things*. For example when God rained manna for the Children of Israel to eat in the wilderness, to them, manna was never recorded anywhere in their law or Bible. Instead, it was something brand new, something they had never heard of. Prophetically speaking, in this end time dispensation, some of the things which believers shall experience are brand new packages directly from the hand of God, something that shall shake the world to its core.

For example, a time shall come shortly in this season whereby raising people from the dead shall become a common experience and an order of the day just like healing a headache. I remember few years ago, when HIV/AIDS was initially declared an incurable disease. No one could believe that HIV/AIDS would one day be cured. But when men of God across the globe caught a revelation of the healing anointing and started praying for HIV/IADs patients and they got healed, it was something new and really amazing. However, there are very few people nowadays who get amazed when HIV/ AIDs is cured because it is now a common experience in the body of Christ. By the same token, the same shall happen with raising the dead. A time is coming where by believers shall catch the revelation of the *resurrection glory,* hence *Resurrection Centres* shall be established across the globe where the dead shall be brought in and be commanded to arise and there shall be mass resurrections ever witnessed in the history of humanity. These are new things which I'm talking about which are about to be unfolded and unleashed in the latter glory.

Prophetically speaking, there is a spiritual invasion, awakening, stirring and shaking that is about to take place in the supernatural. God declared in Haggai 2:7-9 that,

"Once more and in a little while I will shake the heavens, I will shake the sea and I will shake the earth and all people shall come to the desires of all nations" And I will shake all nations, and the desire of all nations shall come: and I will fill this house with glory, saith the Lord of hosts. The silver is mine, and the gold is mine, saith the Lord of hosts. The glory of this latter house shall be greater than of the former, saith the Lord of hosts: and in this place will I give peace, saith the Lord of hosts."

This speaks of an era of great shaking preceding the rapture that shall displace demonic powers operating in the second heavens and culminate in an avalanche or stream flow of billions of souls into the kingdom and that season of the miraculous has just started. We are about to see an acceleration of God's works in every area as well as radical transformations, miracles, signs and wonders such as dominion over nature, physical shaking over cities produced by the glory of God, raising of the dead and other phenomena humanity cannot fathom. On the basis of ample scriptural evidence unveiled above, it is clearly unquestionable that it is perfectly scriptural for believers to unleash expectation for the manifest glory as God promised in what I call a *"pulling"* on the Glory.

CHAPTER FOUR

THE SEVEN DIMENSIONS OF GOD'S GLORY

It is of paramount significance to unveil the divine truth that as much as there are divergent realms, dimensions and depths of the anointing, there are also divergent dimensions of Glory which any believer can tap into in this end time season. A spiritual dimension has greater coverage, as it consists of the width, length, depth and height. The Bible attests in Ephesians 3:18 that *you being rooted and grounded in love, may be able to comprehend with all saints what is the width, length and depth and height of God's presence* This speaks of the *dimensions* of operating in the glory. They are dimensions of glory in the sense that they measure the breath, height and depth of God's glory and explore the different flavours of manifestation of new realms of glory. It must therefore, be put into correct perspective that God cannot be put in a box because He has an endless and perennial supply of His glory which He can manifest in various ways. Although God is the ultimate source of glory, He has placed or imparted His glory in various places for man to make a withdrawal, hence the glory of God has seventh fold manifestations. Therefore, whenever someone is talking about the glory of God, it's either he is talking about the glory as Jesus, the glory as the Spirit or glory as the Father Himself, the glory as man, the glory as creation, the glory as the Word or the glory as a spiritual substance. This is because all these are divergent manifestations of God's glory.

THE GLORY OF JESUS.

"This is the glory of God as Jesus"

The Bible unveils one of the most powerful revelations of Jesus Christ in the New Testament dispensation. Concerning this revelation, Paul declares in Colossians 1:27, *Christ in me, the hope of Glory*. This is the highest revelation of Christianity in the New Testament. This means that Christ is the Glory of God in us. By virtue of His indwelling presence, He is the divine orchestrator and originator of the glory of God in our spirits. Think about it! This is a wonder! How can someone so unimaginably vast and infinitely great live in someone so infinitesimally small? This was a mystery that was hidden for ages but now has been revealed to us. This speaks of an indwelling presence of the God head. Jesus came to reveal the Father and the Spirit has come to reveal Jesus. So, when the Bible says, *"Christ in me the hope of glory"*, it alludes to the fact that Christ dwells in me through the Holy Spirit because it is the Spirit that has come to reveal Jesus. Jesus is the glory of God and if Jesus who is the glory of God is in me, then it implies that I am a career of God's glory. It means that I can influence the world by the glory of God wherever I go. Wherever Jesus went, people gathered around Him as He healed the sick, cast out devils and raised the dead. By the same token, wherever I go, I attract the masses and manifest the Greater glory of God because the same Christ who performed all these miracles is in me. The Bible speaks of *the sufferings of Christ and the glory that should follow*. Now, Christ has come, suffered, crucified, died and rose from the dead and now the glory has come. And that glory is in me. That is why I cannot be sick or broke because the glory of God is in me. Concerning the new creation, the Bible further attests to the divine truth that, *"If any man be* **IN CHRIST,** he is a new creature (2 Corinthians 5:17). In the context of this scripture, the phrase, **"IN CHRIST"** speaks of a place; a realm of glory. It's an environment of glory. Did you know that not only is **CHRIST** a person but also a place, a realm and an anointing? The phrase **"CHRIST IN YOU"** speaks of the *anointing* but **"YOU IN CHRIST"** speaks of a *place or realm of glory*. Therefore, in Him (Christ), you are unshaken by anything because you are at home; it's a peculiar environment of glory where there is neither death, sickness nor decay.

Jesus is the expression of the glory of God; God gave Him that excellent glory which He in turn gave to us. Hence, we have become sharers of His glory: Shortly before His death, Jesus prayed to the father asking for the return of the glory that mankind had lost so that each believer could live in its manifestation. Jesus specifically said, *"Father, the Glory which you gave me, I have given them that they may be one just as we are one"* (John 17:22). This speaks of an impartation of divine glory. Everything that the Father is, His nature, virtue, attributes character, power, authority and grace was manifested in His son. So, Jesus imparted the same nature, attribute and measure of glory of God upon man so that he could in turn manifest the glory and function exactly like God on earth just like what Jesus did. So, we can manifest, exhibit, display and showcase the glory of God in miracles, signs and wonders in the same measure in which Christ functioned while on earth. As He (Jesus) is the glory of God, so are we in this world (1 John 4:17). This is to tell you that there is glory in your life; it's the glory of Jesus, hence you should unreservedly walk in the light of that glory. Bear in mind that Jesus's number one mission was to restore the glory we had lost and as aforementioned in our opening scripture, now He makes a public declaration that His mission has been completed. That is why we can walk in the same dimension of glory, power, miraculous as Jesus did. Concerning Jesus, the Bible affirms in John 1:1, that *the Word became flesh and dwelt among us, and we beheld His glory, the glory as of the only begotten of the father, full of grace and truth.* This implies that Jesus was the glory of God. Jesus came to reveal the glory of the father, the glory that was lost by Adam. Through His death and resurrection, Jesus led us back to that dimension of glory whereby we could walk once more as Adam did in the Garden of Eden and even surpass that dimension of glory.

The ultimate expression of the manifestation of God's glory in the world was when He sent Jesus Christ to earth. Jesus is the highest expression of God to mankind, the complete revelation and manifestation of the glory of the father. The Bible says in Hebrews 1:1-3, that *God has in these last days spoken to us by His son whom He has appointed heir of all things, through whom also he made the worlds, whom being the brightness of His glory and the express image of His person and upholding all things by the word of His power, when he had by Himself purged our sins, sat down at the right hand of the majesty on high.* The Bible further declares in Hebrews 1:3 that Jesus Christ is the perfect revelation of God's glory. It states precisely that, *"The Son is the radiance of God's glory and the exact representation of His being, sustaining all things by the word of His power."* This means that Jesus is the glory of God. He is the exact representation of the glorious radiance of glory and when God's glory touches us, the true, weighty presence of God is being released into our lives. The Bible says in 2 Corinthians 4:6, that *it is the God who commanded light to shine out of darkness, who has shone in our hearts to give the light of the glory of God in the face of Jesus Christ*. This is to show you that our salvation came because of a measure of God's glory that is revealed in our hearts. God places a portion of His glory into our lives when we were born again.

THE GLORY OF THE SPIRIT

"This is the glory of God as the Spirit"

Taking us back to the time of creation, the Bible unveils in Genesis 2:7 that *God breathed His Spirit, which is His glory upon man and man became a living being*. One of the key revelations of the Holy Ghost concerning Jesus is that He is said to be the Spirit of Glory. That means the Holy Spirit Himself is the glory of God. The Bible attests in Job 32:8 that *there is a spirit in a man, the breath of the Almighty give thee understanding*. Logically speaking, this means that since the breath of God is the Spirit of God, then the Spirit of God is actually His glory. The Bible further proclaims that *Jesus Christ was raised from the dead by the glory of God* (Romans 6:4). Now, the question is: Who raised Jesus from the dead? It's the Holy Spirit. Why do I say so? Because the Bible says *the same Spirit that raised Jesus Christ from the dead lives in you*. So, if Jesus Christ was raised from the dead by the glory of God who is clearly the Holy Spirit, this tells me that the Holy Spirit Himself is the glory of God. He needed the body of Jesus, so, He lived in His body while in this world. Through the Spirit, Jesus was the outshining of the Father's glory. That is why Jesus spoke about the Father in Heaven (*Who is God*) and the Father in Him (*Who is the Holy Spirit*). For clarity of purpose, let me refer you to another scripture which depict the highest revelation of Christianity in the New Testament dispensation, whereby Paul declared, *"Christ in me the Hope of Glory"*. In what form is Christ dwelling in you? It's through the Spirit. Tentatively speaking, that means the Spirit is the hope of glory. The manifestation of the indwelling presence of the full God head in humanity is through the Spirit. That means God the Father and Jesus the Son dwells in you through the Spirit. The Spirit is the glory of God because it is the Spirit that reveals God the Father and Jesus Christ. Therefore, when we speak of the glory of God being revealed in the last days, we are actually alluding to the manifestation of the Holy Spirit because He is the one who reveals the glory.

To cement this revelation with reference to further scriptural evidence, the Bible says *the glory of the latter house shall exceed the glory of the former house*. This speaks of a heightened degree of outpouring of the glory of the Spirit because in the former times, i.e the Old Testament dispensation, the Spirit had not yet been revealed in fullness and rested upon a few individuals who functioned as Kings and Prophets but in the last days, there is a tremendous outpouring of the Spirit as prophesied by Prophet Joel. This infers that the glory of God that shall be revealed in greater a measure in the last dispensation of time as compared to former dispensations is actually the Holy Spirit. I have always wondered why the Bible says any sin committed against the Holy Spirit is not forgiven until God dropped a revelation straight into my spirit. It's because the Spirit is the glory of God and no man can tamper or mess with the glory of God and go unpunished. Saphirah, Ananias, Uzah and Simon the sorcerer, just to mention but a few, are quintessential examples of this divine truth.

It is worth exploring the divine truth that while in the old covenant the glory of God was like a cloud inhabiting a place, in the New Testament, the glory of God is placed right into our spirit man when we are born again. The Bible affirms in 2 Corinthians 4:6 that *it is the God who commanded light to shine out of darkness, who has shone in our hearts to give the light of the knowledge of the glory of God in the face of Jesus Christ.* This is to tell you that the glory of God is not only found in Heaven as some have erroneously presumed it to be. Instead, the glory of God is domiciled in your spirit. That is why from time to time, if you ever spend time in God's presence, the glory comes out through your eyes, mouth and body, to the extent of oozing out through every fibre of your being. In John G. Lake's books, you read his experience of flashes of God's glory coming out of his body. In Kathryn Kuhlman's biography, people who knew her before she went into the ministry said her eyes looked sparklingly different after she entered into the ministry. She was not the same Kathryn Kuhlman. Why? Because the illuminating glory of God was now resident in her spirit. The truth is that contrary to the operation of the glory of God in the Old Testament, now the tabernacle has been gotten rid of, hence your body is now the outer court of God's glory, your soul is the inner court of God's glory and your spirit is the inner court of God's Glory. This tells me that you are now the tabernacle of God's glory as your spirit, soul and body is set ablaze or aglore with the glory of God.

In the same manner in which the glory of God descended upon the tabernacle and set it on fire, you are now a blast furnace in the realm of the spirit, exploding with the glory of God. As a custodian of God's glory, the glory dwells in you and you carry it everywhere you go, hence when you show up in any territory, God has arrived because you carry Him in your Spirit. That is why unlike Moses, we are no longer beggars of the glory but carriers of the glory. There are certain statements that are illegal or not permitted for a man to say in the New Testament dispensation which were permitted under the old covenant. For example, you cannot echo Moses statement and say to God, *"Show me your glory"*. This is because the glory of God is no longer an external force but its permanently embedded in the extreme quarters of the spirit. Therefore, praying like Moses is akin to praying amiss because the glory of God is no longer an ethereal or stratospheric force but a tangible spiritual reality resident in your spirit. It's no longer, *"Lord, Show me your glory"* as Moses petitioned, instead, the correct terminology to use in inviting a break out of high realms of glory in your life is, *"Lord, reveal your glory"* because the glory of God is no longer confined to the realm of sight only but revelation.

To substantiate this divine truth further, Paul unveils a striking reality about the new creation in 2 Corinthians 4:7, citing that *we have this treasure in earthly vessels, that the excellency of power may be of God and not of us*. What treasure is he talking about? It's the glory of God. See, the grace of God is tied to the glory of God. The impartation of God's grace is the impartation of His substance and of His very glory. Paul says we have this wonderful treasure, wonderful substance in earthen vessels perambulating inside us. And that is why in verse 8 of the same scripture, it says that *we are hard pressed on every side, yet not crushed*. Why? Because the glory of God cannot be crushed as it represents the essence of who God is. Paul continues to unfold the revelation that we are *perplexed but we are not in despair*. This not a statement of defeat; it is a statement of triumph. *We are persecuted but not forsaken* because the glory of God is in us. And he says *we are struck down but we are not destroyed*. How is that possible? Because the glory of God which represents God's very being, bubbles forth from within us, bullet-proofing every area of our lives. I like what he says in verse 16, *therefore we do not lose heart. Even though our outward man is perishing, yet the inward man is being renewed day by day*. This is the precious experience of the glory of God inside us. While our bodies are subject to adverse circumstances of life, our spirit is preserved as it is a point of contact with the glory of God inside us. The most powerful revelation of this scripture comes out clearly in verse 17 where it says, *for our light affliction, which is but for a moment, is working for us a far more exceeding and eternal weight of glory*. Metaphorically speaking, you can never derive the best taste from a grape fruit unless you squash it. By the same token, there is a certain weight of glory that can never be attained unless we are subjected under persecution. This implies that persecution is the birthplace for greater glory. The more pressure is exerted upon us on the outside, the more the glory of God flows mightily from within us.

THE GLORY OF THE FATHER

"This is the Glory of God as the Father Himself"

The overarching truth in matters relating to glory of God is that the glory is the nature of God. In his prayer for the church at Ephesus, Paul affirmed in Ephesians 1:17 that *I pray to the Father of the Lord Jesus Christ,* **the Father of Glory.** Note that in the context of this scripture, God is addressed as the *"Father of Glory"*, meaning that He is the supreme source, originator and divine orchestrator of the Glory. In fact, God is Glory; His nature or genetic make-up is Glory. The Glory is one of His intrinsic virtues and a quintessence of who He is. In other words, it is the visible splendour and moral beauty of God's manifold perfections. Put differently, it is the total sum of God's attributes, character, and intrinsic virtues, the brilliance of His presence, and the splendour of His majesty. It is the intrinsic essence of who God is manifested by His nature, character, attributes or virtues. This is the same Glory which God imparted upon Adam in the Garden of Eden, which made him an extension of God's glory on earth. Before the fall of man, Adam unreservedly lived a life of overflowing glory. He did not need any spiritual gift to help him contact the realm of the supernatural because he was already thriving in an atmosphere of God's glory, which is a realm beyond gifts.

Did you know that Heaven does not need any light or oxygen for survival as there are no lights in Heaven? Instead, the glory of God administered from the Throne Room is the source of all life in eternity. In essence, the life of God is the glory of God. Eternal life is an impartation of the glory of God upon man; it's a life of overflowing Glory. The essence of life in the spirit realm is the glory of God; the indestructible and incorruptible life that does not have an end. The greater truth is that Heaven and earth shall pass away but life in the Glory of God, manifested in eternity will never come to an end. This is to tell you that unlike other spiritual substances that are perishable, the glory of God doesn't die; neither does it corrodes or depreciates in value. Instead, it persists for ever and its manifestation in a given territory leaves a non-erasable mark in humanity. In view of the above, begin to declare:

I have the life of God in me, in every fibre of my being, in every cell of my blood, in every bone of my body and in every strand of my hair. I have the indestructible and incorruptible life of

God in me, that's why I can never be sick, defeated, despondent or disillusioned because the glory of God is in my spirit, Glory to Jesus!

As you do that, the glory of God in your spirit will begin to rise, driving out sickness, death, poverty and anything that is not consistent with God's will in your life.

THE GLORY OF MAN

"This is the Glory of God as man"

It must be expressly understood that not only is the glory found in Trinity as exuded by Jesus, the Father and the Spirit but it is also resident in man as the first amongst God's creation. Taking us back to the time of creation, the Bible unveils in Genesis 2:7 that *God breathed His Spirit, which is His glory upon man and man became a living being.* This leads us to an inevitable deduction that man is the glory of God since he was created from the breath of God, which is His glory. Did you know that Adam and Eve were the embodiment of God's glory? They were certainly the unique ones eclipsed above any other work of God's hand. As His image bearers, they were set apart from the rest of creation and given unparalleled dignity and status. They were his intimate ones, precious and commissioned with divine purpose, to display the glory of God. Therefore, man is a custodian or carrier of God's gory as an extension of God on earth. Unlike in the days of the Old Testament whereby man had to carry the ark of covenant, which represented the glory of God, from one place to the next, the glory is now resident in man hence, he can also carry it everywhere he goes. However, it must be understood that not only is the glory of man resident in man but man is the glory of God himself.

Concerning our position of glory in Him, God articulated the most powerful declaration concerning man when He declared in Psalms 82:6 that *you are gods and the children of the Most High God.* Note that in the context of this revelation, it is nether Paul, Elijah, Moses nor any other prophets who said that *we are gods.* It is not even Peter, the closest man to Jesus, who said it but it is God Himself in totality who pronounced it. The notion of us being, *"gods"* speaks of a position of elevation in the realm of glory. It speaks of having the glory, which is the nature of God inculcated or imparted into our spirit such that we are able to operate exactly as God on earth. This is to tell you how noble we are in the sight of God in terms of our legitimate birth right, authority and power to move and operate in the dimension of the supernatural glory. The Bible further proclaims in 1 Corinthians 11:7 that *man is the glory of God and women is the glory of man.* What does that mean? This implies that man has the glory of God manifested in his spirit. He has a God-being resident in him. That means, man by God's design or creation has the latent or inherent power to *think like God, walk like God, talk like God, see as God sees and virtually function like God in totality.* Man has a God nature in Him and His spiritual DNA, hence he is capacitated to operate exactly like Him on earth as an extension of His being. That is why the Bible affirms in John 1:13 that *we are born not of the will of man nor of flesh but born of God.* What does that mean? That means by virtue of the indwelling glory of God in us, we are no longer subject to the natural elements of this world. Instead, the glory of God takes pre-eminence over every facet of human existence.

The Bible continues to reinforce the reality *that as many as have received him, to them He gave power or right to become the sons of God* (John 1:12). What does that mean? That means through the Spirit, we have acquired the legitimacy, the right of son-ship and have been granted access to be partakers of Glory together with Christ. We have been given birth to by the glory of God, hence we have the right to call Him, 'Abba, Father!" in the same way Jesus calls Him father. This tells me that man is the Glory of God since he has an indwelling, inherent inhabitation of the glory of God, deeply grounded and permanently embedded in his spirit. That's why Paul says, *"It is no longer I that lives but Christ living in me"* (Galatians 2:19), meaning the indwelling presence of the Christ takes pre-eminence over ever sphere of life as He perambulates in the extreme quarters of our spirit. That is why when we lay hands on the sick; they are instantaneously healed because it is Christ in us who does the work. He uses our faculties to lay hands on the sick such that results are both phenomenal and instantaneous. In fact, when Jesus commissioned us for the work of ministry and declared that, *"Greater things than these shall you do"* (John 14:12), He alluded to the reality of this indwelling presence, that by virtue of Him being able to dwell in each and everyone's spirit, greater and more power will be released and more tasks accomplished for the Kingdom in these end times. This is the reason why the Paul admonished that; *"Whatever you do whether in talk in deed or action do it to the glory of God"* because man is the glory of God, hence functioning in God's glory should be like his second nature. Did you know that a born again man is a type of Jesus? He is an embodiment of everything that Jesus was on earth. Man has taken the place of Jesus on earth, hence if the word describes Jesus as the glory of God, it tentatively means that man is the glory of God because he is a type of Jesus and has assumed the place of Jesus.

A deeper understanding of this revelation comes clearly in Colossians 1:27, where Paul says, *"Christ in me the hope of glory."* And this revelation does not only has reference to a future manifestation of glory but a present one as well because he says, *"The riches of the glory of the mystery of salvation is Christ in you, the hope of glory."* And what he is saying is that between God's revelations of glory in the past and God's revelation of glory in the future, God has not left the world without a revelation of His glory, but the only way the world is ever going to see His glory is when you and I live to manifest that glory. That's where we are all as Christians. That's why whatever we do, whether we eat or drink, we do it to the glory of God. Why? Because manifesting the glory of God should be our lifestyle. We are the temple the world sees. We are the tabernacle. We are the shining face. We are the glory in the world of Christ. And that's why since we have been bought with a price for that purpose, we must glorify God in our body. That's why Paul contended in 2 Corinthians 3:8, that *as we gaze on the glory of the Lord we are transformed from one level of glory to the next by the Holy Spirit.* The focus of the life of a Christian is to gaze on the glory of Jesus. When you look to the Word of God and you see His glory, you go away like Moses. You don't go away proud but you go away manifesting His glory.

THE WORD OF GLORY

"This is the glory of God as His word"

It is worth exploring the divine truth that the word of God is another dimension of His glory. For clarity of purpose, let's look closely at the scripture below: *"The Word was made flesh, and dwelt among us, (and we beheld his glory, the glory as of the only begotten of the Father,) full of grace and truth* (John 1:14). Besides giving the Word of God personality, we also observe in this scripture that the Word of God has glory. Notice it says, *"...we beheld his glory..." meaning* we looked at the glory of the Word. This is because the Word is a person; He's glory-personified. In its original context in Greek, the word, *"Glory"* connotes to splendour, brightness, beauty, holiness, and purity. Since, the Word of God has all these and much more qualities; it means that the word of God is actually the *glory of God.* Now, you can better understand why the Bible refers to Jesus—the Word of God as the brightness of God's glory—the effulgence and out-shining of His glory. The greater truth is that when you study the Word, you receive something much more than inspiration; you receive an impartation of glory that causes you to function in sync with God's perfect will for your life. Because the Word of God is His glory, it has the ability to transform you and make you what it talks about. To further substantiate this divine truth with reference to scriptural evidence, let's consider what the apostle Paul had to say in 2 Corinthians 3:18:*"But we all, with open face beholding as in a glass the glory of the Lord, are changed into the same image from glory to glory, even as by the Spirit of the Lord."* This tells me that the word is like a mirror reflecting God's glory. In a practical sense, we see the glory of God by beholding the mirror of God, which is the Word of God. As you look at the glory of God in the mirror of God, you're changed into the same glory that you see in the Word. That means the more you look—meditate or contemplate the glory of God—in the Word of God, the more you become the glory that you see.

It is affirmed in the scriptures *that Heaven and earth shall pass away but His word shall never pass away*. Why? Because the word is the glory of God and the glory doesn't expire. Neither does it corrode nor is it subject to depreciation. Instead, it is preserved for ever as an integral part of His being. And that glory is the supreme Word of God. The Bible also makes it explicitly clear in Hebrews 1:3, that *Christ is the glory of God*. As aforementioned, we know that Christ is also the Word of God since the scripture says in the *beginning was the Word, the Word was God and the Word was with God*. Therefore logically speaking, if Christ is the glory of God, who is also the Word of God, that means the Word of God is the glory of God. Hence, the phrase *"In the beginning was the Word, the Word was God and the Word was with God"* can also be contextually re-arranged as *"In the beginning was the **Glory**, the **Glory** was God and the **Glory** was with God."* This leads us to an inevitable conclusion that the Word of God is the glory of God. In a similar vein, it also suffices to conclude that in the case of Elijah's encounter with God on mount Horeb in 1 Kings 19:11-13, the small still voice that spoke to Elijah after all diverse manifestations had taken place was actually the glory of God. It was not His power. Neither was it His presence nor His anointing, *but it was His glory* at work. It represented His very being, His nature and His originality. That small still voice came from His being; it proceeded from the Father Himself, hence that voice was His glory. The word of God makes it explicitly clear that there came a fire, storm, wind and even an earthquake but God was not in any of these manifestations. This means that the glory of God was not the fire, earthquake or storm but the word, the very still voice which spoke to Elijah and said, *"Elijah, what are you doing here?"*

To cement this revelation with further scriptural evidence, when Moses asked God to show him His glory in Exodus 33:18, in response, what exactly did God show him? Did He show Him His fire, wind, storm or earthquake, which are the popular manifestations that validates His presence? Definitely not! Instead, God showed Moses five key attributes of His word by proclaiming that *"The Lord, God, merciful, gracious, longsuffering, and abounding in goodness and truth."* This leads us into an inevitable conclusion that the glory of God is neither a storm, wind, earthquake nor any other boisterous manifestation as many have erroneously presumed but it's His *Word.* All these are manifestations of His power but not His glory. The glory of God is His word because whenever God speaks, His glory is manifested. In actual fact, the glory of God is manifested in its intensity through His word. In fact, when the Bible affirms that *in the beginning was the Word,* it alludes to the fact that God's glory was initially His word and the glory is eternal. All the gifts and callings are temporary but the word of God which is His glory, is eternal. In all eternity, angels never new Jesus as a separate entity with the Father, He was always the word of God, always talking. This means that the glory of God is manifested through His word. The Word that proceeded out of the mouth of God breeds life, which is the glory. In the beginning of creation, when God said, *"Let there be light",* His glory was manifested through His word. The Bible says *as heaven and earth shall pass way, His word shall never pass* because His word is His glory and the glory doesn't go extinct.

THE GLORY OF CREATION

"This is the glory of God as His creation"

It is worth exploring the divine truth that the creation is another dimension of God's glory in the universe. The Bible speaks of the glory of *terrestrial* and *celestial* bodies (1 Corinthians 15: 40). It affirms that *there are celestial bodies and terrestrial bodies but the glory of the celestial is one and the glory of the terrestrial is another.* This implies that the creation is the glory of God because every creation reflects and reciprocates the glory of God. That's why David pronounced that *everything that has breath should praise the Lord* (Psalms 150:6). Did you know that even without saying a word or vernacular understandable to man, the planets, the mountain and hills reflect God's glory? But how can mountains, hills and valleys give God glory? Because in them is the glory of God. This is not just a figure of speech but a spiritual reality because everything created has a heavenly sound, a song and a rhythm that sings music in worship of God. For clarity of revelation, lets refer to another scripture that says *the earth is the Lord's and the fullness there in, the heathens and all that dwell in therein, who is the King of Glory, the Lord strong and mighty.* Do you notice that in the context of creation, the Lord is described as *"the King of glory"*? That means anything that is part of creation can retain the glory of God. That is why we are able to impart the anointing upon handkerchiefs and enable them to do miracles when laid upon the sick.

The greater truth is that unknown to many people, God interacts with nature in the same way. Nature exhibits His glory. His glory is revealed to man's mind through the material world in many ways, and often in different ways to different people. One person may be thrilled by the sight of the mountains, and another person may love the beauty of the sea. But that which is behind them both (*God's glory*) speaks to both people and connects them to God. In this way, God is able to reveal Himself to all men, no matter their race, heritage or location. Let me substantiate this divine truth with reference to a quintessential scripture in Psalm 19:1-4:

"The heavens declare the glory of God and the stars proclaim the work of His hands; day to day, they pour forth speech, and night reveals knowledge. There is no speech, nor are there words where their voice is not heard. Their line has gone out through all the earth, and their utterances to the end of the world."

A hermeneutical analysis of this scripture unveils the divine truth that the glory of God is also resident and unreservedly manifested through galaxies. This is the glory of the *First Heaven*. In fact, that's the key to everything that exists. Everything God ever created was designed with a purpose of subscribing to Him, all the glory. That is why the Bible says the Heavens declare the glory of God. Do you notice that in our above opening scripture, the Bible says the stars have a speech and a voice? How is that possible? It's because sound waves are embedded in everything that exists on earth, including stars, rocks, food, trees and everything ever created. Do you know that speech was one of the first ingredients that created everything else you see and the invisible things you don't see? Therefore the idea of stars giving a speech alludes to the spiritual reality that sounds waves can be transmitted through speech from both living and non-living objects.

The greater truth is that when God made the inanimate creation, when He made the heavens and the Earth, they were for His glory and this is an incontestable reality in the spirit realm. Even those who are least inclined to study the Heavens must at times have been stunned by the beauty of a spectacular sunset, especially if we are looking out to the sea beyond a quiet coastline. Even without articulate sounds, and words, the Heavens eloquently declare the glory of God. Graphically speaking, a work of art is the glory of the artist who created it because it's something which brings glory to him. In his work, the artist expresses himself and the artistic master-piece honours the artist's skills. By the same token, the whole creation is a work of art which glorifies God, demonstrating His wisdom and power.

To cement this divine truth with reference to further scriptural evidence, do you notice that even when God made the animate creation, He declared in Isaiah 43 that *the beast of the field shall give Me honour or glory*? But how do beasts give God glory? By releasing sound waves that produces vibrations and a rhythm that goers up to the Father as an aroma of worship. The greater truth is that although our first glimpse of the glory of God has been through the created universe around us, these are only the outskirts of His ways. For instance, think about the wonder of all different kinds of animals like the monarch butterfly with its astounding sequence of genetic reserves and the programmed information by means of which the caterpillar is transformed inside the chrysalis into its very different butterfly form! However, space doesn't al-low me to explore all these wonders, hence I can only make reference to a few quint-essential examples. This is to tell you that God imparted His glory on both living and non-living objects in the universe so that they can in turn reflect that glory.

THE SUBSTANCE OF GLORY

"This is the Gory of God as a spiritual substance"

It is worth exploring the divine truth that the mass and density of the substance which God imparts upon His people especially during worship is actually His glory. The illuminating presence of God is actually His glory. The divine spiritual substance that emanates or proceeds from the father and is imparted upon man is the glory. When Moses asked God to show him His glory, what exactly did he want to see? He wanted to see the visibility and tangibility of the substance of glory of God. In a related incident, the Bible records that *he (Stephen) full of the Holy Ghost, looked up stead-fastly into Heaven and saw* **THE GLORY OF GOD** *and Jesus standing on the right hand of God* (Acts 7:55). Stephen saw something. But what exactly did he see? He saw the effulgence of God's glory radiating from the Throne Room down to the earth. In other words, the curtain was rolled back which allowed him to see in an open vision the visibility and tangibility of the glory of God at the Throne Room.. This is the same degree of glory which rested upon Moses to such an extent that his face was shining and nobody could look at his face. That is the operation of the glory of God as a spiritual substance. Moreover, when Moses petitioned God saying, *"Show me your glory",* he alluded to the divine truth that the glory is a visible and tangible substance because one cannot ask to see something that cannot be made visible in the natural realm. Therefore, when someone says, *"Lord I give you the glory,"* the implication is that the spiritual substance that you have imparted into my spirit, I reciprocate and reflect it back to you, hence it must not come as a surprise that the glory of God is a spiritual substance.

To elucidate on the revelation of the glory of God as a spiritual substance, let's refer to a popular scripture on faith in Hebrews. 11:1: *Now faith is the* **substance** *of things hoped for, the conviction of things not seen.* You need to get that into your heart and into your minds that there is such a thing as a *spiritual substance.* From a scientific point of view, the word, *"substance"* means a matter or something that carries the properties of weight, mass and density sch that can be seen, touched and even commoditised. The truth is that as much as there are natural substances, there are also *spiritual substances.* However, although the concept of spiritual substance is used to illustrate the dynamics of faith as depicted in the above scripture, faith is not the only spiritual substance; the glory is also a tangible spiritual substance. That means the glory can be seen, touched, felt and experienced. The greater truth is that in the spirit realm, everything that leaves Heaven to earth is sent forth as a tangible spiritual substance that has value. The spirit world has its own material form, for example angels and God has a form. When God created angels, He took spiritual substances and brought them together. Later when God made man He created him in a different realm with a spiritual ability. What I want to emphasize here is that there is a substance that is very real. In the book of Psalms it says that the manna which the Israelites ate was angels' food. It was transformed into a physical world so that physical man can eat it and survive in the wilderness. It is remarkably striking in this regard to learn that the spiritual substance can become a physical substance and provide everything that the physical world could have provided. In fact, a lot of the giftings from God actually comes as an impartation of spiritual substance. Everything is a spiritual substance from the spirit world. We have to accept the fact that the glory of God is a spiritual substance. The Holy Spirit is a person but the glory of God, which comes from the Holy Spirit is a spiritual substance. The glory of God is a spiritual substance of God. The power of the Holy Spirit is a spiritual substance of God. Let me redefine the whole system. Practically everything in the spirit world is a spiritual substance.

To further cement the revelation of the glory of God as a substance, the Bible narrates in Exodus 16:10 that *it came to pass, as Aaron spoke to the whole congregation of the children of Israel, that they looked toward the wilderness, and, behold, the glory of the Lord appeared in the cloud.* This was the glory of God manifesting as a tangible spiritual substance. To cement this revelation with reference to further scriptural evidence, the Bible further reports in Exodus 40:34 that *a cloud covered the tent of the congregation, and the glory of the Lord filled the tabernacle.* The idea of the glory of God filling the tabernacle reinforces the divine truth that the glory is a tangible divine substance that can manifest in degrees and measures. The Bible further gives an account of an event during the dedication of a temple that *when Solomon had finished praying, fire came down from heaven and consumed the burnt offering and the sacrifices, and the glory of the Lord filled the house. The priests could not enter into the house of the Lord because the glory of the Lord filled the Lord's house.* Note that the fire which came down was the glory of God manifesting as a visible substance in the natural realm. This was a quintessential example of the glory of God manifesting visibly in the natural realm. The act of the fire coming down and consuming the sacrifice denotes the manifestation of the glory as a spiritual substance. The Bible further records in Numbers 9:15 that, *On the day that the tabernacle was reared up the cloud covered the tabernacle, namely, the tent of the testimony: and at even there was upon the tabernacle as it were the appearance of fire, until the morning.* In view of the above-mentioned catalogue of scriptural references, it is therefore undeniably evident that the *cloud and fire* were visible twin manifestations of the glory of God as a spiritual substance in the natural realm.

CHAPTER FIVE

DEEPER REVELATIONS OF GOD'S GLORY

The glory is a tangible and visible spiritual substance.

It is a divine truth that the glory of God is a spiritual substance. It is a tangible manifestation of God's presence. The glory of God is a substance that manifests in a natural realm. Although it is a spiritual substance, it can manifest in a natural realm. For example, you cannot touch water vapour. You could sort of try to catch water vapour and you cannot because it is in a vaporized state. But when water is condensed into liquid form or crystallised into a solid form, it becomes tangible. In the same manner, the glory of God is invisible in the spirit realm yet God can cause a condensation to take place in the natural realm. God can cause a crystallisation or solidification of His glory upon a place, person or house or any object in the natural realm. God's glory is generally His presence bestowed upon this world, just like air that surrounds this world yet, God can cause His presence to be condensed and solidified in a certain place to make it tangible. Did you know that the spectacular view of the burning bush that Moses experienced was actually the glory of God's presence? The glory of God was so tangible and visible such that the bush burned, yet it was not consumed.

The truth is that the glory of God can rest upon a physical object. Sometimes when we worship God, the glory of God can condense in that place and you feel the presence of God in that place. But when you walk away from that place, suddenly you do not feel the tangible presence anymore. As long as you are in that place, you feel the presence. The glory of God has an ability to hover over an object or over a place. See, God's glory can come on a physical object. It can come on the burning bush and cause it to be lighted. It can come on human flesh, like it came on Moses' face and make it luminous. Can you imagine Moses' face shining with a supernatural illumination that was unexplainable in the natural? It had been exposed to the glory of God.

It is therefore unequivocally evident that God's glory is tangible. Moses who had seen God's glory could not physically enter the Tabernacle when God's glory filled it in fullness. In Exodus 33: 9-1 the Bible says *the glory of God descended and stood at the door of the tent of meeting, allowing Moses to speak with the lord.* That means the glory is something tangible, feel-able and visible. This is to tell you that God had moved from just being a theoretical God to a practical God by manifesting the tangibility and visibility of His glory. Therefore, the idea of the glory held amongst dozens of believers as some kind of ethereal sensation or mysterious spiritual phenomenon is unbiblical. The fact that the Bible says the *glory stood at the door* means that God has a tangible form and has legs to stand. It also says in Exodus 40: 34, that the glory descended and filled the terbanacle and it also filled Solomon's temple (1 Kings 8:10). The idea of the glory *filling* geographical places gives an indication that it is a tangible substance. That is why we speak of *the substance of glory.* Some people think that the glory of God can no longer manifest this way because times have changed. While this is partially true, it must be understood that though times and season have changed, God's principles remain the same and the principle is that the glory must be revealed and manifested in a tangible way. This means if God showed Moses His back, then in this present hour, He must reveal His whole being or form - hands, legs and whole body. That is why we now have hundred percent access to the throne room to behold His glory.

The glory always has a visible and tangible presence.

That is why Moses said, *"Lord show me your glory"*, If the glory was something that cannot be seen, he would have never asked God to show him. There is no way you can drop into a pool and come out dry and by same token there is no way you can be in the presence of glory and stay the same. While it is true that God is omnipresence, however, His glory does not manifest everywhere because He generally manifest where He is worshiped in spirit and truth and where He is continually honoured and revealed. Revelation is very important when it comes to matters of the glory because without revelation, the glory cannot be known or revealed.

> *In the light of this revelation, I recall vividly the days when I started moving in the supernatural power of God. Every time I used to see a visible and tangible pillar of fire just few centimetres over my head and it used to manifest everywhere I go. Whenever I saw it, I would move in greater dimensions of power, miracles, signs and wonders than before. In other words, the glory had moved from the invisible realm and transmuted itself in the physical in the same way God used to lead the children of Israel as a pillar of fire during the night. On a different occasion, as I ministered to people, a visible glory of God manifested in the form of fog or mist which filled the whole auditorium in the same way the glory of god filled the temple in the Old Testament days. Concerning the tangibility of God's glory, Apostle Maldonado concurs with the above practical experience and testifies that while he was preaching in one of his churches, people saw a Shekinah cloud of glory moving in a certain section of the audience. And instantly people in that section started being healed from cancer, developing new body parts, wombs and being delivered without anybody laying hands or doing anything.*

The glory of God is a spiritual environment: It is the atmosphere of Heaven

It is a divine truth that before God created Adam and Eve, He started by creating a perfect environment that would sustain them. God first created the land as an environment then the plants and animals later that would thrive in the soil and minerals. He created oceans and rivers and then created fish and other creatures especially equipped to exist in an environment of water. He created the firmament of the heavens and then created standards and planets that would be placed in it to function according to gravitational laws and orbital paths (Genesis 1:9-25).

By the same token when God created the environment of the Garden of Eden, He designed the perfect setting for human beings. When God created man, He took the dust of the earth which was his predesigned matter which came out of His invisible self and formed man. Then He breathed the breath of life which was also something which was inside Him, into man, man then stood up in a glorifies state, not because that was his choice but because that was his perfect design. Notable is the realisation that the original atmosphere of the earth was the glory of God. Man was created to live in that atmosphere of glory. As a God being, man was created ageless. Aging began the instant Adam fell into sin. If Adam had not sinned, he would have remained younger and good looking forever. Man was created and placed into the Father's ultimate expression of beauty and peace: The Garden of Eden. God put Adam right into the environment of His glory. Outside the Garden of Eden, it was a different story because that was the only environment in which man could be sustained and thrive.

As the ocean is to a fish, so was the environment of Eden to Adam. If something is taken out of its natural environment, you don't have to actively kill it. Instead, it will die on its own. For example, if you take out a fish from the water, it will slowly die of dehydration. Likewise, if you pull up a plant from the earth, it will soon wither and die from a lack of water. By the same token, when Adam sinned, he was taken out of the life or environment of glory and that is why he died spiritually. However, man choose to live outside the parameters of glory so they had to be exiled and this is the reason why human beings die when they are estranged for God's presence. When the decree of banishment was pronounced upon them, their dream was over and the nightmare started. Child birth became labouring nine month ordeal. The sun seemed hotter and the nights turned form cool to freezing cold and the sting of death started ravaging their physical bodies. Therefore, death can be defined as the absence of God's glory in a human body. Every human experiences a process of death due to being disconnected from glory. This process starts from the moment of birth because that is the moment when the curses of living under a *"ticking clock'* and moving towards the inevitability of death, which is associated with fallen humanity, begins to operate.

It is important that we address few questions which perhaps might have pondered but remained unanswered in your mind for a long time. Do you not wonder *why God waited until it was coolness of the day to visit Adam?* The phrase, *"Coolness of the day"* does not refer to a specific time during the day as measured according to human time. Neither does it speak of the number of hours registered on the face of the cloak but a time dimension in the realm of the spirit when the earth was perfectly aligned with the blueprint of Heaven such that it allowed a mass visitation of Heavenly hosts, blessings and other spiritual substances from Heaven. It was a point in time when God granted Heavenly hosts unrestricted access to stand on the *Grand Stand* in Heaven and view the beauty of what He had created on earth. That time coincided with time in the natural realm when the sun was setting and the process of pollination and reproduction which happens in the light of the day was coming to rest. Another question hotly debated by theologians is: *Why did God forbid Adam and Eve from to partaking of the tree of knowledge of good and devil.* It's because it was a part of Him that He did not want them to experience. He did not want them to carry the weight of that knowledge in them. God foreknew what the knowledge would do to them. It would age them, make them weary, have pain and suffering. He knew how to have dominion over it because it was a part of His knowledge. Yet with all that was around them, they wanted equality with God.

> *Eden was not a geographical place but a realm of glory. In that realm, the glory of God was always on the move.*

The glory of God cannot be confounded to one place. Eden was not a geographical place but rather a carefully prepared delightful spot of glory that God designed for mankind to dwell in. In its original context in Hebrew, the word, "Eden" means *"delightful, pleasure"*, and the word garden means *"enclosure, a fenced place, to hedge about"*. It means something that protects, covers, or surrounds. When we are in the glory of God, we are protected by His presence hence as He moves, we also move in Him. Eden was a moment in time because the glory of God is continually moving. That is why when we are in the presence of God we move from glory to glory because the glory of God is constantly moving. No one goes from one place to another without moving. God is active and moving constantly and He manifests Himself where He desires. And when we are in Him, we move with Him. Almost all geographical locations mentioned in the Bible have been found by archaeologist but Eden is the only place which has not yet been discovered because it was a spot, a moment in time where the presence of God came and it was continually moving and as the glory was moving, hence, Adam was also moving.

"If the Holy Ghost does not move, I move the Holy Ghost".

The greater truth is that the glory is not constant but always on the move and that is why we move *from glory to glory* because it is a movement. If you are elevated into the realm of glory and you want to be stagnant, the glory will move you because it is its inherent nature to progressively move, Just like a person who jumps into a moving car is forced to move whether he likes it or not. Smith Wigglesworth utterly understood this principle of moving in the glory, hence he declared, *"If the Holy Ghost does not move, I move the Holy Ghost"*, because he had understood that the realm of glory is always on the move. Eden was therefore not a geographical place per se, but a realm and an environment where the Spirit of God was always on the move just like in the beginning of creation when He was hovering over the surface of the waters. The greater truth is that Adam did not fall from a place, but he fell from God's presence, from an environment of glory. When Adam and Eve fell, the essence of who they were as human beings, made in the image of God, died (Genesis 3). They also began to die physically even though it took more than 930 years for Adam's body to stop functioning. Adam did not need to sustain that human body by eating. The residual of glory that remained in his body kept him physically alive for that long. This is to tell you that the glory is the most durable spiritual substances of the Heavenly realm.

The greater truth is that Eden was a gate to Heaven.

Eden was an environment that was a *gate or geographical portal to heaven* because God manifested His glory there to human beings who were made in His image and were in an unbroken fellowship with Him. God's glory with humanity was also heaven on earth. There is not a time on record that tells you how long Adam was in Eden because eternity was the original atmosphere of the earth. Therefore, Eden was a spot on earth where the presence of God manifested intensely and was a gate to heaven. Jacob caught a glimpse of this glory when he dreamt of a ladder ascending into an opening. However, this gate was shut as man sinned and was exiled from God's presence. When man sinned, he was thrown outside the garden, that's where age began. When age began, Adam had so much glory that he was able to live on the residue 936 years.

The glory realm is the birthplace for all creation; everything was created from the realm of glory.

It is a divine truth that God created the beginning. Before the beginning began, God existed. He always was eternal. Before the beginning, there was nowhere for Him to come from. This is why He had to create *"the beginning"*. While the majority of believers seem to subscribe to this divine truth, some folks erroneously believe that God created the earth out of nothing and that everything came out of the blue, out of the invisible matter. No! That is not the correct picture because everything He created was already in Him. So, when He spoke, and said *let there be light,* light proceeded from within the depths of His being into manifestation in the natural realm. That is why with an indwelling presence of the Holy Spirit, everything you will ever need in life is in you. Therefore, we follow the same pattern which God used to speak things from within our being into existence. Isn't it amazing that God created all things out of himself? As He called, *light be,* light came forth from the depth of His being into existence. When God said, *Let there be light,* what came forth was the voice of the almighty penetrating the vastness of His perception in the eternal realm as He spoke into existence that which He had already created within His being. The very essence of His thought life was thrust into existence, and seen when He spoke. Thoughts became words, words became objective reality. All He had to do was to call out of Himself those things which were a part of His glory and they responded. The sound of His voice preceded the visible manifestation of each creative work.. In this final chapter of human history, the lion of the tribe of Judah is therefore roaring again, unleashing the sound of heaven on earth through the end time generation. It could therefore be deduced that everything that you will ever need in this life, be it miracles, finances, healings, prosperity, is available in the glory realm. Therefore, tap into the atmosphere of glory to speak anything that you want to see happen in this world and it shall be established for you.

As a new creation, we were born into the realm of glory.

In veiw of the above, it is worth exploring the divine truth that the Glory realm is the realm of our birth; it's where we were born into the glory. That's were our true identity and origin is. We were created in the realm of glory. We are from there. Our origin is in the glory, in the Heavenly realm. Heaven is the only place in eternity that is named, and yet, Heaven is created. Heaven is the Capital of the Eternal Realm that is why it is a city. To elucidate more on this divine truth, the Bible speaks of *three* Heavens. The *first Heaven* is the atmosphere around the earth. The *second Heaven* is the atmosphere where Lucifer and his fallen angels were assigned to exist, between the third Heaven and the earth. The *third Heaven* is where we find God's throne room. This is where the Glory of God dwells. This is where we originated. This atmosphere is where we long to be, because it is where we came from. Therefore, when we get hungry for the presence of God, we are actually homesick for the atmosphere He created us in.

Have you ever asked God to take you back in time through the spirit dimension to an epic era before conception when you were a created spirit before His throne?

Only in that realm would you fully comprehend that you were created in the *Throne Room* of Heaven. The reality is that when we are born again, God places His glory in our spirit so that we receive the divine *"breath of life"* and His spiritual DNA. God's DNA contains His glory as His son Jesus. Before being born again, we had Adam's sinful DNA, but now we have God's sanctified DNA hence, we can always carry the glory of God wherever we go. However, the greatest challenge facing us as believers is that we are more comfortable talking about the anointing, instead of manifesting the glory, which is denotes our birth place in the spirit realm. We have already been in this realm before. We were created there. Now, we must learn how to access it once again, and re-enter its atmosphere. That is why Paul uses the phrase *"Whom He foreknew"* to show that we have known this glory realm before. We have functioned and operated in it before the foundations of the earth. Now, we are just replaying the tap in which we have featured as actors before and acting like a man trampling on his own footsteps where he had walked before.

The realm of glory falls outside the time dimension in the natural realm, hence functioning in that realm grants us dominion over time.

It is worth exploring the divine truth that time is not one of the characteristics of God. God is not defined by time because He lives, functions and operates in the eternal realm that is outside our time dimension. Time is not an absolute because it only exists when its parameters are defined by absolutes. God set the earth in time while man was created from the eternal realm. Although man lives on earth, he doesn't operate according to earthly time because he was created in the eternal realm which falls outside the scope or domain of time. Man was never designed to function according to earthly time. It was only after the fall that the clock started ticking. Heaven is governed by the glory which is the realm of eternity where there is no time. Therefore, when we are caught up into the glory, we experience *"timelessness"*. The eternity realm is the womb from which time came. In other words, eternity existed before time. Time is the offspring of the eternal design. Time was created or set in creation after eternity on the fourth day. God set the sun to rule by day and the moon to rule by night, thereby establishing time and season. That is why we have dominion over time because we were created first in the eternal realm which is outside the time dimension of the earth.

With this understanding therefore, when operating in the realm of glory, the key is to learn the art of how to speak from the eternal realm into the realm of time. In the gory realm, time does not exist as we consider it on earth. The only thing that can break the cycle of time is faith. Faith is a higher law than time. It is the ascent out of time into the eternal realm. For a man who knows his rights as a citizen of Heaven, time is made to serve him. Man was not designed to serve time. Time is a part of matter, not a matter of time. Faith is God's matter - the substance or material which represents elements which are made by God to serve an eternal purpose. Time was designed and created specifically for this earth. It doesn't exist outside this planet. The reality is that when people loose track of time and step into the eternal, the eternal becomes real and the supernatural becomes your normal. In this kairos moment, God is bridging you from time into the eternal realm whereby it is naturally supernatural to perfom miracles. That's when you will realise that the eternal is more real than time. The truth is that miracles are in a higher realm, without the influence of time, while our circumstances are the product of time with a beginning and an end. The greater truth is that everything in the eternal realm has already happened- miracles have already taken place and the dead have already been raised. You just have to call it from the realm in which it already exists into the realm in which it will manifest. The key is to be challenged to speak from the eternal realm into time. Therefore, when you step on any death scene, have the mentality that resurrection is a done deal- the dead have already been raised. All you need to do is just turn on the switch and just witness God in action. That is why we are called *witnesses* because at this realm, we watch and see God perform His work.

The realm of glory is a realm of divine speed and acceleration.

It is worth exploring the divine truth that as the Body of Christ, we are about to enter a new season in Church history, a phase that goes beyond the initial Pentecostal experience. When this glory invasion is fully realised, it will usher in a supernatural acceleration of the things of God. To substantiate this truth with reference to a quintessential example, Elijah prayed and saw the first sign as small as a man's hand and the Bible says when he saw it, he gird his loins and outran King Ahab's horse which was probably the fastest and best fed horse in the country. But how possible is it that a man can outrun a horse while he is on foot? Running is a prophetic sign, symbolic of divine speed and acceleration in the realm of the spirit. That was a *dramatic prophetic gesture.* It was a prophetic action of faith, symbolic of how we should move in the spirit dimension to overtake things in the natural realm. While he was seen sprinting in the natural realm, in the spirit realm, that was actually an action of faith. When you read this portion of scripture with the eyes if flesh, you will see Elijah running in the natural realm but if you read with the eye of the spirit, you will see him flying in the spirit. This is a dimension in the spirit called *Holy Ghost transportation.* Elijah was catapulted into a higher realm of glory and divinely transported through the tidal waves of the spirit to Jezreel. Prophetically speaking, as God has already unveiled the first sign of the *glory cloud* heralding a new outpouring of glory in the realm of the spirit, now is the time to run in the dimension of the spirit. As Elijah did, pick up your loins and run so as not to miss the next move of God. Don't just casually walk towards it, but run so you don't miss it. This is the season of the *overtaking anointing.* It's time that you run ahead of everything which represents Ahab's horse in your life.

Did you know that when you are operating in the glory realm, which is outside our time dimension you can actually overtake time in the natural realm. You have two options when operating in the glory realm; it's either you stop the time until you have completed certain divine tasks as exemplified by Joshua or you can simply overtake it. When we stop the cloak, we step backwards in time but when we overtake it, we step forward. That is why the Bible concurs that in this *kairos* moment, we have unequivocally stepped into Amos 9:13— a critical moment in which *the ploughman is overtaking the reaper and the treader of grapes him that sows a seed.* While the *Reaper* is harvesting as fast as he can, on his heels comes the *Ploughman,* who is already preparing another harvest in the soil that the reaper has just harvested. This infers that in this final chapter of human history, all of eternity is pouring into the present, causing us to accelerate forward. In other words, we have entered *the rush hour* of God, a critical moment in God's calendar in which things are moving so fast in the realm of the spirit as we are adjourning quickly towards the second coming of the Lord, Jesus Christ. The truth is that the glory is an accelerator; hence what would normally take years happens in a moment in the gory realm. Those who don't understand the operation of the glory realm are forced to wait for the date the doctor has set for them to receive their healing. This is an error because the glory realm is a realm of speed and acceleration where there is neither procrastination, postponement or delays. If the doctor has told you to wait for six months, just defy the law of time and activate the higher law of faith; reach into the future and take your healing right now!

The realm of glory is a realm of new things.

Did you know that all inventions or latest technologies used either in the spirit realm or natural world flow from the glory realm? The realm of glory is a realm of creativity or proliferation of new things. Without the atmosphere of glory enveloping the earthly realm, we would not be having some of the latest technologies that we have in our modern times. Have you ever asked yourself why as believers we are called the *new creation*? It's because we were born into the realm of glory, which is the realm of new things. It is in that realm that our spirits were recreated or regenerated. However, not only are our spirits made anew but our bodies are also vitalised by the indwelling presence of the Spirit. That is why in the glory realm, new body parts are created because it is a realm of new things. If you have lost any of your body part either an eye, leg or arm due to an accident or any other debilitating life circumstances, don't be troubled, simply get into the atmosphere of glory and call the original blueprint of that body part to be appear and it shall be established for you.

Have you ever asked yourself how Jesus multiplied five loaves and two fish? It's because the glory realm is a realm of new things, hence natural substances are multiplied and new processes are continually given birth to in the spirit realm. This explains how Jesus converted water into wine because in the realm of glory, any substance can be changed into another form without altering its natural properties. Prophetically speaking, a new day in the spirit is dawning. There is a new dimension of glory surfacing on the horizon. The skies are changing and the waves are shifting. The Lord is echoing the voice of Prophet Isaiah and he is saying, *"Behold, I'm doing a new thing! They are created now, and not so long ago, you have not heard of them before today, so you cannot say, "Yes, I knew them"* (Isaiah 48:7). Why is He telling you? Because there are certain things that God is doing in the spirit realm which man in their natural senses does not perceive. He is also telling you so that in tandem with what He is doing in the realm of the spirit, you can also do the same in the natural realm. God is about to do something so brand new that we don't yet have the language to describe it, neither do we have any vocabulary to speak about it. It would be like what Paul described as *"Something inexpressible for man to tell"*. What God is about to do in this *kairos* moment is something unfamiliar to your status quo. You will run to your dictionary and not find its meaning; you will even try and peruse your Bible and not find it because it falls in the realm of unrecorded miracles. The reason why God calls it a *"new thing"* it's because it doesn't have a name as yet. It is a brand new phenomenon unfolding from the throne room of Heaven such that even the angels are still trying to comprehend it. We too will not be able to look at it or recognise it because it will be completely brand new. We cannot call it by the name we used in the past, hence we would need a new vocabulary to describe it in the same way the children of Israel looked at the food of angels that was rained down from Heaven and explained, *"manna"*, meaning *"what is this"* because they had not seen such a thing before.

It's disheartening to note that in some churches some believers have gone to the extent of being puffed up and boast of having people falling under the power or being healed from various sicknesses and being raised from wheelchairs but that's the ordinary level at which every believer ought to be operating because Jesus said, *"these signs will accompany them that believe. In my name, they shall lay hands on the sick and they shall recover…."*So, that's a divine legitimate birth right and an irrevocable inheritance of every believer. Therefore, praying to God to give you the power to heal the sick, cast out devils and raise the cripples is tantamount to asking Him to make you what you already are and to give you what He has already given you. Therefore, as we step into the river of new manifestations of the Spirit, you will realise that what you have seen so far in the arena of signs and wonders, is just a tip of an iceberg and an icing on the cake as there are deeper realms and new territories in the glory realm that we have not yet fully explored. In fact when Jesus said, *'Greater things than these shall you do',* He actually alluded to these deeper realms and great dimensions that believers in these end times shall be elevated into. For ages I have been hearing pastors rant and rave behind the pulpit that God is doing a new thing and I have been asking myself what exactly is this new thing they are always saying and not specifying until God dropped a revelation in my spirit and began to specify the exact details of the old things He is phasing out and the new things He is ushering in the Body of Christ.

Therefore, if you are used to people falling under the power, then I have good news for you because in this season, not only are you going to see people *"falling under the power"* but you will see them spring up into the air and *"floating under the power"*. If you are used to seeing the sick being laid hands on to receive their healing, in this *kairos* moment, you will be shocked to see even the dead jump out of their coffins and running in the streets without anybody laying hands on them. If you are used to seeing the cripples being raised up from wheel chairs, in this season, you will be shocked to see the one who doesn't have a leg at all, suddenly developing a brand new one, a short man suddenly growing into a very tall giant and the one whose head is bald, instantly growing hair right in front of the camera. I'm conscious of the fact that I might be stepping on some religious toes but you will be shocked to see people instantly falling pregnant and giving birth in front of the camera.

In this season, there is a drastic transition and revolutionary leap from the realm of the anointing to the realm of glory. Therefore, if you are used to operating in the realm of the anointing, you will begin to see the visibility of the glory cloud manifesting itself in the natural realm as a solid spiritual substance, precipitating the rain of creative miracles. You will be shocked to see believers under the direction of the Holy Spirit walking through the walls, walking on water and in their air. You will be shocked to see a believer take others to a nearby pool or water reservoir and publicly demonstrate by strolling on the surface of its waters as if he is walking on his own yard. You will be shocked to see your pastor taking a short cut to the pulpit and just emerging on the stage through the wall. After the church service, you will be driving your car at 160 km/hour when suddenly you see a believer that you left at church because he doesn't have a natural mode of transport, comfortably walking past you in the air. While you are still thinking of getting fuel to drive away to a crusade, another believer will just be caught up into the spirit dimension and be carried by the tidal waves of the air and be divinely transported to the venue in another city. Others will disappear and re-appear at their own prerogative just like Elijah.

I'm fully aware that by now, I might have gone too far to be labelled a crazy man but the time has come that the supernatural realm will manifest itself in the natural such that it becomes normal to see, walk and talk to angels. If you are used to sensing angels in an expanded or apparition form, in this season, you will see angels and talk to them face to face just like the way you talk to your friends. A student shall talk to an angel thinking that he is talking to a teacher; a parent shall talk to an angel thinking that she is talking to her own child; a driver shall give a lift to a group of hiking angels thinking that it's pedestrians; a manager shall interview an angel thinking that he is interviewing a candidate for a job; a sports fanatic shall watch a game with an angel at the stadium thinking that it's a another fan. And while you are having a worship service at church, you will see angels accompanying Jesus right into the service. You will see Jesus descending on the stage and walking through the church in a bodily form. If you knew Heaven as some kind of eutrophic sphere far beyond the galaxies, Heaven will tangibly and visibly manifest on the earth such that it will no longer a mystery to believers. You will be caught up in the spirit and catapulted straight into the Throne room of Heaven and walk in the streets of gold in your human attire and have a conversation with the Lord, Jesus Christ. And depending on God's sovereignty and grace, some will be translated straight into Heaven, such that they will neither taste death, corruption nor decay.

The realm of glory is a realm of revelation.

It is worth exploring the divine truth that the glory realm is a realm of revelation. It is a realm whereby everything is known. It is beyond the realm of gifts, faith and the anointing. Figuratively speaking, common sense is to the natural man what revelation is to the man in the Glory of God. Revelation comes before manifestation and without revelation there is no acceleration of the manifestation. Hypothetically speaking, you cannot get fire from water; it takes fire to set a fire in the same way it takes a certain amount of rain to cause a flood. By the same token, without a constant flow of revelation, manifestation will not tarry. *The glory realm is a realm of Revelation.* That is why there is such a thing as *the revelation glory.* This involves allowing God to speak to our spirit when we are basking in the atmosphere of His glory. It incorporates seeing things materialise before they happen and witnessing things happening while they are being spoken.

The greater truth is that what is revelatory to the Heavens is prophetic to the earth. The distinguishing characteristic feature of the glory realm is that things in the Heavens are not learned but they are just known or revealed. It is not possible to study and learn the revelatory realm. It must be revealed and this explains why Paul wrote three quarters of the New Testament when in actual fact he never went to a Bible school. It is possible to learn the operation of the prophetic realm, but not the revelatory realm. There is a world of difference between the *revelatory* and the *prophetic experience.* They are governed by different rules, as the one originates from the throne of Glory, and the other originates from this fallen atmosphere. The truth is that Heaven operates in present tense, while the earth has different time zones or tenses. Here, we have the past, present and future perfect tense. If anything comes to the earth from the Heavens, it has to fit into one of these three tenses in order to remain in the earth and manifest in these three dimensional realms. It has come into the earth, leave the realm of eternity from whence it came and penetrate the realm of time. For this to happen, it must be framed, or claimed by the words of our mouth. Then it remains in our time zone, and will manifest to us in the natural realm.

In view of the above, it is therefore scripturally evident that revelation is such an indispensable necessity to unlocking the supernatural doors to abundance. Without revelation, even prosperity remains a mystery and God's people remain trapped in a morass of debilitating poverty. Did you know that poverty is not a money problem but a glory problem? Poverty is not a lack of money but a lack of perceived access to the glory of God because everything flows from the glory realm. Paul concurs in Philippians 4:2 that *My Lord shall supply all my needs* **according to the riches in glory by christ** Jesus. This tells me that as long as you are born again and you are still in lack, you don't have a money problem. Instead, you have a glory problem. This is because every need or provision is supplied in commensurate with the measure of the glory of God in your life. Therefore, the solution to poverty is to tap into the higher realms of glory where everything is made available and access His glory and poverty will disappear.

The glory of God is not only experienced but revealed.

It must be expressly understood that a move, revival or outpouring of the Holy Spirit does not rest upon any particular person but only upon the revelation of God's glory that an individual holds and imparts to God's people who receive it by faith. The glory of God is more than a biblical doctrine and a theological concept; it is a reality that we can experience. That is why Moses said to God in exodus 33:18 *"Please show me your glory"*. Note that he didn't say , *"Lord teach me your glory"* because the glory is not something that we learn but it is something that is revealed to our spirit. This is because in the realm of the spirit, things are not taught or learnt but revealed. Moses knew that the glory of God was more than just a theological concept and this is why he asked God to show him His glory, the most intimate aspect of His nature. In fact it was after God showed Moses His glory that He gave him the law (Exodus 33:19-34:28). The level of revelation which a man fathoms is directly proportional to the magnitude of glory he can receive from God. God will not visit us beyond the measure of the revelation we have of Him. The glory of God must be revealed, otherwise it cannot be manifested intensely on earth. Many people have no idea what the glory really is because they have never experienced it. Mere religion will never produce a supernatural experience because it is void of the glory of God. The Kingdom, Power and Glory are not just theoretical concepts but spiritual truths. They are heavenly realities that every believer can experience now.

The glory realm supersedes the prophetic realm: There is no prophecy or word of knowledge in the glory realm since there is no past, present or future in the Glory.

It is worth exploring the truth that prophecy is reserved for this earth's time realm but in the glory realm, there is perfection as everything is complete and in the now. The truth is that when one prophesies, he does not speak from the realm of time, but from eternity. Everything is already finished in the Heavens, so there is no need for prophecy. Everything in the Glory is present tense, now knowledge. There is no past, present or future in the Glory. Everything is complete and whole in the Glory. Why? It's because things which are in the future, in the glory realm, they have already happened. Prophecy is reserved for the earth, for the realm of time. It becomes a creative force, reaching into the future and bringing the future into the now. True prophecy never speaks from time, for it would then be distorted. Prophecy speaks from eternity, for it sees the finished result of the declared word. A prophet will not speak from the present to the present tense. He will always speak from the future into the present tense. Prophecy will cease, but the revelatory realm of the Glory will never cease. This is because prophecy is reserved for this earth's time realm, where the future exists. In the Glory there is no future. Everything is present tense. That is why *Second-day prophecy* is different from *third-day prophecy.*

Prophetically speaking, prophecy is about to change dramatically as the two worlds, Heaven with the earth collide. Time on this planet is being dramatically altered as eternity is invading time, and time is being displaced. Since prophecy always ministers through time, it is about to change as well. Because ministry gifts see ahead of time, God does not deal with prophets according to time. The vision of the prophet supersedes time and space, mocking the devil's determination to keep man without hope and a future. Therefore, we need to get up, out of this earth's gravitational pull which keeps us earthbound, in order to hear and see clearly and know what is to come. This information is only available in the Glory, once we break the bonds of time and look back from there. Prophecy is able to touch the past, present and future, that is why we speak of *foretelling, telling* and *forth telling* as key dimensions in the prophetic realm. Time, which is in need of being redeemed for whatever reason, is always in the past tense, never the future tense. So God must take us back to the past in order to redeem the past. If He never redeemed time, we could never enter our future.

Prophecy is the means by which time is created but revelation is the means by which time is known. Too many prophets today are putting into the future what God has already done and is available now. But the time has come that prophecy will no longer be about a future event waiting to come to pass. Instead, as the prophetic words are coming out of the mouths, that which we say will already be created and in motion before we finish speaking. Why? It's because in the glory realm, there is no time. When you speak from the glory realm, you are actually allowing God to create that which you are speaking. It is the same principle that God used in Genesis when He had the Spirit hovering and then He spoke and results were instantaneous. This is to tell you that prophecy sends angels on your behalf to supernaturally arrange things. Therefore, declare God's word in any hopeless situation and angels will swiftly do their part by setting whatever you have decreed in motion.

The greater truth is that the realm of glory supersedes the prophetic realm. Prophecy like any other gift, operates in the absence of glory, but when the glory shows up, prophecy ceases as it is no longer needed as everything is revealed. The glory realm is a realm beyond the gifts and talents. The greatest challenge is that many people in the Body of Christ today are majoring in the prophetic gift but not in the glory. The fact is that you can have a prophetic gift flow at times even when you are not necessarily in the glory. Have you ever wondered why Jesus said in the last day, some will say, "*Lord we prophesied in your name cast out demons in your name, done many wonders in your name*" but He will say I never knew you? It's because these people would have been operating in the gifts alone without the glory. Although your prophecy may be accurate, the weight of the effect of your prophecy will depend on the level of glory of God in your life. The prophetic glory is the Prophetic gifts intertwined with the glory – an invasion of prophetic glory. A prophecy given in the glory has immediate and drastic life changing results. That is why Jesus prophetically declared to a fig tree that it would die and at that moment it started to die. (Mark 11:12-14; 20-24).

In the glory realm, things happen the instant they are declared.

There is a new prophetic dimension in the glory whereby things are coming to pass as they are being said. In the glory realm, there is no procrastination, or delays because time is inconsequential. When God declared in an atmosphere of glory, *let there be light*, light came forth instantly. He didnt have to wait. Instead, results came forth as words were declared. In the glory realm, there is no waiting because waiting is a process in time, of which we have dominion over time; we operate outside the time dimension because we were given birth to in the eternal realm which falls outside our time dimension. The reason why some believers experience delays in their lives is because of the absence of glory. The less you are filled with the glory, the longer it takes for you to cast out darkness and experience victory in your life. Real spiritual warfare takes place in the glory because there, the Lord fights for your battles. Outside the glory, you fight your own battles but inside the glory, God fights for you. That's why God said to the children of Israel, *"This battle is not yours. You do not have to fight for the battles is yours"*. This is because in the glory realm, God assumes total ownership of every battle, and since it is not possible for God to lose any fight, your position is to watch as a spectator. But why does the above scripture connotes that the battle not yours? It's because you are operating in the glory which belongs to God. Therefore, any man who touches you touches the glory of God. Demons know very well that they cannot enter Heaven, hence with the coming down of the glory, they leave instantly because they know that the same rules apply. That is why deliverance happens so fast in the glory zone because demons are not permitted to enter, sickness is rendered illegitimate and death is not permitted to reign. That is why there is such a thing as *Deliverance glory,* meaning conducting deliverance while in the glory zone.

Because we have dominion over time, in the glory realm, you can declare a thing and use your royal prerogative to stipulate the time frame when that thing must come to pass, whether in a day, week or few hours. When the Bible attests that *you shall declare a thing and it shall be established for you,* it doesn't talk about flippantly declaring empty words in any direction but it talks about declaring things while in the glory realm or in an atmosphere of glory. That's when things happen. That is why those who function in higher realms of glory don't wait for things to happen, instead, they make things happen. This is because in the glory realm, it is possible for you to be instantaneously elevated to the reality of *overnight success,* whereby prayers are being answered even before you start praying. Let's look closely at how Ezekiel functioned on the prophetic glory:

So, I prophesied as I was commanded and as I prophesied, there was a noise, and suddenly a rattling and the bones came together bone to bone (Ezekiel 37:7)

The instant Ezekiel prophesied, the noise began and the miracle started the moment the prophecy commenced. This is to tell you that prophecy does not just foretell; it creates that which is being said. It is the tool that brings it to pass. Confessing what you want God to do is different from declaring what He is saying right now while the glory is present. Both Elijah and Elisha walked and lived in the prophetic glory realm and when they spoke, it caused heaven and earth, kings and nations, to react and respond. They prophesied the opening of wombs, rain and drought, provisions, resurrections, and deaths, and the list goes on.

Every created thing has sound waves and responds to sound waves spoken in the glory and Spirit of God

---

It is worth exploring the divine truth that when you speak words of faith directed by God in the glory realm, everything responds to your words. The principle is that every created thing has sound waves and responds to sound waves spoken with the glory and Spirit of God. That is why Jesus spoke to a fig tree and commanded it to wither and it insantly responded because it was created with the capacity to hear and obey. Now, you understand why Jesus said we could speak to a mountain and it is possible for it to be removed (Mathew 17:20). The disciples also marvelled that *even the winds and the surging waters obey him.* The truth is that it's not only diseases that obeys and responds to our commands but the creation itself. Do you notice that God told Moses to speak to the rock so that it would produce water? This is the same principle of operating in the glory that we tap to when healing the sick. Because every body part and object of creation can hear and respond, when praying and commanding broken bones to reconnect, they can hear and respond just as all created things can. This realisation opens a whole new world of authority over creation.

In the biblical account of creation, God spoke for the first time in recorded history in Genesis 1:3 saying, *"let there be light"* and instantly, there was light. Accordingly, everything was created with sound directing it to be a certain thing. This means that if you are in the glory of God, it is possible to redirect an object to be another created thing. If the original raw materials that created a certain object are present (Spirit), then sound can redirect the same created object into another form, especially if you are in the glory realm of God where the Spirit is hovering. The greater truth is that nothing created can be uncreated. According to the *law of thermodynamics*, things created only change form. For example, when you burn wood, it turns to ash but does not disappear completely. Although the ashes seem to dissolve, it is reduced to smaller molecules that still contain imbedded sound particles. This is to show you that one created object can turn into another created thing if directed by sound waves or commanded under the direction of the Holy Spirit.

How do you think Ezekiel was able to prophesy and speak to the bones such that they responded as a proof that they could hear and obey such that the sinews and flesh joined in and reformed? How could the flesh that was dissolved, rotten and now skeletons turn into an army? It's because nothing created is really gone even though it might have disappeared in the natural realm. It only changes form into smaller molecules and atoms we cannot see. It's just that it exists in another realm, in another form; hence, it can be brought back to its original form. Do you notice that Ezekiel even spoke to the dry bones' breath, which is the spirit such that it obeyed and returned? That is why when raising the dead, you must not worry that the death victim is now rotting in the casket or now a skeleton in the grave; simply command the spirit of the dead to come back to life and it will hear and obey such that the dead will instantaneously arise. Imbued with this understanding, you realise that raising the dead is certainly as easy as waking up people from a slumber.

The greater truth is that creation responds to what human beings say or do. That's why the Bible says *the creation itself groans with birth pangs for the manifestation of the sons of God* (Romans 8:19, 22), meaning the earth is eagerly waiting for humanity to command it on what to do. Do you know that the Bible says money is crying out in the hands of those who use it for evil? As a believer, filled with the Spirit and inundated by the word of God, you have the authority over all creation and subjects in the natural realm. In the same manner in which Jesus spoke to the billowing storms and boisterous winds of the sea, you can change weather patterns of geographical territories by speaking or commanding the winds, rain, sun (heat), and other physical phenomenon in the natural realm and they will obey you. For instance, when you wake up in the morning, you can command your morning and determine the exact weather conditions that you would want to see prevail in your neighbourhood and it shall be established.

To cement this divine truth with reference to further scriptural evidence, did you notice that the Bible says *the blood of Jesus speaks better things than that of Abel?* Do you notice in the context of the above scripture that the blood speaks? How possible is it that blood can speak? It's because it has sound waves and responds when commanded. In a similar vein, the Bible also mentions that *the blood of martyrs is crying out* (Genesis 4:10). We need to realise that all things have a voice and their sound can be carried over time to be experienced again. Are you not shocked that after more than

400 years, Elisha's bones still retained the anointing and the sound of God emanating from them such that a dead man who came into contact with Elisha's bones was raised back to life (2 Kings 13:21). This is to inspire you to get into the glory zone and speak forth and the creation will respond to your word.

Sound waves spoken in the glory contain certain levels of energy.

There is a sound of God's glory that is released when we shout to the Lord corporately. Sound is a non-visible element but a very real object that, when in a concentrated form and filled with His glory, is a force to be reckoned with. To give a quintessential example, do you know that the walls of Jericho crumbled when people shouted? What a defiance of the law of gravity! The children of Israel were told not to speak for one week. In this way, they were conserving the power of sound in their voices so that on the day they released it, their shouts would have greater power. Words and sound contain certain levels of energy. Did you know that if you say, "*In the name of Jesus*", dynamite power is released through your mouth? The entire time when the children of Israel spent an entire week not speaking negative words, their minds and spirits were preoccupied with God and with the anticipation of what He would do next.

Then finally, after conserving all their sound waves, on His command, together they released one big shout and shofar blast, such that the power was released like a sonic boom. Sounds waves full of glory and power like a laser were concentrated on the walls around Jericho and down they came. I believe the walls were overpowered by the stream of concentrated sound waves emanating from people's shouts, which blew out all the sound of waves in the rocks. Because the rock wall was essentially made of the building block of sound and it was bombarded with greater sounds waves of glory coming from an army of God's people, the wall crumbled as the very element that held it up was shattered. It has been scientifically proven that if a person signs at a very high pitch long enough, glass will break, especially a fine crystal goblet. The sound pierces right through the glass, which is also made of sounds and shatters it. This is the same reason why a jet aircraft traveling faster than the speed of sound causes things on earth to shake because of the great power of sound waves. This is the same dimension of power that is released when we emit sound waves by declaring things while in the glory realm. Did you also know that even doctors use sound waves to treat cancer? They use a procedure called *high intensity focused ultrasound*, which is high energy sound waves, to destroy cancer cells. The high intensity words you speak to cancer cells that can hear and respond are much more powerful with the Holy Spirit and Glory. This is the reason why when Jesus commanded the fig tree to wither, it obeyed because it was created with the capacity to hear and obey.

The realm of glory is activated by spoken words.

It is a divine truth that what you speak has such a tremendous effect on everything that you do. Speech is so powerful that it is recorded that everything was created by it. Speech was one of the first ingredients that created everything else you see and the invisible things you don't see. In the beginning the Creator spoke in Genesis 1: 3, saying *"let there be light"*, and light came forth instantaneously. The truth is that when you speak over the airwaves, you are invading and taking back the space of, *"the Prince of the power of the air"*, and displacing the enemy so that God can rule over the airwaves and bring His purposes to pass. From a scientific point of view, sound waves created by speech are so small that if you were to divide the smallest particles and atoms into some of the smallest forms inside them, at their core you would find vibration waves called *quarks*. From this scientific reality, comes a spiritual truth that sound waves are embedded in everything on earth, including rocks, food, trees and everything ever created. Therefore, these sounds waves can be altered and respond to other sound waves or speech. According to the studies conducted by a Japanese Researcher Masaru Emoto, water particles and other subatomic particles actually respond to sound and even speech or words spoken to them. If this is the case, then every created thing can hear in a sense and respond in some way, as they were first created with the same core ingredients – sound and light. This understanding can revolutionise your life, including the way you pray, minister and operate in the things of God.

In the light of the above, start to speak things you want to see manifested in your life. If you are going for a job interview, say that you are going to have favour with everyone you meet, and you will be successful. If you are sick, start telling your body that it is strong and healthy and that no sickness can survive in such a healthy state. Create your day each morning by speaking what you believe will be created that you will be successful in all that you do, that you are full of energy and this will cause things to shift from the invisible realm to the visible realm and will also take you from normal to supernatural. This is what we call *commanding your morning*. When you command your morning, you give your reality divine assignments and pull success from the spiritual realm into your day.

The glory travels through space and time.

The glory of God can be carried by invisible sound waves travelling through time and space. That is why it is possible for you to watch a miracle crusade on television that was filmed 3 months back and you get healed while watching it. It's because the glory has travelled through time and space to you. Even though you were not there when the actual crusade took place, whenever you watch it, the same glory is reactivated and you receive the same impartation, healing or blessing as if you had been there 3 months ago. The glory of the meeting that took place at a particular time is frozen and reactivated the moment you watch it. So, the voice waves of the one speaking, the worship and the very atmosphere in that meeting can be contained in sound and light in the form of images and can be reactivated. That is why it is important to watch DVDs of anointed man of God because there is an impartation from these meetings frozen in time, waiting for you to receive it and release it by just pushing the play button of the DVD player.

This is the same principle by which the Bones of Elisha held a reservoir of glory and sound waves of power such that a man who was thrown into the same grave where Elisha had been buried more than four hundred years back was instantly resurrected (1 Kings 13:21). This is simply because the glory travels through space and time and in this case, it had travelled ahead more than four hundred into the future such that the same degree of resurrection glory which soaked into Elisha's body during his life time on earth was still present to raise the dead. As Elisha was now in a higher realm of glory in Heaven, his body was now the only point of contact to transmit the glory between Heaven and earth. This is what we call *Elisha glory,* when a torch of the last generation is passed to the next generation with even greater power. This is to tell you that the glory travels through time and space, which is why in in the glory realm, one can be divinely transported in the spirit dimension to other places just like the experience of Philip in Azotus. That is why multitudes of believers shall experience *divine transportation* in the spirit in the end times days.

The glory of God is always on the move.

Paul made it explicitly clear in his epistles that we move *from glory to glory*, meaning that we migrate or graduate from one plane, realm or dimension of glory into the other. This implies that the realm of glory is constantly on the move as they are inexhaustible dimensions in this realm. The highest realm of glory is found in the *Throne Room* of Heaven. Heaven is the only place in eternity that is named. Heaven is the Capital of the Eternal Realm, that is why it is a city. It's where the headquarters of the glory of God are domiciled. However, the fact that the Bible says God is seated on the throne does not necessarily mean that He is doing nothing. Instead, there are rumblings, movements, shakings, shifting and placements that takes place at the throne room on a daily basis as God unveils, unleashes and reveals new waves of His glory. In essence, the throne of God is not a chair but a central position of governance in the universe. That means the glory of God is always on the move. That is why God declared in Haggai 2:6-8 that *"Once more and in a little while I will shake the heavens, the earth and the seas"* Why? Because the glory of God is always on the move - shaking, displacing, turning, pruning, dismantling and stamping down contrary authority. Even in the Old Testament dispensation, the Ark of the Covenant which represented the glory of God was being carried from one place to the other and would not stay in one place for ever.

Contrary to how we operate in these end times, the Old Testament folks had a limited grace. The glory of God would only manifest when the Ark of the Covenant was carried from one place to the other. However in the New Testament dispensation, the glory of God has taken permanent habitation in us hence, wherever we go, the glory of God is manifested. There is no longer any limitation on the glory, hence, as custodians of the glory, as we move it also moves, that is why there is such a thing as *the propagation of the glory*. That means, whatever ground we set our foot on, whichever territory we tread on, the glory of God is manifested. The Christian life was never designed to stay stagnant but to move from faith to faith, glory to glory, victory to victory until we are transformed into the complete image of Jesus. If the glory of God is moving in a specific season and out of ignorance, you do not move in the direction of God's glory, you become redundant and potentially stuck at the same level. This is what produces friction, spiritual tension that causes prophecies to be delayed and breakthroughs postponed in one's life. The reason why some believers are still trapped in some debilitating life circumstances such as sickness, poverty and death is because the glory of God is moving while they are standing as spectators at a bus stop waiting for something to happen.

The realm of Glory enables us to move, live and function in both the realm of the spirit and the realm of the natural at the same time.

It is only possible through the glory of God to function in both the spiritual world and the natural world concurrently. Although faith connects us to the spirit realm, it is the glory of God that causes us to operate freely in both realms of existence. Faith is a spiritual connection but when the glory comes, it gives way. That is why man is allowed to use faith in the absence of the glory but when the glory comes, man does not need faith to operate in the glory because it is God Himself doing His own work. It is worth exploring the divine truth that man's original state was void of circumstance as we know it because of the Glory in which he lived in the little Heavenly realm on earth called *Eden*. Eden was an epitome of a manifestation of *Heaven on earth*. One of the meanings of the word *"Eden"* in Hebrew is *"a moment in time"*. When God made man, He placed him in one of these moments in time. In that moment in time, he could easily switch between the two realms of existence. Before the fall, Adam operated easily in both realms of existence. He could move into the spirit realm and talk to God and then move back to the natural realm to interact with his animals. Moving from the natural realm into the spiritual realm was like moving from his bedroom into the living room. Enoch is another quintessential example of a man of two realms, by faith living in the unseen. He operated so much in both realms of the existence to the extent that he permanently disappeared into the other world, the eternal one.

Jesus also demonstrated the spiritual reality of living in the two realms of existence at the same time when He declared in prophetic language in John 3:13 that, *"No one has been to Heaven, except the Son of man which is in heaven"*. The question you are probably asking yourself is: How can Jesus be in Heaven and on earth at the same time? It's because of the life in the glory. It is the glory that enables man to see in the spirit and natural realm at the same time as in an open vision. Although Jesus had a ministry to accomplish on earth at that time, He simultaneously operated in the heavenly realm of glory from which He came and that is why miracles and signs and wonders were mightily demonstrated through His hands. Elijah also functioned in both realms, this why he was able to control the economy of heaven, by shutting and opening it at his own discretion. His popular statement of address: *"I stand in the presence of God"*, depicts this dual role which he played across both realms. We have also been catapulted into this realm because the Bible says *we are seated with Christ in the heavenly places.* That means while we walk and work in this earth, our positions of authority, governance and offices are in the spirit realm and as we operate in that realm, we are able to influence activities of heaven and earth. That is why Bible says *whatever we bind on earth shall be bound in heaven.* Why? Because we operate in the heavenly realm of glory which governs both heaven and earth, hence whatever we decree in that realm, heaven is bound to respond with an answer.

Paul, the apostle, said there were times he was *"between and betwixt"*. In other words, he seemed to be in and out of both the spiritual and natural worlds at the same time. He could not tell if it was his spirit only or his body and spirit were taken to the third heaven to see things, many of which he was not allowed to describe. The Apostle Paul speaks in 2 Corinthians 12:1-4 of being caught up to the third Heaven:

"It is not expedient for me doubtless to glory. I will come to visions and revelations of the Lord. I knew a man in Christ above fourteen years ago, (whether in the body, I cannot tell; or whether out of the body, I cannot tell: God knoweth;) such an one caught up to the third heaven. And I knew such a man, (whether in the body, or out of the body, I cannot tell: God knoweth;) How that he was caught up into paradise, and heard unspeakable words, which it is not lawful for a man to utter.

In the context of the above-mentioned scripture, the phrase, *"Caught up"* implies being catapulted into a higher realm of glory". In other words, Paul was simultaneously caught up into the Glory and into the future. Allegorically speaking, the future is up, not somewhere before us in this earthly time zone. While man has a tendency to think horizontally, God manifests vertically, the impact of which issues out horizontally. Our future is in the Glory, where everything comes from. Paul stepped into the world that simultaneously exists with the eternal, or supernatural. As we enter into the *Glory cloud,* we also can experience what the Apostle Paul did. What an exciting possibility! To substantiate this divine truth with reference to experiential evidence, in my person experience in ministry, I have been to Heaven, scripturally referred to as *"being caught up in the spirit"*, walked the streets of gold, stood in the Throne room, seen Jesus, talked to angels and heard mysteries which are not part of the vocabulary of modern man, then came back to the natural realm, taught the masses the deep revelations of Heaven and mightily demonstrated the power of God through miracles signs and wonders. This was only possible because of the atmosphere of glory which enabled me to easily swift between Heaven and earth.

The grand entrance into the realm of glory is through faith.

It is worth exploring the divine truth that faith is the *first dimension* of the supernatural realm, the anointing is the *second dimension* and the glory is the *third dimension*. So, in order to tap into the higher realms of glory, one has to step out or be catapulted from the realm of faith (*first dimension*) through the realm of the anointing (*second dimension*) into the realm of glory (*third dimension*). Faith is the ever empowering awareness of the invisible world and its realities. Faith is the antenna whose frequency is being tuned to the spiritual waves that come directly from the throne room of Heaven. Although faith is a lower plane in the realm of God and a starting point for all humanity endeavouring to reach the realm of eternity, faith is what introduces you to the glory and accentuates an avenue for the glory of God to be revealed.

The greater truth is that faith is a currency of Heaven. You need faith to trade with God at His level and to withdraw from the resourcefulness of His glory. Faith is the time zone in which God dwells. It is, it was, and it is to come. Faith is a higher law than time and it permits us to live, and operate, in that higher law. Through faith, we can access out of time into the eternal. Therefore, faith is the bridge, or passageway, the connection between time or eternity. Without faith the apprehension of an entrance into the eternal realm by the Spirit would not be possible. We are often crises-oriented, meaning that we fail to perceive the Glory of God because we have conformed to the sense realm in which our crises exists. This type of perception or complex makes what we are actually seeing complicated with intellectualism and fact, not truth.

The question you are probably asking yourself is: *How did the concept of faith come about? Surely the first man Adam did not need faith to reach out to God!* The truth is that following the fall of man in the Garden of Eden, God has always had problems in dealing with humanity, in that He is reaching from the eternal realm into a limited realm of time and space. In this respect He speaks a language we cannot understand. We are unable to relate to eternity from within a time realm. How could this gap be bridged? It was up to God to take the initiative and solve this problem of communication failure. It would require a key to decode His thoughts, something that would work in both realms. It had to be a valid medium of exchange in the realm of eternity and the realm of time. Therefore, He provided a medium of exchange, valid in Heaven and on earth when He gave us faith.

Faith is the currency, or gold standard, of the eternal realm, and also an honoured currency, or standard, in the earth. God had to give man faith in order to elevate him above the constraints of time, space and matter so that man could have an intelligent relationship with His Creator. The fallen mind of man cannot understand the eternal realm, nor grasp the fact that he was created for a higher dimension than what time, space and matter would determine for him. The human mind can hardly conceive that he has been given the key to subdue and change his predetermined boundaries set by time and space. The key is faith. God gave us the gift of faith to open the prison door of time and escape, and freely access His glorious realm. The door swings both ways, giving us access to Him, and God direct access to us, without the limitations of doubt. Once the faith key is turned in the lock of time, nothing is impossible to man. He can then freely access the treasures of His loving Father. Unencumbered by the weight of disbelief, we can then enter freely into His presence. We no longer doubt what God said He would do or when He said he would do it. Time is no threat to such a one. This thrills God, as He finds access to such a heart and mind and for that one, nothing shall be impossible in the supernatural dimension of glory.

The glory makes it easy for one to function in the realm of the anointing.

As much as the anointing connects us to the glory of God, it must be understood that in some cases operating and moving in the anointing is dependent on the degree of the glory present. Remember that the *anointing is God's ability imparted upon a vessel but the glory is God himself doing His work* hence, when God manifests His glory in a particular area, the extent to which we can manifest that glory through the anointing is dependent on the measure of the glory that is manifested. We should therefore learn to be sensitive to the varying levels of the glory of manifested if ever we want to move in greater dimension of the anointing. According to the level of God's glory manifested, we can function easily in the anointing. Sometimes in a meeting, everyone's concentration is so perfectly upon the attributes of God, that the glory of God comes into manifestation. When the glory of God is in manifestation, it is easier to function in the ministerial anointing. Do not function beyond the level of God's glory manifested. Each meeting, for various reasons has a different degree of manifested glory and anointing. The realm of glory is what rules or governs the realm of the anointing and not vice versa. There is a limitation for the functions of an anointing set by the manifested glory in each meeting although in the fivefold calling we may actually carry a greater anointing than we are allowed to manifest at that time.

The glory is a quantifiable divine phenomenon: It manifests in degrees, levels and measures.

It must be expressly understood that as much as we have a measure of faith or anointing to operate in the kingdom, *the glory of God is also manifested in degrees and measures* (2Corinthians 3:18). There is ample evidence in the word of God that shows that the glory of God is manifested in measures, for example the glory can fill a house (Acts 2:2); 4:31), a tabernacle (Exodus 40:34), a temple (2 Chronicles 5:14; 7:1), a prison (Acts 16:26) or even a mountain (Exodus 19:8). In other words, whenever the glory of God shows up, it doesn't mean that it will always manifest in the same measure or degree. Depending on the extent to which the right spiritual atmosphere and climate has been cultivated and the level of receptivity and expectation of the congregation and other factors, there are times when the glory of God is manifested to a heightened degree or magnitude while in some other cases it just trickles. Some ministers could get the glory of God and anointing flowing at the stage around them while others could flow in the anointing all over the auditorium even to the extent of having the glory being catapulted beyond church doors and bars to overflow into the streets and market place just like the experience John G. Lake had when the glory of God moved in Johannesburg in the 1950s to such an extent that the power of God was still hitting people in the streets two weeks after he had a conference. That was an extreme degree of manifestation of the glory.

To unveil the intensity and magnitude of manifestation of the glory of God, it is recorded that during the dedication of Solomon's temple, the glory of God was so strongly demonstrated that they could not continue to minister before God (2 Chronicles 5:14). In other words, the presence of God was so strong that all stood in awe, busking under the glory of God. There is a certain dimension of glory that manifests and gets everybody falling under the power to the extent that even the pastor is slain in the power and is just busking in God's presence. After King Solomon prayed, the fire of God came down from heaven and ***the glory of God increased*** to such a level that everybody had to vacate the temple because the glory of God was so thick that nobody could get in (2 Chronicles 7:1-3). This implies that the glory of God is manifested and increased in measures and degrees. That means as we develop in the glory of God in us, we would be able to sense God's glory manifest in a meeting and even measure or detect the intensity of its manifestation.

The glory needs to be awakened, provoked or triggered and diligently sought after in order for it to manifest in the natural realm.

It is a divine truth that God lives, functions and operates in the realm of glory. He is not influenced by time, distance, space or matter. Although He dwells in such a realm of superabundance, God requires you to reach out to Him in faith so as to qualify to partake of His glorious riches. Hence the glory needs to be sought after, desired, admired and searched until it is found. When Moses said to God, *"Lord show me the glory",* he spoke of *awakening the glory of God into manifestation.* This experience is more of an awakening call than just a sight or visual experience because in the spirit realm, if you see something, then you have it. In other words, Moses was not saying that the Lord should just show him where the glory of God is or how big the glory is so that he could just entertain his eyes with the spectacular visual experience just like the burning bush he had seen earlier. Instead, Moses wanted something more than just a visual experience because he had seen so many visual manifestations of God before through thunder, lightning, fire and clouds. He wanted to get the *substance of glory* because in the spirit realm, you receive something by seeing it. Hence, when he said *"show me the glory",* in essence, he actually meant *that "give me the glory"* because in the realm of the spirit, things are procured by vision, hence to show someone something means to give him that particular thing because once you see something, you get it. At times we misinterpret the Bible to mean what it doesn't say. This was an awakening call for God to reveal to him *the essence of what the Glory of God is.* In other words, he was more interested in the manifestation and activation of the *substance of the glory* than just the physical location or movement of the glory. That is why the Bible says in Romans 8:11 *that the same Spirit who raised Jesus Christ from the dead vitalises our mortal bodies.* Why vitalisation? Because the glory of God in us needs to be awakened, activated or energised in order for it to manifest intensely and touch billions of lives across the globe. It's just like the gifts of the Spirit in us. Many have received the gifts but they are not being activated in such a way that they can flow out to touch lives. Even the spirit realm itself needs to be stirred or shaken in order to operate the way God wants it. That's why He declared in Hagai 2:8 that, *"In a little while I will shake the heavens, the earth and the seas".*

When God mentioned the hidden *treasures of darkness and gold*, He actually spoke of the glory which was hidden as a mystery for ages. *Gold* is the most glorious substance in the world but it is not found easily; it is hidden in the depth of the earth and strenuous, assiduous tasks are undertaken to uncover it. As it is in the natural, so it is in the spirit. Just like gold, the glory has to be sought after although the means and process to get to it might not be easy. That is why when Moses asked God, *show me your glory,* God told him that he has asked a *difficult thing* for no man can see God and live. Why did God say it's difficult? Because of the degree of concentration needed by a mortal body to carry the weight of God's glory. Note that God did not say you have asked an *impossible thing* but a *difficult thing.* This implies that although the process of getting the glory might be a daunting task because of the level of concentration, holiness and purity we must exhibit to qualify to be carriers of the glory in the same way the body of a pregnant woman must qualify to carry a child, activating, invigorating and energising that glory is what matters in the kingdom. Having the glory is not a title but a progressive phenomenon. That is why any man can be *defined by the level or degree of the anointing* that is upon their lives but no man can be defined by the glory because no one can own the glory except God. Since we are living in a season of great awakening of glory, we need to seek the glory of God at all costs as God is a rewarded of those who diligently seek after His glory.

The glory of God is sacred, hence it needs to be protected as the most valuable and treasured asset of Heaven.

Immediately after Adam was exiled from Eden, God sent a cherubim to guard the entrance to Eden. Why? God was not trying to guard the fruits or trees of Eden but to guard the glory, to protect His glory. God's glory is pure, uncontaminated hence, needs to be protected. That is why the ark of the covenant which represented the glory of God was guarded in the Old Testament. Protecting the glory does not necessarily mean protection of the glory from abuse by the people. Instead, it means protecting the people from being victims of the repercussions or side effects of the glory when they come into contact with it in sin, wickedness and ignorance, hence the glory of God is protected so that the fire of God will not harm the people. That is why God warned the kings and authorities saying, *"Touch not my anointed ones, Do my prophets no harm"* (1 Chronicles 16:22; Psalms 105:15). By this precaution, God was not protecting the Anointed ones per se, but He was protecting the glory of His anointing so that the ignorant and wicked man are not burnt by His *liquid fire anointing* or at least do not receive instant judgement as a result of tampering with His glorious substance of the anointing. That is why when Uzzah mistakenly touched the ark of glory, he died instantly because the glory of God is holy, sacred, hence should be protected. Therefore, as a new creation, it is important that you safeguard the glory of God and His presence that is upon your life because it is sacred. That is why as ministers of the gospel, not only do we propagate the glory of God to the nations but we also have a divine mandate from Heaven to protect the glory of God by operating within the parameters of God's will when functioning in the realm of glory.

The laws governing the anointing are similar to those governing the glory because the anointing is a product of God's glory. For example, when Eli's children died, because of God's anointing upon him, he was not even allowed to mourn for them. This is to show you how strict it is to operate in the glory of God. Have you ever wondered why Saphira and Ananias received instant judgment by death? Have you ever pondered on why this couple received such a harsh and instant judgement yet even the first man to know sin, Adam, was never sentenced to instant judgement? There is nothing taking place on earth void of spiritual significance. The reason why Saphira and Ananias died is not because they lied in a literal sense because they were not the first people to lie in the New Testament. Instead, they were subjected to a harsh, instant judgement because they tampered with the glory of God, which is the glory of the Spirit, hence they died in the same way Uzzah died when he mistakenly touched the ark of the covenant carrying God's glory. In other words, they attempted to move in the glory of God in sin because the Bible says there was a *prosperity revival* or move of God in those days of which these two were a part such that believers sold everything they had and shared amongst the brethren. Therefore, it is important that we safeguard His glory from extremists that would seek to divert attention from God to themselves hence it is important to know that there are extremes in any Glory Moment.

The glory is a gravity-defying phenomenon that transforms and transcends the natural laws and processes.

It is worth exploring the divine truth that in the glory, all the natural laws and process are altered. To illustrate this scenario with a quintessential example, when Daniel was thrown into a den of lion by king Nebuchadnezzar, what do you think happened? Why do you think the lions did not devour him? Some people think that the lions were not hungry. Others think that God closed the mouths of the lions. These are all mere speculations. As I meditated on this scripture, my spirit began to travel and was divinely transported back in time through the Spirit to the place where the den of lions was. From my vantage point while in that realm, I began to see everything that transpired the minute they threw Daniel into the den. The glory of God filled the den and changed the digestive system and metabolic functions of the lions such that when the lions looked at Daniel, they completely lost appetite because the pangs of hunger got disabled by the atmosphere of glory. In other words, their genetic make-up and nature was completely transformed or metamorphosed by the glory. As they mingled with the glory of God, natural laws and principles had to give way to the supremacy of the law of God's sovereignty in creation. The law of faith closes the mouths of lions but the glory changes the digestive system of a lion. Daniel taped into the realm of original prime glory that filled the Garden of Eden where Adman could interact freely with the lions, without being hurt. Hence, Daniel was to the lions in the den, what Adam was to the lions in the Garden of Eden. When they removed Daniel from the den and the glory lifted, suddenly the metabolic system of the lion was restored and the lions became hungry once again. For experimentation purposes, had someone been thrown into the den of lions immediately after removing Daniel, the lions would have torn him into pieces because the glory would then have lifted. It is the absence of glory that causes the lions and other animals to be malicious to man in the natural realm. That is why you must be ready to embrace the glory because it can change anything and align it to God's original purpose.

> *The glory is the highest concentration of God's Power that raises the dead. That is why there is such a thing as a Resurrection Glory.*

In the realm of glory, in heaven there is neither sickness, decay, nor death. The glory of God in heaven is like oxygen in the natural realm. It is the life blood of all things. Anything that comes into contact with the glory of God receives an impartation of the life of God. That is why in the dimension of Glory the dead are raised because of an impartation of the eternal life of God. Faith is a creative force that pulls back the spirit of a dead man into his body but it is the glory that makes death unacceptable, illegitimate and illegal. The glory changes the natural laws associated with the phenomenon of death and once these laws are transformed by glory, death gives way without struggling. You see how easy it is to raise people from the dead as Jesus commanded? The easiest way is through the glory. You will not have to scratch your head or stretch your faith trying to figure out which spiritual laws to tap into to raise the dead because the glory will automatically change all those laws associated with the spirit of death and give you a divine legitimate right to just wake up the dead by calling them forth just like what Jesus did to Lazarus. People usually get excited about the outcome of a miracle and they hardly get to find out what exactly happened behind the scenes in the realm of the spirit. When Jesus raised Lazarus from the dead, this is what happened in the invisible realm: Jesus tapped into the realm of glory and because of the glory, all the natural laws of death, decay and corruption had to give way and despite the fact that Lazarus had died for 4 days and his body was stinking, he was raised up. How do you explain this? It was not faith or anointing in operation but it was the dimension of Glory which Jesus tapped into.

The most powerful thing is that shortly before His death, Jesus said to God in a prayer, *"Lord, the glory that you have given me, I have also given it to them"* (meaning us). When translated in this context, it would read as, *"the glory which I used to raise Lazarus from the dead, I have given it to them?"* Wow!

This means we have the same measure of glory to raise the dead. This is why Jesus commanded us to go out there and raise the dead, heal the sick and cast out the lepers. How can Jesus command us to go and raise the dead when he knows that we cannot do it? It means Jesus knew that we are already equipped and empowered to call forth the dead back to life. It is only lack of revelation knowledge which inhibits us to tap into the realm of God's power to raise the dead. Jesus even made a remark to authenticate this commission by saying that *"greater things that these shall you do"*. How? Because of the glory. Now this explains why some believers have succeeded to cast out devils, heal the sick but have not been able to operate in the realm of raising the dead. This is because it takes the anointing to cast out devils and heal the sick but it takes the glory of God to raise the dead, because the glory is the highest level of concentration of God's power.

The glory shall be a key divine magnetic force at work during rapture or second coming of Christ.

It is a divine truth that the glory shall play a critical role during rapture. I used to wonder how rapture would take place until God brought me to an understanding of the revelation of glory. The Bible says *when Christ comes back, He shall appear in the clouds.* In other words, He shall be accompanied by clouds. Clouds speak of the glory of God. So Christ shall appear in glory and in a twinkling of an eye, that glory shall be imparted upon the earth and anyone in whom is the glory of God will be captured in glory. In other words, the glory that shall come with Jesus has such a magnetic force that shall attract and capture those upon whom the glory of God rests. In other words Glory attracts glory as much as deep calleth unto deep. The passport or ticket or key to enter heaven is the glory of God. Those who do not have the glory will not make it because in heaven saints live according to the realms of glory. So this is the time to develop the glory in our spirits in preparation of the second coming of Christ so that we are not left behind when rapture takes place.

These scriptures concerning the return of Jesus reveal that it will be associated with the light, the glory of the Lord. According to Matthew 25:31-34,

> *"When the Son of man shall come in his glory, and all the holy angels with him, then shall he sit upon the throne of his glory: And before him shall be gathered all nations: and he shall separate them one from another, as a shepherd divideth his sheep from the goats: And he shall set the sheep on his right hand, but the goats on the left. Then shall the King say unto them on his right hand, Come, you blessed of my Father, inherit the kingdom prepared for you from the foundation of the world."*

This is to tell you how important it is to function in God's glory so that at Jesus's second coming, the glory of God in our spirit will qualify us to see His glory. There are additional scriptures connecting these phenomena to Christ. Matthew 24:29-30 says,

> *Immediately after the tribulation of those days shall the sun be darkened, and the moon shall not give her light, and the stars shall fall from heaven, and the powers of the heavens shall be shaken, And then shall appear the sign of the Son of man in heaven, and then shall all the tribes of the earth mourn, and they shall see the Son of man coming in the clouds of heaven with power and great glory".*

Since the Bible makes it clear that deep calleth unto deep, the glory of God in us is what connects us to the Greater glory which Christ shall come with at His second coming. The Bible says when Jesus comes back, those who did not know him will say to the mountains *"cover us"* and to the rocks *"fall on us"*. This is because of the level of glory that He will be coming with. Sinners will not be able to withstand that kind of glory. Moreover, the Bible makes it clear in 2 Thessalonians that at Jesus's second coming, these shall be punished with everlasting destruction from the presence of the Lord and from the glory of His power. The Bible concurs in Chapter 2:8 *that the lawless one will be revealed, whom the Lord will consume with the breath of His mouth and destroy with the brightness of His coming.* The brightness of His coming refers to His glory. This implies that what is going to completely annihilate the devil is the effulgence of God's glory. The glory will be reflecting an excessively high degree of judgment fire such that the devil will just melt in God's presence. The glory shall become too heavy for the devil to withstand, hence he shall shrink in a flip of a moment, as the radiance of God's glory thrust him into everlasting torment.

At present, the earth is on a collision course with the eternal. The Bible declares that the earth will be filled with the knowledge of the Glory of God, as the waters cover the sea. Presently, the Glory of God contained in the third Heaven is highly concentrated so much that, like a pregnant woman, its waters are ready to break out and precipitate its rain upon the earth. Therefore, for this atmosphere to be poured out upon the earth, the distance between Heaven and earth has to be shortened in order for the earth to be affected by Heaven's Glory. Inevitably, something strikingly revolutional has to happen. Firstly, the earth will collide with the outer sphere or the first Heaven. This is currently taking place. As the first Heaven impacts the earth, the time upon the earth is accelerated in anticipation of the third Heaven's Glory to be poured out. The unseen world is constantly disturbing the seen world because there are things being deposited in the earth from the eternal world that were designed and planned for the now. This collision with the second Heaven will cause the rupturing of demonic forces of evil, which will produce catastrophic events upon the earth, marked by what the Bible calls "*end time events*". Jesus warned of these events when He said *great earthquakes shall be in divers places, and famines, and pestilences; and fearful sights and great signs shall there be from heaven.*"(Luke 21:8-11). This is where the static interference between the Throne room and the earth occurs; making open communication with Heaven more difficult than it was before the fall. For this reason, we see through a glass darkly when in actual fact before the fall, Adam could see clearly into the realm of Glory.

The realm of glory is what's shortening the distance between Heaven and Earth.

Did you know that the distance between Heaven and earth is no longer the same as it used to be in the beginning of creation? Scientists have proven that the further out we go from the earth, the further we become removed from time. The reality is that the distance between Heaven and earth is constantly changing. This is because the Heavens are moving toward the earth in preparation for the day when the earth will be renewed with the Glory of God. The Heavenly Jerusalem is slowly encroaching towards the earth in anticipation of the rapture of the church. God declared that *the earth shall be filled with the knowledge of the Glory of the Lord.* This can only come from the Heavenly realm. The original distance between Heaven and earth today is not what it was after the fall. The two worlds are closer now than ever before. Scientists have made a discovery that the speed of light is slowing down. This is because eternity is invading time and the dominant realm, eternity, displaces time as the two worlds collide. This scenario culminates in a divine phenomenon called *Heaven on earth*. To substantiate this divine revelation with reference to scriptural evidence, Deuteronomy 11:21 (NKJV) reads, *"That your days may be multiplied and the days of your children and the days of Heaven upon the earth."* We see from this that God has intended for man to walk in Heaven's atmosphere right here on this planet.

For the most part, the average Christian is trapped in this time-space warp, a world not native to the born-again believer. However, within every believer is placed the ability to access and be comfortable in the atmosphere God is comfortable in, which specifically includes the timeless zone. Why then would we think it strange to explore the realms of space, time and matter travel? Is this dimension only for scientists? They can never fully understand the ramifications of time-space-matter travel without grasping the spiritual realities behind it: the realm of the spirit, and the realm of the Glory. Once we discover the fragility of time, it becomes obvious that the same laws governing time govern space and matter, and are equally conquerable.

The glory is what connects Heaven to earth through revelatory realms and heavenly portals.

There are certain places on earth that already have an open portal to Heaven, which makes it easier for believers to receive revelation. Webster's dictionary defines a portal as, *"A doorway, gate or entrance, especially a large and imposing one, any point or place of entry"* (John 1:51). In other words, it's an opening into the Heavenly realm. In reality, when we talk about an Open Heaven, we are talking about an opening of a portal – a window of opportunity when the portal is opened over individuals, cities and nations. In Genesis 28:10-12, the Bible speaks of Jacob's ladder type of portal, set up on the earth, with its top reaching Heaven such that angels of God were ascending and descending on it. This is a quintessential example of *a revelatory realm and portal.* Jerusalem is the largest open-heaven portal on earth as people experience angelic appearances, open visions, a huge wave of glory and third heaven encounters. Such third Heaven experiences can alter and accelerate years of your life and ministry because of one heavenly encounter. Bethel is another portal on earth that was opened by Jacob in Genesis 28:17. The truth is that once a portal has been opened, there is a permanent door in that place allowing it to be reopened much more easily in successive generations because someone already paved the way. Some portals were opened during ancient times while others were opened during the greatest revivals in the past generations. When Jacob eventually realised that the place where he laid his head was a geographical portal, connecting the earth directly with Heaven, he exclaimed, *"This is a gate of Heaven"*. This tells me that a portal serves as a gate or leeway to Heaven, through which angels, answered prayers and blessings are transferred from earth to Heaven and vice versa.

The attainment of higher realms of glory is the ultimate purpose of the church.

The ultimate aim of the end time church is for saints to develop the quality of their spirit through ministerial activities to the extent that they attain the level of glory required to function in God's kingdom. Hence, life is a spiritual journey into the dimension of the glory of God. The anointing, faith, miracles, signs and wonders are just a means of taking us to higher realms of glory but they are not the ultimate goal of the kingdom. That is why Jesus said at judgement, many will come and say that they cast out demons, healed the sick in His name but then He will say that He doesn't know them. Why? This is because they would have been operating in the anointing and using their own faith to move in the realm of the spirit, but devoid of the glory which qualifies them for heaven. The principle is that in order for one to enter heaven which is a place of glory, he must have the glory of God in his spirit. That means our walk with God is not a fight to get more power, or anointing but a greater weight of the glory. That is why at the end of Paul's ministry, he said, *"I have fought a good fight and now I await the greater weight of glory"*. In other words, after fighting, preaching, teaching and moving in signs and wonders, he didn't say, *"Now, I await for more power or anointing"* but he said, *"Now, I await for greater glory"*. That means the glory is out ultimate purpose in the kingdom. We are not defined by the measure of power or anointing that we have but by the dimension of glory we have been elevated into. The Bible reveals *three* key dimensions of the supernatural realm, that is, faith, anointing and the glory. Faith (*the first dimension*) and the anointing (*the second dimension*) are to connect us to the glory (*the third dimension*) but their pursuit is not our ultimate endeavour. However, in the current church set up, people are erroneously advertising and celebrating more of the power and the anointing and in the process neglecting the glory which is our ultimate possession. When you get the anointing, you don't dare to celebrate and stay at that level forever. Instead, let that anointing connect you to a higher spiritual plane, which is the realm of glory.

Moreover, there is ample evidence that Jesus is coming back for a church that is perfect and all ministerial activities are conducted in a view to bring the Body of Christ to such a state of completeness or perfection. The state of perfection is the state of glory because the glory of God is perfect. In Revelation 22:5, the Bible declares that, *"And there shall be no night there, and they need no candle, neither light of the sun, for the Lord God giveth them light, and they shall reign for ever and ever."*

This implies that in the end of time, God shall rule or govern the universe through His glory. This is to tell you how important God's glory is above everything else in the universe.

The glory of God is the government of the universe. That is why there is such a thing as the Government Glory.

The truth is that while God uses spiritual laws and principles to govern the universe, at times these laws are limited or restricted. The glory is the overarching plan of authority that governs the universe and prevails in all matters where law cannot suffice. The glory transcends all laws and principles. It does not have a boundary or limitation. That is why David said, *"Lord where can I go from your presence, to the highest heavens you are there, to the lowest part of the earth you are there"*. This is because the glory of God is the monitoring mechanism of the universe. While angels are actively involved in some matters relating to the government of the kingdom, God does not rely on angels to monitor how things run in the universe. He does the monitoring process through His glory.

It is His glory that supervises, controls, leads, governs, rules and reigns across the universe. Even angels are dependent of the glory as they regularly appear before God to receive an impartation of new garments of glory in order for them to operate effectively in the spirit. That is why angels cannot lose a fight against powers of darkness because they are covered in glory. If ever there is something that the devil is most terrified of, it is the glory. In her book, exposition to Satanism, Grace Iwhere testifies of her experiences in the spirit world whereby the devil wept bitterly and regrettably whenever he thought of the glory that he had and how it was stripped off him as a result of rebellion. The devil is heartless and will not regret anything but the fact that the only thing he regrets of is the glory tells you how valuable the glory is to every creation.

As much as faith is a way of life, the gory is also a way of living.

The Bible describes the glory in 1 Corinthians 10:31 as a *way of life* and an integral aspect of humanity. Allow me to draw your undivided attention to this verse so that you can learn some truths that elucidates its meaning as we share together in the culmination of this end time season. The Apostle Paul says, *"Whether therefore you eat or drink or whatever you do, do all to the glory of God."* He points out eating and drinking because those are the most mundane routine necessary things of life that occupy us whether we desire them to or not, that's just the routine of life. And what Paul is saying is everything, even those very mundane routine normal things in life are to be done to the glory of God. That's the bottom line in all of our living. Everything we do we are to do for the glory of God. That is the most important thing in the universe. This is the call in simplicity to Christian living, we are to live to the glory of God. As much as faith is a way of life, the glory is also a way of living because through the glory, we live, move and have our being. As much as a body cannot live without oxygen, a spirit man cannot live without the glory. Every sphere of life, whether in Heaven or earth is grossly dependent on the glory of God, without which there is no life.

As darkness intensifies, there is a contrasting proportional increase in glory.

In the revelation of God's glory prophesied in Isaiah 60:1-5, Isaiah says, *"See, darkness covers the earth, thick darkness covers the people, but upon thee, the glory of God is risen"*. This implies that the glory of God manifests intensely where there is prevalence or pre-eminence of sin just like the light shines more brightly when there is intense darkness. It is a fact that the darker the night, the more brightly the light shines. The window of opportunity or the most opportunistic time to rise to higher realms of glory is when there is manifestation of wickedness in the world. The greatness of the light is shown in darkness. In the absence of darkness, one would not know how powerful light is. By the same token our light, power, glory is manifested more when there is trouble in the world. Moreover, the glory of God is an exemption to the problems of this world. While the world is in deep trouble, we are exempted by the glory not to suffer the consequences of people's wickedness.

Unlike other heavenly spiritual substances, the glory takes a permanent abode or habitation in humanity.

It is an incontestable reality that the glory of God dwells in a man and perambulates in the extreme quarters of his spirit. This is the reason why Paul unveiled the highest revelation of Christianity in the New Testament dispensation that *Christ in me the hope of glory.* This implies that *the glory of God manifested through Christ dwells in our spirit.* However, for it to be manifested intensely in the universe, there must be a habitation or it must take up residence in man. The use of ark of covenant representing God's glory and its dwelling with man in the Old Testament days was a foretaste of this habitation. God has always wanted man to dwell where His glory is. That is why God did not create man and put him in a desert. Instead, Adam was created and put in Eden, a perfect environment or place full of God's glory. There was a concentration of God's glory is Eden more than any other place in the earth. The place where one could find the glory of God in its highest, intensity was in Eden because God was demonstrating a divine principle that He has always wanted to dwell with men. The anointing comes upon human vessels and then takes off once certain tasks has been accomplished but the glory takes a permanent residence in our spirits. That is why we speak of the anointing upon but when it comes to the description of the glory we only speak of the glory within.

The glory is reciprocated as a two way divine phenomenon, hence there is such a thing as a divine transaction of glory.

It's manifestation is a two way process or phenomenon. The Bible unveils this divine exchange when it says *when His praises go up, His glory comes down* (Psalms 67:3). That means for it to flow, there must be a corresponding input or divine exchange made to God in the form of praises, worship, honour, acknowledgement, reverence and majesty. During worship sessions or prayer, the glory that is in our spirit is lifted or rises up and enter the realm of God. Everything we offer to God is offered through the glory. That is why the Bible speaks of our offerings rising up as an aroma of incense pleasing to God. When the glory that we offer to God reaches heaven, it attracts more glory, blessings, anointing, power, and causes riches in glory to manifest in our lives. The more God receives the glory, the more He releases the glory. All things held constant, the amount of glory which God can release at any particular time is to a larger extent dependent on the amount of glory that we can release to God from our spirit. This is what I call a *divine exchange or transaction of glory.*

There is a dimension or weight of glory that cannot be withstood by everyone and only a few people can stand in that atmosphere of Glory.

While it is God's original master plan to manifest His glory everywhere in its intensity, it must however be understood that there is a certain level of weight of God's glory which cannot be withstood by everybody. To cement this revelation with reference to scriptural evidence, God spoke to Moses in a thick cloud in Exodus 19:9 God saying, *"Behold, I Will come to you in a thick cloud, that the people may hear when I speak with you and believe you forever".* The thick cloud represents *the weight, heaviness, and thickness of the glory of God.* The people could hear but not enter a cloud because if they did, they would immediately die. Why? It's because there are certain levels of glory that cannot be entered by man in his sin. Only Moses could enter that glory, hence he had to build a small tent in which to meet face to face with God (Exodus 33:7-11). He was drenched into the substance of glory so much that when he exited the tent, his face glowed with the fire of God's presence. His energy was renewed and his body revitalised because the weight of the glory of God always strengthens. Few people have access to this atmosphere because they are not suited for it. Although the glory of God is unreservedly available for exploration by humanity, it is worth noting that one has to qualify to move in higher realms of glory. The glory is our credentials in the realm of God. That is why a high degree of consecration is essential for one to qualify to stand in the atmosphere of His glory.

However, it is a typical scenario in the modern day church that many believers want the glory of God and its associated benefits such as healing, health and prosperity but they don't want the ways of God and His holiness. The atmosphere of glory is only for those who hunger and thirst for His presence, those who continually enter His presence, purifying and sanctifying themselves. It is recorded that during the dedication of Solomon's temple, the glory of God was so strongly manifested such that even priests could not enter the temple to minister before God (2 Chronicles 5:14). In other words, the advent of the glory in its heightened degree, tampered with their religious programmes and messed up their spiritual agenda such that nothing was business as usual. To give a quintessential example of this scenario, it is said that Smith Wigglesworth, a man who ushered an unquestionable heavy weight of God's glory, to the extent of being mightily used to raise the dead, once invited several pastors to pray with him. When they began to worship God, His glory was manifested to a greater magnitude and intensity such that the atmosphere began to feel heavy and one by one, pastors began to leave because they could not withstand it. The glory of God filled that place and pastors felt like they were going to explode, hence they never dared to invite Smith Wigglesworth again. They acknowledged that very few men could withstand that atmosphere of glory. How do you explain this? It's because there are levels, depths and degrees in operating in the realm of glory. There are certain realms which are so deep and sacred such that only a few people like Smith Wigglesworth could enter. This has more to do with the quality of your spirit and the extent to which your inner man has been developed.

Paul described this realm of glory as *a far more exceeding and eternal weight of glory* (2 Corinthians 4:17). This is because in the glory realm, there are different degrees of glory. When we go to Heaven, there are still different degrees of glory. We can all have access to God's throne but there are different degrees of glory. So those who are in a higher stage of glory when they visit the lower stage of glory, they would have to be clothed with a special covering so that those on the lower glory can stand the depths of the glory that the higher ones are carrying in their person. It has to do with the quality of the development of their spirit. Sadhu Sundar Singh in his book *"The Spiritual World"* speaks about how he was taken on a trip to Heaven and God showed him all the different realms of glory. And he asked a question to the angel who was instructing him. *"Can they visit one another?"* And the angel told him that they can for they put on different degrees of glory and covering as they move to different levels. Then those who are not used to the depths of God's glory, when they move into a higher glory they are also given a covering so that they can stand the greater glory that they are experiencing.

> *The glory has its side effects. It is a highly inflammable and explosive spiritual substance.*

It is worth mentioning that while the glory of God is such a blessing, upon which every sphere of human existence is grossly dependent, tampering with the glory has its own consequences. To substantiate this revelation with reference to scriptural evidence, the Bible records in 2 Samuel 6:7 that Uzzah was killed by God for messing up while operating in the glory of God. Likewise, Ananias and Saphirah died in the glory of God (Acts 5:1-11). Moreover, hundreds of Israelites died in the wilderness when they grumbled in the glory of God. God takes His glory seriously such that He cannot share it with any man. No man can glory in His presence, hence God demands that the one who operates or functions in the realm of glory be fully and completely depended on Him in all humility. Anyone who messes up with the glory of God suffers consequences, either by death, reduction in life span or other ways known to God. That is why the Bible says *it is impossible for one who once tested the goodness of God and the powers of this age to fall away and be brought back to repentance* (Hebrews 6:6). Why? Because tampering with the glory of God has consequences. The goodness of God mentioned in the above scripture is His nature and glory. You cannot function in the glory of God and then go back and entertain sin or live like a sinful man.

The Bible says *nothing is impossible or too hard for the Lord* but the only instance in the Bible where God say something is impossible is in the area of tampering or messing up with His glory. In the context of the above scripture, crucifying Christ over and over means stripping him of all the glory which He obtained through the power of the cross hence, God is not prepared to have His glory above all things messed up with. That is why He is strict and His rules for operating in the glory are stringent and He goes to the extent of killing to have His glory honoured. We know that He cannot come very near us as long as we are in the flesh. If we were to stand too close to His glory, our flesh would be rent from our bones and we would be totally consumed, since flesh cannot withstand the glory of God.

There are some strikingly interesting things that we can learn about the glory of God through His dealings with the children of Israel in the wilderness. God instructed Moses in Exodus 32:34 saying, *"Now, therefore, go, lead the people to the place of which I have spoken to you. Behold, My angel shall go before you"*. So, God promised His angel to go with them. Initially, God wanted to go with them but later He said, *"If I go with them My presence is so strong they will all die off."* So, God decided, *"I will send My angel with you."* Moses was not satisfied; he is a second miler. So, in Exodus 33 when a pillar of cloud appeared and God was speaking to Moses, he said in verse 13 , *"Now therefore, I pray, if I have found grace in Your sight, show me now Your way, that I may know You and that I may find grace in Your sight. And consider that this nation is your people."* And He said, *"My presence will go with you, and I will give you rest"* (Exodus 33:14). Then he said to Him, *"If your presence does not go with us, do not bring us up from here"*. The reason why God later changed His mind and wanted His angel to go with the children of Israel instead of Him it's because He wanted to protect them from the side effects of tampering with His glory. He was aware that if He were to go with them in all their sins and rebellion, there would all be consumed by the fire of His glory.

The greater the glory the greater the judgement.

It is worth exploring the divine truth that the greater the glory, the quicker things will happen. Jesus prophesied that the centurion's servant would be healed and at that very hour she was healed. The greater the glory is, the greater the miracles will be but also the greater the judgement. Swift miracles will happen but also swift correction or judgement. Both will accelerate as the glory is accelerated, depending on our response. Zachariah received a prophecy from an angel and when he doubted, he received another one that he will be mute. All happened quickly because the prophecies were in the glory realm when the Spirit was moving. Why did God have to make Zacharias mute? It's because the same power that is released through the spoken prophetic word in the glory can bring life and death. Zechariah had the power to kill the prophecy in the same way it had come to life, by speaking in unbelief while in the glory and allowing the opposite to occur, he thus nearly created a disaster by negative declarations in the glory. In order to stop this from happening, God had to take away his words by allowing him to be mute so he would not undo the prophetic declaration or prophesy the wrong thing altogether. When the glory is present, there is greater power in our words. Paul had a similar experience as he was trying to convert the Roman leader of Cyprus but a sorcerer was hindering his efforts. Paul in the spirit realm was warring with the demonic power so it would not prevent the proconsul leader's salvation. In the spirit of glory, Paul used a great weapon that dealt a blow to the sorcerer- the weapon of prophetic glory where he prophesied that he would be blind and instantly the sorcerer went blind for days.

Did you notice that when Peter prophesied to Ananias and Saphirah, concerning their death, the glory of God was moving? Multitudes were joining the apostles and the glory of the Spirit was everywhere, which culminated in what I call a *prosperity revival*. Because of their deception in the gory, Peter prophetically declared that they would die and after questioning them, they instantly died. (Acts 5:1-12). This is a very striking narrative which many people have a hard time comprehending. Why was this sin so harshly and swiftly judged when surely there were greater sins committed in the New Testament church? Why were the people who mocked those speaking in new tongues at Pentecost not judged as harshly? It's because the glory in Acts 5 was considerably greater and had increased from glory to glory. This is what I call *judgement glory*. The apostles were not just laying hands on the sick anymore but Peter's shadow alone was healing the sick. Because the glory had gone to a greater level, so did the prophetic gift and the swiftness of its fulfilment. God did not want this new move to be hindered because of sin. That is why you need to be careful of careless words you speak flippantly while in the glory realm. I believe a new chapter of judgement glory may be on the horizon, just as it was with Ananias and Saphirah, hence believers are strongly cautioned to consecrate themselves before operating in the glory realm.

Death is a manifestation or a result of the departure of the glory of God.

It is worth exploring the divine truth that there is no life outside the environment of God's glory and that is why immediately after being disconnected from the glory of God, Adam and Eve started developing symptoms of aging which eventually lead to the degradation of their mortal bodies and death. There is a spiritual law that states that life corresponds to the environment. When you take a fish from water, it dies. When you pull a tree from the ground, it perishes. By the same token, when you separate a man from the environment of glory, he dies. That is why death is said to be the absence of God's glory.

The greatest tragedy in life is to lose the glory of God. The Bible records in 1 Samuel 4:21, an incident whereby the departure of the glory on earth was a tragedy graphically illustrated in the death of Eli, the high priest and judge of Israel. When he heard that the Ark of the Covenant, (*which represented the place where the glory of God manifested*), was captured by the philistines, he fell backwards and died of a broken neck. When Eli's daughter in law heard of his death as well as the death of her husband, she went into premature labour and gave birth to a son and before she died, she named him "*Ichabod*" which means, "*the glory of God has departed*" from Israel. Shiloh had been the centre of worship but until that moment, it never recovered that distinction. Philosophically speaking, death is the absence of the glory of God. Therefore, when we say that someone has died, what that actually means is that the glory of God, which is His spirit, has departed from the body. This is a typical scenario in the world today. The reason why there are alarming reports of deaths, constant wars, corruption, and infestation of evil in the world today is because of the absence of glory. The reason why government of nations are failing in all their economic and political endeavours is because of the absence of glory. Where churches fail to move in the supernatural to heal the sick, deliver the oppressed and raise the dead, it's because of the absence of the glory since it is the glory of God that raises the dead. Jesus taped into the realm of glory when he commanded Lazarus to come forth, hence, in the absence of God's glory, death continues to wreak havoc in the world. Becoming stagnant or settling for less than God's best because of circumstances is a sign that the glory of God is gone.

There is an intricate connection between the Kingdom, the Power and the Glory.

The relationship between the Kingdom, the Power and the Glory is that the Kingdom is what produces power and power is what reveals the glory. In Mathew 6:13, Jesus taught His disciples that whenever they pray, they should say, *"Yours is the kingdom, the power and the glory"*. This implies that each of these aspects is distinct. In simple terms, the Kingdom is *the message of heaven*. The power is the *ability of heaven*. And the glory is *the atmosphere or environment of heaven*. Jesus powerfully demonstrated the message of the gospel He carried and brought the environment of heaven to earth. This means that the kingdom is *the government of God,* the power is *the ability of God* and the glory is *the nature of God*. Therefore, the kingdom of heaven is in us hence, power flows through us to reveal the glory of God. The word *kingdom* refers to the *government of people under the authority of a king*. This implies that in our capacity as Kings and Priests, the kingdom of God is in us hence we can manifest the power of that kingdom anytime, anywhere for the glory of God to be revealed. Philosophically speaking, the kingdom must demonstrate the power so that the power will reveal the glory of God.

Everything in the Kingdom revolves around the glory of God. The purpose of a Kingdom is to produce power and power is supposed to reveals God's glory. God will not allow anything to happen that will not bring glory to him. If it does not bring glory to Him, that thing will not happen. Nothing will happen that will not bring glory unto the Lord (Romans 8:28-30). In the midst of our most harrowing experiences and defining moments, in a time when everything looks bleak and sober, non- repairable, and hard to imagine otherwise, the Lord is redeeming each and every moment in our time for us to ascribe honour, glory, power, dominion, majesty, and might, glory to Jesus!

There is a certain level of persecution that produces a greater weight of glory.

It is important to unveil the divine truth that contrary to what many people would want to hear, persecution produces a greater weight of glory. To cement this revelation with reference to scriptural evidence, Paul contends that *tribulation brings forth perseverance, and perseverance, character and character hope* (Romans 5:3, 4). In a related scripture, He continues to emphasise that *For our light afflictions and suffering, which is but for a moment, is working for us a far more exceeding and eternal weight of glory* (2 Corinthians 4:17). He concludes this revelation by admonishing the saints that *if you are reproached for the Name of Christ, blessed are you, for the Spirit of glory and of God rests upon you* (1 Peter 4:14). In other words, there is a measure of glory that rests upon an individual for having gone through persecution. Take note that in the context of this scripture, the phrase *"Suffering for Christ"* does not mean suffering sicknesses nor suffering for our mistakes, instead, it means persecution for His name's sake. This is because some people bring persecution on themselves because of their own foolishness, sin and error, thinking that they are actually suffering for Christ. This is not what persecution for Christ means. Suffering for Christ is when you receive persecution for being Christ-like or for obeying and acting on His Word. However, this revelation does not infer that believers should go around looking for opportunities to be persecuted because the glory of God can still rest upon an individual through other millions ways besides persecution.

The life of God "Zoe" is grossly manifested in the glory realm.

In the natural realm, there are different kinds of lives, such as animal life, plant life and human life. By the same token, there is only one kind of life that rules and governs in the supernatural and the most fundamental life is the *"Zoe,"* which is the *God kind of life* which He has invested upon humanity. This is the life which God uses. It is the spiritual oxygen which God breathes; it flows profusely from God, like a river to touch every life, creation, object in both the spirit and natural realm. If that life for example is imparted upon the ground, even the soul will start to be productive. That is why God declared in 2 Chronicles 7:14 that *"If my people called by my name will humble themselves and seek my face I will answer them and heal their land"*. In the context of this scripture, the phrase *"heal their land"* speaks of this impartation of the God kind of life upon human soil. If this God kind of life flows through the air, it changes the atmosphere and if it flows through the land, it makes it fertile and if it flows through the seas, it makes bitter waters sweet. Anything that comes into contact with the life of God receives life. That is why when the glory of God comes, we witness extraordinary miracles where by malfunctioning electric gargets such a stoves, refrigerators, ovens and even cars are supernaturally repaired such that they start functioning normally.

The glory of God is what produces this "Zoe" the God kind of life hence if you want to operate in the realm where you are continually filled with the life of God, just bask in His glory. To cement this revelation with reference to further scriptural evidence, the Bible records an incident whereby *a dry piece of wood was laid in the presence of God and on the following day, it had developed buds and produced almond fruits* (Numbers 17:1). This implies that the life of God had flowed through the dry piece of wood and caused it to produced something amazing. That is why the glory of God can be imparted upon broken or dysfunctional electric gargets such as cars, refrigerators Television sets, cell phones, stoves and other sound appliances such that they start functioning properly. In other words the same life of God that flows through a sick body and brings about a healing is the same life that flows through any object either steel, iron or wood and makes it work. This is the same dimension of Glory that raises the dead back to life.

The glory provides a spiritual covering to subjects in the natural realm.

In the modern Christian cycles, there is a principle that is so overemphasised by those who intend to groom upcoming ministers and that's a principle of *spiritual covering*. Unknown to the masses, when someone seek for a spiritual covering from another minister, he is actually seeking for the covering of the glory because a spiritual covering can only be provided for in the *Glory Realm*. Therefore, when a minister undertakes to provide a spiritual covering to a ministry, what he is saying is that he is connecting that ministry to a greater dimension of God's glory. Without the glory of God, no one can provide any significant spiritual covering. Concerning the spiritual covering of the glory, it is recorded in Exodus 13: 21-22 that,

The Lord went before them by day in a pillar of a cloud, to lead them the way; and by night in a pillar of fire, to give them light. ; to go by day and night. He took not away the pillar of cloud by day, nor the pillar of fire by night, from before the people.

It is evident in the above scripture that the cloud by day and fire by night were divergent manifestations of the glory of God. When the children of Israel came out of Egypt, they carried their own atmosphere of glory with them. As they journeyed in the wilderness for forty years, the heat didn't scorch them by day, neither did they freeze to death in the biting cold at night. Why? Because of the atmosphere of glory which protected them. At night, they were canopied by a pillar of fire that kept them warm, while a pillar of cloud was present during the day to keep the heat away. The spiritual covering is therefore God's spiritual clouds that envelop a ministry and provides a thick protection from the stratagems of the enemy. That is why the Bible *says he who dwells in the secret place shall abide in the shadow of the almighty*. A secret place is a realm of glory; it's a perfect environment or covering where the glory of God is highly contracted. It is called a *secret place* because in that realm, the glory of God has not yet been revealed to the masses, except to the one who dwells in it. In that realm of glory, sickness is declared illegal, poverty is considered illegitimate, demons are not allowed to enter, and death is not permitted to reign. If we stay in the Glory realm, the enemy's not a problem because he's not there. Some people are staying in the realm where he is. That is why they are always huffing and puffing, fighting the fight of faith. They haven't learned to enter God's rest. When you enter the rest of God, you know the victory is yours, but the battle is the Lord's. He wants you to stay before His face and praise Him. As you praise Him, you're unaware of what is going on around you because the atmosphere changes when you praise.

CHAPTER SIX

THE HIGHER REALMS AND DEGREES OF MANIFESTATION OF GOD'S GLORY

It is worth exploring the divine truth that multitudes of Christians have not yet discovered what they can do in the glory of God. In other words, they are not aware of the limitless opportunities available for them in glory. The greater truth is that there are new realms, higher dimensions and greater depths in God's glory which are available for exploration and discovery by the new creation believer. When Paul declared in 1Corinthians 2:9 that *no eye has seen nor has it entered into the heart of man what He has prepared for those who love Him*, He spoke of these new realms of glory which mankind have not yet fully comprehended in this end time season. This concurs with God's call in Jeremiah 33:3 that, *"Call unto me and I will answer thee and show you great and mighty things which you knowest not."* This speaks of the availability of boundless opportunities which God has prepared for us in the glory. Moreover, the riches in Christ glory described by Paul in Philippians 4:19 speaks of these realms, depths and dimensions of glory.

It is a divine truth that Christianity is characterised by a progressive spiritual momentum and drive, heaven ward in Christ Jesus. According to the scripture, our lives are programmed to move progressively from one realm or level of glory to a higher one. Now, the problem here is that when we overstay our time in the outer court, or refuse to migrate into the glory of the Holiest of all, we potentially become a people of multiple personalities failing to see beyond the confines of this limited dimension. For example, in the principle of the Ark of the Covenant as it crossed over Jordan, the Israelites were instructed to follow in progressive spiritual momentum with the ark, for they had not passed this way before (Joshua 3:4).

The word of God tells us that we migrate from glory to glory, from faith to faith and I believe from realm to realm. This implies that according to God's original plan and purpose for humanity, we are designed to constantly change in every sphere of our spiritual endeavours and never stay stagnant. We are constantly evolving into the image and likeness of God, moving into the next realm of glory. However, it must be expressly understood in this regard that our old nature cannot take us into the places and territories of the spirit God wants us to walk in. In order to move into the next season or realm of glory, we must let the old traditions, methods and mentalities to fall away so that we can step into newer and deeper territories of glory in Christ. That is why in this end time season, there is a new company and unique breed of people arising, who shall move in the dimension of the Spirit to unreservedly exhibit the glory of God like the abundance of clouds releasing rain. There is a greater dimension of glory that God has called us to walk into but we must learn to step out of the boat and trust God that He will lead us to a place called, *"there"* so that we can bring *"there"* which is the glory into *"here"*, which is the present. The Bible further unveils the divine truth that *in Him we live, move and have our being* and this implies that to *"move"* is the call of living the God kind of life.

There are pivotally important revelations the Lord gave me while in the midst of prophetic worship pertaining how we could constantly move or migrate to higher realms of glory. The abundance of these revelations shared below has a lot to do specifically with continuous, progressive and forceful spiritual momentum, the active rhythm of the Spirit in remaining still or moving forward with the *cloud* and not with the *crowd*, going forward without distraction and despair, hence with this type of knowledge, nothing will either deny, defy, delay or dismay God's eternal purpose in your life.

The Realm of Transfiguration

Transfiguration is a spectacular change in the countenance of either a human or physical object into a glorious spiritual form under the influence of the glory.

In its original context in Greek, the word for transfigure imply that whatever is inside has come out and the true essence has been expressed. This is a higher realm of glory which believers can enter into especially in this end time dispensation. Jesus made a physical demonstration of how we can be elevated into this realm through His appearance in glory with Elijah and Moses. The Bible records in Mathew 17:2-3 that,

> *During Jesus's transfiguration, His face shone like the sun, and His clothes became as white as the light. And behold Moses and Elijah appeared to them, talking with him. Behold a bright cloud overshadowed them and suddenly, a voice came out of the cloud saying "This is My beloved son, in whom I am pleased, listen to Him".*

It must be expressly understood right form the onset that transfiguration was not just a once off spiritual phenomenon as some believers presume, but a realm which is available for believers in the New Testament to tap into. If it was a secret, then Jesus would not have dared showing the glory publicly to His disciples. Multitudes of people across a broad spectrum of charismatic faith inadvertently presume that transfiguration is a once in a life time experience which only Jesus encountered and non-one else can tap into that realm. But, the question is: If this realm was not for us, then why would Jesus let his disciples to see or have a divine experience which never concerned them? The greater truth is that such an overwhelming divine experience was pointing to the unimaginable rays of God's glory which believers would be able to practically display to the nations of the world hence, Jesus had to allow them to catch a glimpse of what they were about to do.

I never understood how Jesus would take Peter, John and James to the Mount of Transfiguration. You would think Jesus would want them to evangelise with what they had seen and experienced. Peter was caught up in the height of that glory when Jesus came out and said, *"Tell no man"* (Marks 9:9). Why? Because Peter saw the realm but he had not conceived the realm. This is evidenced by his immature remark that, *"Lord, let us build three houses, one for you, one for Elijah and one for Moses"*. The secret of it is, when you have conceived a realm, your voice carries that realm. Peter could have said, *"Lord, let the same dimension of glory that is upon you, Elijah and Moses come upon us"* and it could have been granted. But Peter had not yet received that realm and that is why Jesus told him not to say anything. You see, you have to catch the realm. A day has come when you will not necessarily have to minister what you have studied, instead, you have to catch the flow of the river to know the stream of God.

Moreover, when Jesus declared to us that, *"Greater things than these shall you do"* (John 14:12), transfiguration is one of those greater things which Jesus manifested on earth and that realm of Glory is available to be explored by believers in this season. As a matter of fact, when Jesus declared in the first part of this verse that, *"The things which I do, you shall do them also"*, He was not just talking about healing the sick and casting out devils. Instead, that portion of the scripture also incorporates His divine experiences in the glory, one of which is the transfiguration.

Now the question is: What was the purpose of Jesus's transfiguration?

Firstly, to manifest the glory of God publicly, unreservedly and unconditionally, as a way of granting access to humanity in all extreme quarters of life, to experience God's glory. At the moment of transfiguration, the disciples were able to see who Jesus was on the inside in a physical, visible and tangible way. Likewise, the expression of transfiguration reveals the fact that what is contained within us, the glory is not a secret hence, can no longer be hidden or held back, but must explode, burst forth and overcome the flesh. His transfiguration demonstrates what we can experience in Him. In other words, He has opened a way for us to walk in the glory. Secondly, until the moment of transfiguration, Jesus had operated under the *anointing* of the Holy Spirit but through this manifestation, He showed three of His disciples *the glory that was available for them to explore.* In other words, He ushered a paradigm shift and drastic transition *from the realm of the anointing into the realm of glory.* When they were transfigured they were able to see Moses and Elijah with Jesus. Metaphorically speaking, Moses represents the *law,* which is the logos or written word; Elijah represents the church or God's power; Jesus represents the Kingdom of God while the cloud represents the glory. Therefore through this revelation and manifestation, Jesus revealed to His disciples that He would bring or usher His kingdom, His power and His glory in abundance. *But, how did his disciples know that the two figures standing next to Jesus were Moses and Elijah?.* This is because in the presence of God people are known as they are regardless of the time that may have separated them. In other words, in the glory, things are not learnt but revealed. In the spirit, we do not learn things. Instead, we supernaturally know things. This is revelation knowledge which automatically comes from the spirit realm as an impartation into our spirit without any study.

The truth is that the glory of God has a traceable progressive record of impact since its unveiling in the Garden of Eden till transfiguration. Now, throughout the Old Testament, God had been calling men to operate in His glory progressively in divergent ways. Initially, His glory came in the garden, then it came on the face of a man in Mount Sinai, then it came in a tent in the wilderness, then it came in a building or temple in Jerusalem and finally He sent out His glory in abundance and without measure and this time He sent it in the form of a man, His only Son, and when Jesus Christ came into the world, He was the glory of God in a body and that is why the bible proclaims in John 1:14 that *the Word became flesh and dwelt amongst us and* that, *"We beheld His glory."* So during transfiguration, Jesus pulled back His flesh and He revealed the effulgence of His glory. In other words, He showed that He was none other than the Shekinah, the same glory, the same essential reality of God revealed in light in the Old Testament that dwell in the temple, that dwell in the tabernacle, that shone in the face of Moses and that came in the garden and walked with man. That glory was now back and God in Christ was saying, *"Will you receive my glory?* That is why God cried out, *"This is My beloved Son, in whom I'm pleased, Listen to Him."* By these words, God figuratively meant that, *"I have released My Glory for you in fullness, receive it, walk in it and demonstrate it".*

This is the same measure of glory which God has made available for every believer in this end time season, to unreservedly exhibit, propagate and proliferate to the nations of the world on behalf of the kingdom. That is why in this end time season which marks the conclusion of God's eternal plan for the earth, many believers across the globe are going to have divine experiences of transfiguration as God unreservedly manifests His latter glory on planet earth.

The Realm of Transformation

Transformation refers to a deep, profound, radical and remarkable change in the quality of a human spirit, resulting from a direct contact with God's glory and whose effects are drastically felt on the human body and mind in the natural realm.

The difference between *transformation* and *transfiguration* is that while transformation is the change in the quality of the human spirit, transfiguration is so profound such that it even changes the countenance of the physical body. It is of paramount importance to unveil the divine truth that the greatest weight of glory is *transformation*. The absolute demonstration of God's power takes place when the heart of an individual is transformed in the spirit man right from the time he is born again until eternity.

Therefore, God is calling every believer to change because He wants to take us into another level. He wants to do a new thing (Isaiah 43:19). As a matter of fact, a generation that does not embrace change will not impact the world. However, the only movement that can generate transformation in society is the outpouring of the glory of God. In Mount Sinai, *Moses' face was transformed into a shining face by the glory and no one dared to stare at him* (Exodus 34:29-35). This was an epitome of transformation by the glory of God. The Bible concurs that we are transformed by the glory. Stephen saw heaven open up and the glory of God. In other words, he was caught up into the glory. Paul admonishes us in Romans 12:2 saying,

"Do not be conformed to this world but be **TRANSFORMED** *by the renewing of your mind that you may prove what is the good and perfect will of God".*

The Greek word for transformed is *"metamorphoo"*. *Meta* means among, with, after, behind and *"morphoor"* means to form or fashion. Metamorphosis, therefore means to change into another form, to transform or transfigure just like a caterpillar dies in its old form in order to be transformed into a beautiful butterfly. The same term is used in Matthew 17:2 with regard to the transfiguration of Jesus. The main idea of the verb is to die to one form of life in order to be born into another. The opposite of transformed is *"conformed"*. The Greek word for conformed is *suschematizo* . This term comes from the two route words, *sun* which means with and *schema* which means figure, form, shape or appearance. Thus to be *"conformed"* refers to adaptation or taking the shape, form or appearance of the pattern of this world. When we *conform* to something, we stop being *transformed.*

The question that you are probably asking yourself is: How do I get transformed by the glory of God? In reality, as we spend time in the presence of God, we are transformed into His likeness. The greater truth is that what changes the person is not the time spent in church but time spent in God's presence. For example, if we were to expose a new believer to the presence of God for one hour and then compare him to a Christian who has been born again for ten years but has never experienced the presence of God, the new believer will look more like Jesus than the old born again because of exposure to the presence. There are many changes that we have to submit to such as renewed minds, character, approaches to worship, preaching styles, manner and length of services and the removal of rigid structures that impede the Holy Spirit from freely moving.

Secondly, transformation comes when we continually inundate our spirit with God's word. The Bible affirms in 2 Corinthians 3:18 that,

All of us as with unveiled face (because we continued to behold (in the word of God) as in a mirror the glory of God, are constantly being trans formed into His very own image in ever increasing splendour and from one degree of glory to another, for this comes from the Lord, who is the spirit.

To provide a historical background to this revelation, when the glory was present on Moses's face, he covered it with a veil so that people would not see the glory depart from his face (Exodus 34:29-35). That glory was temporary but we now have unrestricted freedom in the glory. The veil has been removed and we can look upon the glory of God in the face of Jesus continually as if we were looking at it through a mirror. Each time we look into the *"mirror"*, which is the word of God, a direct and positive effect is produced in our hearts and minds. Imagine standing in front of a mirror in which the reflected image is the perfect version of you. As you look upon that image, you begin to see yourself in the spirit as God sees you, His completed work, created in His likeness and image. This experience causes two things to happen. Firstly, you begin to change and conform into the image you see in a mirror, which is Jesus. Secondly, you begin to reflect and manifest the glory within you in front of other people.

In a view to present a more elaborative discussion on the revelation of transformation by the glory, the verb *transformed* occurs in the continuous present, which indicates that we are constantly being transformed and moving from glory to glory. When Aaron's leadership was challenged, the Bible tells us in Numbers 16:5 that *he spoke to Korah and all his company saying, "Tomorrow morning the Lord will show who is His and who is holy, and will cause him to come near to Him".*

Then in Chapter 17:2, God said to Moses,

"Speak to the children of Israel, and get from them a rod from each father's house, all their leaders according to their fathers' houses – twelve rods. Write each man's name on his rod. And you shall write Aaron's name on the rod of Levi. For there shall be one rod for the head of each father's House".

Then Moses placed the rods before the Lord in the tabernacle of witness. Bear in mind that the tabernacle of witness points to the Ark of the Covenant and that is where the glory of God dwells. So, twelve rods were placed in the tabernacle of witness. *Now it came to pass on the next day that Moses went into the tabernacle of witness, and behold, the rod of Aaron of the house of Levi, had sprouted and brought forth buds, had produced blossoms and yielded ripe almonds.* Wow! A dry rod producing flowers and fruits within 24 hours!! This is a manifestation of transformation in the glory. This was a creative miracle. That is what the glory of God can do, when a conducive platform or atmosphere is created for it to manifest. When we focus on God's glory, when we seek His glory, when we hunger for His glory, when we sit in the glory of His presence, a transformation takes place in our lives. And in order to understand how that transformation takes place in our life, we need to see the breakdown of God's glory in order that we can grow in God's glory. That is why in the glory creative miracles takes place, old people become younger, bald heads grow hair and toothless people are filled with teeth and even the dead are raised.

Evidently, there is transformation in the glory. Ideally speaking, no one can jump into a pool of water and comes out dry. By the same token, no one can mingle with the glory of God and come out the same. The evidence of having dwelt, mingled or stayed in the presence of God's glory is transformation that takes place in our spirits. To cement this revelation with further scriptural evidence, After Meshach, Shadrack and Abednego refused to partake of the delicacies of the King's palace (Daniel 1: 15), at the end of ten days their features appeared better and well-nourished in the flesh than all the young men who ate the portion of the King's delicacies. Moreover, God gave them knowledge and skill in all literature and wisdom and Daniel had understanding in all visions and dreams. These kids were ten times smarter than the rest. They had deeper knowledge in the arts, science, and literature of the Chaldeans, even though they had gone for such a long time without food. How possible could that happen in the natural realm? They had so rubbed in, mingled and infused themselves with the glory of God such that their bodies were renewed to the extent that they even functioned in super intelligence. That is why it is possible for an old person to be changed to look younger if he constantly stays or comes into contact with the glory of God. That is why even dead bodies are raised back to life in the glory because there is a transformation that takes place as a result of coming into contact with God's glory. That is why in this end time season where God unleashes the fullness of this glory on humanity, deep creative miracles such as the growth of new body parts, increase or decrease in height, change in natural complexion are going to increasingly become a common phenomenon in the Body of Christ due to transformation by the glory. Glory to the Most High God!

The Realm of Translation

This is a temporary or permanent movement of earthly objects specifically humans under the influence of God's glory, from the realm of the natural into the realm of the spirit without reversing backwards.

This is a product of divine orchestration in the spirit realm where God allows believers through His grace to have a foretaste of His glory. It is of paramount significance to highlight right from the onset the fact that translation can either be *permanent* or *temporary* depending on God's sovereign will and purpose. In order to unveil an in-depth understanding of the concept of *translation,* it is best that we illustrate it with reference to natural phenomenon because the realm of the natural is an exact representation of the spiritual realm. According to the law of gravity, if you throw an object for a limited distance upwards into the atmosphere, it will always come down due to the force of gravity. However, if the same object is thrown upwards and reaches a certain distance into the atmosphere, it does not come down to earth. Instead, it continues to migrate upward and forward only. The same applies to the glory. If you stay in the glory for a limited time period, you may always bounce back to your earthy realm and senses. However, if you stay constantly or long enough in the glory, there is a breakthrough line or point which you can reach in the spirit dimension whereby you just get caught up into the glory of God to such an extent that it becomes like your second nature. In that realm, you continue to migrate heavenward and you might not come back to the natural realm anymore. Enoch was catapulted right into God's throne room this way. In other words, he walked into the glory of God and was caught up. Elijah was also caught up in glory in a similar fashion as he stood in the presence of God 24/7. Likewise, Jesus was caught up in the cloud, which represents God's glory, right into heaven after His resurrection from the dead. Therefore, believers are cautioned never to put God in a box because in the atmosphere of glory, it is possible for anybody in this end time season to be caught up in the like manner, glory to God!

In fact, the glory of God is such that if there is a great measure of it upon our lives, it will cause a transformation and a lifting up. I believe one of the things that will happen in the last days is that God will place His glory in a greater measure in the church until the church is so full of God's glory that the very glory of God causes us to be translated into His presence. The first was Enoch who walked with God and he was translated. The second was Moses because he had tasted God's glory so much that even though he died, the Bible says in Deuteronomy 34 that God buried him. God specially sent an angel to bury Moses because of the dimension of glory that he had operated in. We even see in this context, the devil contending over the body of Moses because he wanted an impartation of glory form Moses's body. The book of Jude recorded how Michael, the Archangel came to collect Moses' body. Now that was unusual. It was special. In the Old Testament, there is no record of God collecting the corpses of any saints besides Moses. The Old Testament saints who died were kept in a place until Jesus came. Moses went there but because he had tasted and touched the glory of God so much, God sent an angel Michael to set him free, took him out from Hades, resurrected his body and raised him up again. This is why in Matthew 17: 2-3, we see him talking to Jesus on the mount of Transfiguration. He was translated into God's glory. Why did God do that for Moses? Because Moses had partaken of God's glory to a level that provoked elevation and promotion in the dimension of the spirit, by God Himself. God's glory can cause the dead to rise again and become living. The third person is Elijah, who was caught up in a chariot of fire and his mantle fell on Elisha.

Prophetically speaking, in the last days, many believers will be translated, some permanently while others temporary. Many shall be catapulted right into the throne room of God to explore the glory of the heavenly realm. This dimension of glory is already surfacing in the Body of Christ in this season. For example, in our ministry, almost every Sunday, we send some of our members on study tours to heaven. During these ministerial sessions, some people are translated into the future where they see God's plan and purpose for their lives. Since we are fast approaching the end times, the Holy Spirit wants to accelerate our learning. These study tours of heaven will reveal many secrets for our times. Under the direction of the Holy Spirit, the minister randomly picks a few members who were chosen by the Holy Spirit to make a trip to heaven. He asks them to prepare by confessing their sins and asking for grace. Once they are ready, the minister points his forefinger at them, one by one, and they fall to the ground like dead men and women. He asks the ushers to examine them and roll them on the floor and there is no response from them. Their breathing and their heartbeats even slows down considerably. They are then carried to the stage for some time before the minister claps his hands to wake them up. They then go to the mike to make their reports to the congregation about their experiences in the spirit world.

This is the highest level of operation or life in God's glory. The Bible says in Genesis 5:24 that *Enoch walked with God and was caught up to heaven.* In other words, you start with walking with God first and when you have matured in that realm, God can translate you straight to heaven. *Why was Enoch translated?* Because he functioned so much in the realm of God's glory to the extent that his whole physical body got transformed. In other words, he found he was no more breathing in the natural. He was breathing in the spiritual just like angels. He lived like a spirit being on earth and that was when the translation took place. Elijah was another man who walked close with God and there was no one who moved and functioned in the realm of God's glory like he did. Elijah walked with God, performed miracles, closed and opened heavens at his own discretion and reached a certain quality of the spirit which qualified him to be catapulted into this glorious realm and chariots of fire came and took him.

Elijah walked so close with God that angelic visitations were like contact with human beings. You see him at the end of his life, in 2 Kings 1 and 2; he seemed to be always with God. He even made a remarkable statement: *"I am Elijah who stands in the presence of God."* This is to tell you that he stood in such presence of God's glory that earthy mortals could not reach. When he was lonely, God sent His angels because there were not many saints in the Old Testament who had entered that realm. There was a level whereby he reached, he walked so close with God that when he was about to complete his ministry, the Lord said, *"Come straight home".*

Jesus was translated to heaven after His resurrection and the Bible records that as they looked up, they saw Him enter a cloud until he was no more. *This is the highest realm that a man will ever enter in God.* In this realm, you don't taste death or decay but you are taken to heaven straight away. Unknown to multitudes of believers, it is possible not to taste death or the grave. If Old Testament folks walked with God without the regenerate spirit but functioned so much in the glory to the extent that they were translated to heaven, how much more us, the new creation with the indwelling presence of God's glory in our spirit? If only you could catch this revelation, you will be the next wonder in this world. The difference between the realm of visitation and translation is that visitation is temporary while translation can be both temporary and permanent. In both realms, the will of God is paramount for one to encounter such a divine experience. Paul spoke about the abundance of revelations in the *6th dimension* which is the realm of visitation but in this last dispensation, we will talk about the abundance of revelations of the *7th dimension* which is the realm of translation, as it becomes a widespread global phenomenon, glory to God!

The Realm of Transition

Transition refers to the progressive spiritual migration and paradigm shift from one condition, form, stage, place or activity into the next level. It is a drastic, profound and impactful change from one level, dimension, sphere or realm of glory into a distinctively new realm of glory in the spirit.

It is of paramount significance to unveil the divine truth that the life of a believer is designed in such a way that involves progressively migrating forwardly from one dimension, realm, sphere, and glory of the Spirit into a distinctively new realm of glory for Kingdom advancement. That is why the life of a Christian is designed to move and function progressively upwards and forward only, there is no other alternative route in the spirit dimension. By the same token, the Church is programmed to transition from glory to glory, from faith to faith, from conception to perfection, from the cross to the throne and from the realm of the anointing to the realm of glory. Likewise, the apostolic dimension shifts and launches the church's mentality from church to kingdom, from visitation to habitation, from encouragement to equipping, from schooling to retooling, from teaching to training, from impartation to activation, from revelation to demonstration, and from global apostolic reformation to global transformation.

That is why we have described transition as the passing from one condition, form, stage, place, and activity to another. Spiritually speaking, it is the period of passing out of Egypt, through the wilderness, to the Promised Land. Transitioning involves a delicate and intense process of change. It may even involve *transformation* and *translation* (Colossians 1:13; 2 Samuel 3:10; 1 Thessalonians 4:6-18; Hebrews 11:5; 12:26-28 Romans 12:2). Transitioning is *purpose through process.* Transitioning requires personal confrontation of oppressive positions and limited mentalities (2 Corinthians 10:3-5; Deuteronomy 7:1-5; 12:1-2: 1 Tim. 1:18; Acts 10:38). Transitioning is linked with spiritual maturity. It is one aspect to be spiritual and yet another to be mature. Transitioning is not exclusive to the spiritual dimension only, but is applicable to the natural as well. That is why it is evident in physical and mental growth, from childhood to adulthood, through various stages (1 Corinthians 13:11; 14:20; 15:46; 1 Peter 2:2; 2 Peter 3:18). In a spiritual sense, there is a transition from a state of being spiritual babies into spiritual infants and from spiritual teenagers to the mature level of son ship in Christ

Transitioning is *apostolic* and *prophetic* in principle, nature, character, scope and dimension. Transition recognizes the important stages and development of the saints. Whether individual or corporate in calibre, transitioning acknowledges the need to migrate into greater spheres and frequencies of the Spirit through the active force of Spiritual momentum. Thus, transitioning here enables you to pioneer new calibrations in the Spirit. (Hebrews 6:5; Deuteronomy 31:2-3; Romans 8:37-39). Moreover, transitioning is seen in the scripture from name change to nature change. For example, Abram became Abraham, Sarai to Sarah, and Jacob becoming Israel. Jacob was created but Israel was formed (Isaiah 43:1; 44:1-2; Galatians 4:19). Transitioning is a way of life. From so called losses to gains. It is inevitable. From kindergarten to College, and from being single to become one in marriage, transition is inevitable. Being married doesn't make you a man or a woman. You must develop manhood before marriage or ministry (Genesis 2:24).

The three dimensions of Moses' Tabernacle reveals the present truth of the progressive spiritual maturity of the saints. It reveals the maturing process, and the migration into new realities and thresholds of the Spirit (Exodus 25:9). Transition takes place from outer court to Holy Place and from holy place to Holy of Holies, from water baptism to Spirit baptism to fire baptism, from the Called to the chosen, from Egypt through the wilderness to the Promised Land, from Justification through sanctification to glorification, from Divine healing to divine health, from Workers to worshipers, from the former rain to the Latter, from Gleanings to harvest, from 1st Heavens 2nd Heavens to the 3rd Heavens, from the door to the gate, from Visitation to manifestation, from habitation to glorification, from blessing to inheritance. This speaks of being progressively catapulted into higher realms of glory.

In this end time season, there is a definitely new pattern being developed, a kingdom people who are defining new ways and technologies through new frequencies in relating one another to the eternal purposes of God. There is a new breed of apostolic people, now and on the rise, whose message is sweeping across all the frontiers of Christian traditions and knowledge into a higher realm of glory by taking over the world and populating it with the glory of God, to make it the headquarters of God's glory. However, the new paradigm and dimensional shifting will not be embraced by all, especially the general masses. Therefore, don't expect a lot of folks to align themselves with what the Lord is speaking into the corporate progression of His people. For there remains the civil war between *"dispensational mathematicians"* and proponents of *"Kingdom Now."* Many still hold to a particular scheme of teaching of defeatism, a negative gospel and industry of fear. Such fear has become the basis for sprawling organizations world over, with no hint or view of the glorious church of the end times.

Nevertheless, there is a cry of the Spirit for radical change and transitioning for the body of Christ to a glorious church in perfection and glory. It is a people who are consumed in the eternal purpose of God, who live by His design and not by personal crisis. These people are none other than the corporate glory of the Lord, a people of His manifest and eternal purpose, a people of a brand new day. A unique breed of people who shall excel into new frontiers of knowledge. A people who shall vanquish beyond into new thresholds and portals of His unlimited glory into a realm where they become His life in the midst of death, His joy in the midst of sorrow, and His peace in the midst of the storm. A people who shall become that venue and vehicle of expression, which brings light out of shadows and dark worlds, with more impartation and activation following. This is the calibre of believers God is raising in this end time season, to function in the realm of His glory like never before.

The Realm of Divine Transportation

Transportation is a divinely orchestrated migration or movement of a natural object from the realm of the natural through the tidal waves of the spirit into the realm of the spirit under the directorship of the Holy Spirit and without changing its physical properties.

There is a realm of God's glory called *divine transportation* in the spirit. This is a divine experience whereby believers are divinely transported to various places in the spirit when the Holy Spirit wants to accomplish certain tasks with speed and acceleration. Although this is a spectacular realm, it is not a new spiritual phenomenon in the Bible. The reality of this divine experience was manifested when Philip was caught up in the glory of the spirit to Azotus, when Elijah used to disappear into the spirit dimension and when Paul was caught up into the third heavens to behold the glory of God and when Paul was divinely transported in the spirit to behold the order in the Colossian churches.

This is the most spectacular and peculiar realm in the spirit dimension. It is a much higher realm than the realm of trances and open vision in that in this realm, not only do you see and associate with angels, not only is the spirit world revealed to you but you begin to explore the whole spirit world. It is a realm of exploration and discovery. The scripture records in Isaiah 5:8 that *"They that wait upon Lord shall be renewed of their strength. They shall rise of the wings like eagles, they shall walk and not faint, they shall run and not get tired"*. In most cases people who interpret this scripture usually emphasize a lot on the aspect of waiting and they hardly get to catch a revelation of what it says one would be able to do after the waiting process. In essence, this scripture gives a revelation and insight of dimensions of transportation in the realm of the spirit. It provides a foundation and background for understanding how transportation takes place in the realm of the spirit. In essence, when the scripture says that those that wait upon Lord will *walk, run and fly,* it is not talking about physical walking, running and flying. God has nothing to do with your physical walking and running since physical exercise profits a little but Godly exercise profits unto all things. Instead, what the scripture is talking about are dimensions in the spirit where one walks, runs and flies in the spirit. When someone is moving in the realm of transportation, it's either he is flying, running or walking in the spirit. This implies that in the Christian journey or race, there are different types of people, that is; *those who are walking in the spirit, those who are running in the spirit and those who are flying in the spirit.* The question is: In which category do you belong? I know that it might sounds a little bit strange but you got to experience it. There are different ways and means of Holy Ghost transportation. In the physical realm, there are different modes of transportation such as cars, bikes and planes hence, as it is in the natural realm, so it is in the spirit realm.

It is of paramount importance therefore to highlight at this stage that due to its diverse nature or form, this realm has THREE different dimensions: Walking in the spirit, running in the spirit and disappearance in the spirit. In a view to enhance a significant level of understanding of the phenomenon of divine transportation, it is of paramount importance that we understand the tripartite nature of humanity. A human being is a triune being, meaning that you are a spirit, with a soul and live inside a body. The body relates to the physical world, the soul relates to the intellectual world and the spirit enables you to move, live and function in the realm of the spirit. However, it must be understood that while your body, soul and spirit are linked or interwoven to form a complete human being, your spirit is not limited to the body. Instead, it has the liberty to leave the body for a while and enter the spirit world without necessarily rendering the body lifeless. This understanding is the basis for *divine transportation*. Paul says in Galatians 5: 16-19,

"But I say, walk by the Spirit, and do not gratify the desires of the flesh. For the desires of the flesh are against the Spirit, and the desires of the Spirit are against the flesh; for these are opposed to each other to prevent you from doing what you would. But if you are led by the Spirit you are not under the law". And in Verse 25, he proceeds to say, *"If we live by the Spirit, let us also walk by the Spirit".*

This is a dimension in which your spirit is no more earth-bound or pulled by gravitational force of the law of sin and death. Instead, the spirit begins to soar into the heights of the heavenly realm. The experience in this dimension is like a leap of faith into the spirit realm. In the natural realm, we start by walking before we could run. The spirit realm is just like the physical realm in comparison. When a person is born and is a little child, they don't know how to walk yet. They learn to walk. They toddle at first, they stumble and fall, but after sometime your child learns to walk. In the spirit realm, it is the same way. When a person's spirit is newly born, they are like spiritual babies. The sad thing is, many people remain spiritual babies. But when our spirit man grows, it grows to the extent where it is not limited by the physical body. I'm not talking about astral travelling or forcibly doing things that are outside of God. I am not talking about desiring it either or purposefully trying to project yourself. Instead, I'm talking about fellowshipping with the Holy Spirit to the extent of yielding to God. When your spirit ascends to the deepest heavenly place, it is no more limited by the earthly realm and it becomes very easy for your spirit to enter the realm of transportation. When you pray, suddenly your spirit is there, and you know what is going on.

The Bible unveils the reality of this dimension in 2 Kings 5, whereby Elisha the prophet healed a man called Naaman from Leprosy. Naaman then offered some gifts to Elisha as a token of appreciation but he refused. It happened that Gehazi, Elisha's servant was covetous and went after those gifts. After that he then went back and stood before his master, and Elisha said to him, *"Where have you been Gehazi?"* And he said, *"Your servant went nowhere."* But Elisha said to him,

*"Did I not go with you in spirit when the man turned from his chariot to meet you?
Was it a time to accept money and garments, olive orchards and vineyards, sheep and oxen,
menservants and maidservants?*

This means that Elisha followed Gehazi in the Spirit. Elisha was taken up right at the moment as Gehazi was turning back not as he was going. The moment the man was turning back, Elisha was there in the spirit and he saw the whole thing and heard the whole thing except they could not see him for he was in the spirit world. His body was at home but it's only his spirit that followed him. In the context of the scripture, Elisha says, *"was I not with you when you went?"* and since Gehazi and Naaman were not running but walking, it means that even Elisha's spirit was walking with them.

In the realm of the spirit, there were times when in prayer the Lord can take us into various places, and homes of people, usually for certain purposes and reasons, to pray for them or just to show something and it is through this realm that you get to be enlightened on what happens in people's lives behind the scenes. For example, Kenneth Hagin had an experience where one day he was transported in the spirit and he got into the car with a young girl and a young boy. And he was seated in the car behind them and went with them all the way as they drove into the park, committed sin and drove back. All the time Kenneth Hagin was sitting there. This implies that you might be in a certain country and want to go and see how thing are like in another country and you could just can go peep and then come back and on the following day people will be shocked when you call them to tell them of how things are in that country when in actual fact you have not been there for the whole year. I remember the day I was transported in the spirit to America. I had never been to America before but I was caught up in the spirit and I went and prayed for people and actually stopped someone who was about to have a medical operation. This is how powerful this dimension is in the area of ministry.

Moreover, sometimes it is possible for our spirits to leave our bodies and enter the spirit realm to impart other lives just like in the case of Paul where he says in Colossians 2: 5, *"For though I am absent in the flesh, yet I am with you in spirit, rejoicing to see your good order and the steadfastness of your faith in Christ."* Note that when he says *"my spirit is with you"*, it's not just a figure of speech because a figure of speech does not have the quality or the ability to see what is going on. But Paul says: *"I can see you and I can behold what you are doing."* This implies that his spirit was divinely transported into the Colossian churches and he could see, understand experience and know what they were going through. There are times when God gave him to know what was happening in the church of Colossae by a *supernatural visitation*. So, there are times in the spirit that you can be transported like Paul, where you are able to watch in the human level not so high up just like Paul could behold the order of the Colossians. I have heard some people say, giving testimonies that when they were in trouble they dreamt that I came and prayed for them at night. In reality, I was transported in the spirit and was actually there praying for them though they could not see me in the physical realm.

The Bible records an incident in 1 Kings 18:41 whereby Elijah declared that ", *I hear the sound of heavy rain*" and then he ran faster than King Ahab although the King was riding on a horse and he was on foot. This was not a physical run but a transportation in the spirit dimension. There is no record in the Bible of Elijah being an athlete. Elijah was not an athlete but he physically outran the King's horse which by nature was probably the fastest and most well fed horse in the country. How do you explain that phenomenon? This was not a physical run, it was a dimension of transportation in the spirit which Elijah tapped into. This is a realm and dimension in the spirit which Elijah entered and moved into and was carried by the wings of the spirit. Such a dimension is going to increasingly become a common phenomenon in the Body of Christ in these end times. I have heard a testimony of two man who were coming from a crusade and on their way home, rain caught up with them and the younger one ran faster ahead of the older one leaving him far behind. But then the Holy Spirit caught up with the older man who could not run physically and he was instantly catapulted into that realm of transportation and began to run extremely faster in the spirit such that he was home in few seconds. The distance of ten miles that could have taken an hour to reach, he actually covered it in seconds. The younger brother was shocked when he found him already home. This is the dimension of running in the spirit which I'm talking about.

When a person is transported in the dimension of the spirit, it is just his physical body tagging along with the spirit. But when your spirit is so used to that, the day will come when the revival of God will move so powerfully that people will be transported from different corners of the earth to various places to preach the gospel and then be transported back. But that will be a normal consequence because the spirit has been travelling a lot. When you are an intercessor, when you pray, your spirit can travel into a different realm, into a higher realm, and you do battle with spiritual forces. That is happening all the time. But when you have grown in God and your spirit has developed, it is no longer limited by any earthly boundaries. Instead, it moves and travels in the dimension of the spirit.

There is something about the development of our human spirit when it attains a certain quality and ability. The bible says in Acts 8:26-40 that *immediately after baptising the Ethiopian Eunuch in water, Philip was carried by the spirit to Azotus such that the Eunuch saw him no more.* In other words, he was carried by the tidal waves of the spirit in the spirit all the way to Azotus. In other words his physical body was transported and he few in the spirit. In essence, Philip was transported physically. His body had to take on a different physical quality in order to break the force of gravity. This is something that is physically not possible. So, under this dimension, the body takes on a very supernatural quality. There is a realm whereby your body crosses the line of the spirit. If your body doesn't cross that line, it is just subject to the spirit. But when your body crosses that line and enters into the spirit world the body takes on a different quality. This is a migration that takes place in the spirit when the Holy Spirit wants His job to be done with a sense of urgency. This is a realm of transportation. Such a realm is going to be popular in this last dispensation as the Holy Ghost wants to accomplish God's work with speed.

How is transportation in this dimension possible?

In this type of transportation, your physical body has yielded to a certain extent. It has to do with our relationship with our spirit, soul and our body. Some of us are not related properly to our physical bodies. If you are not related properly to your physical body you won't be able to experience all these manifestations. You must have a right relationship with our physical body. *So, when your physical body knows its place and is very yielded to the realm of the spirit, it can reach a stage where your spirit just carries it along.* The Spirit of God coming upon you, carries your body along. And at that time your physical body seem to take on a peculiar quality, which was never there in the natural. That is why the size of the blessing which a man can receive is proportional to the size of his spirit because the larger the spirit, the greater the blessing.

How does one enter the dimension of divine transportation in the spirit?

In the occult realm, which is a non-Christian realm, they have what you call *astral travelling*. Those who yield themselves to the occult state of spirit realm seem to be able to travel into that realm. But there is a realm that even the unbelievers who yield themselves utterly to the realm of the spirit seem to be able to move into. And for the unbelievers and the occult people to do that, they need a certain level of freedom from their body. There are different levels in which our body is related to our soul and our spirit. Let's say this bible is the body and your human spirit is the hand. Your body can be under the dominion of your mind and your spirit or your body can be dominating your soul and your spirit. The spirit, soul and body are in different types of relationship. It's just like a husband and wife relationship. There are some wives who dominates their husbands and there are some husbands who dominate over their wives. There are some who have a perfect relationship of equality and consultation. And you could see many couples have different types and degrees of relationship. In a similar comparison there is a relation between our spirit, soul and body. And some people have their body and soul control them so much that they are never able to move into the spirit realm, whether they are unbelievers or Christians. Even the unbeliever who wants to move into the realm of the spirit and experience astral traveling has a price to pay. They either go on a vegetarian fast or they try to seclude themselves from worldly activities. They give themselves to concentration of what they call meditation in order to enter that realm. The principle behind it is the isolation of the body from the soul so that the soul is free. This happens in the same way if you try to concentrate after a heavy meal, your body seems to be enlarged and your soul reduced and your spirit absent. If you have been on a long fast, you will notice you feel very light. It is just not physical lightness although you will loose a few pounds. But there is another realm of lightness where your spirit and your soul are related to the body but not so firmly gripped by the body. Its like your spirit and soul are floating above your body. That kind of lightness is necessary in order for a person to move into the spirit world, which is why a Christian needs to have a fasted life.

This is also a dimension or level whereby one disappears in the spirit. For example, it was a common experience for Elijah to disappear and reappear. In this realm, your whole body disappears from the natural world. You become invisible in the natural world but only those in the spirit world are able to see you. It is not only witches who are able to move in this dimension for that's a counterfeit. If witches think they can fy, wait until they see you fy higher. In this last dispensation of time, many people are going to experience deeper dimensions in God. You will be walking with some brethren to a crusade and all of a sudden you disappear. By the time they are look- ing for you, you will be preaching the word of God and moving in the power. I have heard of a man whom God told to go and preach in another country but did not have enough money for transportation. So, he took his luggage and went to airport and Holy Ghost told him to enter a room and he suddenly appeared in that country where he ministered powerfully. When he was coming back, he went to the airport and entered the same room and all of a sudden he appeared again in his living room together with his luggage. This is a realm of transportation. Such a realm is going to be popular in this last dispensation as the Holy Ghost wants to accomplish God's work with speed. It must be expressly understood that disappearance in the spirit di- mension did not originate with witches or astral travelling. Instead, it originated with

God and the devil copied or counterfeited it. The fact that the devil is copying does not make it his. You might not have entered this realm before but wait until the day God wants to use you in the global arena and you urgently require a plane to go for a crusade in a distant place.

The Realm of Transmutation

Transmutation is the permanent movement or migration of spiritual subjects or substances from the realm of the spirit into a visible and tangible manifestation in the natural realm. It could also incorporate a supernatural change in the state of a natural substance from one form to another.

There is a realm in the dimension of God's glory whereby the spirit realm crystallises or transmutes itself into the natural realm to the extent that it can be seen, felt and touched. For example, angels, miracle money and other spiritual substances manifest through this way. The bible records an incident in Exodus 16, whereby Manna fell from heaven and was gathered for food every morning, for the children of Israel to eat in the wilderness. In other words, manna which is the food of angels transmuted itself into the natural realm as a spiritual substance for earthly beings to partake of. Moreover, the Bible records in Mathew 14:13-21 that Jesus prayed and food fell from heaven to such an extent that about 5000 people were fed. The question is: Where did all that food came from? The answer is simple. From heaven. That means, there is a readily available supply of food in the heavenly storehouses and when a miracle of this nature was performed, there was a transference or transmutation of food from the heavenly storehouses into the earthly realm. This means that there is a blue print for everything in the spirit realm. Creative miracles occur this way. For example one without a leg can receive an original blue print of that leg directly from heaven, one without an eye, hand, teeth or any other body part can receive these brand new parts in a similar fashion. Moreover, the Bible records another incident whereby *Jesus turned water into wine*. This was a special form of transmutation involving a supernatural change in the state of a natural substance from one form to another. This is a realm that breeds mighty signs and wonders.

However, in its purest form, transmutation denotes the manifestation of the realm of the spirit in to the realm of the natural. In other words, it is the manifestation of heaven on earth. It must be expressly understood that the realm of the spirit and the realm of the natural are distinct and separate realms and these have been separate entities even since the fall of man in the Garden of Eden. However, as God permits, the realm of the spirit can move and manifest itself into the realm of the natural so as to synchronise it with the perfect will of the father. Transmutation is therefore an invasion of the natural realm by the realm of the supernatural in order to fulfil God's divine plans and purpose. However, there are specific spiritual laws that govern this phenomenon. It has always been God's will for these distinct realms to function together in harmony and synchronisation just before the fall of man in the garden of Eden. Adam used to move easily and effortlessly between both realms, for example he would move in the spirit dimension and talk to God and then move into the natural and talk with animals.

For example, when the Bible says that at the end of the age, Heavens shall come down and the New Jerusalem shall rest upon the earth, that speaks of an intensive degree of transmutation where the whole of heaven comes down into the earthly realm. However, at the present moment God permits some part of the spirit or heavenly realm to transmute itself or move into the natural realm so that miracles, signs and wonders take space. That means miracles takes place when the spirit realm overlays or rest upon the natural realm. This is what I call *Heaven on earth* or a visitation of heaven to earth. In this end time season which marks the last wave of signs and wonders, there is an undeniably concrete evidence of the transmutation of spiritual substances on the earth. For example, gold dust, silver stones, diamonds and other precious stones are seen falling down in places of worship as God manifest the wealth of heaven to all His creation.

The Realm of visitation to the Throne Room

Visitation is a spectacular divine experience in which man is caught up or catapulted into God's Throne Room in the Third Heavens (either in the body or outside the body) for a specific purpose or on a study tour to explore the glory of the Heavenly realm, so as to update the inhabitants of the earth concerning the current happenings of Heaven.

This is a realm that we can tap into when we have walked, fellowshipped and communed with God so much that by His grace, He grants us permission to temporarily visit His throne in heaven in order to get a foretaste or glimpse of how things are like in His throne. Prophetically speaking this is a characteristic feature of the end time dispensation and in this season of visitation, many believers will be catapulted right into the throne room on a study tour to explore the glory of God. This is the realm that Paul tapped into in 2 Corinthians 12:2, when *he was caught up to the third heavens*. We also have testimonies of some believers around the world who are still entering that realm as God pleases. For example, the seven Columbian youths whom Jesus took to both heaven and hell to see what is happening there. Concerning Throne room visitations, God said,

> *"My people insist that I should go down there and fix things. I have already done that. It's no your turn for you to come up here".*

This is to tell you how expedient it is to be catapulted into God's throne to behold the beauty of the Heavenly realm so that you can come back and update the inhabitants of the earth about the knowledge of the glory of God. This is another ways through which we shall fill the earth with the knowledge of the glory of God in this final chapter of human history. Paul unveiled the mystery of Throne Room visitation when he figuratively declared in 2 Corinthians 12:1-4 that,

> *I know a man in Christ who fourteen years ago was caught up to the third heaven, whether in the body or out of the body I do not know, God knows. And I know that this man was caught up into Paradise, whether in the body or out of the body I do not know, God knows and he heard things that that cannot be told, which man may not utter.*

Now, Paul was educated and he would not be short of words to describe his experience of visitation to the throne room as far as the average man is concerned. So, you could imagine the impact of what he is saying here. This is not an ordinary man who lacks the vocabulary talking, but an intelligent and well educated man. To provide a background of the man, Paul was brought up at Gamaliel's feet as one of the most highly educated people in his days. And for him to make a statement that he has been in the spirit realm, and that when he came back he could not describe what it was like, imagine the impact of that! It was just like a Noble prize scientist who is on the top echelon of intellectual ability coming back from the spirit realm and say, *"I could describe atoms, molecules but I can't describe what is there"*. It would have the same impact. Paul was above the ordinary in everything that he pursued in God. This implies that there is a spirit realm, which is quite hard to comprehend, and there is something in that area that could motivate us deeper into that realm.

In the context of the above quoted scripture, when Paul says *"I know of a man"*, we know he is talking about himself because later on he says, *"Because of the abundance of these revelations a thorn in the flesh came into my life"*. So, we know it was him in the end. He is of course referring to himself because in verse 7 he wrote, *"Unless I should be exalted above measure by the abundance of revelations"*. So, we know that he is speaking about himself *in the third person* and of the abundance of the revelations that has come into his life. And he made use of a phrase that says, *"He heard things that were inexpressible for man to tell"*. He could not find an appropriate vocabulary or vernacular in the natural realm to accurately describe the undiscerned things of the glory realm. This is to tell you that the spirit world is a realm that doesn't operate on logic as is the case in our natural world. The spirit is a realm where our natural logic breaks down. There is an experience in the spirit world where Paul was not sure whether he was just there in the spirit or whether his body was also there. That qualifies our statement that transportation in the realm of the spirit has no distance. There is a degree where we move in God and only our spirit is able to transcend geographical distance.

How and when do we qualify to visit the Throne Room?

The most important thing about visitations of God is the timing. It is not just in preparations alone, which is important for we need to have a right heart before God. It is not how holy you are, or spiritual or how much good works you have done for God, but it is the fullness of the timing of God that determines the visitation of God upon your life. God has a place and time for it. At times there is some spiritual knowledge which God wants us to built up first before He could reveal the Throne Room. It is to make the visitation more permanent in our lives. That is what I mean about proper timing. We cannot afford to be anxious about the visitations of God upon our life in any way. We need to tell Him, *"Lord, it doesn't matter how you manifest or when you do it, we just want to be in the perfect will of God to receive the right things at the right time."* If it is not God's time for your visitation and it happens, the impact and the effect of that visitation would not be permanent.

CHAPTER SEVEN

THE SEVEN-FOLD DIVINE PRINCIPLES OF OPERATING IN THE GLORY REALM

It is worth exploring the divine truth that as much as God reveals His glory in every fabric of His creation, these are certain key principles that we can tap into in order to provoke the glory of God into greater manifestation in the natural realm. These are principles that one can tap into in order to walk into the deeper depths of God's glory in this final chapter of human history. Notable is the realisation that these laws of the supernatural complement each other and are progressions to enter into the greater depths of God. Each of these laws has a specific manifestation that produces something special. However, it's unfortunate that many believers are failing to operate in the realm of the God's glory because they do not understand spiritual laws and principles which they could take advantage of to generate positive results. Spiritual laws and principles are therefore vital keys that unlock the doors into the supernatural and accentuate an avenue through which the glory of God can flow in the natural realm. Learning how to tap into these spiritual laws and principle is vital to birth forth supernatural manifestations of God's glory. Therefore, you are definitely guaranteed to launch into the depths of glory if these spiritual laws and principles are correctly applied, practised and activated. The following are the *seventh-fold principles* of inviting God's glory to manifest unreservedly either during your personal times of prayer, or during corporate worship at church.

Creating or building an atmosphere of the glory.

It is important that we know how to create a conducive spiritual atmosphere of worship so that the glory of God can descend upon our meetings. In order for the rain of God's glory to precipitate unreservedly upon the nations, the *glory cloud,* which symbolically represents the glory of God, must be formed. The *glory cloud* is a quintessence of God's presence since God is always known to speak in a cloud (Exodus 16:10-11). To substantiate this divine truth, let's refer to a few quintessential portraits from the word of God: When Jesus was transfigured, God spoke from a cloud (Matthew 17:1- 5); when Jesus ascended to Heaven after His resurrection, a cloud received Him out of their sight (Acts 1:9) and the day Jesus returns, He will be *"Coming out of the clouds of Heaven with power and great glory"*. This is to tell you how important it is to build a cloud of God's glory, because it is through the cloud that His presence manifest intensely. Although it is true that the glory of God dwells in us, in our closets and churches, we must also create or build a cloud of His presence and a spiritual atmosphere where the glory of God permanently dwells. When we do, it takes few seconds to enter into His presence when we worship in those places.

It is worth mentioning that the glory of God is tripartite in terms of diversity of its manifestation. There is the glory of God in Heaven, then there is the glory of God in an environment and there is the glory of God in our spirit. But the one I'm referring to here is the glory of God in the atmosphere. For a lack of better word, this is what we call an *atmospheric glory*. To cement this divine truth with reference to scriptural evidence, the Bible confirms in Ecclesiastics 11:3, that *If clouds be full of rain, they empty themselves on earth*. It is interesting to note that the writer of the book of Ecclesiastes used physical phenomena to derive this revelation. In the natural realm, before rain could be anticipated, clouds must be formed first and when they are saturated to the maximum capacity, they inevitably release the contents of rain on to the earth. As it is in the natural, so it is in the spiritual realm. This means that you must start with building the glory cloud first before you can even anticipate the rain of God's glory because once the glory cloud is ready, the precipitation of the rain of God's glory is inevitable. The secret is therefore in learning the art of how to get the clouds saturated so that they are ready to precipitate the rain of glory upon the masses who desperately need the glory of God.

How is this cloud of glory formed?

The truth is that when we worship God, we form a spiritual cloud that is the glory or presence of God. Spiritual clouds create the right atmosphere for God to speak and do creative miracles. The formation of the spiritual cloud depends on the depth of our worship. Practically speaking, during a service, as the Holy spirit moves from one person to the next, He stops by each person, takes in the substance of his worship, and with it, forms the cloud for that service, which allows the presence of God to descend. Everyone who contributed worship to form that cloud, will receive what is in it. That is why at times the Holy Spirit begins at the front stage and at times at the centre of the congregation during worship because people in those areas formed the cloud.

It is of paramount significance to advance the divine truth that creating the right atmosphere builds God's throne. The glory will always manifest where the throne is built. Therefore, the sign that indicates that the throne is complete is when we experience the outpouring of His glory. In one of his writings, Apostle Maldonado contends that *we must praise until the spirit of worship comes and worship until the glory descends or until His spiritual throne is built.* This implies that believers who do not participate in the corporal ascension of praise into the presence of God, become obstacles in the service. They can hinder or kill the atmosphere because they did not partake of the corporal ascension. The atmosphere must be created from the bottom up by worshiping so that everyone can ascend to the throne and enter into worship in harmony as one body.

Perceiving the glory.

As aforementioned, the spiritual atmosphere is created through worship but the cloud must be discerned to release its contents. Discerning or perceiving the ingredients or contents of the cloud of glory is key to releasing its contents. In the natural realm, geographers and weather forecasters engage in a perception expedition to determine the contents of the cloud so that they can accurately project to the world what to expect from the prevailing whether conditions. There is a realm in which the *glory cloud* gets so highly concentrated in the natural realm such that if you were to bring weather forecasters to measure or perceive the humidity of that atmosphere, they would say, *"there is a possibility of rain and thunderstorms."* As it is in the natural realm, so it is in the spirit. Our ability to release the cloud of glory depends on the ability to discern its contents. In addition to receiving what the cloud of glory contains, we must also discern what is in it. The glory cloud will sometimes contain tangible spiritual substances of healing, deliverance, provision, breakthrough or resurrection anointing. The other reason why the contents of a divine cloud may not be realised is because we have not learnt how to pull from that atmosphere. When the glory of God manifests, we must take our miracles by declaring them and doing corresponding actions. Making a *"pulling"* on the glory implies placing a demand for the glory cloud to release its contents. Once the cloud and throne are edified, we can perceive the spiritual atmosphere of glory. In the natural realm, the atmosphere contains *a gaseous substance surrounding a celestial body formed by ingredients in the environment*. In the spiritual realm, it works basically the same way. The ingredients in the atmosphere of glory are continuous prayers, offerings, intercessions, praise, worship, obedience and honour directed to God's throne. When these ingredients exist in an environment, they produce an *open heaven* and build a divine spiritual atmosphere which is ripe for creative miracles.

The truth is that the reason why multitudes of believers don't experience a torrential down pour of glory from the glory cloud in Heaven is because we aren't discerning what God is releasing. If we have our spiritual senses opened and attuned to the frequency of God in the realm of the spirit, we will be able to see what is coming from the realm of glory. In other words, we will be able to project through the heavenly airways the extent to which the glory cloud is impregnated with the presence of God, the speed at which the glory waves are moving as well as the direction in which the glory cloud is moving. If we take what we see in the glory cloud and decree it, it will be framed in time and manifest in the natural. The dilemma that people often run into is that by the time they see into the realm of glory and act on it, the window of opportunity has closed. Then they have to open it up again through praise and thanksgiving which is such a daunting task culminating in a spiritual recession of God's glory in the church. No wonder multitudes are in a recession where the power of God is concerned.

Releasing the atmosphere of glory

It is worth noting that in order for the glory of God to manifest abundantly in a specific territory, it must be released. Releasing the glory gives Heaven permission to legally to endorse the propagation of the glory. There is a divine principle that in the spirit realm, anything remains locked until it is released. For clarity of purpose, let's take another closer look at our opening scripture in Ecclesiastics 11:3: *if clouds be full of rain, they empty themselves upon the earth.* As aforementioned, in the natural realm, there can never be any rain without clouds. Likewise, worship creates a cloud so that manifestations of God's glory can shower down upon us. But what will happen if clouds were formed and full of water and it doesn't rain?. In order to create or encourage rainfall, some researchers have discovered a technique called *cloud seeding.* Through this method, a rain storm happens after moisture collects around naturally occurring particles, in the air causing the air to reach a level of saturation at which point it can no longer hold that atmosphere. Cloud seeding essentially helps that process along, providing additional *"nuclei"* around which water condenses. These nuclei can be salt, calcium chloride, dry ice or iodide. A similar thing happens in the spirit. Sometimes a cloud is formed and there is so much potential in the atmosphere but there is no visible manifestation of His presence. As much as it is important to know how to create a spiritual cloud, it is also important to learn how to release the atmosphere or what is in the cloud of glory. Just like in the case of cloud seeding in the natural, sometimes we need to learn how to sprinkle the cloud with more seeds of worship, until His glory descends.

The glory of God releases and produces something in the hearts of people that cannot be received directly through hearing teachings, reading books, listening to anointed worship music or receiving an anointing through laying on of hands. What the glory releases can be released only in His presence when the people's spiritual DNA is enlivened. Their vision is enlarged and a passion for the kingdom and souls is ignited within them. Therefore, if we sincerely want to be changed and transformed, we must dare enter into His presence and stay in His movement from glory to glory. Although the prophetic glory is resident within us as Paul attested: *Christ in me the hope (anticipation and expectation) of glory* (Colossians 1:27), it must be fully understood that the substance of God's glory is not in you as a dead lake but a river that should flow out and influence those in your sphere of contact. That is why with regard to the release of God's glory, we speak of an *outflow* and *inflow* of glory. The *inflow* speaks of the flow of glory into the human spirit usually through *impartation* while the *outflow* of glory speaks of the oozing out or bubbling forth of the glory of God from within the depths of your being to impact your world.

According to the law of manifestation, not only is the active rhythm of the river of glory received but it is also released. To cement this divine truth with reference to scriptural evidence, let me refer you to a provocative question which Peter asked some believers in Corinth: *"Have you* **received** *the Holy Ghost since you've believed?* While this question was asked to a generation that had just received the outpouring of the glory of the Spirit which is about 2000 years ago, let me rephrase it and ask the same question to this generation that has had the Spirit in full operation for the past 2000 years: *Have you* **released** *the Holy Ghost since you've received?* I leave you to do a self-introspection on this one! Note that not only does God wants to release the greater glory for now but for future generations as well. Heaven operates on the basis of the *principle of irrevocability* which states that once something (glory, blessings, anointing, and impartations) has been released from Heaven to earth, it permanently belongs to earth and does not return to heaven as there is a *certificate of ownership* attached to it. For example, when the glory of God is released over a territory in the natural realm, it lingers in the natural environment for years so that it can even impact the future generations. That is how mantles are preserved to fall on the next generations. There are makes that have lain on the earth for ages that are waiting for you to pick up. The mantle of raising the dead left by Smith Wigglesworth when he was translated into glory is available on earth for you to pick it up and invade death infested territories such as the mortuaries and hospitals with resurrection power of Christ.

How then do I release the glory of God?

Note that releasing the glory of God is largely dependent on its location. As afore-mentioned, there is the glory of God in Heaven, then there is the glory of God embedded in the human spirit, then there is the glory of God in the atmosphere or natural environment. Releasing the glory of God from each of these locations requires a different technique. For example the glory of God in Heaven is harnessed and released through *radical worship* because that's the only substance that enters heaven to contact or magnetise God's glory. The glory of God in the atmosphere is released through *territorial dominion* (Prophetic decrees issued over territorial regions) while the glory of God in a human spirit is released through *Prophetic action* (activating your spirit by praying in the Holy Ghost, confessing and preaching God's word and practically demonstrating God's power during ministration). Overall, in order to see a greater manifestation of God's glory in your life, declare the word of the Lord that what He has spoken concerning you, is coming to pass and that all has been done already and is only manifesting now in our appointed time. Every promise of the Father is simply becoming a manifestation in our time from eternity. His time is always on time. Therefore, speak it, declare it, prophesy it, proclaim it, decree it, and release it. Jesus said, *"He that believes in Me as the scripture says, out of your belly shall flow as rivers of living water"*. Let the rivers flow abundantly. He has put them within you to come forth and flows like a river in flood. Therefore, begin to declare: *"O river of God! Come forth and water the nations! Spring forth, as a fountain of life. O, river of the Living God, the Lord would declare your release this day!"* Practically speaking, release the river of the Lord from within the depths of your inner most being; release the streams of life from within your belly; release the rain of God's glory from the centre of your spirit; release the flow of power from the inner corridors of your heart and release abundance of glory the from the extreme quarters of your spirit, glory to God!. This is how the glory of God is made manifest in this generation.

Imparting the substance of glory.

The glory of God is not just a theological or ethereal concept as some have erroneously presumed but a tangible spiritual substance that emanates from God. The substance of glory can be imparted upon human vessels just like the anointing. As a spiritual substance, it is a quintessence of God's virtue and the exact representation of His being hence it can be divinely transacted or imparted upon its recipients when humanity comes into contact with God in the natural realm. Jesus declared in John 17:22 that, *"The glory which you gave me I have given it to them that they may be one just as we are one"*. This is the basis of *the law of impartation of glory*. In the context of the above scripture, the phrase, *"I have given it to them"*, means that I have *imparted* it upon them because the glory can only be given through impartation. This is to tell you that we have already received an impartation of glory in our spirit. Our responsibility is to draw the reservoir of glory from within the depths of our spirit to bless those in our sphere of contact. When Jesus was resurrected, He reclaimed the glory and gave it back to His people, the church so they could be transformed and shaped according to the glory of the father. In this context, impartation means *the act of transferring the glory either upon human recipients or geographical places or territories such as buildings, streets as well as the prevailing atmosphere over cities and nations*. That is why there is such a thing as *atmospheric glory* which results from the invasion of glory on the natural atmosphere. If the glory of God descends upon a city, town or nation, it becomes easy for other geographical territories to catch that flame of glory through *impartation*. Hence, our experiences in His glory must be imparted or taken to our workplaces, schools, community organisations, departmental stores, streets and the public arena.

The Realm of Glory

Do you remember when Moses asked God, *"Please show me your glory?"* What exactly was he asking for? Was he just asking to watch a movie of God parading on the mountain or there is something specific that he needed? He was simply asking for an *impartation of the substance of glory.* You need to understand that in the realm of the spirit, things are received or imparted through sight or vision. Once you see something, you have it. So, what Moses meant by this remarkable request is that if God could grant him an opportunity to see him, the glory would be imparted upon him. Let me awaken you to another questioning spree? Do you remember when Paul said to believers in Corinth, *"Brethren, I long to see you that I may impart a spiritual Gift?"* How did he intend to do it? Through sight or vision. Why do I say so? Because he says I long **to see you**, meaning once he sets his eyes of them, they would receive an impartation. This is the same principle by which the sick and demon possessed received a healing impartation through the reflection of the shadow of Peter. Since the shadow of Peter was a reflection of God's glory in his spirit, radiated through a shadow as a point of divine contact, it means that the glory can be imparted.

How then do I receive an impartation of Glory?

The reality is that some people erroneously presume that the glory of God is only found in Heaven, hence upon ministration in a specific locality, it goes back to its original source. No! That is not the correct picture because while the glory originates from Heaven, it does only thrive there. Upon its release in the natural realm, it permanently abides in the human spirit, which explains how the sick got an impartation from handkerchiefs and aprons that were taken from the body of Paul. However, some of the glory lingers in the natural atmosphere, in the air, clouds, upon trees, buildings, on the streets and in every sphere of the natural environment such that those who come into contact with these objects can actually receive a direct impartation of God's glory. However, impartation of glory can also come in divergent ways such as laying on of hands, coming into contact with an anointed vessel, listening to anointed worship music, watching DVDs and taps of anointed men of God, watching anointed television programmes, reading anointed books, through corporate worship in church so forth. Other means of impartation which are increasingly becoming a norm across the Body of Christ are through dreams and open visions, trances, divine transportation in the spirit, direct contact with angels during their visitation on earth, through out-of-body and inside-the-body experiences, divine experiences of visitations to the throne room of Heaven. In this season of glory invasion, the glory will be imparted even in interesting ways such as handshakes and mere greetings.

Responding to the glory.

To experience continuous transformation, we need to know how to respond to the glory when it manifests during our meetings. Responding to the glory means *developing a significant level of sensitivity and quickness in apprehension of the move of God such that we are rightly positioned to act and move in the direction in which the glory is moving*. It means aligning our spirit in the glory realm with the blueprint of what God wants to do, how He wants it done and when He wants it done. The most effective way to respond when God's presence manifest is to worship and totally surrender to him. If we refuse to respond when God visits us, we will be judged. Sometimes God's presence comes to heal, deliver and people are not even aware of it, but they do nothing about it, they don't respond in faith but are mere spectators rather than participators. Even though God acts according to His sovereign will, our part is to respond when His presence comes by declaring, *"Lord I receive the glory, I receive my healing"*. Sometimes our faulty attitudes are reflected in our body language, our expressions may appear to be different or lack reverence or talk to him in a casual manner. By so doing, we grieve the Holy Spirit because God doesn't come where He is tolerated but He comes where He is celebrated. Jacob had not been aware that the presence of God was there with him. In Genesis 28:16, Jacob woke up from his sleep and said, *"Surely the Lord is in this place, and I did not know it"*. This is to tell you that it is possible to be in a service where the presence of God is so powerful such that people are falling under the weight of God's glory to the extent of lying prostrate on the floor but others are just unaware of what was happening.

In other words, they did not realise that God is present. It is possible to be in a place where the glory of God is present and not realise it. This is because at times we are totally absorbed in our own problems so that our spiritual perception is completely turned off or we are just caught up in our own agenda or predetermined programs. Our priority should always be to allow His glory to manifest. We need to remain sensitive to how the Spirit of God is moving. If God in His sovereignty decides not to take action, only then can we take hold of faith and the anointing and heal the sick.

How do we respond to the glory?

The best way to respond to the glory of God manifested in a particular locality is through *expressions of faith* and *radical worship*. This is exemplified by the expressions of Jacob whom the minute he realised that the presence of God was invading the geographical territory in which he lay, he hastily set up, marked the place and anointed it with oil. When the glory of God comes, you might want to cry, worship, lay hands on people, cast out demons, prophesy, preach and so forth but depending on what the glory is leading you to do, you need to follow suit. Concerning our response to the glory, there are *five groups* of people who seem to surface. Firstly, there are those who *follow the glory*, meaning they are spectators who are satisfied with watching from afar what the glory is doing through others and never dare to enter the river of the Spirit to encounter a personal experience. Secondly, there are those who *carry the glory*, meaning they are active carriers of His glory as they assume the mandate to propagate it to the furthest extremes of the world. Thirdly, there are those who *reveal the glory* by teaching others the revelation knowledge of the Glory Realm. Fourthly, there are those who move from revelation to manifestation by *manifesting the glory* and putting their revelation knowledge into practice through visible demonstrations. Finally, there are those who function in an apostolic dimension to *protect or safeguard the glory* from being taken to extreme or losing its original purpose and relevance in a generation. In a nut shell, whichever role you adopt, you must learn the art of how to respond to the glory of God when it shows up in a meeting. This is very critical because how much of God's blessings you can receive from Him is dependent of how you respond to His glory when it shows up.

Activating and accelerating the cloud of glory.

The glory of God does not need spectators. It needs to be provoked or awakened into manifestation. The glory is not an automatic phenomenon. God requires man to reciprocate His actions while in the glory zone. Even though God takes action, however He requires man to actively participate in the glory. God uses man in the affairs of man, hence for the glory of God to make an impact across the world, man has to be at the fore front as a vehicle to propagate the glory. That is why in this end time seasons, people who shall see the unimaginable manifestation of the glory of God are those who are practically involved in demonstrating it through actions of faith manifested through signs and wonders.

It is a divine truth that the supernatural needs to be provoked into manifestation in the physical realm, in what I call a *spiritual awakening*. Moses taped into this spiritual law when he asked God to show Him the glory. Paul unveils the greater revelation that *the same Spirit that raised Jesus Christ from the dead vitalises our mortal bodies*. Why? Because the supernatural needs to be vitalised, quickened, activated, even the gifts of the spirit needs to be stirred up in order to function in the full measure of God. The supernatural realm needs to be cultivated in order to manifest in the physical realm. This is the *law of manifestation*. That is why God declared that, "*Once and in a little while, I will shake the heavens, the earth and the seas and the desire of nations shall come to Me*". (Hagai 2:8). In other words, the spiritual realm needs to be shaken in order for souls across the globe to stream into the kingdom.

The truth is that the glory of God needs to be activated in order for it to break forth in the natural realm. Activating the glory leads to a supernatural acceleration of the things of God. For you to fully comprehend this truth, let me refer you to a quintessential example that you will easily understand. There is a technique used by geographers to accelerate rain formation called *cloud seeding*. During this process, an aeroplane is used to hover over the clouds and pray a chemical or substance that would trigger or impregnate the clouds with humidity. Once that happens, the clouds will become saturated and instantaneously release raindrops. As it is in the natural, so it is in the spirit realm. There are instances when the glory cloud needs to be heavenly seeded or impregnated with the humidity of our worship so that it can give birth to supernatural manifestations. At times the glory cloud hovers over the atmosphere but doesn't have much humidity to release the rain of glory. Under the circumstance, it can be provoked, activated and triggered through an atmosphere of radical worship in order to accelerate its manifestation in the natural realm. That is why the quickest way of getting breakthroughs, healings, deliverance and blessings is in the glory because there, things are accelerated because the cloak is not ticking.

How then do I activate the glory of God?

Active participation in the glory leads to the growth and development in the glory. The development of the glory of God in our lives would ultimately have to do with the alignment and tuning of our nature and attributes with the nature and attributes of God. There are no short cuts to the development of God's glory in us. Activating the glory of God comes through a biblical principle called *the practice of the presence of God*. This holistically incorporates spending time in His presence fellowshipping with the Holy Spirit (2 Corinthians 3:18), extensive study and meditating on the Word of

God (2 Peter 1:4), activating your spirit by praying a lot in the Holy Ghost even for three hours or the whole day, cultivating an atmosphere of worship, practical use and activation of spiritual gifts, stepping out in faith to practically demonstrate the power of God during ministration.

Revealing the Glory.

It is worth exploring the divine truth that unless the glory of God is revealed, it remains a mystery- hidden, and unexplored and concealed. To cement this truth with reference to scriptural evidence, Proverbs 25:2 affirms that, *"It is the glory of God to conceal a thing, but the honour of kings is to search out a matter."* The principle is that for the glory of God to be manifested, it must be *revealed*. A mystery appears unto many as *"knowledge withheld,"* and a revelation as *"knowledge revealed."* The mysteries of the kingdom are not to imply that the word of God is something merely ethereal, or out of reach. Rather, that in discovering the depths *(The Deep things of God)* of the Person of the Holy Spirit, we find that there is an undiscovered realm and so much more that awaits us (1 Corinthians 2:9-16. Romans 11:33; Deuteronomy 29:29; Psalms 42:7; 2 Corinthians 12:1-4; Colossians 2:3).

It is of paramount importance in this regard that we clarify the difference between a *mystery* and *revelation*. Something becomes a mystery in that it is a place that requires our spirit, mind, and imagination to enter in by the invitation of the Spirit. On the other hand, something becomes a revelation in that it reveals the intimate and spiritual knowledge of that which the Spirit initiates our understanding into. From here, knowledge apparently withheld becomes knowledge now revealed. But some may argue that *"No good thing will he withhold from them that walk uprightly* (Psalms 84:11). The truth is that the Father places a premium on seeking after Him. Some call it *"God Chasing,"* and others call it *"God Chastening,"* smile. However, you dare to admit this; the Lord places a demand on the principle of seeking after Him. There is something significant in pursuing all of Him, as He intentionally hides Himself for a season, only for you and me to press in. He is, in a sense, a God of hide and seek in the intimate sense, veiled to an extent, but revealed to those of His timing and choosing.

There are both physical and spiritual requirements for releasing the miraculous. If we don't speak, nothing will happen. If the cloud isn't present, nothing will happen. We need the cloud of glory present, and we need to speak into it. It's time for us to switch gears and begin to operate in spiritual understanding and revelation. In the natural world we learn by gathering information with our five senses. In the spirit realm we gain revelation with our spiritual senses. Revelation is nothing more than the revealed mechanics of God that enables us to think and operate from the supernatural dimension. We must stop questioning God. Instead of always looking for logical answers to natural problems, why don't we respond to God in faith? As we do we will ascend into higher levels of glory and see a greater manifestation of the miraculous.

Transacting the glory

It is worth exploring the divine truth that the substance of God's glory is a transaction or two way process. Hence, there is such a thing as *transacting the glory*. David understood this principle of transacting God's glory, hence he affirmed, *"When His praises go up, His glory comes down"*. This means that the worship that we render to the Heavens forms a matter, tangible substance and material with which God uses to build the glory cloud. Without the substance of worship, the glory cloud is not created because the material needed to create it is absent. In the glory realm, God inhales our worship and exhales His glory. This is the basis of transacting the glory. The challenge is that many believers want to be receipts of the glory but they never want to transact or reciprocate the glory back to God. In other words, they want to receive from the glory cloud yet they do not want to build the cloud. The reason why God issued a stern warning that *no flesh shall glory in my presence* is because He was aware of the prevalence of this syndrome in the church. It's only fair that if you are not ready to transact the glory, you rather not operate in that realm at all because there are consequences. When you analyse the context in which the word *glory* is used in the above-mentioned scripture, you will realise that it doesn't refer to the spiritual substance or *Shekinah glory* that emanates from the throne of God but it alludes to self-exaltation, which hinders the free flow of God's glory.

The truth is that the glory of God is transacted. That is a secret to provoking the rain of God's glory into manifestation in the natural realm. Sadly, some people have a negative balance of glory in their spiritual account because they have not transacted the glory. They have been recipients of God's anointing and received alarming breakthroughs in every facet of human existence but they have not transacted it back to the creator. That is why they are in a spiritual recession where the power of God is concerned. The truth is that when you transact the glory back to God, there is an addition in your spiritual account. As matter of fact anything miracle that is not declared or transacted on the earth remains illegitimate in Heaven because transaction gives a license for Heaven to ordain, authenticate and seal the miracle. Have you ever heard of some people who received miracles and shortly after that they lost them? What exactly do you think happened? It's because those miracles were never transacted back to Heaven, hence they were not endorsed and certified as legal so that they can be declared as permanent possession of recipients. This is to show you how imperative it is to transact the glory through worship and thanks giving.

It is saddening to note that while the *Receiving Department* in Heaven is always highly congested and tightly packed as a beehive flooded with prayers, petitions, appeals and requests of a diverse nature directed to God, the *Acknowledgment Department* that receives acknowledgements and thanks to answered prayers from the earth is always empty as very few believers often transact the glory after receiving so much from Heaven. That's why most people's prayers are clouded with requests and appeals yet devoid of thanksgiving and you wonder why things are not moving as they ought to. This is to tell you that a lifestyle of radical worship and thanksgiving should be an integral aspect of your life. This is a secret to unlocking the glory realm and launching the masses into greater depths of the miraculous.

Transitioning the Glory.

Transition is a radical change or drastic shift in the dimension of glory from one level, usually a lower one to the next. Note that it is rendered illegal by Heavens for anybody to operate at the same level, depth and dimension of glory. No one can permanently dwell in the realm of glory because the glory of God is always on the move. That is why Paul insists that *we move from glory to glory*. This is part of the transition process. The fact that we are instructed in the Bible to migrate from glory to glory means that there are many level, depths and degrees through which we can migrate as we explore and adventure into this unknown dimension. That is why no one can ever claim to have fully comprehended the glory realm because it is inexhaustible. That is why God demands that we keep moving, shifting and migrating so as to explore the new, hidden and deeper territories in that realm. The idea of transitioning in the glory is exemplified by Jesus's words when he stepped on the scene and instructed Peter to shift his position, *cast into the deep and let down the nets for a catch*. In other words, Jesus was unveiling a very important principle of transitioning. Note that the problem was not with the skill per se since Peter was an experienced fisherman. Instead, the problem was his position. Why do I say so? Because it is when Peter shifted his position and cast the nets into the deep that he obtained instantaneous results. He caught a large amount of fish to the extent that it appeared as if the fish themselves were now competing to enter his nets.

Another dimension of transition in the glory involves developing an understanding of the times and seasons of God so that we are able to determine the direction in which the glory is moving. This is because the act of transitioning goes hand in glove with the times and seasons. For example, you change according to time or in line with changes in seasons. You need to understand that in the same way natural seasons change from summer to autumn then winter to spring, the glory has its own seasons as stipulated in the calendar of God. There is the *archaic season* which depicts the dimension of glory or level at which you have been operating in the past; then there is the *contemporary season* which depicts the status quo or where you are currently operating in the now. Then there is the *neoteric season* which denotes what you should step into now, the deeper realm and higher dimension that is available for exploration. This unknown dimension is what Isaiah described in prophetic language as a "*new thing*".

In view of the times and seasons as stipulated in the calendar of God, it is therefore imperative that we develop a *prophetic perception* just like the Sons of Issachar so that we are able to detect the times and seasons of the glory and prepare ourselves for delving into the next level of glory. Prophetically speaking, we are on a prophetic era, a *"Kairos"* moment now that presents a great opportunity for the children of God to be catapulted into the highest realms of glory. This move, God wants to position His people for opportunities that will affect the destiny of the masses across the globe and touching generations into the future. God spoke to Joshua and said, *"Prepare provisions for yourselves, for within three days you will cross over this Jordan, to go in to possess the land which the Lord your God is giving you to possess"*(Joshua1:11). The children of Israel had been in transition for forty years and now God was giving them a window of opportunity, just seventy two hours to prepare for the change that would shift them into their inheritance. By the same token, God is preparing you for a change that will impact thousands of generations in the future.

Conceiving and incubating the Glory.

The reality is that many people are never able to make the shift of transition that will move them into a new season because they did not take the necessary steps of preparation. This is a season of transition for many people. During transition you feel that you are in a state of being in- between; you feel that you are starting all over. Transitions are the vehicle that God uses to bring promotion or elevation in the realm of the spirit. So, how you handle your transition will determine your promotion or position in the dimension of the spirit. Let me illustrate this divine truth with reference to a quintessential example you will easily comprehend. If you have been in transition in a job, you understand that how you left your last job will often affect the prospect of new jobs. If you want to be a possessor, then you must take the steps of preparation during your season of transition. Once you begin to prepare, God is then able to accelerate you into your prophetic promise. Only those that were prepared were the ones invited when God was getting ready to move. God wants to move you into a new season, out of transition into prophetic promise. If you want God to move in your life, you must exercise *radical faith* and prepare your provisions. What is it that you have been putting off that will prepare you for your tomorrow? Once that window of opportunity is open, you must go through it. Many people miss great opportunities because they were not prepared. Preparation precedes occupation. You will never be able to occupy that which you are not prepared for. When the Bible announces the state of affairs of the earth in Genesis 1 that *the Spirit of God was hovering over the surface of the deep,* what do you think God was doing? Resting! No! This was a preparation phase. The best word to describe this divine act is *incubation*. God was contemplating through the vastness of His perception the exact design and proto-type of a world He wanted to create such that when the idea of a new world was fully conceived in His imagination, He spoke it into existence. That is why He didn't just utter words flippantly but He tapped from His inner resources and spoke and said, *Light be* and light which was an integral part of Himself proceeded from within the depths of His being into visible manifestation in the natural realm. Before you step into a new realm of glory, you need to conceive the realm and when conception has been fully realised, there will be a rebirth of new manifestations in that realm.

This is also a time for you to put things in order to create an atmosphere for God to move in your life. The Bible records in 2 Chronicles 5: 1 that,

"All the work that Solomon had done for the house of the Lord was finished; and Solomon brought in the things which his father David had dedicated, the silver and the gold and all the furnishings. And he put them in the treasuries of the house of God. Then the house of the Lord was filled with a cloud, so that the priests could not continue ministering because of the cloud, for the glory of the Lord filled the house of God.

David communicated to Solomon as to how the house of God was to be built. David had the dream but was unable to complete it. Solomon completed the house of God. Once he finished the house of God, he brought in all the things that his father had dedicated and put them in the treasuries of the house. This was the prerequisite for the glory, or the presence of God coming into the house. God was looking to make sure that all things were in order. Once everything is in order, it creates a climate where God's presence, His seal of approval can come. This is a season to get things prioritized in your life, and do the first things first. I want to challenge you to think about those areas of your life that are not in order and to make it a point to put order into those areas so that you can create an atmosphere that is inviting to the presence of God. Since God is a God of order, then order is the atmosphere where His presence is manifest.

Perhaps, you may be in the midst of transition and want to break out of that cycle and prepare for your prophetic promise and if you will prepare your provisions during transition and get things in order which was lacking. You will be in position when the window of opportunity comes to shift you into your new season. Once you step into that new window, you will be welcomed by a new presence, a new grace, a new anointing and a new realm of glory. Prophetically speaking, we are in a time spiritually where there is an awakening occurring in the Body of Christ. As this awakening occurs God then shifts us into a place of acceleration. However, there are many people, churches, and ministries that are not functioning at their full potential. The spirit that has lulled the Body of Christ to sleep is robbing people to walk in the fullness of their inheritance. The good news is that in this end time season, paradigms are shifting, tables are turning and lids are being lifted off the pots as the glory of God is exploding in the extreme quarters of the earth as the waters covers the sea.

CHAPTER EIGHT

HOW TO TAP INTO THE HIGHER REALMS OF GOD'S GLORY

It is worth exploring the divine truth that persistently seeking after the substance of God's glory is every man's dream in this season which marks the conclusion of God's eternal plan on earth. The Word of God speaks of progressively being transformed from one realm of glory to the other and migrating from one dimension of glory to the other (2 Corinthians 3: 18). The beginning is not set; it is something that already was, a constant activity that goes from one point to another. That is why the glory of God is a movement. The Bible confirms this when it mentions the Shekinah cloud of the Lord continually moving in the desert. The greater truth is that the life of a Christian must exhibit a progressive pattern from glory to glory, conception to perfection, from faith to faith and from grace to grace. This is the process of renouncing the lower life to abound in the higher life, from mere *"Psuche"* to *"Zoe"*, from beneath to above and from the natural realm to the spirit realm (John 12:25).

There is something specific that we need to do and if we do it, we provoke the glory of God into boundless manifestation. In essence, the glory of God does not manifest automatically. Man has a say when it comes to initiating the degree of its manifestation. To cement this revelation with reference to scriptural evidence, let's look at a quintessential example of how Moses was catapulted into the highest realms of glory. This is what Moses commanded Aaron to do in order to awaken the glory of God into manifestation in the natural realm: *"This is the thing which the Lord commanded you to do, and the glory of the Lord will appear to you."*(Leviticus 9). It is evident that the glory of God is not something mystical but a tangible spiritual reality that manifest whenever we do the right thing. Doing the right thing implies positioning ourselves in a birthing position by appropriately applying the right spiritual principles to provoke the glory of God into manifestation. The glory of God will always come whenever we move in the right direction. And here Moses, the man who had abundantly experienced the effulgence of God's glory, says to Aaron *"You do this thing and the glory of God will come"* Note that Moses did not say that the glory *may appear.* God's glory will not tentatively come. Moses said *it will appear.* God's glory will definitely come. Hence, doing the right thing at the right time with the right motive is such a multipurpose key that can trigger or provoke the glory of God into manifestation.

The following are vital keys which one could use to open every door into the supernatural in order to manifest the glory of God. These are keys that we need to employ to unlock the realm of glory in this end time season:

Diligently and rigorously seek after the face of God and the substance of glory

It is worth noting that God is the source of glory, hence it matters most to seek the provider first before one could seek after the substance of glory. The glory comes as a reward for having sought the face of God. When God says *He is a rewarder of those who diligently seek him,* one of the ways through which He rewards us is by the glory. It is like a lifetime achievement, that is why in heaven people will be rewarded by crowns. The glory is a symbol of honour, achievement and promotion. When God promotes a man in the spirit, He gives him His glory. Moses said to God, *"Lord show me your glory",* and when God granted him that window of opportunity to behold the glory of God in its fullness, he was instantly promoted into a higher dimension in the spirit. In your quest to get soaked in the glory, you must pursue the glory of God like Moses, Elijah and Enoch and be elevated into the realm of endless glory. The Bible unveils a mystery in Genesis 5:24, that *Enoch walked with God, and he was seen no more, for God took him.* The expression *"walked with God"* denotes a devout life of glory, lived in close communion with God, while the reference to his end has always been understood, as the writer of Hebrews confirmed that, *"By faith, Enoch was translated that he should not see death, and he was not found, because God translated him"* (H e b r e w s 11:5). In other words, he was permanently catapulted into the higher realms of glory.

The Realm of Glory

It is of paramount significance to highlight the fact that if ever we want to see a greater manifestation, we need to cry out more for the glory. For God to bring us into another level, we need to have growing pains, we need to get hungry and even desperate. If you are just not hungry enough, nor desperate enough, you might not see alarming results. God wants you to want Him more than anything.

I recall vividly the day I earnestly and persistently prayed and told Jesus how much I wanted His glory. Spiritually speaking, I walked in the footsteps of Moses, cried out to know Him and said, *"Lord show me your glory"*. I understood clearly that the glory of God resident in my spirit but I needed more than just habitation – a vitalising and electrifying experience in the glory. Suddenly, in the middle of seeking God, I felt His presence visit me like thunder. It was so thick that I couldn't stand. The glory was like a hovering electric liquid honey cloud. There was an electric current in the air. The weight of God's glory enveloped me and hit me just below my knees. It felt like water, but it was electricity coursing through my body. It travelled downward and then filled me right up into my head. I spread myself prostate on the floor convulsing, barely able to breathe, experiencing rapturous realms of joy, delight, ecstasy, and pleasure. This was the filling of the glory. It felt euphoric, awesome, a baptism of glory. I have had many God encounters, but I tell you, this was like nothing I had ever experienced before. This was different. The weight of His glory was so intense that it was like breathing glory.

It was on the basis of my divine encounters and individual peculiarities in the spirit that I learnt that we must seek the glory above all else. We have to want this weighty presence, this river, more than anything else. The only way we can keep going, the only way we can truly live, is to live in the glory. We cannot just live on dutiful devotions, not on words of prophecy, nothing else, but desperation and hunger for the glory. Our appetites direct our lives. Why nibble when you can feast on God's glory? Does the passionate desire for anything of the world supersede your longing for God? Hunger for anything besides Him is dangerous. Only hunger for God assures victory. Therefore drink deeply of God's glory.

In this end time season, not only should we seek the glory but we should also get to the extent that we breathe in the glory. There is a place where you can get deep enough in realms of glory, and stay there, wanting nothing but the Shekinah glory to fill and refill you to the brink of spiritual capacity. When you pray, seek nothing but the glory, not His hand, but His face, and you can become so filled with the glory that you will carry it for all to see. In order to experience a sudden turnaround in your life, you need to get to apace whereby you challenge God in an area He Loves the most just like I proclaimed,

"My God, I'm hungry for Your glory. I'm tired of a powerless gospel, of powerless Christianity, give me power". I had to have the atmosphere of heaven. I had to have the Kingdom of God in word. I couldn't handle hype any more. I couldn't handle talk. I had to have the pure glory of Jesus. I had to have it, right then, and right there! His glory, His presence had to be on everything I did. I had to have the glory I just had to. I tell you, I want His glory to drip down the walls of my room. I want my carpet stained with my tears of holy desperation.. Every time I would try to preach on something else, the glory came out of my mouth! I preached and talked about nothing but holy hunger, desperation, and seeking His presence for months, and there was an outbreak of God's glory in realms I have never imagined before.

Prophetically speaking, the glory of God is coming into the church in dimensions that will amaze even believers. The glory cloud is manifesting across the body of Christ evidenced by gold dust, supernatural oil, dental miracles, gold fakes, and angel feathers falling down from heaven during worship sessions. These are already happening and this is to tell you that the Shekinah glory has already begun to move in the supernatural realm. Therefore, the world is going to witness the sweeping power of the glory of Jesus and the Shekinah is going to change people in an instant. The glory is the atmosphere of heaven. The glory is the very atmosphere where God dwells. In this atmosphere is extreme living. We are living in these extreme days of Christianity and living. The supernatural is going to be natural and real, a common occurrence, in everything we do, and everywhere we go, as believers. God and His kingdom can so advance, and Jesus can be so manifest, that the glory can change the spiritual climate of a meeting, city, region or a nation. When we get into the river of glory enough, people will remark as they did to Peter and John, *"You've been with Jesus and you've been with Him!"*

The question is: How desperate are you for God's glory?

Are you willing to do what it takes to be in God's glory until the glory touches you? You have to hunger, thirst, pursue the glory, and usually it happens in your quiet place, without distraction. Then, you don't have to worry what others are thinking, and you can let loose, and go all out for God in your desperation. You can seek His glory anywhere. It doesn't matter who's smiling at you when you look up into heaven and see your Father smiling, delighted with your holy desperation. Seek His smile, seek His face and seek His glory. If you have His smile, His kiss, the river of His glory, nothing else matters in this world except His presence.

In line with this new move, God is raising up a generation of people who aren't focused on anything else, but rather, His face for those who want to get hold of who God is, so that God's glory alone will transform them, their families, cities, and nations. Who will stand in His holy place? Is it you? Find out how you can prepare your heart to ascend the holy hill, to meet God face-to-face, as Moses did. Examine the hearts and motives of Moses and Jacob, and understand how God's glory changed them, and then apply those principles to your life for extreme living and living life victoriously and to the maximum in the river of God's glory.

Graduate into higher dimensions in the realm of the anointing

There is an intricate connection between *the anointing* and *the glory*. This is because the anointing is what brings the glory, hence, you need to grow, graduate and develop further in the realm of the anointing. The anointing is what provokes the glory of God into manifestation. Therefore, acquire the anointing first and the substance of God's glory will illuminate your life. The anointing is given to bring the glory of God into manifestation. This is its ultimate purpose in the kingdom. You get to see the glory of God through the anointing. The anointing is what connects you to the glory of God. God's presence and power are resident in the anointing, hence any man of God who taps into the realm of the anointing and manifests miracles, signs and wonders ushers the glory of God on the scene. The anointing reveals or manifests the glory of God. In Acts:10:38, the Bible speaks *of how God anointed Jesus of Nazareth with the Holy Ghost and with power: who went about doing good, and healing all that were oppressed of the devil; for God was with him.* This implies that the anointing is what certifies, reinforces, establishes and authenticates God's unwavering supremacy, divine plans, purpose in the light of His creation. In the absence of the anointing, the glory is not revealed.

Some people think that the anointing and the glory is one and the same thing. On the other extreme there are those who are just so obsessed about the anointing that in the process, they neglect the glory that brings that anointing. That is why in this end time dispensation there is an emphasis in the supernatural for a progressive transition from the realm of the anointing to the realm of God's glory. The anointing is like the light. The light is what manifest the glory of the sun. Without the sun, there is no light and by the same token without the glory, there is no anointing. But it is the light which makes manifest the glory of the sun. In the same manner, it is the anointing that manifest the glory of God. For a deeper understanding of how you can function in the realm of the anointing, I would like to kindly refer you to one of my books titled, *"Deeper Revelations Of The Anointing"*

Launch into a Deep, intensified and elevated worship

It is a divine truth that your praise changes the atmosphere and your worship sustains that realm. Praise and worship are the keys that unlocks the pathway into the glory realm. We enter into His presence with praise (Psalm 100:1, 1 Thessalonians 5:17, Isaiah 61:11, Isaiah 45:8). When His praises goes up, His glory comes down, hence it is advisable that believers don't just sing songs about God but worship deeply in truth and in spirit. As we worship, we are creating the cloud of glory. As we praise God, the atmosphere thickens and become spiritually heavy and pregnant with the possibilities of God. It's here, when the spiritual climate is ripe, that we can speak into the cloud of glory and see a release of greater miracles. The Bible declares in 2 Chronicles 5:13 that,

"Indeed it came to pass, when the trumpeters and singers were as one, to make one sound to be heard in praising and thanking the Lord, and when they lift up their voice with the trumpets and cymbals and instruments of music, and praise the Lord, saying, For He is good. For His mercy endures forever."

As they were exalting the mercy of God, the house of the Lord was filled with a cloud. That means that what they said was also as important as the music. It did not say when the music was as one that the glory of God came although it may include that. Instead, it says that when the musicians were as one, they made one sound to be heard and when they praised the Lord saying, *"For He is good and His mercy endures forever, "*then the glory of God came into the place. Let's consider how Solomon prayed:

"Now therefore, arise, O Lord God, to Your resting place. You and the ark of Your strength. Let Your priests, O Lord God, be clothed with salvation and let Your saints rejoice in goodness. O Lord God, do not turn away the face of your Anointed. Remember the mercies of your servant David" (2 Chronicles 6:42).

Note that it's when they sang and praised the mercy of the Lord, that the house of the Lord was filled with the cloud. That was God's glory in manifestation. In other words, it is the dimension of worship that provoked the glory of God into manifestation in the natural realm. The moment the mercies of David were mentioned, the glory of God was manifested in its intensity. Let's consider exactly what transpired following their heightened degree of praise and worship:

> *When Solomon had finished praying, fire came down from heaven and consumed the burnt offering of the sacrifices, and the glory of the Lord filled the temple. When all the children of Israel saw how the fire came down and the glory of the Lord on the temple, they bowed their faces to the ground on the pavement, and worshiped and praised the Lord, saying, "For He is good, For His mercy endures forever"* (2 Chronicles 7:1).

Noticeably, you feel and sense the glory of God wanting to arise when we exalt His mercy. Therefore we must strive to get in the Glory through high praise, and worship. Many times while ministering in a corporate setting, I would start with praise and worship as this brings the anointing. From there, I'll minister under the anointing seeing healings and miracles. When people begin to praise the Lord and give Him glory for the miracles, their faith level begins to rise. Faith and high praise will usher in the glory cloud, creating an ideal atmosphere for greater miracles. As the people's expectation increases, so does the glory.

The most important thing with regard to manifestation of the glory of God is that we must learn to cooperate in forming the cloud of glory by participating with all of our being, dancing, shouting, and singing with all of our heart. This releases the glory and the Kingdom of God within us and mixes with the glory in the atmosphere. When we do this, we are partnering with heaven to create the glory cloud. You must therefore praise higher and worship Him with all your might like David did. Your worship will create the cloud of His presence and then He will come in all of His glory. Worship is a key for manifesting the glory by releasing a new song. I have often been in meetings where the songs that are being sung have long outlived their day. Don't get me wrong, at one time they had power and carried revelation and a weighty anointing, but they've become familiar and stale. In these services where such songs are sung, rarely will there be a fresh release from heaven because the atmosphere that's being created is not filled with faith, passion, and fresh revelation. People just get stuck in song mode.

Our worship is the key to bringing the new sounds and realms of glory into the earth

It's the song of the Lord that flows from His heart through ours. As we worship, we usher in streams of heaven that changes the atmosphere in which we live. As we join together and our worship intensifies, it will lift us into another realm, the glory realm. The new sound that is being released is the sound of His voice riding on the praises of His people. God sings His song through us; releasing the sound of heaven on earth. The angels listen for the new sound; when they hear it, they come down just to worship with us. Do you know that at times angels join us when we worship? I had a recording of a worship song whereby angels joined saints during a worship session in Bethany in 1985. That was the most beautiful sound I have ever heard in my life. All of Heaven and earth long to worship and see what God may reveal next. Anyone can worship—but not everyone will worship with the new song of God. Until we sing the new song, the greater realm of the Spirit will not be released in our midst.

There is a song in our spirits that can take us to new places in the glory realm

Nobody can do it for us; we need to do it ourselves. When we release the song that lies dormant in our spirit, it will lift into a greater glory of His presence. The new song is the prophetic word of the Lord that must be sung. The angels search for the aroma that is released from the new song, drawing them like bees to a flower. When they come they begin to stir the atmosphere of glory and help release the miraculous. The devil, however, hates when we step over into the new song. He is powerless against it and is locked out of the glory as the high praises are released. I have been in worship services where the cloud becomes so thick that a golden dew begins to form in the atmosphere. However, when God's people hold back their praises, it doesn't seed the heavens for the much needed glory rain.

However, many people get caught in asking God to rend the heavens and come down. They cry and call out to God for a visitation when all the while God is saying, *"You come up here!"* The heavens are open—Jesus has already cleared the way for us to access the Father. *"You come to Me!"* Our praises rise like incense to the Lord drawing Him to us. Our praise goes up and the glory comes down. As we sing the new song, God releases His Word which brings the framework of Heaven into the now. This is why spontaneous supernatural explosions of glory manifest when His presence is in the room. The superior realm of heaven literally collides with the inferior, natural realm of earth, causing the inferior dimension to be instantly affected and changed. Anything that is inferior in the presence of God will be changed! This is why it's mandatory that we change the way we worship. We need to learn what brings heaven—the old ways just won't cut it. Only the high praises of God will release the new dimensions we long for.

Unveil the glory through Deeper Revelation.

It is a greater truth that revelation is what unveils the mysteries of God's glory. In the absence of revelation, God's glory remains a mystery. Revelation is what unveils, unpacks and uncovers the package of God's glory. The Bible speaks of *hidden treasures of darkness* (Isaiah 45:3). The glory is one of the hidden treasures of darkness which God is revealing by His spirit. The Holy Spirit is said to be the Spirit of glory, hence His duty is to reveal God's glory to us. To us, the glory is no longer a mystery because we can walk into it and manifest it everywhere. When you touch God's glory, He will always give you unusual instructions.

The glory realm is the atmosphere of revelatory knowledge.

Whatever is revealed in the Heavens becomes prophetic to the Earth (Amos 3:7). This realm is also considered as the hidden life, as revealed in Proverbs 25:2, that *it is the glory of God to conceal a thing, but the honour of kings is to search out a matter.* This is to tell you that the dimension of glory which a man can be catapulted into is directly proportional to the level of revelation he has about God. God will not reveal His glory beyond the level of revelation that you have of Him.

The truth is that God has to reveal Himself in order for us to understand Him. It is not just man finding God; it is rather God revealing Himself. No matter how much we try to understand God with our finite understanding, unless God chooses to reveal Himself, there is no way we could have understood Him. Unless God chooses to reveal by His Spirit, we will never grow and understand. That is why we are to ask for the Spirit of wisdom and revelation. For God is such that no human mind can understand Him. The only way is for God to come down to our level and reveal Himself.

Christianity is a revelation of God to man and not just man finding their way to God.

We have set the fact that man cannot come to know God by himself. All the philosophy of man has never led him any closer to God. All the great minds and brains that have ever lived and died could not even come close to a hair breath of the wisdom of God. They have tried to comprehend this earth and this existence that we are in. You remember Jesus told His disciples that they are blessed for God has chosen to reveal to them what many wise men longed to hear what they hear and to see what they see.

The greater truth is that it is only when God reveals that we can receive. Without revelation, there is no reception. Revelation comes first followed by reception. If Christ did not reveal His salvation, we would have nothing to receive. It is the revelation that must come first, and so, there is a progressive revelation from God. The only way we can grow in God is by His grace. The grace of God is God's revelation of Himself to us. As He reveals we receive. And if we are faithful to His revelations, He will reveal more. Revelation is progressive until we have grown in His fullness. Therefore, acquire revelation knowledge of the glory. Many walk with God, but don't know the glory, or intimacy with Him. There are times in my bedroom where the glory of God comes and I think, whoa! I'm going to heaven! Knowing the glory is not knowing about Him, but knowing Him for who He is and the inner reality of who He is. It's about knowing the glory of the Lord in such a way, that the presence is as thick as honey – rich and weighty. It's the *kabod*, the weighty glory of the Lord. It's about wanting His glory more than anything else and wanting to be with Jesus, for the Glory of the Lord is His manifest presence, Jesus.

As reiterated before, *Kabod* is the Hebrew word for glory, and it means literally, *"weightiness" or "substance."* That means there's weightiness, a density, and a substance of God that is found nowhere else except in His presence. His splendour is weighty and awesome. One time, God's *"kabowd"* fell on me with such intensity, that it left me speechless. I couldn't muster any words, but that was just as well for they would have messed up the experience. His splendour weighed on me until I was breathless. It takes a long time to recover from such visitations of glory. The Lord spoke to me about the revelation of raising the dead, which I compiled into a life transforming book, titled, *"The Realm Of Power To Raise The Dead"*. This was after a season of soaking in His presence for sometimes up to twelve hours a day. It was a time I would just saturate myself in His presence and bask in the glory. The visions of this global ministry, including the 21 books which I authored were all birthed out of that time.

Foster Deeper dimensions of consecration.

It must be expressly understood that contrary to how some folks have portrayed it, the glory of God does not come that easy. Instead, it must be tapped, provoked, triggered and channelled into manifestation. There is a price to pay to see the glory of God into manifestation. God instructed Moses to consecrate people for three days so that on the third day, He would manifest His glory. Consecration entails the absence of sin, dying to self and devotion to God. It enlarges one's spiritual capacity to receive the glory. God said, *no flesh can glory in His presence.* Therefore, He imparts His glory upon those who are selfless and have crucified the flesh. Consecration causes us to receive an impartation that will cause us to access the glory realm at a greater degree than ever before.

God told Moses, *"You cannot see My glory. No man can see My glory and live. But I will show you the back part of My glory"* (Exodus 33:23). Moses lived in the old covenant where Jesus had not shed His blood yet. The entire animal sacrifices point to the blood of Jesus that was to be shed. But in the New Covenant, many times people pray to God, *"Lord, show me Your glory. Lord, let Your glory come upon me."* Sometimes they do not realize what they are asking. If the glory of God comes when there is sin in your life, it would kill and destroy you. See the glory of God will react very much to sin and destroy it. If sin is a part of our life, we would be destroyed by God's glory. That is why we need to look closely at 2 Thessalonians 1:9: *These shall be punished with everlasting destruction from the presence of the Lord and from the glory of His power.* You say, *"I did not realize that the glory of God is an instrument to punish the wicked."* If the glory of God comes upon you, and the blood of Jesus is not upon you, it will destroy you. When people say, *"Lord, give me Your glory,"* when God really sends His glory and sin is present in your life, the glory of God will destroy you. We are talking about God's sacred presence. The glory of God can only come on a place where the blood of Jesus has come. The blood must be present first before the glory can come. The blood must touch the place first before the glory touches it. The blood represents the mercy of God. This is why a high degree of consecration is highly imperative for us to function in the realm of God's glory.

Practically demonstrate or manifest the glory wherever you are.

It must be expressly understood that the glory of God is not for personal use for no one can bank the glory. Instead, it is to be showcased, exhibited, displayed and demonstrated in every sphere of human existence. A man who becomes a recipient of God's glory and does not do anything about it stands a chance to loose that glory. The glory has to be manifested. That is why God was angry at Moses for crying out to Him when in actual fact he had received glory. God said to him, "W*hy are you crying to me? What is it that is in your hand? Stretch it forth and your way will open".* God demands that we demonstrate His glory, propagate it and populate it to the extreme ends of the world on His behalf. This is because according to God's original plan about man-kind, man was created to display the glory of God.

The greater truth is that the Lord has always chosen to release His glory through signs and wonders. It must therefore be understood that the glory of God is meant to be publicly and unreservedly demonstrated. God has ordained us to demonstrate His glory on earth. It is not for us to store up for our personal benefit alone. Paul revealed in 2 Corinthians 4:7, *that we have this treasure in earthly vessels, that the excellence of power may be of God and not for us.* In the context of this scripture the word *"treasure"* refers to the *glory* and *"earthly vessels"* refers to *our bodies.* Therefore the treasure, which is the glory of God is manifested through us when God, not sin is continually glorified in our lives. We are therefore chosen vessels to manifest the realities of heaven when there is a need, to exhibit the virtues of God and to display the Excellency of the father. This treasure that dwells in us have the ability to save, heal, deliver, raise dead and the only requisite for having this treasure is to make ourselves available to manifest His glory. It must be further understood that the glory of God is not only demonstrated in the church during services but it is revealed everywhere the vessels of clay go whether in the restaurants, classrooms, workplace, sports arenas or anywhere.

Consider what Paul had to say about God in Romans 9: 23: *That he might make known the riches of His glory on the vessels of mercy, which he had prepared beforehand for glory.* That means every believer who receives Jesus as Lord and Saviour is chosen to be a vessel of mercy to manifest His glory on earth regardless of age, culture, nationality, race, gender or any other human disparity. Paul further unveils the reality of manifesting

God's glory when he says that *the earnest expectation of creation eagerly waits for the revealing of the sons of God* (Romans 8:19). This means that every creation has an earnest expectation, an ardent desire to see the manifestation of carriers of God's glory. That creation is in fact vigilant now, waiting for the moment when a child of God will walk into a hospital and declare a word and all the sick will be healed. It is waiting for a child of God to enter a funeral parlour and command the dead to rise, to the glory of God. This is the promise of the last days for every believer.

In this last wave of God's glory, we need to take or manifest the glory outside the confines of the church. The glory of God can no longer be confined within the vicinity of church bars and doors. You don't have to wait for the next church service to see a healing or miracle for the glory of God to manifest everywhere you go. Many believers erroneously presume that for God to become visible or tangible, it is imperative to have a musical group and corporate worship, otherwise God cannot flow. This is an error. Corporate worship does produce the cloud of glory that makes all things possible. It fills and renews the oil in our lamps giving us the fire we need and bringing forth spontaneous miracles. However, it is not true that you cannot manifest God's glory outside such a setting through raw faith, without choirs, music or any built up atmosphere of glory because the Holy Spirit in us is more than enough to give birth to God's glory. You can be God's instrument anywhere in the world because you are a mobile tabernacle of glory of the Holy Spirit. In this season, great supernatural manifestations will take place not only in church but in stadiums, arenas, theatres, parks, public places, streets and everywhere a believer who is full of the glory goes and is willing to manifest it.

There is a great gulf fixed, a line of demarcation, a dividing asunder between being a preserving Christian and becoming an instrument for kingdom advancement. For one generally has the view of leaving earth while the other sees the eternal purpose of God to inherit it. One sees a way out of this mess, but the other is being positioned to pierce, penetrate, and to pioneer new thresholds and frontiers, apostolic colonization, new core and corporate dynamics of the King and His kingdom among the masses. One sees the church going and the other sees the Christ in awesome splendour and radiant glory progressively manifesting, not merely to His church, but through His church. One sees the dire need to disappear, while the other is anticipating the fullness of Christ and His eternal purposes to reappear. The bible says in Mathew 11:12, that *from the days of John the Baptist, until now, the kingdom of heaven has been forcefully advancing and forceful men lay hold of it.* This means that we carry with us the dominion, Lordship and will of the king, thereby possessing the potential to manifest the reality of His kingdom to each person and in each situation we encounter, establishing it forcefully by practical demonstrations.

Develop a perennial hunger, unquenchable thirst and insatiable appetite for the supernatural.

It is a fact that the supernatural is provoked or tapped by desire. God said, *"Call unto me and I will answer thee and show you great and mighty things which you did not know"* (Jeremiah 33:3). One of the things which God promised to show in the context of this scripture is the glory. God said if you call Him, He will show you the glory just like He showed Moses and even greater than that. Addressing a situation that involved questioning God's sovereign will in the administration of His glory, God said, *"I speak to a prophet through visions but as for My servant Moses, I speak face to face with him"*. Why. Because Moses had the glory of God , hence glory speaks to glory. Moses was the only one who qualified to go up the mountain because of the substance of glory upon him. The glory is what will qualify you to enter certain territories and to access certain treasures in God which multitudes only know of as a mystery. You can never enter heaven without the glory because the glory is the access point into heaven. *Deep calleth unto deep* (Psalms 42:7) *and* by the same token, *Glory calleth unto Glory*. In other words it takes glory to see glory. We can only see God in the glory. If Moses did not have the glory and saw God, he would have died. This is because during that time the Bible says, *no man could see God and live at any moment*. So what saved him was the glory of God. It is therefore imperative that we develop an appetite for God's glory if ever we want to see Him move mightily in this season.

Progressively pursue a dense network of the SEVEN most critical spiritual exercises.

As part of what we call, *"The practice of God's Presence"*, there are certain spiritual exercises which when properly executed, can catapult a man to the realm of glory. These includes praying in the Holy Ghost, fasting, having a deep fellowship with the Holy Ghost, diligently studying the word of God, constant meditation on the word of God and creating an atmosphere of continuous worship. Praying in the Holy Ghost is the highest level of spiritual communication in the spirit realm that builds up your faith according to Jude 1:20. Fasting on the other hand, sharpens your spiritual antenna so that you are rightly positioned in the spirit dimension to access the glory. It propels your spirit into the glory much like the rocket boosters and the enormous power that propels a space shuttle into orbit. Once in that realm, you tend to hear God better and you are attuned to the frequency of the Holy Ghost as the power and the presence of God increases upon you and your faith deepens. At that level, your spirit is totally focused on the spirit realm and distractions tend to lose their grip. On the extreme end, meditation takes God's word directly into your spirit. In other words, it makes God's word an integral part of your spirit and with the word of God in your spirit, the glory of God is provoked into manifestation. Lastly, creating an atmosphere of worship attracts the glory of God because when His praises goes up, His glory comes down. If you make an optimum mix of these exercises your spirit will be activated and spiritual capacity enlarged to receive the glory. The glory requires a place of habitation hence your spirit and body needs to be thoroughly prepared to inhabit or carry that glory. Many people desire to receive the glory but they are not able to carry the glory. Just like some people desire to be pregnant but then their bodies are not able to carry the baby for nine months. Rigorously embarking in any of the above mentioned spiritual exercises will enlarge your spiritual capacity and place you in a position whereby you qualify to be a recipient and carrier of God's glory.

Develop an understanding of how to respond to the glory of God

In the natural realm, the presence of clouds does not always guarantee rain. It depends on the amount of atmospheric pressure on the clouds. By the same token, our desperate hunger and thirst for God is what will cause His rain to come. However, we must learn how to respond to Him with great longing and faith, believing that what will soon follow is a great cloudburst of rain and a resulting harvest. How you respond to the glory will determine how much you can receive from that glory.

There are three different types of people that I would like to highlight with regard to responding to the glory. Firstly, there are those who have never experienced the glory, hence there have no clue whatsoever concerning operating in the glory. Then there are those who have experienced the glory but have not known what to do or how to respond when the glory is present. Thirdly, there are those who do not recognise the presence of the glory. The above scenario can cause people not to respond to the glory as they should. This is the reason why Uzzah mistakenly put out his hand and touched the ark of God and the anger of God was aroused and He struck him there for his error because he did not know how to respond to the glory of God(2 Samuel 6:6-7). The reason why Paul says some people are sick and dead because of failure to handle the Holy Communion is because of failure to respond to the glory of God. This should demonstrate for us that we shouldn't be too casual about the presence of God when we gather as believers, that is an atrocity. Uzzah's fate teaches us to be relevant towards God. It also teaches us about the importance of knowing and understanding the glory of God so that we can walk in it, live in it, experience it without offending him.

When in the presence of God, don't keep your arms crossed as if you are a spectator. Instead, celebrate His presence and learn to receive from Him. Respond to Him. Don't quench the Holy Spirit. When you move in the glory of God, you just have two things you can count on, *the leading of the Holy Spirit* and the *rhema word.* There is no specific pattern or structure that exists for you to go by. If the glory comes but you don't respond, then you cannot partake of the blessings it brings because with the glory comes blessings, breakthrough, elevation, promotion, healing and creative miracles. It is therefore evident that in order to awaken the glory of God into manifestation, you need to learn the art of responding to the glory. This has more to do with developing a significant level of sensitivity to His presence, hearing His voice accurately, and walking in the obedience and direction of the Holy Spirit. If you could only do that, then your spirit will become sensitive, hence responding to His glory will be like a stroll through a park.

Tap into the dimension of glory by demonstrating actions of faith.

In order to be fully inundated with God's glory, it's essential that we begin to see things in the realm of faith, and out of the realm of faith. Without faith, we can't hear what God is saying. Faith operates from a higher law than the natural laws of matter, space, and time. The person of faith believes and speaks from the eternal realm of the now, releasing the unseen realm of glory into the natural. *Faith is the Spiritual Language of Heaven.* There are many ways to enter into the spirit realm, but there is only one way to enter into the realm of the glory, that is only through *faith* in Jesus Christ. In order to access the glory realm, you must primarily have faith in Jesus Christ (Matthew 7:13-14, John 14:6, Galatians 3:26, 4:6-7, Romans 3:22). Jesus is the ultimate manifestation of God's glory (John 1:14), hence we need to have a deep relationship with Him that goes beyond our natural sense realm – that moves us into the *"supernatural"* sense realm of believing God's Word by faith. In order to walk in the glory realm you must believe the Word of God (John 20:27-3). Believing the Word will cause us to live in the realm of glory (Psalm 37:3). The *"signs"* or evidence of the glory realm will begin to manifest and follow you as you simply believe (Mark 16:15-20 Acts 2:42-47).

There is an intricate connection between *faith* and the *glory of God*. Jesus said to Martha in John 11:40, *"Did I not say to you that if you would believe you would see the glory of God?"*. Jesus gave us the key to seeing the tangible and visible glory of God, that is to believe, above all reason-and intellect and beyond your circumstances. We have access to God by faith. Faith is a higher law than the natural laws. By faith we can bypass space and time, stepping into the timeless realm. Faith is the door between the natural and supernatural dimensions—without faith we can't enter the spiritual realm—without faith we can't even please God (Hebrews 11:6). It's essential that our faith level rises, if ever we want to see the glory of God abundantly manifested in our lives.

Faith operates from the Spirit of Revelation. When we believe and decree by faith, we are reaching out of the natural realm of limited matter into the spiritual realm of unlimited creative resources. Faith is the language that moves the realm of glory. The natural man doesn't understand this language (I Corinthians 2:14), neither can he comprehend the reality of the glory realm. The fallen mind of man doesn't know or understand that he is living below his created potential. After the fall, God gave man faith to lift him so he could see into the unseen realm and have hope. When Adam fell, he was banished from the realm of glory and unable to see the place from where he came. But God in His love gave him faith so he could see and have hope of returning from where he fell. Without faith, he would have died. Likewise, we access our home of glory as we pull on it by faith. The faith realm supersedes the lower realm. We must get high in order to have authority over the low. God is calling this Glory Generation to go higher than we've ever been before.

"Now Faith is the assurance (the confirmation, the title deed) of the things [we hope for, being the proof of things [we] do not see and the conviction of their reality [faith perceiving as real fact what is not revealed to the senses]." (Hebrews 11:1).

Notice the word that this verse begins with: *Now*. When the glory cloud appears, by faith we have the authority to decree the *"Now!"* and the substance from the supernatural realm will manifest and materialize in the natural. For this to happen, it takes knowing God by revelation which ignites the faith to produce the substance of a miracle.

The nature of God is faith, so without faith it's impossible to please God.

Faith must become who we are or God's glory cannot abide with us. When we fall back on our fallen Adamic nature we cut ourselves off from our Life-Source. Sin weakens faith, and when unrepentant of it, faith will eventually cease to operate completely. The scripture confirms that God will beautify the humble (Psalm 149:4). When we humble ourselves we are able to step into the place from where we fell and operate from that glorious realm.

Miracles are of this higher dimension and are not influenced by time. Faith is a higher law that exists out of time and operates from the law of higher truth, not based on fact. The truth is, *"By His stripes you are healed"*, but the fact is you are sick. Which is dominant, *truth or fact?* Because truth is from the higher realm of God's presence and promise, it exceedingly triumphs over fact, human intellect, and reasoning—you are healed. Faith is like a tuner in a radio. A tuner picks up the radio waves in the atmosphere and releases them as sound in the natural. When we tune into the frequency of heaven by faith, we can pull back through time and space the new sounds and matter from the realm of the Kingdom. Metaphorically speaking, we are radios that are able to speak and decree the sounds of Heaven on *earth.* Jesus declared that,

> *"I will give you the keys of the kingdom of heaven, and whatever you bind (declare to be improper and unlawful) on earth must be what is already bound in heaven; and whatever you loose (declare lawful) on earth must be what is already loosed in heaven* (Matthew 16:19).

This is to tell you that supernatural matter will only be loosed on the earth in the faith realm if it is already loosed in the glory realm. It's necessary for us to understand the nature and ways of God, as well as the spiritual Kingdom laws that govern the universe, if we want to operate in the dimension of the glory.

Operating in the Glory means operating in new faith realms.

Prophetically speaking, the church is about to enter a new realm of faith where we are going to see an increase in the miraculous. In this place of faith, there will be opportunity for us to learn how to operate in the realm of glory. In order for us to do this, it's first necessary that we understand a little bit about the realm of the spirit in correlation with the natural realm. The physical world was created and birthed from the spiritual realm. Everything in the natural was birthed from a realm we cannot detect with our natural senses. As aforementioned, the natural man cannot receive the things of the spirit—therefore, it's our spirits that are able to sense, recognize, and experience the spiritual realm. It's your spirit man that receives revelation from the spirit realm. Supernatural substance is constantly being released between these two realms; both the natural and the spiritual. That is why faith is what joins the *"super"* to the *"natural"* to produce the *"supernatural"*.

Let Go of the Old and Press into the New realms of glory.

It is worth mentioning that although God's glory is set forth to manifest intensely in this season, many will not accept this new cloud of glory. They will evaluate it and give their stamp of disapproval; they will discourage others from diverting to this type of unrestrained worship. We will need to make decisions about where we want to go. Are we hungry for God? Will we pursue Him no matter how it looks or what it costs? When Jesus came to earth and performed miracles, signs, and wonders He said, *"Blessed is he who does not take offense at Me"* (Luke 7:23). I don't care how the cloud of His presence comes or what it looks like, as long as He keeps coming. We must be willing to lose our grasp of the old and reach out for the new. The glory altogether is new. People tend to be comfortable talking about the anointing—the manifest realm of glory. However, the glory is the new terrain the corporate body of Christ is beginning to trek into. God is offering this rising glory generation new dimensions of glory—we're going to touch places no generation before us has gone.

We were birthed from this realm of glory and it's where we should feel the most comfortable—the most fulfilled. This is because the Bible says *we were born in Zion, In Holy Jerusalem, in a numerable company of angels* (Hebrews 12:22). Moreover, when we worship God and give Him praise, we are fulfilling our very purpose—our destiny. In this place of glory your past sees your future and realizes it can't go where you are heading—it loses its grip on you. When we step into the glory, we are experiencing the future, we taste the eternal—our past simply falls away. As we step into the cloud of glory, we are stepping into the realm of *all things are possible*. We cannot go to a worship service thinking God is going to do something new while we hang onto the old—it doesn't work that way. We need to worship God in the now and minister to

Him in the new. We need fresh expectation—fresh faith. God is demanding that we operate by His principles—we must align ourselves with this new move and let go of the old.

It's impossible for the old schools of thought to mix with the renewed mind set of this Glory Generation. This new paradigm shift is being brought forth and backed up by the revelation and manifestation of the glory of God by the Holy Spirit. This will not come about in a conventional manner, but rather by a corporate body of believers who are connected to the Head of the body, which is Christ. Each person is a living stone that will make up a beautiful spiritual house, with Jesus Christ Himself being the chief cornerstone (I Peter 2:5; Ephesians 2:20-22).

Step into the new- the realm of new things.

It is worth exploring the divine truth that when we are in the Glory zone, we are able to declare the word of the Lord and see it supernaturally manifest. In other words, we would have stepped into Job 22:28, *"You shall decree a thing, and it shall be established for you."* In essence, when God said you shall declare a thing and it be established for you, It doesn't necessarily mean that you shall flippantly declare words but you shall declare things while in the glory zone and reap immediate results because words get to be established in the atmosphere of glory. God has given us access to the storehouses of heaven—provision, miracles, gifts, mantles, blessings, favour—you name it! As we encounter new realms of the Glory in this season, we will see a swift manifestation of the words we speak. Now is the time for us to decree a thing—it will be established. We are being commissioned by the Lord to step into new realms of Glory through worship and high praise. As we do this together, we are going to see the Kingdom of Power and Glory made manifest. God's Kingdom is taking dominion upon the earth and is displacing every stronghold of the enemy. Psalm 149:6 says, *"Let the high praises of God be in their mouth, and a two-edged sword in their hand."* To demonstrate the reality of this kingdom, the Bible confirms that, *"Christ will reign until all enemies are under His feet* (I Corinthians 15:25).

In our quest to migrate into higher realm of glory, we have also stepped into Amos 9:13, whereby *the plough man shall overtake the reaper.* That means we have stepped into a dimension whereby immediately after we sow a seed, we see a harvest. We are stepping into a realm of timelessness where the miracles in His presence are being made known to us in almost unimaginable ways. As we continue heavenward, we are breaking the constraints of the natural realm and shaking off old paradigms. The doors of heaven are opening wider than we've ever seen before and we are witnessing the unfolding of the scrolls of destiny. Both the seen and unseen worlds are being changed from one degree of Glory to another, and all are being transformed by this ever-increasing Glory of God.

Posture yourself into a birthing position for God's Glory.

There's one thing above all else that God wants from His people, that is to know His presence. He desires us to know His presence in our lives and He really is calling us to know that He is with us. God's presence is His glory, and He is calling us into the river of His glory. God wants us hungry, thirsty and desperate for His presence. Everything, He does comes out of His glory. That's where the power is. The power is in the glory, the glory river of His presence. *Everything is in the river.* Do you know the glory of God as God wants you to know it? God wants to give you His glory! It's going to permeate, saturate, and cover everything you do. He's calling His church into the river, into the glory. Everything He does comes out of the river. Everything God is going to do will come out of that river. Do you need healing? Position yourself in a birthing position by soaking into the river of His glory. That's where the creative miracles are, that's where the blind see, the deaf hear, and the mute speak, that's where broken hearts mend, and disease washes away. Are you contending for harvest? Get into the river and marinate yourself in His glory. Harvest is there - not just one or two fish, but an abundance of fish. Are you in bondage? Jump into the river. Make a big splash. Do you need a financial miracle? Dive into the river, joy is there, and sins are washed away in the glorious river of His presence. When we encounter the glory of the living God, the glory presence of Jesus the Healer is manifest, we are set free from sickness, disease, sin, lack and bondage.

All God calls us to do, therefore, is to go deep into the glory, deep into the river of His presence. The power is in the river. In the river is everything. God is calling you into the river. He is calling you to desire that place more than any place, or anything else. And when you desire, hunger, and thirst for His presence, you will glimpse the face of Jesus. *How badly do you want to see Jesus?.* God's glory is manifesting on the earth and in the lives of hungry believers in a fresh, new way. I believe that desperate saints will come into the glory of the Lord and see Jesus as they've never seen Him before. They will talk to God face-to-face, as Moses did. When you know Him and when you are obsessed with this one thing, that you would know Him, you'll know the power of His resurrection, Paul says, *"That I may know Him and the power of His resurrection"* (Philippians 3:10). You will just manifest the power of God everywhere you go because God will trust you with it. God is calling you into the river. Jump in! *There is a river, just locate the source.* Where is the river? The river flows from heaven, from God's throne, where His presence is. If you want to experience the river, first contend for the presence of the Source by positioning yourself before the Throne.

Position yourself before the One who is Life. Get into the glory of God, into relationship, and into knowing Him. This is far and above your daily devotional time, far above duty or obligation. This is hungering to be in His presence more than hungering for His power, or the work of His hand. It is a hunger for Him above all else. It's saying, *"Lord, even if I never know, see or experience your power, it's okay. I just want to be in your presence. I want you for who you are, not for what you do."* God is calling us into His glory to be ones satisfied by visitations of His presence, more than blessings or great demonstrations of power. He's calling us to know Him, to soak and saturate in the river of His awesome glory. Much too often we seek other things first, and yet, the Bible tells us to *"seek first the kingdom of God and His righteousness, and all these things shall be added to you"* (Matthew 6:33). God is asking us to seek His glory. Therefore, dive deeper into the river of His presence in order to experience the effulgence of His glory manifest more than ever before.

Develop an in-depth understanding of the Three Dimensions of the Supernatural realm.

In the word of God, three key dimensions of the supernatural realm are revealed, namely *faith,* the *anointing* and the *glory.* Likewise, there are three feasts that correspondingly represent the *three realms* of the supernatural namely, the *Feast of Passover,* the *Feast of Pentecost* and the *Feast of Tabernacles.* Passover symbolises faith, Pentecost symbolises the *anointing* and Tabernacles symbolises the *glory.* The truth is that you cannot understand the glory if you don't first understand *anointing* and you cannot understand the anointing if you don't have faith to catapult you into that higher dimension. The battle many preachers always have is introducing people into the glory of God. Faith is a voluntary act based on our knowledge or conviction. Faith is the first dimension into the supernatural. It is the legal entry into the invisible or super-natural realm. It is the key to operate and work in the eternal realm. It is the ability of the believer to believe something that is unreasonable. Faith is NOW and requires a revelation from now. You cannot have a present faith without a present revelation. We don't see a heightened degree of miracles today in the church because miracles occur in the NOW, not yesterday. Most of the decisions we make are based on time, not on faith. If it is not now, it is not faith. Faith is the prerequisite to enter into the glory. Many people want to enter the glory but don't even know what faith is. In essence, it is the substance of the spiritual world. When Jesus heard that, He said, *"This sickness is not unto death, but for the glory of God, that the Son of God may be glorified through it."* (John 11:4). Martha wanted to enter into the glory for Jesus to raise Lazarus from the dead but Jesus corrected her faith first. This is evidenced by His statement, *"Didn't I tell you that you must believe to see the glory of God?"* That means believing is what introduces us to the realm of glory. The glory of God is not revealed to everybody but only to those who would step into that dimension through faith. Faith has been given to each and every one of us by measure. You must first believe in order to see the glory of God. Entering in His glory is a reward of your faith; it is His greatest reward. Faith is supernatural but we have reduced it to something natural. We have reduced it to optimism and motivational messages. But when you preach faith, the most amazing miracles take place because it is NOW from a present revelation.

The next dimension (*Second dimension*) of the supernatural that introduces us into the realm of glory is *the anointing*. The anointing is an aspect of the supernatural power of God that empowers us to fulfil the purpose and calling here on earth. It is one of the aspects of His power working through us. It has been given to each and every one of us by measure. We need each other because we have measures that others don't have, and vice versa. But to each one of us grace was given according to the measure of Christ's gift. (Ephesians 4:7). We don't have it all in ourselves; we need each other. Anointing is the power of God working through you. It is the seal in your spirit you to experience the glory. In Him you also trusted, after you heard the word of truth, the gospel of your salvation; in whom also, having believed, you were sealed with the Holy Spirit of promise, (Ephesians 1:13). The anointing was given to us for the earth. There are no blind, deaf or sick people in heaven. There are none who are broken hearted and oppressed. You do not need anointing in heaven; it is for the earth. It is not for your pride or for your fame. God wants to release His anointing to humble people who love His people. If you are a pastor and you wanted to die with that mantle, it is best if you start transferring it on the next generation.

"The Spirit of the LORD is upon Me, Because He has anointed Me to preach the gospel to the poor; He has sent Me to heal the broken hearted, to proclaim liberty to the captives and recovery of sight to the blind, to set at liberty those who are oppressed (Luke 4:18).

God give us anointing because we all fell short of the glory of God (Romans 3:23). Man was under the glory, not the anointing, before sin and so God gave us anointing so that we are able to move in the supernatural realm. In other words, after falling short of the glory of God (Romans 3:23), God gave man the anointing as a back-up.

The next dimension into the supernatural realm is the glory. The glory is the third dimension. The glory of God is the manifested presence of God Himself. It is the realm of eternity. It is eternity revealed, without limits or restrictions. It is the atmosphere of God Himself. Each manifestation is from the nature and character of God Himself. It is not His power operating through us, but rather it is God Himself doing His own works. We have limited God because we think He has to do His works through a human being. While this is true in the anointing and in faith, in His glory He works by His own initiative. It is beyond your measure of faith and anointing. It is God Himself, in all of His attributes and majesty. When God performs a miracle in you without you having the faith to believe for it or the anointing to manifest it, it is God Himself touching you directly. I had been in meetings where, without even touching anyone, miracle after miracle begins taking place. It had nothing to do with people's faith, anointing or gifts but the glory of God!

15. Get rid of sin, distraction or anything that might hinder you from seeing the glory.

It is true that sin can be a major impediment to operating in the glory. Isaiah testified in Isaiah 6:1 saying, *"In the year King Uzziah died, I saw the glory of God"*. That means Uzziah was a major obstacle that was hindering the move of the glory of God. Isaiah couldn't see the glory because of the presence of Uzziah whom he feared, reverenced and honoured. In a natural context there are certain things that need to die such as flesh, pride, relationships in order for us to see the glory of God. It is the death or separation to the old man, that leads to the arising of a new. It is the putting away of the old mind through the mind of Christ. It is establishing where our true-life source is, and where our treasures and values are. It is death to the old order ideas that life consist of the abundance of things we possess (Luke 12:15).

It is the death of those things that we sometimes hold dear, value and esteem. In the year that king Uzziah died or my pet formula, my pet doctrine, my pet song, whatever I admire and is driven for (Isaiah 6:1), the things that we feel make us important inside and out. It is the deaths of what we merit, the death (separation and distinction) to what we argue as of that which brings us happiness. It may even by our Isaac, on the third day (Genesis 22) ready to be offered up. No, it is not to make us miserable, or to strip us of a happy life. But it is putting things into perspective. For when we lose or let go of the pull and tug of the lower life, we find to enjoy ever more the higher life. That's why the overcoming sons need more than to rightly divide the word of truth, but to rightly divide asunder soul from spirit.

For when we are walking below at the exclusion from the above dimensions of the higher life, we potentially reflect Adam, who was just a living soul. Sure, we have chores to do, and Martha had a legitimate concern, although it was not the time to spring clean, so-to-speak. But the truth is, whether higher or lower, natural or spiritual, above or beneath, or visible and invisible, there is to be a distinction made between soul and spirit. The dwellers of the heavens can also live on earth, but they have the mind of Christ, his thoughts, feelings, and purposes. Those that inhabit (in many cases those that are inhabited by) the earth and sea can very well speak of some who are tossed to and from by every sea billow. It could also mean the earth, every wind of doctrine, relegating life to the dust, just surviving, just getting by, life as usual, the "self" same thing.

---

16. Arise! Shine! For the glory of the Lord is risen upon thee.

It is of paramount significance to highlight the fact that although countless messages have been preached behind the pulpit on the glory, the glory realm can never be exhausted as there are deeper territories, higher dimensions and greater heights in this unknown dimension. As we embark on a voyage or expedition to explorer the mysteries of this unknown dimension, lets refer to the Biblical account of Isaiah sixty, which presents a striking description of how we are to demonstrate the glory of God to the furthest extremes of the world: This scripture unveils *9 key elements* that are crucial in provoking the glory of God into manifestation. Let's look closely at how this scripture is chronologically presented as there are deep revelations gleaned in its narrative:

Arise (from the depression and procrastination in which the circumstances have kept you- rise to a new life)! Shine (be radiant with the glory of the Lord), for your light has come, and the glory of the Lord has risen upon you! And His glory will be seen upon you. See, darkness covers the earth and gross darkness the people, but upon thee, the glory of God is risen. Kings shall come to the brightness of your rising and your sons shall come from afar. And the wealth of the nations shall come to you (Isaiah 60:1 AMP).

In the context of the above-mentioned scripture, do you notice that verse 1 is connected to verse 2 and verse 2 is connected to 3? This is because verse 2 begins with the word *and*, and verse 3 begins with the word *of*. Meaning the story is not complete until you get to verse 3. In other words, this is a *spiritual chain of action-and-reaction* because your shining is dependent on your rising and revelation (the reflection of light) is connected to your shining and the impartation of glory is a consequence of revelation, the manifestation of glory is dependent on the degree of its impartation and favour, spiritual influence and wealth transfer are the products of impartation of glory.

ARISE!

This speaks of a response to a "DIVINE CALLING"

The word *arise* is a verb, an act and a doing word. This is a *calling* to undertake a specific assignment. It's not a request, petition or negotiation but a *statement of instruction*. It's a directive, order and mandate from the Master Himself. It is an order to make a decision and take action. Sadly, indifference is the condition of many believers today when faced with great challenges imposed by the world. They are passive, domicile and lethargic, waiting for something to happen, instead of making things happen. They are coiled in their comfort zones and potentially wired in a mundane word of religion, complacency and mediocrity to the extent of drowning in depression, confusion and ambivalence. As a consequence, many are sick, busted and wounded. But God says *arise* from that depression, *arise* from failure, *arise* from death and *arise* to a new life. In other words, come out of your comfort zone, step out from the crowd and set your sail through the glory realm.

The reason why multitudes are entangled in a morass of debilitating poverty, sickness and death is because they are not arising. You see, the solution to the prevalence of your unrelenting circumstances is not in running from church to church seeking for an impartation but it's in your arising. God is calling you to arise! This is a wake-up call for radical revivalists and revolutionaries to rise up on this epic transition and take their rightful place on earth by curtailing the mass rampage instigated by the devil through alarming deaths and eradicating the syndrome of sickness, poverty and calamity that has gripped the masses for ages. Therefore, if you are tired of being a sailor or existing on the shores of tradition and religion, make up your mind today that you will never be broke another single day in your life. Make up your mind that you will never be ordinary, ever again. Make up your mind that you will never be sick in your body. As you make that decision, you are already stepping out of the plane of the ordinary, out of spiritual lethargy and the negative spiritual gravity that keeps you conformed to the status quo. Did you know that the life of a Christian is programmed to progressively move in one direction, upward and forward only? Therefore, break camp and move forward. You see, God is raising a distinct breed of people who are revolutionaries and world changers.

The voice of God is echoing throughout the earth, calling for man and woman to step out of their comfort zones and delve into the higher realms of His glory. In other words, God is raising a distinct breed of people who are modern day, 'minute men', ready at the drop of a hat to bring about abundant life into situations where the enemy would have stolen, killed and destroyed; a distinct breed of believers who shall curtail the rampage instigated by the devil through alarming deaths by de-program-ming his operations, while installing the agenda of Heaven. God is setting a global stage for this new breed of people to step out of the crowd, out of the convictions of ordinary life of mediocrity and complacency, to parade on the global scene and be rightly positioned in the spirit to take over territories of the world on behalf of the Kingdom. God is therefore breaking forth every man and woman into a season of great spiritual awakening. Therefore, don't you dare stay in the same place; there is more for you in God in terms of deeper territories, newer realities and higher realms of glory than what you might be currently experiencing. Hence, you need to take your foot off the brakes of religion and tradition so that you can accelerate into the new realms of glory which God is unfolding from the Heavenly realm. In this end time season, you will have to stop clinging on the shoreline and delve into the river of glory as God is calling men and women to step out of the convictions of ordinary life of mediocrity and complacency into a realm of overflowing, explosive and electrify-ing glory, to manifest the glorious expressions of the Heavenly Father from within the *third dimension*. This is to tell you that there is a new type of man coming forth on the earth rising beyond the confines and dictates of the realm of time, to access the glory. The truth of the matter is that yu are that man whom God has singled out by His grace to be a chanel of His glory on earth. The question is: *Are you ready to arise?*

To provide a quintessential example of this scenario, I'm reminded of how Peter stepped out of his boat and confronted the surging waters of the sea and began to walk on water when Jesus called him and said, "Peter come". Peter had previously seen every miracle that you could name, but when he saw Jesus walk in water, he perceived there was another deeper realm that he had not experienced before. Hence, he stepped out of his boat, he stepped out of religion; out of the confines of the realm of senses and began to walk on water. But in order for him to see the power of God being demonstrated by walking on water, he had to first step out of the boat. The truth is that unless and if you come out of the boat, you will not see the power of God being displayed through you. Your boat is your comfort zone, your status quo and your environment that confines you to a place of mediocrity, complacency and average thinking. Hence, you have to come out of that artificial environment in which the circumstances of life have entangled you. Just like Peter, begin to put your foot out of the boat and God will make the waters solid under your feet. Do you remember when Peter toiled the whole night in an endeavour to catch fish but could not catch anything until Jesus stepped on the scene and gave him a revelation to cast into the deep? While it seemed as if the fish were previously refusing to enter his nets, following the revelation of casting the nets into a deeper realm, it appeared as if the fish themselves started competing to enter his nets. You see, the problem was not with the gifting per se, for Peter was an experienced fisherman. Instead, the problem was the depth, dimension or level of operation, that's why Jesus told him to shift his position and cast into the deeper realm. You see, you need to cast your faith into the deeper realm and push beyond the dictates and confines of your comfort zone to a realm that is unfamiliar to your status quo.

This is a season to step out in faith and confront the surging waters of the sea of world problems. Do you know what happens when you step up higher? Your legs start to dangle because God removes the step on which you previously rested your feet. When your legs start to dangle, they are not touching anything familiar. It's a new realm that you are catapulted into. The reason why multitudes seem to be entangled in a morass of debilitating poverty, sickness and disease is because the level and dimension in which they operate is too shallow to give birth to a breakthrough in the realm of the spirit. Do you notice that when you are in the air, you are not conscious of the plane's speed when it is in its height? You are only conscious of speed, the more you descend. By the same token, you are only conscious of your debilitating circumstances of disease, sickness or debt because of the lower plane of life in which you live. When you go higher, you learn that your circumstance can't come where you are going. The higher we ascend, the less we are aware of ourselves. This scenario is exemplified by Peter who stepped out of the boat when he saw Jesus walking on water and confronted the billowing storms, the boisterous winds and the surging waters of the sea and in response, God gave him a foretaste of His supernatural power.

Prophetically speaking, paradigms are shifting as God is calling and raising a new generation of people with the audacity to leave the comfort of the boat and walk on water and perform miracles for His glory. A new day is birthing a distinct calibre of believers who will dare to step out of the mundane world of religion into the supernatural realm. God is stirring up a company of believers who will not accept the status quo; a unique breed of people who shall step out of their comfort zones to emerge at the centre of the world stage to influence the nations for Christ through a practical display of God's power. It is an incontestable fact that you have been called, divinely ordained by God and duly mandated by Heaven to perform miracles, signs and wonders for His glory. In other words, you have been given a divine apostolic and prophetic mandate, certified by a stamp of God's approval, and authenticated by the seal of His own handwriting that you should uncompromisingly move in the supernatural power of God. But for that to happen, you must first arise.

Prophetically speaking, many of you have shifted from the position God established for you that's why you are no longer connecting properly. You see, in order for an Ariel to access the airwaves and transmit them to a television set, it must be rightly positioned and connected. By the same token, in order for you to access the heavenly airways and the frequency of the Holy Ghost in the realm of the spirit, you must be rightly positioned. That is why immediately after the fall of man in the Garden of Eden, God called Adam, "*Adam, where are you*". Not because God was not seeing him per se, but because he had shifted from his usual position where God had placed him. Many of you ought to be raising the dead, raising cripples from wheel chairs, healing the sick and waking on water but you haven't attained those levels because you are not arising. Many of you ought to be operating in the five-fold offices of an apostle, prophet, evangelist, pastor and teacher but your offices are vacant because you are not arising. Many of you ought to be occupying key positions of leadership and governance in the business, economic and political world in the capacity of company directors, CEOs, ministers, and parliamentarians but you are far below those standards because you are not arising. Many of you ought to be millionaires by now and impacting this world with Kingdom financial resources but you are still centinaires because you are not arising. But it's never too late, hence, God says, Arise!

SHINE!

This speaks of "EXUDING EXCELLENCE"

The word *shine* is translated from the Hebrew word, *owr,* which means to be the *light,* to be luminous, to show light or to be set on fire. Therefore, to shine means to *exude excellence* in every facet of human existence as your spirit is *aglow* with the glory of God. In order for you to shine, you must first become the *light* and be set ablaze. This is the reason why Jesus said, *"You are the light of the world"*, in the very sense of the word. As you shine, the glory of God is manifested, darkness is dispelled and everything is aligned according to its original blue print in Heaven. However, in order to shine, you have to first arise. This shining occurs when you arise from that spiritual condition of lethargy, passivity and conformity. That means shining is a consequence or product of your arising. When you eventually make a decision to arise by stepping out of your comfort zone, instantaneously, you start shining. When a bird makes a decision to flip its wings and take off into the sky, automatically, it starts flying. By the same token, when you release your faith and step into a higher realm of glory, you start shining. As much as it is inherently genetic for a bird to fly, it is also part of our genetic make-up or DNA as a new creation believer to shine with the glory of God. When you take out light from the position in which it was previously hidden and you place it on the table, it doesn't struggle to give light; it shines automatically. By the same token, when you come out of your hiding, your light becomes evident to all without any hustles, wimping and huffing. The truth is that God is ready to grossly manifest His glory through you but for that to happen, you need to take action Your shining is dependent on your rising and that is why some actions that we take have either a negative or positive bearing on the destinies of those we are connected to. In the same way your preaching is dependent on the level of understanding of the Word, your shining is dependent on your degree of arising. Unless and if you take action and step out of the boat, out of your comfort zone and convictions of ordinary life of complacency and mediocrity, you will not shine.

Did you know that the *glory* is the beauty of light embedded in your spirit but that beauty or glory will not be seen or made manifest unless you shine. It's only when you shine that the beauty of the glory of God in your spirit will be reflected. *But in a practical sense, how do we shine?* Shining is the act of displaying the beauty, virtues, perfections and excellences of the father. When we raise the dead, we are shining; when we raise cripples from their wheel chairs, we are shining; when we heal every manner of sickness and disease, we are shining; when we become Kingdom Millionaires and we take over the wealth and property of the nations, we are shining, glory to God!. Did you know that everybody has a star which denotes a symbol of greatness in life? Depending on the extent of pursuit of the calling of God, others have their stars shining brightly while others are just dim. The extent to which your light is shining is what determines your sphere of influence. You can only influence people in your sphere of contact as far as your light shines. Shining is an imperative action, hence you cannot but shine, in your family, office, business, church and every sphere of life. If you can shine in your family, then you can shine in your street, and if you can shine in your street, then you can shine in your city and if you can shine in your city, then you can shine in your nation and the whole world, glory to God! It's only through your shining that you will be able to influence man and take over the territories of the world on behalf of the Kingdom.

FOR YOUR LIGHT HAS COME.

This speaks of "REVELATION"

It is an incontestable fact that the reason why God gives us His light is to make us shine. So, your shining is dependent on the intensity, magnitude and severity of your light. The greater the light, the greater the shining. As much as gross darkness is the intensity of darkness, the glory is the intensity of Light. In essence, light is the reflection of the glory of God. Therefore, when Isaiah prophetically announces that your light has come, what he implies is that the glory of God is being reflected or radiated from your spirit. But why is he telling you? Because not everything is obvious to everybody. There are people who receives an impartation of the glory manifested though breakthroughs, open doors and answers to prayers but they don't even know it. Hence, Isaiah breaks the ice and says, "*Hey look, your light has come*". This light is the life to carry out everything God has commanded. Whenever we go, that light transforms our surroundings and impacts our world. With God's light, we can determine what dimension of glory or what proportion of his light we will allow to manifest on earth. The light we reflect is like the sun that shines brightly on earth. The amount of God's light you choose to shine will determine the range of your influence and dominion. In this Year of Shining, let it be ingrained in your thinking that you were born to make history; hence, it is time to shine through the darkness of this world.

The truth is that light speaks of *revelation*. The Bible speaks of the two lights in Genesis 1:16, that is, the *greater light* and the *lesser light* representing the dimensions of truths or revelation of God's word. The greater light speaks of the *greater truth* while the lesser light speaks of the *lesser truth*. But you are the *Greater light* because you carry the greater revelation of God's word. It is worth exploring the divine truth that the glory realm is a realm of *revelation*. That is why there is such a thing as *the revelation glory*. It is a realm whereby everything is known. It is beyond the realm of gifts, faith and the anointing. Figuratively speaking, common sense is to the natural man what revelation is to the man in the Glory of God. Revelation is such a multipurpose key in the realm of glory. It is an indispensable necessity to unlocking the door to the new realms, unknown teritories and greater depths of the glory realm. While manifestation precedes *revelation*, it is revelation that produces the manifestation. Revelation is the *birthplace* for every supernatural manifestation. Metaphorically speaking, manifestation is revelation realized in operational design, in divine rhythm and motion. Therefore, it is revelation that gives birth to a manifestation. Hypothetically speaking, you cannot get fire from water; it takes fire to set a fire. It takes a certain amount of rain to cause a flood. By the same token, without a constant flow of revelation into your spirit, the glory of God will not be intensely manifested. And truth be told: Where there is no widespread revelation on the glory realm, it remains an unknown dimension.

THE GLORY OF THE LORD IS RISEN UPON YOU.

This speaks of the "IMPARTATION" and "PERAMBULATION" of the glory.

It is worth exploring the divine truth that impartation precedes revelation. In order for the glory to be received as an impartation into your spirit, you must have revelation of how to receive it. Traditionally, we always expect the glory of God to fall from above, because that is how it happened in the Old Testament, today the glory can still come upon us as it did upon the early church but it is also within us, *perambulating* in the extreme quarters of our spirit. It is a treasure that is birthed in us and revealed knowledge will bring about its manifestation. I'm reminded of how the glory of God descended upon Jesus in the form of a dove and rested upon His spirit such that immediately He became a wonder in the world. Therefore, *the Glory of God rising upon you* speaks of the manifestation of the glory of God in your spirit that makes you operate with heavenly efficiency. It is worth exploring the divine truth that while in the old covenant the glory of God was like a cloud inhabiting a place, in the New Testament, the glory of God is placed right into our spirit man when we are born again. Once the glory of God rises upon you, it starts to perambulate inside your spirit, driving out darkness, sickness and any trace of poverty.

This is to tell you that the glory of God is not only found in Heaven as some have erroneously presumed it to be. Instead, the glory of God is domiciled in your spirit. That is why from time to time, if you ever spend time in God's presence, the glory comes out through your eyes, mouth and body, to the extent of oozing out through every fibre of your being. In John G. Lake's books, you read his experience of flashes of God's glory coming out of his body. In Kathryn Kuhlman's biography, people who knew her before she went into the ministry said her eyes looked sparklingly different after she entered into the ministry. She was not the same Kathryn Kuhlman. Why? Because the illuminating glory of God was now resident in her spirit to the extent that she was so mingled and infused in the glory of God such that she became the glory. The truth is that contrary to the operation of the glory of God in the Old Testament, now the tabernacle has been gotten rid of, hence your body is now the outer court of God's glory, your soul is the inner court of God's glory and your spirit is the inner court of God's Glory. This tells me that you are now the tabernacle of God's glory as your spirit, soul and body is set ablaze or aglore with the glory of God. In essence, you are now the glory of God manifested on the earth on behalf of heaven.

In the same manner in which the glory of God descended upon the tabernacle and set it on fire, you are now a blast furnace in the realm of the spirit, exploding with the glory of God. As a custodian of God's glory, the glory dwells in you and you carry it everywhere you go, hence when you show up in any territory, God has arrived because you carry Him in your Spirit. That is why unlike Moses, we are no longer beggars of the glory but carriers of the glory. There are certain statements that are illegal or not permitted for a man to say in the New Testament dispensation which were permitted under the old covenant. For example, you cannot echo Moses statement and say to God, *"Show me your glory"*. This is because the glory of God is no longer an external force but its permanently embedded in the extreme quarters of the spirit. Therefore, praying like Moses is akin to praying amiss because the glory of God is no longer an ethereal or stratospheric force but a tangible spiritual reality resident in your spirit. It's no longer, *"Lord, Show me your glory"* as Moses petitioned, instead, the correct terminology to use in inviting a break out of high realms of glory in your life is, *"Lord, reveal your glory"* because the glory of God is no longer confined to the realm of sight only but revelation.

HIS GLORY WILL BE SEEN UPON YOU.

This speaks of the "MANIFESTATION" of glory.

The glory of God will manifest in a visible and tangible way when we arise. Manifestation precedes impartation. In other words, in order for the glory of God to be visibly and tangibly manifested or seen, it must be imparted upon the spirit of a vessel. The glory of God is not just theory, a pretty concept or theology that is impossible to demonstrate in the natural realm. When the glory of God is displayed in the church, streets, market place and the public arena, the whole world will see it with its own eyes. Note that the glory of God cannot be hidden. You see, it's not just enough to be a recipient of the glory, it must be visibly and tangibly seen in the natural realm. Unless and if the glory of God is seen in the natural realm, it will not influence man. The truth is that God desires that His glory be publically demonstrated so that the millions who are lost can see and turn to Jesus. The world will see the glory in us but how will it manifest? It's simple. God will do things that will attract multitudes to the church and cause billions of souls to stream into the church in an unprecedented manner. That is why in this season, God is raining the *golden glory* in the form of gold dust, silver, diamonds and other precious stones coupled with miracle money so that people will see the glory and believe in Jesus Christ. In this end time season which marks the summation of ages, during worship sessions, angels shall be visibly seen imparting the substance of glory upon its recipients.

It is worth mentioning that the glory of God is not an ethereal force but a visible and tangible spiritual substance. In the same way the glory of God led the children of Israel as a pillar of fire by night and a pillar of could by day, the glory of God shall be visibly seen upon you. That means you are now the pillar of fire and the pillar of cloud because the glory of God is in you; in the extreme quarters of your spirit. That means you are now a custodian of God's glory on earth, hence whenever you show up, God has arrived because His glory is seen through you. In the same way Elijah saw the glory of God as small as the man's hand, the glory of God shall be seen upon you but this time it shall not be as small as a man's hand but as big as a man's body. The dimension of the glory manifesting as small as a man's hand speak of the beginning, or entry level point into the glory realm. However, there are deeper territories, realms and dimensions that we have to migrate to. There is another very important revelation gleaned in Prophet Isaiah's declaration that, *"The glory of God will be seen upon you"* and that is the principle of *vision*. Bearing in mind that in the realm of the spirit, things are procured or possessed through sight or vision, as the glory of God is seen upon you, many will receive it because in the spirit, once you see something, you have it. This is what we call *Prophetic perception*. This is a spiritual sight necessary to see what God is doing in the invisible arena and in tandem with Him, you do exactly the same in the visible realm. It incorporates the ability to see the unseen, hear the unheard and then speak the unspeakable. This means that your imagination was intended by God to be the lens through which you apprehend the realms of spiritual realities.

DARKNESS SHALL COVER THE EARTH AND GROSS DARKNESS THE PEOPLE.

This speaks of "SUBJUGATING THE INFLUENCE OF THE DEMONIC KINGDOM"

The word *darkness* referred to in the scripture above does not refer to physical darkness but the terrifying influence of Satan's kingdom on earth. There are two dimensions of darkness unveiled in the above scripture and those are; *ordinary darkness* which is an entry level in the realm of evil and is said to cover the earth and *gross darkness* which is the intensity of darkness or darkness manifested to its highest degree and is said to cover the people. The darkness that covers the earth refers to the veracity of natural disasters while the gross darkness that covers the people refers to the debilitating circumstances facing humanity such as death, sickness and poverty. The reality is that spiritual darkness covers the earth and its manifestation is getting thicker while the people have no idea what to do about it. The strongest evidences of this state of affairs include the escalating natural disasters taking place around the world, multitudes drying of starvation, endless wars amongst nations and global economic crises. The truth is that the world is terribly spinning out of order on its way to absolute destruction, hence the masses are starving for the glory of God to intervene and stop the madness. Taking into account a myriad of horrific, traumatic and appalling events which are unfolding in different parts of the world in the current times, it suffices to adjudicate that the world is in a state of crisis, pandemonium and disarray and conforms to the exact pattern of deformity and darkness in which it was just before creation.

Furthermore, as the influence of darkness covers the earth, economies are crumbling, governments are crushing, and this has culminated in incredibly alarming deaths of millions of innocent souls across the globe. Moreover, the frequency and veracity of natural disasters such as earthquakes, hurricanes and tsunamis seem to be on the rise and rebellion, wars and rumours of war continues to wreak havoc as they dominate the daily headlines and fill the evening newscasts. The staggering pace of modern society continues to bombard us in every newscast with disturbing events unfolding throughout the world. As if that is not enough, starvation and malnutrition has become the order of the day as humanity in the extreme quarters of life is being plunged into a morass of debilitating poverty. A saddening and darkening global economic outlook has become a common experience as economies of the world are shaken right to their foundations. Moreover, a financial crisis is eroding countries around the globe where corruption, insecurity and fear abound as the fate of humanity seems to be determined by the principles of a morally degenerating world. All this is classed as negative spiritual gravity emanating from the influence of the kingdom of darkness.

The question that you are probably asking yourself is: But why is gross darkness covering the people? It's because they have allowed themselves to be under the influence of evil and have given the devil a legal foot hold to influence their lives. This is the reason why Jesus labelled the Pharisees and Sadducees as the children of the devil because through their envy, anger and grief, they had opened a door for the devil to rule over their hearts. Due to the influence of darkness, many people have returned into the world in search of other alternative sources of power and some have yielded themselves to the demonic realm to the extent that they are used as agents of darkness operating in the capacity of devil worshipers, Satanists, magicians and witches.

The pervasive rise in occult activity, coupled with the Church's naiveté in matters of the supernatural are main factors that have beguiled some Christians into displacing Christ's throne with the virtually extinct deities of the secular world. That is why there is such a heightened degree of counterfeit demonstration of fake power in the kingdom of darkness manifested through magic, witchcraft, divination and sorcery because in some instances the power of God has been substituted for evil. The Church's inability to demonstrate the supernatural power of God has therefore created a vortex for every dark spirit to suck the masses into its clutches.

However, the good news is that the glory we carry has the power to subjugate the darkness by curtailing the mass rampage instigated by the devil all around the world through alarming deaths, sickness and poverty. Although the darkness in the world becomes denser each day and wickedness continues to multiply, the manifestation of God's glory on earth is correspondingly becoming more powerful and weighty with each passing moment (Isaiah 60:3). We are therefore not shaken by the presence of darkness in our world because *the darker the night, the more brightly the light shines.* In other words the severity of our glory is revealed more when darkness is intensified. We are an exemption to the darkness of this world because we are superior to Satan and his cohorts. In the same way God provided light to the children of Israel in Goshen while there was horrific and terrifying darkness on the side of Egypt, we operate under *the covenant of exemption,* hence we are exempted from the darkness of this word.

KINGS SHALL COME TO THE BRIGHTNESS OF YOUR RISING.

This speaks of "GLOBAL IIMPACT" and "DIVINE FAVOUR"

In the context of this scripture, the word *Kings* speak of those who occupy the highest positions of authority and governance in our business, economic, social and political world. Note that the *kings* are not coming to you per se, but to the brightness of your rising. In other words, it is when you arose that they realised that they brightness they saw was because of you, hence they are streaming in your direction. The truth is that your lack of arising is what is actually delaying your own breakthrough and divine appointment with these influential people. The implication is that once God manifests His glory upon us and it becomes visible to the world, then the world's leaders in the capacity of Presidents, Prime Ministers, Governors, Senators, Mayors, and many of those who hold high positions of authority and governance in politics, business world and in the communities, will seek our guidance and direction. When they see the glory of God being publicly displayed and manifested through signs and wonders such as the raising of the dead, they will stream to our churches clamouring to know more about the new move of God and how they can financially support it. They will understand that they do not have the answers for the people whom they govern in the midst of such dense darkness; hence they will constitutionally endorse Jesus Christ as the Lord of their nations. Mind you, many of those leaders have already consulted witchdoctors, sorcerers and soothsayers but have found no viable answers. The world is therefore desperately looking for answers to major worldwide crises and all these fundamental problems but neither governments, world political leaders, nor religious systems seem to be able to offer valid solutions. We therefore live in a generation filled with unanswered questions because religion has dismally failed to provide any valid answers to the horrendous plight of humanity and the debilitating cicumstances of life facing the masss. Therefore, when God manifest His glory upon us, we will not give them answers based on human understanding, religion or natural reasoning but on the revelation of the Spirit of God. We will give them supernatural prophetic words that will speak specifically to their lives, cities and nations. This is indeed a season of global impact and global demonstration of the glory of God!

Notable is the realisation that the act of Kings coming to the brightness of your rising is coupled with *favour*. Favour is the outshining of God's glory. It is the outworking of the magnetic power of the glory. The glory of God has such a strong magnetic force that attracts those with power, influence and resources to stream to our churches in search for solutions to the worldwide crises. It releases a supernatural influence that trigger divine arrangement of circumstances in the realm of the spirit that will bring to you the right people, at the right time, with the right resources. Do you know that some countries are paying their tithes to men of God? This is the reality of the divine truth which I'm talking about, which shall become a common phenomenon in the Body of Christ as believers in the extreme ends of the earth are catapulted right the climax of God's glory.

YOUR SONS SHALL COME FROM AFAR.

This speaks of "SPIRITUAL INFLUENCE AND MENTORSHIP"

The phrase, *your sons shall come to you* speaks of your spiritual influence. How does this influence come about? It is connected to the previous verse. As Kings come to the brightness of your rising, your scope of influence of spiritual domain shall correspondingly broaden as you influence the world through the effulgence of God's glory. The word *sons* in the context of the above scripture speak of *discipleship or mentorship*. As the *Kings* and those connected to your destiny come to you, you shall provide them with spiritual guidance, direction and mentorship in the things of God. In other words, you shall be a centre of attention. The truth is that God is bringing home a generation of prodigal sons and daughters to save them and raise them up in this movement of His glory. He is bringing them from afar, releasing them from the prison of alcohol abuse, drug addiction, immorality and other debilitating circumstances facing humanity. This generation yearns for the supernatural and is running towards the light. Do you know that spiritual sonship also infers a covering of the glory? In 1 Samuel 19:23, the Bible records a remarkable story about *Saul who was not a prophet but when he joined or came under the influence of prophets, he too started prophesying* to the extent that people were amazed. When he came under the spiritual covering of the prophets, he received a prophetic impartation and started prophesying. In a similar vein, as your scope of influence enlarges, it is possible that those who come under your spiritual covering will be able to operate in the higher realms of glory that you have tapped into. It is through the law of influence that God precipitates the substance of His glory to not only those in our immediate sphere of contact but also to those from the extreme ends of the world. This is what we call *a spill over of blessings.*

There is a realm in which you can operate whereby you determine everything that happens in your street and as you continue to operate in the glory of God, your sphere of influence enlarges to the extent that you are able to influence the whole city. As you continue to explore the deeper territories in the glory realm, you will realise that there is a dimension in the glory realm that you reach whereby you are able to control what happens in your nation and your prolonged stay in this realm will eventually catapult you to a level whereby you literally take over the extreme ends of the world. I read of how God used Smith Wigglesworth mightily to such an extent that he permitted no one in his locality to die without his permission. This is to show you how broad his sphere of influence had extended. Some people command authority over cities, others over regions, while others over continents. Your sphere of influence is determined by the degree of authority you can command in the realm of the spirit, the level of your revelation as well as the size of your God-given dream. It is through your influence that many believers shall come from the extreme ends of the world seeking for mentorship in the matters of the Kingdom. It is for this reason that we have established the *Global School of Resurrection* whereby believers come from different parts of the world to receive deeper revelations on resurrection and an impartation to raise the dead in their areas of influence.

THE WEALTH OF THE NATIONS SHALL COME TO YOU.

This speaks of "WEALTH TRANSFER"

Do you know that the term *glory* also means *wealth*, hence wealth is a symbol of glory. Philosophically speaking, show me a man with wealth and I will show you one who has received a greater weight of glory. Remember that one aspect of the glory, the *kabowd* of God is *wealth*. The phrase *the wealth of the gentiles shall come to you* speaks of wealth transfer, which shall become a common occurrence in the Body of Christ in these end times. It refers to the top riches of this world, expressed in the form of gold, diamonds and the top currencies of the world, held as reserves in the world banks or local banks. It also incorporates the best territories which are producing riches all around the world such as land, property, mines, city buildings, banks, multinational companies which God is *transferring* to the hands of believers as part of His end time agenda on earth. The basis of wealth transfer is Proverbs 13: 22: *the wealth of gentiles shall be transferred to the righteous.* The word *gentiles* as used in the context of the above scripture is not an insult per se, but a collective term used to mean unbelievers or all those who have not yet received Christ. This means that the wealth of the gentiles, who are unbelievers, will come to the righteous in the manifestation of the glory, just as Israelites received wealth from Egyptians when they left Egypt by the powerful hand of the Lord.

Wealth transfer involves a supernatural transfer of money or financial resources from the hands of the wicked (Unbelievers, sinners, devil's cohorts) into the hands of the righteous (believers) in such a way that is inexpiable in the natural realm. This Biblical phenomenon denotes a supernatural transfer of heaven's wealth and resources in the form of money, gold, silver, oil, investments, property and a myriad of other riches in glory from the worldly systems in possession of unbelievers into the hands of believers whom God has ordained or set apart to finance His end time agenda, plans and purposes. It is worth noting that in this end time season whereby God shall lift up his people especially in the arena of financial provision so that they can quickly expedite His divine plans and purpose on earth. It must be understood that while it is possible to rain miracle money directly from heaven, some of the financial resources which God is going to unleash upon His people will not come directly from Heaven. Instead, they are already located in the earth realm in possession of unbelievers. What God simply does is to transfer, shift or move these finances from corrupt, bogus, wicked people of this world into the hands of His children who are ready to use them to for propagate the gospel of the Lord Jesus to the furthest extremes of the world. This supernatural transfer will take place in a way that ordinary people will not understand; even bank experts will not be able to comprehend the dynamics of this divine phenomenon. This shall be a time when God separates the righteous from the wicked. The Bible records a spectacular or striking event in Exodus 10:21-11:10 whereby on a given day, while there was thick darkness which covered the whole of Egypt, there lights in Goshen, which was a place inhabited by the Children of Israel. In other words there was a *transfer* of light from the wicked to the righteous. This is the same principle by which God uses to transfer wealth from hands of the wicked to the righteous. While there is financial darkness for the wicked characterised by crash of markets and loss of wealth, there shall be abundance, increase, and alarming profits for the righteous.

As far as God is concerned, wealth transfer is not a new biblical concept in the realm of prosperity but a divine phenomenon that has transpired across past generations. However the gravity and intensity of its manifestation shall be heightened in this end times in what is called *the final wave of prosperity*. In a Biblical context, this phenomenon of wealth transfer has already transpired six times. The first wealth transfer took place in Genesis 12:10 in Egypt when famine struck the land, Abram went down to Egypt and believing that Sarai was Abram's sister, Pharaoh entreated Abram and gave him sheep, oxen, servants, cattle, and much wealth such that he left Egypt a very rich man in cattle, in silver, and in gold (Genesis 13:1-2). It was the first recorded wealth transfer from the wicked to the righteous. The second one took place in Genesis 26:1 when Isaac was about to go to Egypt and God interrupted him and caused him to meet Abimelech of the Philistines and God transferred the wealth of Abimelech to Isaac. The third wealth transfer took place in Genesis 30:25-31 when God blessed Jacob after working for Laban for seven years and God gave Jacob the wealth of Laban. The fourth wealth transfer transpired in Genesis 41 when God gave Joseph favour to interpret dreams and became the wealthiest man in Egypt within a flip of a moment such that Pharaoh gave Joseph control of all of Egypt's business and economy. The fifth wealth transfer is recorded in Exodus 12: 35-36 when the children of Israel stripped the Egyptians of humongous wealth that belonged to them and left Egypt with alarming wealth resources after being in bondage for four hundred years. In the sixth biblical wealth transfer in 1 Kings 10:23, God Almighty not only gave Solomon the wealth of one nation, but the wealth of the nations of the world, making him the richest man on planet earth. The seventh wealth transfer is the portion of the end time dispensation. It is the one which God is pouring out upon the church in this present hour. It is the *7th blessing* of the last dispensation and marks the beginning of the final wave of prosperity. Next in line for this great wealth transfer is you!

This implies that there shall be a sudden transition from Worldly Billionaires into God's Billionaires as wealth and property supernaturally slips from the hands of unbelievers into believers or the furtherance of the gospel. The question is; how will this transfer take place? Firstly, investment or business doors will be shut against the wicked unbelievers while opportunities are opened and available to believers. The process shall be well managed by angels such that there shall be no flaws. Unbelievers will just wake up and in a flip of a moment all their millions and billions worth of investments will be gone. When this happens, no theory or monetary principle shall be able to provide a viable explanation, solution or answer to this phenomenon. Believers shall therefore rise with such alarming financial power to direct the world economy through establishing banks, malls, trade centres, and be in possession of the best properties and assets in the word. Secondly there shall be an unexpected crash in the stock markets such that at the end of the process, humongous investments will have slipped into accounts of believers. Thirdly, this shall be made possible through a supernatural appearance of unusual or miracle money directly into the accounts of believers through angelic deposits. This is indeed the best time for one to become a Kingdom Millionaire. Therefore, the above stated scriptural reference is an ample evidence of the reality of wealth transfer which God has planned for His church especially in these end times.

The Realm of Glory

Prophetically speaking, there is a coming the greatest financial invasion ever witnessed in the history of humanity. The manifestation of this blessing is at an all-time high and imminent as we are approaching a *"Blessing manifestation of glory"* which is a supernatural explosion of wealth in ways and intensity that the human race has never seen before. It must be expressly understood that everything the world has and is using it for evil shall be claimed by believers and used for the propagation of the gospel across the world. In the current end time dispensation, there are a multitude of wealth reservoirs that shall be taped and drained into the gospel of Jesus Christ as the Lord is restoring the earth to its rightful ownership position. There shall be a large scale supernatural transfer of wealth into the bank accounts, investments, houses, bags and even wallets of Christian for the purpose of propagating the gospel of Christ.

CHAPTER NINE

THE ROLE OF WORSHIP IN PROVOKING THE GLORY OF GOD INTO MANIFESTATION

Worship Is The Master Key To Unlocking The Glory Realm.

It is worth exploring the truth that presenting yourself as a vessel of worship is the key to accessing the higher realms of God's glory. In worship, we experience the original atmosphere of the glory God intended us to be in with Him. Worship is an atmosphere or realm in which we were given birth to by God before His throne in Heaven. Therefore, when we worship God, we are home seek as we long to be in this very original atmosphere of glory He created us in. In worship, you are not concerned with the elements of matter because God becomes the matter you worship for *without Him was not anything made that was made* (John 1:3). He is everything that is and is to be, all the while waiting for us to simply worship who He is. Oxygen is to a natural man what worship correspondingly is to a spiritual man. During worship, God inhales our worship and He exhales His glory. Hence, worship is a *divine transaction,* so to speak. That is why there is such a thing as the *transaction of the glory,* meaning the pouring out of our very being in exchange with the breath of life from God's presence. In the very breath of God is where you will find the atmosphere ripe for the miraculous. That's where you find the supernatural mass that provokes a torrent of miracles, signs and wonders to break out, culminating in a perennial stream flow of praise and worship to the Father.

However, it is disheartening to note that most believers have not fully compre-hended the difference between *praise* and *worship*. The difference between praise and worship is that praise is an affirmation of God's works while worship is an affirma-tion of God's presence. Prophetically speaking, God said, *"Worship is an affirmation of My presence, that is why when I am affirmed, I have to manifests Myself"*. We praise God for what He has done but we worship Him for who He is. The Praiser says to God, *"Lord I thank you for my lucrative job, amazing family, blooming business and all that you have blessed me with"* but the Worshiper says, *"Lord, I worship you for who you are, even if I don't have anything, you are God, you mean so much to me, You are the King of Kings and Lords of Lords"*. Therefore, praise is the proclamation of the great and powerful works of God expressed by singing, playing musical instruments and giving shouts of joy as well as by different postures of the body such as clapping, dancing and raising hands. Notable is the realisation that praise is not about singing the fast–tempo songs that makes you dance, jump and shout. Neither does worship imply the slow paced songs that people sing emotionally and present as a prelude to the preaching of the word. Instead, praise is an exuberant, clamorous and enthusiastic expression that often in-cludes many words and a physical display. Worship on the other hand involves fewer words, at times no words are needed at all as there is total silence because it has more to do with inwardly pouring out our hearts before God. I'm reminded of how Han-nah poured out her spirit in worship before God such that words could not come out although her silence spoke louder than her weeping. This is the essence of true worship. She worshiped God so deeply to the extent that her worship was mistaken by the Priest as drunkenness. You see, there are times when you are so absorbed, mingled and infused in an atmosphere of worship such that even those around you will think you are out of your mind.

It is worth exploring the divine truth that the greatest depths of worship are reached without uttering any meaningful words to the mind. Did you know that every element of nature or creation emits deep sounds of worship to God, even without uttering a single word? That is why the Bible says *Heavens declare the glory of God and the stars and the moon proclaim the work of His hands*. This is to tell you that there is silent com-munication taking place between God and His creation during worship, even without any sounds, voices or words emitted. David, a man who understood the depths of worship more than any other person in the past generations concur in Psalms 148 that *God commands the moon, sun and stars to praise Him*. But in essence, how can the moon, sun and stars praise God? This is because all creation has the ability to hear, listen, obey and respond and worship the Creator. Even inanimate objects respond in worship to Him. Often, we listen to music and worship tapes to help us get into the presence of God because music is the international sound of the earth but when you are outdoors, in touch with creation, you sense God's presence without man-made music because there is a natural on-going orchestra of worship via the creation. Did you know that rock samples from distant planets emit sounds of worship that we can hear when put under special machines that track sound waves and energy? The truth is that creation emits sound waves of worship that are invisible to your ear but your spirit receives them.

It is an incontestable reality that worship is the highest form of intimacy with God. This is because worship brings us into the third Heaven, right before the Throne Room of God. That is why in worship, we experience the atmosphere of Heaven on earth. Worship is the catalyst that brings about the substance of Glory from God's Throne down to the earth. Therefore, true worship opens the new Heavenly sound in the earth, a sweet melody resonating from your innermost being and not just the mimic of worship from your flesh. The greater truth is that as we worship corporately, we build a supernatural mass such that as our worship intensifies, along with the sound of all those around us worshiping, the sound gains mass. As that mass of worship takes on more energy, it begins to lift the entire group of worshipers into another realm, the glory realm. That is why the greatest miracles are expected to happen during worship. It's because miracles are within the mass of His presence which is known as the *glory*. During ministration, we therefore speak into that mass and then the mass takes on the word we speak and miracles happen. The reason why we don't see miracles as we ought to in the church today is because there is not enough mass in the service to manifest miracles. The truth is that the realm of worship is the realm of the miraculous. In other words, miracles and worship goes hand in glove just like praise and worship. If you can praise, it's easy to enter the realm of worship. By the same token, if you worship long and deep enough, it's easy to enter the realm of the miraculous. The truth is that when we worship God, the eternal become our reality and the impossible becomes our possibility. Can you imagine the day when we would worship and every wheelchair is emptied, every blind eye is opened, every deaf ear is opened, every cancer-ridden body is healed and every death victim is raised from the dead? This is the true essence of worship which shall become a common occurrence in the Body of Christ in these end times.

THE ESSENCE OF WORSHIP

It is of paramount significance that we define worship and see what the essence of worship fully entails. This is because so many believers are involved in worship activities but somehow lack a revelation of what worship really is. Worship is all that we are responding to all that He is. Webster dictionary defines worship as *an act of paying homage to a dignitary or somebody higher than you*. In a spiritual sense, it is a divine act of adoration, honour and reverence directed to God, the bases of which is His Word, which is a vehicle by which a man pours out all his heart to Him. In a deeper sense, it is a direct contact between the human spirit and the Holy Spirit in the realm of the spirit, the result of which the *lesser spirit* is yielded, mingled and infused into the *Greater one*, culminating in what we call the *drinking together of spirits*. In other words, your spirit is flowing into the Holy Spirit in the same way the waters of a river are ushered into the sea. From a scientific point of view, unless and if the terminals (positive and negative) contact each other, there is no flow of current. By the same token, unless your spirit has contacted the Holy Spirit during worship, you have not worshipped at all. To understand the true essence of worship, let's look closely at the revelation that is gleaned in the narrative in John 4, when Jesus spoke to the Samaritan woman at the well:

> *"Woman, believe Me the hour is coming when you will neither on this mountain nor in Jerusalem worship the Father. You worship what you do not know; we know what we worship, for salvation is of the Jews. But the hour is coming, and now is, when the true worshippers will worship the Father in spirit and truth for the Father is seeking such to worship Him. God is Spirit, and those who worship Him must worship in spirit and truth".*

In order for us to fully comprehend the depths of worship, let's first examine what worship is not by looking at the use of the word *worship* in both Hebrew and Greek terminology as used in the Bible. Let's look at what the Bible says about worship so that we will be able to define worship and see what the essence of worship fully involves. There are *Seven Greek words* used in the scriptures for worship and most of the definitions touch on some of the things that we do and some of the things that God expects. There is one main word in the Hebrew for true worship and one main word in the Greek that reflects the true measure of worship. The Hebrew word for worship that carries the fullness of God's expectation and desire is the word *shachah*.

The Greek word for true worship is *proskuneo*. However, there are many side words for worship that we need to consider so that we can come to a fuller understanding of what worship really means. We are going to look at some of the Hebrew words for worship that is not that kind of worship that that we should give to our Father God.

The first word used for worship in Hebrew is the word *segad*. It means to bow down before a superior. This comes out clearly in Daniel 3:3, where the Bible narrates that: *All the officials of the provinces gathered together for the dedication of the image that King Nebuchadnezzar had set up, and they stood before the image that Nebuchadnezzar had set up. Then a herald cried aloud "To you it is commanded, O peoples, nations and languages that at the time you hear the sound of the horn, flute, harp, lyre and psaltery, in symphony with all kinds of music, you shall fall down and worship the gold image that King Nebuchadnezzar has set up.* .In the context of the above scripture, the Hebrew word used for worship here is *segad*, which means *to bow down* and is never used in a true sense of real worship to our God. This tells us that God doesn't just want our outward form of worship, our physical worship or posture alone. Worship doesn't mean all those things that we do. Worship is in our heart. You could bow down and your heart could still have pride.

The other word which refers to worship unveiled in Jeremiah 44:19 is *atsab* which means to give or sacrifice something. *The women also said, "And when we burned incense to the queen of heaven and poured out drink offerings to her, did we make cakes for her, to worship (atsab) her, and pour out drink offerings to her without our husbands' permission?"* This is a worldly form of worship as it involves the dimension of worshiping objects, burning incense or giving offerings. This doesn't portray a true reflection of worship because you could do *atsab* or give something like the Pharisees and the Sadducees who gave things to the temple but they have pride in their hearts. You can give those gifts but if those gifts come from pride, worship is automatically gone out although worship involves giving ourselves to God. Have you ever wondered why some people give a lot in tithes and offerings but it appears that their lives are not changing? It's because they are focused on this type of worship. At times we confuse between the result of worship and the essence of worship. The essence of worship is a humble heart. It's not just what you say. You can give God your tithes of a million rands and it means nothing if your heart is proud, there is no worship.

The other word popularly used for worship is *abad*, which means to serve. Let's look at 2 Kings 10: *Then Jehu sent throughout all Israel; and all the worshippers of Baal came, so that there was not a man left who did not come.* The word *abad* is used here to refer to Baal worshippers. The full essence of the word means to serve. But does it mean that when I am serving Him, that is my worshipping? No, if it's just pure service alone without love it's not that kind of worship that God wants. *Abad* worship is the kind of worship that only dwells in service; Just doing something all the time. That is how the spirit of religion starts to creep in. Have you ever wondered why some people are always serving in the church but then their lifestyles seem not to reflect their service? It's because they are focused on this form of worship. They mistakenly think that God is worshiped through service only.

The other word for worship expressed in the book of Acts 16:14 is *sebazo*. *Now a certain woman named Lydia heard us. She was a seller of purple from the city of Thyatira who worshiped God.* The word worship is the word *sebazo*, which means to venerate. To venerate is to pay homage and respect to. Now, Lydia has not come to know Jesus yet but she has a deep respect for God in her heart. She would not take God's name in vain. When God's name is mentioned in general, she is the type who really respected God and that indicates her openness to God because she was already having some respect and direction toward God. Now, some need to have that kind of *sebazo* or respect for God because they don't have respect for God in the way they refer to God in their conversation and daily life. In Heaven, every word is so vital. I mean you dare not say anything except what God wanted you to say. This is why in Heaven those who have been there talk about a place where angels teach you the proper protocol of how to enter God's presence. We talk about entering His gates with thanksgiving; enter His court with praise. However, respect alone is not good enough. It didn't bring Lydia to salvation. Respect of God in your life will build a form of devoutness and outward holiness but in itself it is not good enough.

The other Greek word which refers to worship unveiled in Acts 17:22 is the word *eusebeo*. *Then Paul stood in the midst of the Areopagus and said "Men of Athens, I perceive that in all things you are very religious, for as I was passing through and considering the objects of your worship. I even found an altar with this inscription: TO THE UNKNOWN GOD.* The word used in this context for worship in Greek *eusebeo*. *Eusebeo* is reverential fear. And that's what those Greek fellows were like in Acts 17. They had many idols in the temple of their many gods from their Greek mythology. The strange thing is that as Paul was looking at all these idols, they did not affect him at all. Because greater is He that is in me than he that is in the world. A lot of people get intimidated when they see a huge imposing pagan altar. Paul was right there looking around then he noticed that these people are afraid in case they missed out on any god. *"Let's build an altar and leave it empty. Let us dedicate it to the unknown god whom we do not know in case there is one more that we missed."* And Paul said, *"I have come to tell you about this unknown God."* He said this unknown God is the main God that they all should worship. He talked about Jesus and the resurrection from the dead. *Eusebeo* is a worship based on fear. It says, *"If I don't worship Him, He is going to punish me. If I don't worship God, something bad is going to happen to me. If I don't say my prayers, then something bad is going to happen to me".* It is a religion based on fear, hence that is not the worship that God wants. The truth is that God doesn't use fear to force us to worship Him because our worship would not be true. So many Christians have a *eusebeo* form of worship. They worship God to avoid the wrong things happening to them and that is unscriptural.

The other Hebrew word for worship is *threskei,* which refers to the *skilful art of playing musical instruments.* Let's closely refer to Colossians 2:18: *Let no one cheat you of your reward, taking delight in false humility and worship of angels, intruding into those things which he has not seen, vainly puffed up by his fleshly mind.* The word used for worship here is *threskeia*, which refers to a religious observance or being religious about something. This does reflect the true essence of worship because you can sing the loudest, play music instruments the most skilfully but if there is no humility in your heart, there is no worship. The Father doesn't seek such worshippers. He looks for a heart that humbles before Him. It is not just ritualistic worship that the Father desires. People sometimes have ritual and they are proud of their ritual. They wear special robes in worship and they take pride in it. The essence of true worship is a humble heart. A broken and a contrite spirit He will not reject.

The other Greek word which is normally used for worship is *Therapeuo* which is found in Acts 17:25: *Nor is He worshiped with men's hands, as though He needed anything since He gives to all life, breath, and all things.* The word here is a word that's seldom translated worship. It's the word *therapeuo* where we get the word *therapy.* In essence, it means healing, wholeness and also means a kind of service. It speaks about worshipping God because of its therapeutic value. It's a bit selfish in that it takes worship like a medicine. You say, *"What can God do for us? Let's worship Him because He can do this and that for you."* This kind of worship still isn't right because of the therapeutic value of worship. We get something out of it. We get healing, blessings, anointing, glory and power from Him. Yes, all those things are divinely transacted when you really worship but when you worship because of that, this is not the essence of what He wants.

What then is the true reflection of worship?

The true measure of worship is from the heart; the very depths of your being. The Hebrew word *shachah* and the Greek word *proskuneo* denote the essence of true worship as an inward condition of the heart. The truth is that God desires worshippers and not just a bunch of people who seek to be blessed by His presence. That is why Jesus said to the woman at the well that *the hour is coming, and now is, when the true worshippers will worship the Father in* **spirit and truth** *for the Father is seeking such to worship Him.* Worshiping God in *truth* means basing your worship on God's word because His word is the truth. The Word of God is the binding force of all atoms and molecules and is the only material given to man to build a supernatural mass that produces a greater weight of God's glory. On the other hand, worshiping God in *spirit* depicts a scenario in which your spirit gets so infused, blended and mingled with the Holy Spirit such that your spirit and the Holy Spirit becomes one. However, both dimensions of worship flow from the heart, which denotes the Headquarters or Operational centre of your spirit. The reality is that some worship God from their minds, others worship God from their bodies, in what we call *lip service* but the true essence of worship is when it flows as a river from your spirit to join the river of the Spirit of God in the realm of the spirit.

Part of the theological understanding of the redemption of man is that since one third of angels in Heaven have fallen, there are a lot of vacancies up there in Heaven for worshippers of God. So, God seeks after worshippers; that is why your worship is critical in the pursuit of the agenda of Heaven at this time. But beyond that, God also decided to manifest a dimension of worship that possibly the angels have never heard before. For instance, angels can never sing *"Amazing grace how sweet the sound that saved a wretch like me"* for they have never been lost. But we have experienced the reality of God's salvation; hence we can sing that song for ten thousand years. So, there is a clear-cut difference between angels and us and that difference is in the art of worship. Our worship is different because we can move into a dimension that the angels could not. Therefore, one of God's purposes for the redemption of men is to bring forth a worship that was unattainable by angels.

There are two main instances whereby man can reach the purest, highest and deepest worship to God, firstly it's during *celebration time* and secondly during the *hardest times of trials.* The sad thing is that the most important times when we need to worship God, when God can get the purest, highest and deepest worship out of our lives are exactly those times when we forget God easily and that is when you would have received the fullness of God's presence. When your spirit is at rest, it's easy to infiltrate the realm of the spirit and enter the greater depths of worship. That is when your spirit is open to receive an uninterrupted flow of revelations directly from the Throne Room of Heaven. On the other hand, the best moment to enter the greater depths of worship is when you are in the greatest difficulty. The reality is that all the rest of the times when things are normal, we remember to worship God. But when things are difficult and it is so hard to say, *"Praise the Lord for He is good and His mercy endures forever,"* we should continue to worship God regardless of prevailing circumstances. Even sometimes, when things are most difficult, tears are rolling down your cheeks, your shield of faith is full of arrows from the enemy and your hands are so tied, you still have to say, *"Praise the Lord."* Do you know why? Strangely, it is precisely at those times that we release the most beautiful and highest praise tunes during worship.

Do you remember that it was during the most difficult moments when Paul and Silas were in prison that they released the most beautiful worship to God which provoked angels to break the chains and open their prison doors? Let me illustrate this scenario with reference to another quintessential example. When the Israelites were groaning under the burdens imposed by Pharaoh, they were crying to God. If they had worshipped God in that difficult season, I believe that they would have seen something more powerful. The power of God would have broken out to set them free from the bondage of Pharaoh earlier than expected. The truth is that when we go through difficult seasons in our lives, when life seems full of setbacks, financial troubles or sickness, we may not have the desire to worship God, yet this is precisely the time when God will ask us to present a sacrifice of our worship. Your worship when you are in the midst of difficulties touches Him even more than all of the worship of Heaven. When you worship in His glory in the midst of your trials, that is worship in Spirit and in truth and carries the greater weight of glory. Undoubtedly, the Father seeks such to be His worshippers.

THE FOUR DIMENSIONS OF WORSHIP.

There are four key dimensions of worshiping God in the realm of the spirit. A spiritual dimension has greater coverage, as it consists of the width, length, depth and height. They are dimensions of worship in the sense that they measure the breath, height, length and depth of God's glory in worship and explore the different flavours of worshiping Him. These are clearly expounded by Paul in Ephesians 3:14:

> *For this reason I bow my knees to the Father of our Lord Jesus Christ from whom the whole family in heaven and earth is named, that He would grant you, according to the riches of His glory, to be strengthened with might through His Spirit in the inner man, that Christ may dwell in your hearts through faith, that you being rooted and grounded in love, may be able to comprehend with all the saints what is the width and length and depth and height to know the love of Christ which passes knowledge that you may be filled with all the fullness of God.*

Do you notice that in the above-mentioned scripture, Paul says that you may be filled with all the fullness of God? That's God's desire for our lives that we will be full of His fullness. But to be filled with God's glory to the brink of full spiritual capacity involves these *four dimensions* of width, length, depth and height. What do these four dimensions speak of? Of course, they relate directly to our experience of God in the glory realm. Firstly, the length speaks of our expression in relationship with God, how we intimately relate to God, how we enrich our lives in His presence. There are many different styles of expression in worship. For example, one could express himself in a spiritual song, a heavenly sound or a prophetic tongue. It's about how we express ourselves to God through our relationships with Him, and enrich our expression. Each type of style develops one particular aspect of our soul. Therefore, we need a relationship and fellowship with Him so that our soul muscles can develop proportionally. See, if you do weight lifting, you would find that just lifting the dumb-bells in a different way would cause different muscles to be developed. It is undeniably through relationship that the glory, anointing, power and signs and wonders flow.

Secondly, the dimension of *width* speaks about our personal experience with God. It speaks of our encounter with God in the realm of the spirit. You see, you need to have a divine encounter with God in order for you to fully comprehend who He is and how He ought to be worshiped. Your encounter will determine the depth of your worship. That is why you need a direct contact between your spirit and the Spirit of God during worship. The width also speaks of the length of time we spend in the presence of God. It is true that people who spend more hours worshiping God tend to be more sensitive to the move of the Spirit than those who are visitors in the realm of the spirit. In order for us to experience the glory of God in worship, we need to invest more time in His presence. The difference between Moses and the rest of the children of Israel was in this dimension - he spent more time in God's presence such that when he came out, his face was glowing with unquenchable fire of His glory. However, in the New Testament dispensation, where the manifestation of God's glory surpasses that of the former times, the glory of God is glowing in our spirit, hence as we spend more time in His presence, our spirit is made aglow with the beauty of His glory.

The third dimension of worship is *depth*. Depth has more to do with the Word of God. If your worship lacks the Word, it lacks depth; it is very superficial. When we say that a certain type of worship is weak, what we imply is that it is devoid of God's word. The sound might be nice but there is a lack of depth since the worshiper is not firmly grounded in the Word. If your worship lacks the Word, it lacks eternity. It only has a temporal power because God ascertained that, *"Heaven and earth shall pass away but My Word shall not pass away."* This is to tell you that only the Word has eternity, hence your worship should have the ingredient of the word if ever you want to enter the greater depths of God. The Word that God speaks is the binding force of all atoms and molecules. That is why we need the Word in our worship as much as we need oxygen to breathe. When we worship God, we build a supernatural mass and the word of God is the only material given to man to build this supernatural mass that produces a greater weight of God's glory. When our worship is full of the Word, the music sounds different. The depth of the music has the Word and of course, the Word is expressed in languages too. Do you notice that the Father seek those who worship him in *truth and in spirit*. Notable is the realisation that in every worship set up, there are songs that talks about God, there are those that talks to God, then there are those that talks with God, but the difference is in the Word content. Whichever way you worship, the ingredient of the Word must be present to provoke the glory of God into manifestation because the glory of God is like a current; it gravitates in the direction in which the Word is flowing.

The Realm of Glory

The fourth dimension of worship is the *height*. Height speaks of ascension or catapult-action into the Heavenly realm. You need to understand that as much as our soul, spirit and body are interwoven into a collective total man, our spirit is not earthly bound. During worship, it vacates the body and enters the realm of God in what we call an *outside-the-body experience*. However, if a man is catapulted into the Heavenly realm while in His body, that is called an *inside-the-body experience*. This is the dimension of worship which Paul spoke about when he testified about being caught up to the Third Heaven. But how did Paul get to be caught up to such greater heights in God? Was he just sleeping and all of a sudden he found himself parading at the Throne room? Definitely not! It was during one of his private worship sessions that he had the inside-the-body experience as he was catapulted to God's Throne. This parallels the kind of worship rendered by Stephen in Acts as the mob stoned him. You see, the Bible records Jesus as sitting at the right hand of God but at the sound of deep agonising worship emanating form the Deacon, Stephen, Jesus stood up! In other words, Stephen rendered to the Heavens such a radical worship from the depths of his being that caused Jesus to stand up and receive his spirit. This is akin to how Paul and Silas earlier worshiped God in prison and entered the greater heights of the angelic realm of worship such that angels were provoked to break their chains and open prison doors in the natural realm. Do you also notice that the Bible says that *we are seated in the Heavenly places with Christ Jesus?* But how do we get to that position where we are seated at the Throne room in Heaven? Do we just slumber and wake up to find ourselves incidentally at God's throne. No! It is through ascension during the depths of worship that we are catapulted to such greater heights in God. The reality of this scripture is only possible when we reach the higher depths or dimension of worship. It's not something that you just claim with your mouth as is the practice in the modern day church. Instead, it's a practical experience in the glory realm whereby you worship God and enter the greater heights such that you just appear before the Throne Room. This is what we call *being lost in His presence*. Allegorically speaking, the glory realm is the *"there"* and worship is what gets us from *"here"* to *"there"*. This is to tell you that you need to ascend to the Heavenly realm during worship to catch a glimpse of the beauty of the Heavenly realm. Worship is a public parade displayed in the streets of Heaven; hence you unequivocally need to be catapulted into the Third Heaven especially in these end times which mark the summation of ages. That way, your worship will have a significant impact in the realm of the spirit. That is why when we worship, we enter the Heavens and join angels before the Throne room.

THE THREE DEGREES OF GLORY IN WORSHIP

It is worth exploring the divine truth that when you enter the depths of worship, there are degrees of manifestation of the glory of God. The average Christian gets content when they see the glory of God but that's enough. There are many degrees and unexplored territories of glory you enter into when you worship God. Like a sailor on a sailing expedition, you enter into one and you flow in it. Chronologically, you enter into another one level and step into another one until it brings you into the greater heights of God's glory. The Bible concurs with this divine truth that we are being transformed from glory to glory. That means, the glories of God are the mountain peaks in our life as there are many Mounts of Transfiguration that we move into from glory to glory to glory until we reached the heights of His glory. Don't be satisfied with the first degree of glory. Instead, enter the deeper territories in the glory realm as there are more depths of God's glory. At first degree, your worship changes the atmosphere or environment, at second degree, your worship changes you and at third degree, your worship changes the world.

The First Degree of Worship

This is when the glory of God is highly concentrated in the natural realm such that it changes the natural atmosphere of a territory. To catch a glimpse of the first degree of manifestation of God's glory, let's closely consider the following scripture in 2 Chronicles 7:1:

> *When Solomon had finished praying, fire came down from heaven and consumed the burnt offering and the sacrifices and the glory of the Lord filled the temple. And the priests could not enter the house of the Lord, because the glory of the Lord had filled the Lord's house.*

This is what we call a *glory invasion* in the natural realm. Now, that's the greater glory but at an entry level. There are many people who see the first glory of God in manifestation and then pitch their tent in its atmosphere and don't enter deeper. They think the first degree is all there is yet there is a deeper glory that you can tap into when you are in covenant with Him. As you enter deeper into worshiping Him, you not only have the glory of God but you have the fire of God coming down with His glory. In the context of the above-mentioned scripture, it is in the fire that the burnt offering outside keeps on burning. So, the fire came on the brazen altar and consumed the sacrifice. Normally if the fire did not come down on the brazen altar, the Priests had to light the fire themselves. But now, the fire came directly from Heaven. In other words, God Himself ignited the spark of light and burnt the offerings. That is where human works comes to an end and God's Spirit takes over a hundred percent. That's what we want, to be totally infused, marinated and mingled with the manifestation of the Holy Spirit such that the Holy Spirit fully blows you. All you do is to set sail and the wind of the Spirit blows you. However, the gravest mistake which some believers usually make with regard to worship is that immediately they sense the glory of God descending in a meeting, they start praying for the sick, casting out devils and inviting people to the alter, instead of basking in an atmosphere of worship. Many at times, results are less spectacular compared to what could have been had they waited for the moving of the Spirit, not just the coming of the Spirit. It is one thing to get the glory and Spirit of God to come and it's another thing to get Him to move. Somehow the Israelites were able to have the ark of the glory in their midst but they did not have a revelation about the ways of God and how He moves and operates. That is why they missed out on a number of things, including their destiny to the Promised Land, but this must not be your portion.

The Second Degree of Worship

It is worth mentioning that it's not just enough for the glory of God to manifest in an atmosphere of a meeting. The most important question is: What did you get from that atmosphere? There are people who get into powerful meetings where the glory of God is moving and there are just spectators to the extent that they come out of the river of God's presence as dry as a duck. So, at the second degree of manifestation of the glory, the glory of God does not just change the atmosphere but is changes you. This is what we call *transformation*. The second degree is when the glory of God intensifies to such an extent that it changes the total man. In other words, it transforms both your soul, spirit and even your physical countenance. At this level, the body or flesh pulls back as in the case of transfiguration such that the glory inside your spiririt is pulled out and unveiled. At that level, the flesh is invisible such that only the glory of the human spirit is made visible. Enoch walked with God and walked in such greater glory that he was so physically transformed and enraptured into the depths of God's glory until he disappeared in the natural realm.

The Third Degree of Worship

At this level, man is catapulted right to the highest degree of glory at the Throne room of Heaven. The third degree is the manifestation of the glory of God at the *Throne room*. This is what Paul experienced when he spoke of being "*caught up to the Third Heaven*". At the third degree, it's no longer Heavens coming down to you but you being catapulted to the Throne room. This is the highest degree of worship in glory which any man can ever experience. That's where you experience the tangibility of the glory, raw and undiluted from its original source, the Throne Room itself. So many believers are brainwashed into thinking that the highest form of worship is attained when the glory of God comes down in a meeting but that's only the second degree. The highest degree is when God personally invites you to worship Him not in your church or meeting but at His Throne in Heaven. That is why visitations to the Throne Room in Heaven are increasingly becoming a common phenomenon in the Body of Christ as believers in the extreme ends of the earth are catapulted right into the climax of God's glory in this end time season.

THE THREE LEVELS OF WORSHIP

There are these three different levels of worship in the realm of God. These levels are dependent on the extent to which the quality of our spirit have been developed and also on the degree of intimacy and relationship with the Holy Ghost. For illustrative purposes, we use the pattern of the tabernacle of Moses to graphically portray these levels of worship. There is the first veil that separates the Outer court from the Holy place. Only the priests in the Old Covenant can enter the Holy place. There are three pieces of furniture there; the candle stick, the table of showbread and the altar of incense just before the second veil. When you cross the second veil, you enter into the Most Holy place where there is an ark of covenant. In case you don't understand, in Heaven, there is an Outer Court, a Holy place and the Most Holy place. Heaven is not just heaven. Some Christians have no idea of what things are like in

Heaven. What Moses made was only a shadow and a pattern of what God gave him a peek. Once in a while, there were prophets like Isaiah who had a glimpse of the temple of God in Heaven. In Heaven, there is a real Outer Court. Of course, it's much bigger and larger than we can imagine. It accommodates millions. There is a real Holy place and there is a real Holy of holies. When Jesus Christ rose from the dead, He entered the Most Holy place so that you and I don't have to be in the Outer Court although we can enjoy all the blessings in the Outer Court. We don't have to be just in the Holy place. We can be in the Most Holy place where He lives.

It is worth exploring the truth that the tabernacle was a shadow or representation of God's pattern of worship in Heaven. Therefore, basing our analysis on the pattern of the tabernacle, there are *three* different levels of worship that we need to enter into and each one has its special touch or special principles involved. If only you could understand them, it will help us to enter into the highest worship. There is a certain level of worship that takes place in the *Outer court*; then there is a level of worship that takes place in the *Holy place*; and there is a dimension of worship that takes place in the *Most Holy place*. All these can be lined up as different dimensions of worship. The word dimensions indicate some equality in a sense. For example, we live in a soul dimension and a physical dimension at the same time. And when we are born again, we live in a spiritual dimension. So, the dimensions are simultaneous and they take place at the same time. However, *levels* speak about one at a time. The highest level is built upon the lower level. Therefore, we will use the word *levels* to reinforce a deeper understanding of this divine truth.

The Outer Court level of worship

At the level of outer court, worship is regarded as a routine exercise that is done merely done in church every Sunday. It is more of a ritual or religious exercise or gathering than a life style. Although Sunday was set aside as a day of universal worship because of convenience, God is not a Sunday God; He is not only found on Sunday. The greatest challenge in the Body of Christ today is that the majority of Christians are Sunday Christians. They are so filled up by the word on a Sunday service but during the week, they crash back to their normal habits. Hence, their worship cannot make any significant impact in the realm of the spirit. Others believe that God can only be worshiped in church, hence they would not dare activate an altar of worship in their homes, workplaces and private places. In the tabernacle of Moses, the people who worshiped God at the outer court were outsiders, those who did not have a covenant with God. By the same token, at the level of outer court, the believer has not committed himself to a life of developing an intimate relationship with God. He is more of a visitor in the realm of the spirit and a part timer in the things of God, rather than being a permanent residence of that realm. At the outer court level, a believer might love God but then be inhibited by sin or habits to enter the sacred territories of God. At this level, when believers meet for corporate worship, they worship only for 15 minutes and before they could even breakthrough into the next level, they are already interrupted by their programmes and agendas hence the glory of God is not invited.

The Inner Court level of worship

At the inner court level of worship, the believer has begun to grasp the significance of consecration in worship, hence his life is set apart as a vessel of worship. At this level, worship is perennial, it's not dependent on circumstances, whether during great times or the worst circumstances, the believer worships God intimately and has developed a deep, intimate and personal relationship with God and can also lead others to greater depths of worship. In the tabernacle of Moses, there were three main vessels, in the Holy place, that is the table of show bread which represents the *word of God*, the brazen alter of incense which represents *the essence of worship* and the candle stick which represents *the revelation of God* Therefore, at the level of worship in the Holy place, worship is based on the *revelation of God's word* and *consecration*. At this level of worship, the believer has mastered the twin principles of sacrifice and maintaining a high degree of holiness as a lifestyle of worship. Hence, prayers are made from the depths of one's spirit which significantly impacts on the realm of the spirit and sphere of contact. Intercessors are raised at this level of worship and churches that enter this level of worship begin to shake the nations and influence communities by their prayers. Based on this realisation, it therefore suffices to adjudicate that the majority of the churches are currently operating at this level.

The Holy of Holies level of worship

At the level of Holy of Holies, the believer is catapulted to God's throne in Heaven to worship him. This is what we call *Throne room worship*. It is the climax of worship and depicts the highest level of worshiping God which any human being can ever attain. Let me refer you to a quintessential example of Moses's tabernacle to shade more light on this divine truth. In the tabernacle of Moses, there is only one instrument found in the Holy of Holies, that is, the Ark of Covenant shadowed by the Seraphim and Cherubim, which represents the presence of God. Therefore, the level of worship at the Holy of Holies depicts worshiping in the presence of God. The believer is so mingled with God's presence such that he is catapulted right into the *Throne room of Heaven*. The believer has attained a dimension of worshiping God which Jesus described as *the truth and spirit dimension of worship* (John 4:24). This is worship that is based on the truth of God's word and a direct spirit-to-Spirit contact with the Spirit of God, in what we call a *drinking together of spirits*. In other words, the believer is so infused, marinated and drenched in the Holy Ghost such that if you were to observe his spirit and the Holy Spirit, you would not be able to tell the difference.

The portrait of a Seraphim and Cherubim covering the Ark of the Covenant in the Holy of Holies symbolises angelic presence. Therefore, the dimension of worship at the Holy of Holies is tantamount to the level of angelic worship. In other words, any man who enters this level would have entered the level, degree and dimension of angelic worship, and would have acquired the grace or ability to worship at the same level as angels. That is why at times when you worship God at that level in a meeting, angels can join you just like what happened in Bethany in 1985 when angels joined the worshiping saints with an unusual Heavenly sound that infiltrated the whole atmosphere in the natural realm. When you enter the atmosphere of worship at this level, you are completely lost at His presence. At times you worship God and you are not even conscious of time and might check the cloak only to found that you have been worshiping God for 7 hours non-stop. Some ministries who embark on a 24 hour non-stop worship sessions have tapped into this level. This is a level of the miraculous whereby we worship God until the blind eyes are opened, cripples rise up from wheel chairs by themselves and the dead rises up on their own accord without anybody praying for them. At this level, tumours disappear, cancer cells die and demons evaporate without any instruction. In other words, healings and deliverance take place without any prayer line and prayers are answered the instantaneously without any huffing and whining.

Paul worshiped God until he entered this level and was catapulted right into God's throne in what he described as "*being caught up to the Third Heaven*". This is a dimension whereby a man beholds God face to face. This is not a level of crowds but individuals and this explains why only a few ministries have entered this realm. Because of the extent to which the quality of the human spirit is developed, believers at this level are able to float about through the air like a butterfly, walk on water as though on dry ground, go through walls, disappear in the natural realm and be divinely transported through the spirit realm to the furthest territories of the world. This is a level where the supernatural realm is manifested in the natural to the extent that it's normal to see angels worshiping in the church and the substance of glory, visibly manifested as the glory cloud, supernatural rains, supernatural light and supernatural earthquake becomes a normal occurrence. Many believers get surprised when they enter into the supernatural realm but at this level of worshiping God at the Throne room, walking through the golden streets of Heaven, talking to Jesus and parading through the extreme corridors of the spirit world becomes a norm.

The question is: Are you ready to enter this deeper level NOW?

CHAPTER TEN

THE VISIBLE SIGNS OF MANIFESTATION OF GOD'S GLORY

It is worth exploring the divine truth that the glory of God is no longer a mystical spiritual phenomenon because in this end time season, God is causing His glory to manifest visibly in such a way that everybody can see it in the same manner in which the Israelites saw a pillar of fire by night and a pillar of cloud by day. Throughout the scriptures, we read about the glory of God manifesting itself in a tangible and visible way in the natural realm and such an enthralling spectacle is going to intensity in these end times as we are adjourning quickly towards the second coming of the Lord Jesus Christ for the Grand Finale of the earth. But why does God manifest Himself in a visible and tangible way? Because He wants to draw your attention to Him. The Lord knows how to get your attention because when He appears, it's not just business as usual. You cannot ignore Him or escape from what He is about to do or be casual about it. For example, you cannot pretend that nothing is happening when the earth beneath your feet is shaking and quaking just like the experience of the Children of Israel whose legs became jelly and their knees became almost rattled with the trembling of God's presence. Neither can you ignore the bone chilling sound of a mighty trumpet blast, the thunder and lightning when it echoes audibly through your very own ears.

The pages of Scripture are filled with miraculous other accounts of the glory of God appearing for His children. The greater truth is that the Lord has always chosen to manifest His glory through signs and wonders. Therefore, don't be sceptical if you see spiritual phenomena tangibly manifesting itself as a physical substance in the natural realm. It may come as thunder and lightning or a very loud trumpet blast (Exodus 19:9, 16). Sometimes the glory comes as a *cloud* (2 Chronicles 5:13-14, Exodus 40:36); sometimes it comes as a *flame of fire* (Exodus 40:38, Acts 2:3). Sometimes the glory comes as *dew* upon our clothes (Judges 6:37-38), or as a *mighty rushing wind* (Acts 2:2). Sometimes the glory comes as *manna* or provision from above (Exodus 16). Other manifestations of the glory includes miracles like a pool of healing water (John 5:1-15), water transformed into Heavenly wine (John 2:1-11), angelic encounters (1 Kings 19:5-7, Acts 10:3, Acts 12:7- 11) and even financial miracles released in unexpected ways (Matthew 17:27). An understanding of this tangible and visible glory of God is such a key which one could use to open every door into the supernatural in order to manifest the glory of God mightily in this end time season.

THE GLORY FIRE.

It is worth exploring the divine truth that *fire* is one of the popular manifestations of God's glory in the pages of the Bible. However, being creatures quick to become fearful, we have a tendency to dwell on the negative side of things and so usually associate divine fire with wrath (Leviticus 10:1). This has been a serious mistake of the church throughout much of its existence. On the contrary, fire represents the power of the Word of God. To provide an introductory perspective to the divine revelation of fire, God asked Jeremiah a rhetoric question in Jeremiah 23:29: *"Is not My word like fire, declares the Lord, and like a hammer that breaks the rock into pieces?"* Why is the analogy of fire used to describe God's word? It's because God's Word either burns or tempers with those who hear it. It can bring energy and power or great and total destruction. In Ezekiel 10:2, God commanded Ezekiel saying *"Go in between the wheels and fill your hand with coals of fire from between the cherubim and scatter them over the city."* To give a historical background of the events culminating in this prophetic word, this symbolic imagery concerns the power of God present in dealing with the people who were left in Jerusalem during the first part of the Babylonian captivity. The city would soon be destroyed for the sins and apostasies of the people. Fire came from between the cherubim, from within the image of God. Thus, fire represents the power of God manifested toward his sinful people. That is why God declared in Zephaniah 1:18; 3:8 that *"In the fire of his Jealousy, the whole world will be consumed.*

However, God's power is not always used in anger, of course. Here, we see a picture of the great positive power of God in a vision of the present spiritual kingdom.

In Zechariah 2:4-5, it says *"Jerusalem will be a city without walls because of the great number of men and livestock in it. And I myself will be a wall of fire around it, declares the Lord, and I will be its glory within."* This is how God protects and glorifies the spiritual church that Christians live in today. Fire that defines and protects the kingdom is the Word of God, as we shall see in the New Testament references.

It is not surprising that fire plays such a significant role in the Bible. The Creator Himself is described as a *"consuming fire"* (Deuteronomy 4:24). Doesn't it seem rather strange to our understanding to call the Creator a consuming fire? In Hebrews 12:29, Paul says *"For our God is a consuming fire."* This verse is one of the most powerful metaphors in the Bible. But in what way is God a consuming fire? The passage in Jeremiah 23:29 tells us *His word is like fire* and John 1:1 confirms that *the Word was God.* It is the power of God manifested in what God calls into being by willing or stating it, and activated through the person of Christ. The Bible narrates in Revelation 8:5 that *"then the angel took the censer, filled it with fire from the altar, and hurled it on the earth.* Notice the parallel with Ezekiel 10:2. Here again, the fire originates in the altar, meaning it comes from God himself, and then it is taken and *"hurled on the earth."* This symbolizes the power of God, whose word caused the destructions to come upon those disobedient to Him.

The Bible further records a spectacular display of God's glory in 1 Kings 19:11-13:

"A great and powerful wind tore the mountains apart and shattered the rocks before the LORD, but the LORD was not in the wind. After the wind there was an earthquake, but the LORD was not in the earthquake. After the earthquake came a FIRE, but the LORD was not in the FIRE. And after the FIRE came a gentle whisper. When Elijah heard it, he pulled his cloak over his face and went out and stood at the mouth of the cave. Then a voice said to him, 'What are you doing here, Elijah?'" (1 Kings 19:11-13).

Note that there are various manifestations of God's glory depicted in this portion of the scripture above, namely, *wind, earthquake* and *fire.* In this context, fire depicts a manifestation of the glory of God. In other words, the glory of God had transmuted itself from the spiritual realm and was now manifesting as a visible and tangible flame of fire in the natural realm.

On Pentecost, we meet yet another visible manifestation of the glory of the Holy Spirit as fire. Along with the sound of a mighty rushing Wind, *there appeared unto them cloven tongues of FIRE, and sat upon each of them* (Acts 2:3). The question is: Where did that FIRE come from? This was the glory of the Spirit that was manifested as a tangible and visible spiritual substance in the natural realm. Fire generally signifies either destruction or purging as in the refining of metals. The term *"tongues of fire"* appears only here and in the American Standard Version translation of Isaiah 5:24 (*"the tongue of fire devoureth the stubble"*). *"Tongues of fire"* in the Acts account conveys the double significance of enlightenment and the giving of utterance to this enlightenment. The Greek word *glossa*, here translated *"tongues,"* is frequently used for language and is the same word used when referring to the speaking in tongues in verse 4. (However, the word translated *"language"* in verses 6 and 8 is a different word and corresponds to *"dialect."*) The thought is that the various *"tongues"* split off a central luminary source, somewhat analogous to the lampstand picture of Zechariah, where the oil to light the lamps came from the two olive trees. The Holy Spirit enlightened the minds of the waiting disciples and then authorized and enabled them to speak (*or at least be understood*) by the Jews who had travelled to Jerusalem from many parts of the Roman empire.

Notable is the realisation that when tongues of fire came upon the 120 disciples, they shifted them from the Upper room and drove them into the streets of Jerusalem. The tongues of fire caused them to open their mouths which were previously shut by the fear of man. And what did they declare? The wonderful works of God! And what was the result? Three thousand were added unto them. Do you find it a coincidence that when Moses' Law was given under a fiery mountain, three thousand Israelites were killed? But when the Law of the Life in Christ Jesus was made manifest under a different kind of fire in the upper room, three thousand were added unto them!? (Exodus 32:28; Acts 2:41) Both laws were connected with fire. One brought fear, wrath, and death; the other brought liberty, forgiveness and Life.

Clearly, the writers of the Bible employed the use of fire in many different ways. However, when it came to the spiritual use of fire, they usually attributed fire to God. God manifested Himself in various forms of fire on many different occasions. We find some of these manifestations in the making of the Covenant with Abraham (Genesis 15:17), the burning bush (Exodus 3:2-4), pillar of fire (Exodus 13:21), on Sinai (Exodus 19:18), in the fame on the altar (Judges 13:20), and God answering by fire (1 Kings 18:24, 38). Sacrifices and offerings (*including incense which represented the prayers of the people*) were to be made by fire. (Exodus 12:8,9,10; Leviticus 1) Fire often meant the acceptance of a sacrifice by Yahweh (Judges 6:21; 1 Kings. 18:38; 1 Chronicles 21:26). Leviticus 9:24 tells us that the sacrificial fire *"came forth from Yahweh."* The fire on the altar was to be continually burning. (Leviticus 6:12,13) Fire came down from heaven at the consecration of Solomon's Temple. God said He would dwell there *"forever"* according to the King James Bible, yet we know the Temple was destroyed and the fire put out. Is the Bible in error? Definitely not!

I believe, in order to understand our English Bible translation, we must know something about the culture of the people who wrote the original text in their native languages. Aramaic, Hebrew, and Greek are highly figurative, extremely expressive languages, full of many kinds of idiomatic expressions and figures of speech.. We must understand how *they* used the word *"fire"* if we are to understand the meaning of the word *"fire"* in the Bible. Christians who have allowed the fire of God to enter the very recesses of their lives will see His fire in a totally different light. Rather than being utterly destroyed by the fire, they are purified, corrected, cleansed. God's fire within brings forth a love that desires to bring healing and restoration to all mankind. The more spiritually minded, desirous to be changed, and willing to be conformed to the image of Christ one is, the less fear they have of fire in the Bible. The latter group is more likely to use the word *"fire"* in a positive sense. I think the latter group is also more likely to be spiritually alive.

In order for us to catch an in-depth understanding of supernatural fire, it is important that we first understand the character of physical fire. What does natural fire do? It usually takes dense matter composed of different atoms and breaks them apart into simpler elements, usually gases. Have you ever noticed that fames naturally flicker upward, higher? It is the gases ignited which produce the fame. Fire produces fame (light) and heat, two very useful properties in the natural world. The more we seem to understand the scientific properties of fire, the more useful fire seems to become to mankind. Science and the business community are finding all kinds of uses for the energy waves which come forth from fire, whether the fire is from the sun, or from the splitting of an atom, or other sources.

It has only been in recent years that mankind has discovered that fire never really permanently destroys or annihilates anything. Fire just stirs up the molecules until they reach a point of agitation great enough for atoms within a molecule to be released from one another. Fire divides. The same thing happened when Jesus sent forth the fire of which He spoke. He sent forth a seed (spark) of faith which broke the power of tradition which held people together to a lower form of government. Some, through His fiery word, were released to serve in a higher kingdom, the kingdom of God in which dwelt righteousness, peace, and joy. Others stayed behind and became the ashes or remains of the Levitical System. While the Old Mosaic System was destroyed in one sense, its destruction brought forth something better, higher. This fire loosened a force which would literally change the course of mankind. Fire is never static. It moves. It seeks to consume. It always produces change. It will force one to act.

In this end time season, in the same way the children if Israel saw a pillar of fire guiding them by night, supernatural fire shall manifest visibly as the glory of God illuminates the nations. This fire shall perform various purposes such as burning tools of darkness, demonstrating before unbelievers that Jesus is Lord so as to daw multitudes in faith in Him. Fire shall be demonstrated physically during ministerial sessions as the presence and glory of God invades places of worship.

Testimony of Divine encounter with the Glory Fire:

I recall vividly that since the time I started practically demonstrating the power of God, I used to see a visible pillar of fire in front of me and wherever I saw it, it ignited a flame in my spirit such that I moved in greater dimension of signs and wonders than ever before. The manifestation of that pillar of fire had so heightened to the extent that in an open vision, I could visibly see it at a level slightly above my head while at the same time being conscious of the things in the natural realm. I remember on a certain day as I was still relating to one of my brethren about my experiences with the pillar of fire, it came right in the midst of the conversation. It was so tangible and visible such that I could literally point at it as it moved just above my head. This is exactly what the disciples of the early church encountered, which launched them into the greater depths of the realm of the miraculous. At Pentecost, the Bible says that tongues as of fire appeared over the heads of each of those who gathered together (Acts 2:3). The Holy Spirit comes as fire to work something deep into the substance of our lives that will shape things around us, rather than us taking on the shape of the world. As fire, He works in a dual way, to probe the inner recesses of our life and to refine us as gold or silver is refined in the fire; and to temper our personalities by causing a penetration of fire into our system.

THE GLORY CLOUD.

It is a divine truth that God has always been known to speak from a cloud. The *cloud* of His presence represents God's glory. God led the Israelites as a *pillar of cloud* during the day and a pillar of fire during the night as they journeyed from Succoth. A *cloud* speaks of divine protection. It is one thing to feel the cloud of His presence in a meeting, and it is quite another thing to have that glory manifested. Miracles make the glory real to us. The glory is a cloud that hovers over our lives, and in the glory cloud, there is the greatest potential for miracles, revival and harvest. Remember what happened when the glory cloud descended upon the temple in 1 Kings 8:10. The Bible attests that *when the priests had come out of the holy place,* **the cloud** *filled the house of the Lord, So that the priests could not stand to minister because of the cloud: for the glory of the Lord had filled the house of the Lord.* In Acts 1: 9, Jesus ascended to the Father through the glory cloud: *"And when he had spoken these things, while they beheld, he was taken up; and a cloud received him out of their sight."* According to the scriptures, Jesus was taken up in the *Shekinah* cloud in which He will return again during His second coming. Did you notice that when Jesus was taken up in a *glory cloud,* His disciples were so much fascinated by the glory cloud as they gazed up in the Heavens? Sadly, most Christians are content with the presence of the cloud. They are just happy if its hovering over them. They never think of tapping into the resourcefulness of the cloud to birth miracles and a greater harvest. There are multiple clouds in the realm of the spirit; you have got to discern the difference between a *personal cloud* and a *corporate cloud*. There is a *healing cloud* and a *prosperity cloud*. You need to know how to create a cloud, for without a cloud, there is no rain.

When a natural cloud hovers over a city, the weather forecasters say, *"There is a possibility of rain and thunderstorms today."* The presence of the cloud presents those very real possibilities. In the same way, when the glory cloud hovers over us, a sense of expectancy fills us, for we know that anything is possible. The Bible affirms that *if the clouds be full of heavy rains, they empty themselves on earth.* This is to tell you that when spiritual clouds are hanging over the church, miracles, signs and wonders are bound to happen. Far too many people rest in the fact that the cloud is present, and are content to wait for its manifestation - in rain, revival, miracles or unprecedented harvest. Some of these people become discouraged and wonder why the presence of the cloud has not manifested itself. In order for a cloud to produce rain, it is not enough that it be seen and felt. There must be an atmospheric pressure in the air to cause rain. This is a scientific fact in the natural, and it is true in the spiritual as well. The pressure needed is our continued hunger, unquenchable thirst and insatiable appetite to see and experience the glory. Like Moses, we must pursue the glory of God until the manifestation comes.

Mary was not content with the fact that Jesus was present at the marriage in Cana of Galilee. A miracle was needed, and she sought Him until it was accomplished. Elijah prophesied that rain would come during a time of extended drought. Then he began to travail before God until he saw a sign, a cloud of the size of a man's hand. When he saw it, he said to his servant, *"Run."* He was just that sure that rain was coming, and it did rain over the dry land. Elijah did not stop pressing in until he saw the manifestation of the glory. In our ministry, some believers have testified that while they gathered for worship, a cloud appeared out of nowhere in the middle of the congregation and floated around the congregation for a time, leaving many covered in specks of gold dust. It was reported that the glory cloud moved and swirled, going up and down over the congregation. Such a movement brought forth an atmosphere of greater miracles, signs and wonders.

A Testimony Of An Encounter With The Glory Cloud:

I recall vividly the day the glory cloud literally came into my room and filled the whole atmosphere. I was awake and literally breathing in the vapour of the cloud into my nose. I began to breathe very deeply in that atmosphere of glory. As I continued in that atmosphere, God literally opened my sense of smell and I began to smell strong incense. I was so drenched in the glory of God such that I was now smelling God like perfume. I could literally feel the moisture from the cloud touch my face. I could feel the cool presence and moisture go down my nostrils as though I had put my face in front of a vaporizer. Then as I breathed in the air, I could smell it's purity and freshness. As the experience occurred, I knew it was the Lord's glory cloud. I had literally breathed His very presence.

There is another record of a direct counter with the glory cloud in our ministry and this time it came right into the church. As we gathered for worship, we could literally see a small cloud just below the lights, extending through and past the white glow. We were all amazed as we watched the fog or vapour begin to descend up and down from that place. It went in waves where it ascended, then came back down to just above people's heads in the congregation. It seemed highly saturated, full of humidity and ready to precipitate itself upon the congregation. A couple times, it moved over to almost the centre of the stage, but most of the time it stayed on the right side. As I went to the section where it seemed to be highly concentrated, I breathed in the fog like vapour through my nose. I immediately recognized the difference between the hot dry air in the back of the church and this cool moist air and remembered my past experiences with the glory cloud. It was like the smell and moisture of putting your head into a vaporizer when it is on its lightest setting. This is one of the notable experiences we had in the glory cloud.

THE GLORY LIGHT.

The Bible concurs with the divine truth that Jesus is the light of man and that light is a manifestation of the glory of God. As people see Jesus, the glory of the light is manifested. In these end times, there are records and testimonies of people who have been translated to heaven and the first thing which they testify to have seen is the light. That light is the glory of God. However, it is possible for that supernatural light to move from the spirit realm to manifest in the physical realm as a visible and tangible spiritual substance. As believers are worshiping God in truth and in spirit, the light of God's glory shall be visibly seen in the natural realm in these end times. It must be expressly understood that God is not in the hiding so that His children would seek Him. Instead, He is revealing Himself in fullness so that humanity can experience the warmth of His presence. That is why He manifests Himself in the form of supernatural light.

Did you know that the first specific creative act of God in Genesis 1 was the creation of the beauty of light? The creation of light was the initial step in the creation of life. The authoritative command, *"Let there be light"* in Genesis 1:3, was the first word of God spoken after His creative Spirit *"moved"* upon the primary material out of which He created the heavens and the earth, and which lay, until the utterance of that word, in the chaos of darkness and desolation. Something akin, possibly, to the all-pervasive electro- magnetic activity of the aurora borealis penetrated the chaotic night of the world. The ultimate focusing of light (on the 4th day of creation, Genesis 1:14 in suns, stars, and solar systems brought the initial creative process to completion, as the essential condition of all organic life. The origin of light thus finds its explanation in the purpose and very nature of God whom John defines as not only the Author of light but, in an all-inclusive sense, as light itself: *"God is light"* (1 John 1:5). The word *"light"* is divinely rich in its comprehensiveness and meaning. Its material splendour is used throughout the Scriptures as the symbol and synonym of all that is luminous and radiant in the mental, moral and spiritual life of men and angels; while the eternal God, because of His holiness and moral perfection, is pictured as *"dwelling in light"* (1 Timothy 6:16). Light is not just the absence of darkness. When natural light fails, man by discovery or invention provides himself with some temporary substitute, however dim and inadequate.

In view of the above, it is therefore unequivocally evident that light is a reflection of the glory of God. *When the appalling plague of "thick darkness," for three days, enveloped the Egyptians, terrified and rendered them helpless, "all the children of Israel had light in their dwellings"* (Exodus 10:23). That light was the glory of God in action in the natural realm. Whether the darkness was due to a Divinely-ordered natural cause or the light was the natural light of day, the process that preserved the interspersed Israelites from the encompassing darkness was supernatural. Miraculous, also, even though through natural agency, was the *"pillar of fire" that gave light to the Israelites escaping from Pharaoh* (Exodus 13:21; 14:20; Psalms 78:14), God led them all the night with a *light of fire."* Moreover, supernatural was the effulgence at Christ's transfiguration that made "His garments as white as the *light"* (Matthew 17:2). Under the same category, Paul classifies `*the great light*' that `suddenly shone round about him from heaven' on the way to Damascus (Acts 22:6; compare 9:3). That light was a visible manifestation of the glory of God. The glory is what illuminate the peoples. The light of God's glory strike on the way to Damascus and Paul fell under the power. This was a manifestation of the glory of God. In these rare instances, the supernatural light was not only symbolic of an inner spiritual light, but instrumental in revealing the glory of God.

The phenomena of natural light have their counterpart in the inner life of man. Few words lend themselves with such beauty and appropriateness to the experiences, conditions, and radiance of the spiritual life. For this reason the Scriptures use *"light"* largely in the figurative sense. Borrowed from the natural world, it is, nevertheless, inherently suited to portray spiritual realities. In secular life a distinct line of demarcation is drawn between intellectual and spiritual knowledge and illumination. Education that enlightens the mind may leave the moral man untouched. This distinction rarely obtains in the Bible, which deals with man as a spiritual being and looks upon his faculties as interdependent in their action.

The Bible says in Psalm 119:105 that *the Word is a lamp, a light that illuminates the darkness*. If a person walks through the woods at night, he is well served to have a flashlight with him to shine it on the ground in front of him so that his feet do not trip over a snag in the path, or his shins do not encounter a boulder or fallen log. That is what light does: It illuminates or reveals. God's Word illuminates the path of our lives. If we keep God's Word shining along the way, then we will be far less likely to trip. We will not be easily deceived. Because we are following the light, we will see what the light reveals in the path ahead of us. It is only when we turn the light off (*before we have actually arrived at our destination*) that something could spring up in the dark and trip us. Therefore, if we keep the light of God's truth shining brightly ahead of us, then we have a greater chance of avoiding deception.

Have you ever given yourself a second to meditate on the spectacular display of the glory light which took place on the way to the Red sea as the Egyptian army pursued the Israelites? The Bible says God brought light to the side of the Children of Israel while there was horrific darkness on the side of Egyptians. Where did that light come from? From the sun? Definitely not! That light was not natural light. Instead, it was supernatural light because the whole territory was infested with unusual darkness. Have you ever wondered why the Bible says when God brought forth judgement against Pharoah, in Goshen, where the children of Israel lived, there was light while there was gross darkness in Egypt? It doesn't necessarily mean that God allowed natural light to prevail over Goshen while He rained darkness over Egypt. What it simply means is that when God brought forth judgement, both territories were subjected under intense darkness because of the wrath of God. However, as a redemption plan to rescue His own people, God brought *supernatural light* in Goshen. That light was not physical but *supernatural light* shining through the darkness of His judgement. Prophetically speaking, in this end time season, believers in the furthest extremes of the word shall demonstrate supernatural light to accomplish God's work. For example, in territories like Africa where load shading is rife, a believer can actually command *supernatural light* in darkness such that there shall be lights wherever you are, while the rests of the country is in darkness in the same way there were lights in Goshen while there was thick darkness in Egypt.

A Testimony Of A Practical Demonstration Of A Glory Light

I recall vividly the day I demonstrated the Glory Light in the physical realm while still at High School. It happened that I returned home after spending a Semester study at a Boarding School. During my first night at home, while I slept, I saw a dark figure in the shape of a human body coming towards me. It was very dark in my room and as that figure came to me, it attempted to sit on my stomach. Suddenly, bolts of light came out of my body, thrust that figure, flung it high in the air and as it attempted to escape, I waved my hands under the direction of the Spirit and pointed at it while shouting "Jesus!". What amazed me is that as I pointed at it, bolts of sparkling lightning proceeded out of my finger like a volcanic eruption and brought visible lightning into the room such that everything in the room could be seen visibly as if there was day light. That demonic figure was mercilessly busted out through the door into the darkness. The most spectacular experience is that those whom I was sleeping with, woke up and were amazed to see light shining in the room yet the lights were off. The experience of demonstrating the glory light was so spectacular such that it was as if I were watching a movie. This is how the Glory Light operates. It brings light to scatter the powers of the devil.

Prophetically speaking, in this send time season, many believers across the globe shall experience the visibility of the glory of God manifesting as light. This shall be symbolic of God's presence and direction in the affairs of humanity. In areas around the world that are infested by physical darkness, believers shall be elevated to the dimension of glory whereby they shall command light to supernaturally shine through the darkness and it shall be established. Say, you are having a crusade in a remote area with poor lightning or it happens that lights goes off while you are still ministering. Under the circumstances, you have the right to command light to supernaturally shine through in the same way God spoke into the darkness of the deformed earth and said, *"Let there be light"* and light came forth (Genesis 1:3). This is how the glory of God will be manifested as a greater light in this end time season.

THE GLORY SMOKE.

Smoke is one of the manifestations of the glory of God revealed in the Bible. In Genesis 15:10, 17, the *smoking oven* and burning torch symbolizes the glory of God. In many instances in the Bible, God represents His glory through the image of smoke. In the Old Testament especially, God represents Himself through the image of fire and smoke- the burning bush and the pillar of fire in the wilderness. The manifestation of smoke goes hand in glove with fire because there is no smoke without fire. This is evidenced by the manifestation of both the smoking oven and the burning torch in Genesis 15:17. It is likely that, as God passed through the divided sacrifice, the fire consumed it, showing His acceptance. The burning of the sacrifice by fire is symbolic of the manifestation of God's glory out of heaven onto the natural realm. When the Tabernacle was built, God ignited the first sacrifice. When the Levitical ministry and the priesthood under Aaron were consecrated, God ignited the sacrifice, as He did in Genesis 15:17. God consumed it out of Heaven. To cement the revelation of smoke as the glory of God, the Bible says when God descended on Mount Sinai, *the mountain was covered in smoke and God spoke* (Exodus 19:18). This was a visible manifestation of the glory of God. Such supernatural experiences shall be come a common experience in these end times. As believers gather in worship meetings, smoke, mist, fog or any other related substance shall cover the place as the glory of God is intensified or manifested in the natural realm.

However, although smoke is a symbol of the glory of God, it also reveals the dangerous side of God. All of the SMOKES in Revelation are symbolic of the same thing: the *destruction and desolation* of the city of Jerusalem and the nation of Judaism of which it was the capital. It is recorded in Revelation 15:8 that *the temple was filled with smoke from the glory of God and from his power.* This means that smoke is a manifestation of the glory of God. It is a symbolic picture of the destruction of the Temple. The temple was filled with symbolic SMOKE as well as literal smoke when it was burned to the ground. The symbol stands for the destruction of the Temple as the physical abode of the spiritual God. He desolated it by removing His presence from it forever and destroyed it with the symbolic contents of the seven golden bowls, which were "filled with the wrath of God" (verse 7). This event would show Gods power and His glory, which represents victory. The Bible further declares in Revelation 18:9 that *when the kings of the earth...see the smoke of her burning, they will weep and mourn over her.* The many merchants who had become rich in Judea, along with the Jewish leaders who had rejected Christ and had led the people into a degraded spiritual lifestyle, would see the destruction of their land and nation and would truly mourn. The SMOKE of the desolation and destruction of the Jewish state would rise forever in the impact it had on the affairs of man and God.

A Testimony Of The Glory Smoke

I recall vividly the day when I led a prayer meeting with my brethren at University. It happened that as I ministered on the anointing of the Holy Spirit, what appeared to be smoke, mist or fog appeared and filled the whole auditorium such that it could be visibly seen in the natural realm. If anybody had passed by and witnessed that divine experience, he would have thought that the auditorium was on fire. I was instantaneously catapulted into a higher realm of glory whereby I demonstrated the power of God in miracles, signs and wonders like never before. This was a unique manifestation of God's glory which shall increasingly become a common occurrence in the Body of Christ in this season as God reveals more of Himself on behalf of humanity.

SUPERNATURAL WIND.

At times God manifests His glory though a supernatural wind. The Greek and Hebrew words translated "spirit"*(pneuma* and *ruach*) are also translated either "*wind*" or "*breath*" Both the words wind and breath are also used in close conjunction with the Holy Spirit, as can be seen from these texts:

"And when the day of Pentecost was fully come, they were all with one accord in one place. And suddenly there came a sound from heaven as of a mighty rushing wind, and it filled all the house where they were sitting and they were all filled with the Holy Spirit." (Acts 2:1).

The rushing wind referred to in the context of this scripture is symbolic of the visible manifestation of the glory of God. That was a move of God. In other words, that wind originated in the spirit realm and was now transmuted into a tangible and visible form in the natural realm. Let's refer to another scripture in order to get more clarification on the revelation of the supernatural wind. It is recorded that Jesus breathed upon His disciples and said, *"Receive Yee the Holy Ghost"* (John 20:22). That breath was an impartation of the glory of God from the spirit upon the disciples. Remember that the glory of God dwells in our spirit, hence we can release that glory as *"wind"* or breath to give birth to healings, impartations, miracles, signs and wonders.

To cement the revelation of the supernatural manifestation of wind with reference to further scriptural evidence, we find, in the original creative process of humanity, that the breath of God was the activating force in giving life to Adam: *"The LORD God formed man of the dust of the ground, and breathed into his nostrils the breath of life, and man became a living soul"* (Genesis 2:7). Likewise it is the spirit that gives life to the true Christian and it is the same spirit that will eventually raise all mankind from the grave and endow them with new life. Wind is perhaps the first representation of the glory of God's Spirit in the Bible. It says, *'In the beginning, God created heavens and the earth. The Spirit of the Lord was hovering over the surface of the deep...".* *The* phrase, *"Hovering over the surface of the deep'* describes the movement or manifestation of the glory of God's Spirit as *"wind'.*

The wind represents the presence of the Holy Ghost as He performs various functions. A wind speaks of a revival but that depends on the character of its manifestation whether it's a south, west, north or east wind. The Holy Spirit, coming as wind, depicts His power, guidance and direction. When Jesus tells Nicodemus about the new birth experience (John 3:8), He tells him that it is not like a tangible birth where you can see the baby being born and check the clock for its time of arrival. The work of the Spirit breathes into a life, and something transpires that people cannot recognize. There's a dynamism but also a gentleness, like the wisp of a breeze. You can't necessarily see where it came from or where it goes, but all of us can attest to times when God has come and dealt with us, and no human being knew how it happened. At Pentecost (Acts 2:3), it wasn't a wind that blew in; it was the sound of a rushing wind—like a hurricane. That sound, not the sound of the people speaking in tongues, is what drew the crowd in. The Holy Spirit as sovereign God is dynamic, irresistible, and unstoppable. Prophetically speaking, in this end time season as people worship, a cool breeze shall blow over geographical territories. In some extremely hot places characterised by aridity, a supernatural wind shall be released to bring forth the su-pernatural presence of God.

A Testimony Of The Supernatural Wind

I recall vividly the day we had an all-night prayer service at our church premises. Since the masses were hungry for the supernatural, it happened that the auditorium got filled up with people to the extent that some where even standing. The fans in that auditorium were not functioning properly, hence the ventilation was very poor as the small fitted windows could not do justice in granting entrance of any air into the venue. The situation was further exacerbated by the fact that it was extremely hot, hence people started suffocating and expressing signs of discomfort due to the extreme heat. Under the direction of the Holy Ghost, I was prompted to command a supernatural wind to blow over that place and instantly, what appeared to be a gentle cool breeze blew across the hall bringing a fresh and rejuvenating atmosphere which enabled us to proceed with the programme of the night. That was a supernatural wind in operation.

SUPERNATURAL THUNDER AND LIGHTNING.

At times the glory of God can be manifested in the physical realm in the form of thunder and lightning. On the way to Damascus, the Bible says Jesus appeared to Saul and manifested *lightning and thunder* (Acts 9:3-9). How do I know that? Because of the response which his companions articulated. Other said it had thundered. This was supernatural thunder. At first, light shone around them then Paul fell under the power. That means this lightning was accompanied by thunder in the supernatural. This was a manifestation of God's glory in the physical realm. Such manifestations shall become a popular phenomenon or a common occurrence in the Body of Christ as God reveals the fullness of His glory. in these end times. It might not occur spiritually but physically as thunder roars to terrify agents of darkness. Thunder and lightning roared and the people trembled and hid themselves. When Paul fell under the power, others said it roared while others said it thundered. In other words, they had different versions of the same divine experience. They had mixed emotions, hence they could not accurately describe the glory of God from a natural perspective.

SUPERNATURAL EARTH QUAKE.

In some cases, God manifests His glory on earth in the form of a supernatural earthquake, depending of course on the nature of tasks which He wants accomplished. An earthquake represents revolution – a drastic shift or radical change. It speaks of a movement, shaking, stirring, and brewing that is taking place in the realm of the spirit but whose effects are felt on the physical realm. Revelation 16:18 speaks of a mighty earthquake, such as was never seen on the earth before. This great revolution will overthrow everything that is not of the Lord's establishment and approval. This revolution will affect all the governments of the world, socially, politically, financially and ecclesiastically. It reads: *"...And there was a great earthquake, such as was not since men were upon the earth, so mighty an earthquake, and so great"* (Revelation 16:18). "Again Jesus said that wars, famine and pestilence would be followed by earthquakes It was not unusual for Jesus to use symbolic language; in fact, He often used symbolic language or dark sayings to conceal the real meaning until the due time should come. In Biblical symbology, an earthquake means a revolution. Or a radical shifting in the spirit realm that impacts on subjects in the natural realm.

The Bible further unveils a striking or spectacular incident involving a visible and tangible display of God's glory in the natural realm through a supernatural earthquake. It emphatically states that in the early church as believers gathered together in prayer, the pace where they met was visibly shaken (Acts 4:31). This was a supernatural earthquake. It was a visible manifestation of God's glory in the natural realm. It was a sign that God is present. This is the same manifestation that took place when Elijah was on the mountain after he had run away from Jezebel (1 Kings 19:11-13). An earthquake symbolises God's power in the supernatural. Moreover, it represents the movement of God's power from the spirit realm into the natural realm. God declared in Hagai 2:8) that, *"Once more and in a little while I will shake the heavens, seas and the earth and the desires of nations shall come to me"*. This shaking represents the move of God as He displaces powers of evil and establishes his rein on earth.. Especially in this end time season, shakings of this nature are paramount in that people could see the power of God being displayed practically so that they can stream into the kingdom in billions. Where the power of God is visibly demonstrated in the form of an earthquake, no one can resist but give themselves to Christ.

The Visible Signs of Manifestation of God's Glory

I have often interpreted dreams where people have found themselves in an earthquake. Often the interpretation has been that there is coming a shaking in their lives to remove those things that are not of the Lord. Often I have seen this occur when someone is about to enter into a new realm of ministry. In a positive context, an earthquake means that a shaking and a dramatic change for the good, is about to occur in the life of that person! The verses below shows this kind of shaking that took place when Jesus died, signifying a close or end of the old and the beginning of the new era (Matthew 27:50) *"Jesus, when he had cried again with a loud voice, yielded up the spirit. And, behold, the veil of the temple was torn apart from the top to the bottom, and the earth quaked, and the rocks split"*. This shaking occurred once again to signify something new: Matthew 28:2 *"And, behold, there was a great earthquake: for the angel of the Lord descended from heaven, and came and rolled back the stone from the door, and sat upon it"* (GMR Version). As the glory of God is manifested through a supernatural earthquake, many believers will be shifted, lifted and catapulted not the realm of new things – creative miracles and new waves of the anointing.

In a negative sense, an earthquake can also speak of an attack from the enemy as he attempts to destroy people's lives and to remove their feet from under them. In such a case, I would advise the one having such a supernatural encounter to run to the solid rock, which is Jesus Christ, to ensure that their footing remains sure, throughout this attack. This spiritual reality is evident in the scripture below: Psalms 82:4 *"Rescue the weak and needy; deliver them from the hand of the wicked. "They know nothing, they understand nothing. They walk about in darkness; all the foundations of the earth are shaken."* This is the power of God manifested in attacking human armies. Another related scenario that substantiates the revelation of the supernatural earthquake is found in (Jeremiah 51:29): *"For the land shall tremble and sorrow, for every purpose of the Lord shall be performed against Babylon, to make the land of Babylon a desolation without an inhabitant."* In this powerful prophecy of the downfall of Babylon, we see that the trembling or earth-quaking of the land is symbolic of the God directed destruction of that land. This passage is filled with other similar symbols which speak the same message with poetic imagery. The Bible records in Ezekiel 38:19-20 that *"Surely, in that day there shall be a great shaking in the land of Israel and all that are upon the face of the earth shall shake at my presence."* This is the essence of supernatural earthquake. Prophetically speaking, in this end time season, believers are going to experience visible shakings of geographical territories as a result of the power of God being released on earth. This shaking shall culminate in the destruction of the strongholds of the enemy and the subsequent stream flow of the lost souls into the Kingdom.

A Testimony Of The Supernatural Earthquake

I recall vividly the day I demonstrated a supernatural earthquake during one of our Deliverance services. It happened that while I ministered to the congregation, demons started manifesting everywhere. Under the direction of the Holy Ghost, I Suddenly declared, "I command a physical shaking of the foundations of this building in the name of Jesus! I release a supernatural earthquake to shake every demonic stronghold in this territory in Jesus Name" As I uttered these words, suddenly a tremor went through the building causing a shaking which was tangibly and literally felt on the floor of the building. As the masses fell under the power, the demon possessed lost balance and fell on the floor with loud screams and instantly departed. Within few minutes, the situation was back to normal as I continued with the service and documented numerous testimonies of people who got delivered and healed as a result of that supernatural shaking. This is how mass deliverance is conducted. A supernatural earthquake releases a shaking that dismantles the strongholds of demons and sets the masses free from oppression.

SUPERNATURAL OIL.

The glory of God can also be manifested through supernatural oil and this is increasingly becoming a common occurrence in the Body of Christ in these end times. The manifestation of God's glory though supernatural oil is an evidence of the presence of the Holy Spirit since He is the one who administers the anointing. The oil of Scripture is directly related to the Holy Spirit's work in our lives (2 Corinthians 1:21-22). The anointing is a supernatural impartation of God's ability on a vessel and with the anointing, comes an enablement to accomplish tasks with speed. The Holy Spirit, by His anointing and presence, confirms what He is—the Spirit of Truth, of Holiness, of Wisdom. Obeying the Holy Spirit means that He will give us wisdom when we need it in the practical of our everyday life. The Lord also wants to anoint those who have been overcome by the spirit of mourning with the oil of rejoicing. That anointing brings the lifting of our heads with the refreshing of seeing beyond today—not with superficial optimism, but with a deep abiding of hope that has been begotten in

279

us by God. In our ministry, we experienced an unusual supernatural occurrence of appearance of oil from heaven which rained down and covered the ceiling of the church and then gracefully dripped or oozed down its walls and eventually soaked the carpet until it became wet with oil. This supernatural oil initially began to saturate and pour out of the atmosphere with the smell of rose. After that it started flowing with the smell of nard. After that it continued flowing out but this time with a new fragrance or smell of myrrh. As if that was not enough, all sudden diamond stones started falling heavily on people's heads during worship sessions like hail stones.

A Testimony Of The Glory Of The anointing Oil

Sometimes as I stand in the glory, my hands and feet begins to drip with supernatural oil, representing the miracle anointing of God. Many times I will use this supernatural oil to pray for the sick and have seen tremendous healing miracles take place. The supernatural oil that flows from my hands often carries a heavenly aroma – the fragrance of Jesus (Song of Songs 2:1). In Psalm 23:5 David says, "You have anointed my head with [fresh] oil."). God is anointing us with a fresh new impartation from His Spirit! Other times while in the glory of God, I have seen tiny sparkles appear in the air or on people. Sometimes the glory will come as a shower of golden rain; sometimes this golden substance will come out from the pores of my skin. One day, while praying a woman's hands suddenly became wet with a thin sheen of oil and she began anointing people with it. We found that we could wipe her hands dry, only to have the oil come back just out of her hands. It also was scentless when it was left on her hands but as soon as she anointed people they could smell it. This is how the phenomenon of supernatural oil is raining upon God's people in this season.

SUPERNATURAL RAINS.

The glory of God can also be manifested through a phenomenon of called *supernatural rain*. This involves the precipitation of showers of rain from the spirit realm into the natural realm. By supernatural rains, we are not referring to the normal rain which comes during the rainy season. Instead, we are talking about the rain that comes from the spirit and is manifested in the natural realm as if it is natural. The difference between the rain of the spirit and natural rain is that natural rain comes from the *clouds* while the rain of the spirit comes from *heaven*. Rain has a dual implication in the word of God. Firstly, as refreshing where there has been dryness and barrenness (Joel 2:23-29). Secondly, as restoration where there has been loss (Isaiah 28:11-12). The *"pouring out"* Peter refers to at Pentecost (Acts 2:17) is not an abstract use of the word; it has to do with the *"latter rain"* that brought about the hastening of the harvest and fruitful crops. The Lord is saying that He will send rain to fields [people] that are totally barren as a promise of hope. Needing to be refreshed doesn't mean that I've backslid or sinned. When the lawn endures a hot day, it dries up and needs the refreshing of rain. The Holy Spirit, coming as rain, comes to bring refreshing and restoration Rivers are channels or conduits to places where the refreshing of water is needed. John pinpoints that the work of the Spirit as *"rivers of living water"* was to become available after Jesus' ascension (John 7:37-39). The Holy Spirit is manifest in rivers in order that the rain not only be a refreshing upon you, but also that the Lord would make you an overflowing tributary of His Holy Spirit fullness, life, and love to others. The Lord wants people to get in touch with who He is, and that takes people who will let the rivers of living water be awakened in them and then gush out of their lives. So the Holy Spirit is manifest in rivers.

There's what God calls the *rain of the spirit*. As much as natural rain falls on the earth, so the rain of the spirit falls on the church of Christ. The physical natural rains comes from clouds in the sky above. But the rain of the spirit comes from heaven. It's a great programme of heaven to open its window for the rains to fall. In Isaiah 32: 15-18 it says: *"Until the spirit he poured upon us from on high and the wilderness be a fruitful field, and the fruitful field be counted for a forest"*. The prophet saw the pouring of the spirit upon Israel and what looked as a wilderness became a fruitful field. A fruitful field soon became a forest. Everything changed from wilderness to forest. Today the church is receiving the same. We as the church have our wildernesses and places in our lives which could never change for any reason but with the supernatural rains, anything is possible.

It is divine truth that part of God's end time programme is to release great transforming rainfall of His spirit on the earth. Hence, there is such a thing as supernatural rain which shall become a central theme and a common experience amongst God's children in this season that marks the conclusion of God's eternal plan for the earth. To cement this revelation with reference to scriptural evidence, it is recorded in Genesis 8: 22, that; *"God said that while the earth remaineth, seedtime and harvest, and cold and heat, and simmer and winter, and day and night shall not cease"*. It's very exciting to know that there is a winter time. During this time, the heavens are open and great storms of rain and snow begin to fall on the earth. Everything changes. Most of the animals and birds go into hibernation. The skies are dark and loaded with waters. The days of heat are over. It's now winter time. The same applies with supernatural rains. As it is in the physical world, so it is in the spiritual. There are spiritual seasons. As farmers can tell the rainy season with precision, so children of God also know these seasons with spiritual precision.

Prophetically speaking, supernatural rains are coming down upon the body of Christ like never before in this end time season. These rains are to prepare the body of Christ for His second coming. The apostle Paul saw this mystery of the church. He used the example of husband and wife. The husband marries a wife when she has been decked as a bride. God also is preparing his bride which is the church. It's about time for the wedding of the book of Revelation to take place. In Ephesians 5:26 – 27, the Spirit through Paul said, *"That he might sanctify and cleanse it with the washing of water by the word. That He might present it to himself a glorious church, not having sport or wrinkle, or any such thing, but that it should be holy and without blemish"*.

That's why God is releasing great supernatural rains upon the church so that all spots, wrinkles and all such things which had failed the church all these years can be dealt with once and for all. The reason is that God is about to present the church to Himself as a bride is presented to her husband. This great rainfall is a result of God's great love for the church. As we take a journey into these great revelations, make sure you catch a portion, begin to process that which belongs to you. It's great supernatural rainfall time. Don't stay behind. It's your time. In Psalms 102:13 the Spirit said through the prophet; *"Thou shalt arise, and have mercy upon Zion: for the time to favour her, yea, the set time is come"*. Since you have this revelation now, your favour is beginning to flow to you. God is arising in Heaven to pour down mercy and favour upon Zion, which is His church. There's always a set time for God to do certain things in His church. Your set time is now. In the context of the above scripture, the Psalmist was praying with such confidence, asking the Lord to arise and have mercy upon Zion. The church of Christ has to be confident as it commands the supernatural rains to come down.

To further substantiate this revelation with reference to scriptural evidence, it is recorded in Psalms 29:10 that *"The Lord sits upon the flood, yea, the Lord sits as a King forever"*. This implies that our God sits upon foods of supernatural rains and sits in command as King. The church is experiencing the rains that flow from these foods. The Lord wants to beautify His church with rains from His foods. Just like in the days of the prophet Elijah it says in I Kings 18:41 that "Elijah said to Ahab, *"Get up, eat and drink, for there is a sound of abundance of rain."* The prophet saw a great storm coming and told Ahab the king to go and begin to eat and drink. In simpler terms, he was telling him to go and begin to celebrate for the rains had come. The king who was sad because of the long drought, was to go and celebrate the beginning of heavy rains as evidenced by verse 45 which says,

"It came to pass in the meanwhile, that the heaven was black with clouds and wind, and there was a great rain".

It came to pass exactly, as the prophet of God had said. Joy came back to Israel and people rejoiced. The same is happening right now. God has sent storms of supernatural rains to the church of Christ. It's time to celebrate and rejoice because the supernatural rains are beginning to cleanse the church, beautifying her and making her glorious. If you are part of the church, then great things are beginning to happen in your life. As it begins to rain on you, God is Omniscient, so, He knows what you want exactly. These supernatural rains open up barren wombs, it opens up new jobs, this rainfall cleans your mind of all bad memories. This rainfall will cause young ministries to flourish. It will draw good things from the kingdom ground just for you. This rainfall will answer in your finances. Welcome the season of great rains of the spirit of God. It means a lot. It goes beyond the rains of Pentecost which flooded the early church.

Prophetically speaking, great rain is about to fall on you. So get set! The rains of the spirit will transform your life so dramatically that even your friends will begin querying your advancements. Believe me; your life will be different. Just open up and read on. You have been wondering why Christians are not making any head-way. In fact, some Christians are getting discouraged world-wide. It appears, Satan is gaining more and more access into the Church. Reception is being baptized by convenience. Sin is turning its face. But no! This is a powerful moment for the church. All we need is *revelation knowledge*. It's good to fast and pray. But these two can't deliver the knowledge you need to you. Go for revelation and throw off every force that discourages you.

The spirit is being poured upon your life now for a very special programme and reason. God knows what you are going through. He knows what is happening at your place of work. He has seen your wilderness. He has seen how you can do nothing about it. This is the wrinkle the apostle Paul saw that's troubling you. The good news is that God has released the rain of His Spirit to deal with your wilderness. God wants to deal with that desert condition in your finances, health, studies or family. Just lift up your right hand and call on the rain to fall right now. The rain of the spirit is yours to deal with the wilderness. That sickness which has been in your family all this long, the rains will wash it away. The rain of the spirit is falling to deal with that impossible case. Rise up on your feet and command the rain of the Spirit to fall on you. And the wilderness will become a fruit field! That's amazing! It takes the rain of the spirit for the wilderness to produce. It shall become a fruit field. Though it had been a wilderness previously, a desert, an impossible story today, change is coming. Just believe the word of God.

Whenever God sees a messed up life, a confusing situation or a circumstance that we can't handle, learn it today, God releases the rain of the spirit. This rain of the spirit comes in the form of word, into your life. God will whisper certain keys into your ears. This rain can come as a person who will transform your business. It can fall as an advice from a friend. The rain of the spirit is the spirit of God himself coming down as rain. In Genesis 1:2 it says: *"And the earth was without form, and void, and darkness was upon the face of the deep. And the spirit of God moved upon the face of the waters.* You see, in such confusion and chaos, God sent His spirit to control the situation. This was before He ever spoke a word to recreate the world. I know that in some area you are without form, you are insecure, you feel such a vacuum, there is longing to be satisfied. May be you are struggling with certain memories. You know what! Become ever bolder now and command the rain of the spirit into that situation, say it: *'Lord I command the rain of the spirit into this breaking home, or dying business in Jesus' name'*.

Now, something is beginning to happen. Begin to expect a change. It won't take so long. Begin to give thanks for your victories! And the wilderness be a fruit field and the fruitful field be counted for a forest. So, this means that that every wilderness, and desert-like condition will eventually become a forest. Have you thought about it? A wilderness to become a forest!! Is that natural? No. It's a mystery. So don't struggle trying to understand with your mind. Only believe. Your wilderness will become a fruitful field. Your fruitful field will become a forest. Stop the tears now. Let's believe in God and his prophets. In Ezekiel 39:29, it says:

The Realm of Glory

"Neither will I hide my face anymore from them: for I have poured out my spirit upon the house of Israel, saith the Lord God."

This means that this rain of the spirit brings with it, the ever-abiding presence of God in your life. God has promised never to hide His face after he pours out his spirit upon the house of Israel, the church. His Spirit when poured out upon us carries His face. God is good. I don't think that this is a simple thing. It's great. You can't afford to remain the same. We should avoid those habits of begging God for His face to appear. Let's instead believe God for the rains of the spirit to be poured out. The truth is – if you have declared the rain of the spirit upon your life, things are going to change. The face of the Lord, or His eyes will be on you continually.

As His spirit foods your life, this rain will cause you to be in His presence wherever you go. What a joy your life should be! You see, I am tired of seeing children of God languish as though they are orphans. Our Father is the great God, who is also King sitting on foods. Why would His children suffer hunger? Let's rise up one more time and declare the rain of the spirit on our families, our professions and ourselves. We will be amazed at what the Lord will do. We will begin to gain favour from our bosses. Something good will happen to your husband and he will begin to change. Life will cease to drag. I see your forest where there has been a desert. That wrinkle has been removed. For a wilderness to become a forest, something miraculous must have happened. So, go ahead and rejoice. You know a forest is impenetrable; it organizes its own rainfall called relief rainfall. A forest is a great asset compared with a desert. So, that's what comes from the rain of the spirit. You don't have to be stranded. People like Peter and the Apostles, no devil could stand in front of them. They had the rainfall of the spirit of God. Persecution simply enlarged the church. Mighty signs and wonders showed forth. Peter's shadow could heal the sick. That was the early church with the early rains of the spirit. How much more this end time church! In Job 8:7 it says: *"Though your beginning was small, yet your latter end should greatly increase".*

The rain of the spirit of God which the early church saw was only the beginning. The early church however saw a great move of God where thousands upon thousands came to the Lord and were filled with the Holy Spirit. The end-time church's move of the Spirit of God will be bigger and greater and more wonderful. If Peter's shadow healed the sick by the beginning of the rains of the spirit, how much more us who are in the rains of the greatest harvest ever? I see you manifest in a dimension that has never been known. In Joel 2:28 it says,

The Visible Signs of Manifestation of God's Glory

"And it shall come to pass afterward, that I will pour out my spirit upon all fresh: and your sons and your daughters shall prophecy, your old men shall dream dreams, young men shall see visions; And also upon the servants and the handmaids in those days I will pour out my spirit".

So, according to God's programme, we are in the days of great supernatural rainfall of the spirit of God. He's raining down great wisdom, great understanding, judgment, knowledge and others. That's why when our Lord Jesus appeared to John in the book of Revelation, He always said: *"He that hath an ear, let him hear what the Spirit says to the churches"*. He is the great rain coming down upon the church. During the rainy season, farmers know that it's time to go and plant. They get that message from that rain. We too ought to hear what the Spirit of God is saying because He is our rain. So, open your ears and hear what the spirit of God is saying to you concerning your business or family or that sickness on your mother. That's why the Spirit has been poured out in these last days in a greater measure. He's the speaker lets listen. He knows everything. He's the one who made Peter's shadow to heal the sick at the beginning of His rains, how much more us who are in the rains of the greatest harvest ever? I see you manifest in a dimension that has never been known.

As you experience the glory of the supernatural rains, you need to be conscious of the presence of the Holy Spirit in your life. You see, the spirit of God is a person. He has emotions, feelings and wants to be loved and worshipped. You see his manifestation because of the way you relate to Him. Our Lord Jesus said in John 14:26 that: *"But the comforter, the Holy Ghost, whom the Father will send in my name, he shall teach you all things and bring all things to your remembrance, whatsoever I have said unto you"*. So, from Jesus' time, the Holy Spirit has been there to fulfil that special task: to comfort our lives as he deals with our wildernesses, to teach us all things, so that we are full of wisdom, and causing us to remember these great truth always. And that's how your wilderness will disappear for ever. This is what God had in mind when He promised to pour out the spirit like rain in the book of Joel 2:28.

Therefore, begin to consciously relate with the spirit of God. He wants to comfort you. It's His ministry and area of specialisation. For you to stay crying renders Him useless. Let Him come in and comfort you. Open your ears to His teachings. All your ignorance will disappear. Your ignorance is what your mountains are made of. Begin to have a separate program for you and the Holy Ghost. Give Him time as you study God's word to illuminate your mind. He's the author of the written word of God, so invite Him as you study it. I see a change come on you. Do these things on a daily basis. Allot him (*the Spirit*) time for worshipping in His presence. I don't mind the circumstance you are in now, it has to change. Remember, how you relate with Him is what matters most. Because He is a person. Mishandling Him is like physical rain falling and no one goes out to dig the softened ground and plant crops for food. That rain would be wasted. It's time for the rain of the spirit. Let there be rain upon your life. Let there be rain upon your wilderness. Let there be rain upon your soul, in Jesus' name.

Again in Hosea 10:12 it says, *"Break up your fallow ground: for it's time to see the Lord, till he come and rain righteousness upon you."* So many think that seeking the Lord is trying to find out where He has hidden. No! God never hides in that sense If He ever hides, no man can search out His ways, no man can locate him. Not even devils can try to locate His whereabouts. God never hides for the people to search for Him and find Him. Look at that scripture again. It says, *"break up the fallow ground: for it is time to seek the Lord"* so we seek the Lord by breaking our fallow grounds. By enlarging our capacities, by stretching forth our sights, by accommodating more of what we didn't have of Him. By breaking up the fallow ground, it means to break our religious beliefs and routines, to break into God's new things. Practically, it's searching out in scriptures for truths, it's waiting on Him in prayer according to the truths we have discovered from the word and God. I can suggest fasting here while you are on your personal search. Otherwise, seeking the Lord is your personal effort on your part to put things in order. To fight off those sins which entangle you easily, It is recorded in 1 Kings 18:41-45 that:

Elijah said to Ahab, "Go up, eat and drink; for there is the sound of abundance of rain." So Ahab went up to eat and drink. And Elijah went up to the top of Carmel; then he bowed down on the ground, and put his face between his knees, and said to his servant, "Go up now, look toward the sea." So he went up and looked, and said, "There is nothing." And seven times he said, "Go again." Then it came to pass the seventh time, that he said, "There is a cloud, as small as a man's hand, rising out of the sea!" So he said, "Go up, say to Ahab, 'Prepare your chariot, and go down before the rain stops you.' Now it happened in the meantime that the sky became black with clouds and wind, and there was a heavy rain.

This is a quintessential example of how the supernatural rains shall overtake man's programmes in the natural realm in this end time season. Conclusively, it is worth mentioning that supernatural rains shall increasingly become a common occurrence in these end times as God manifests the fullness of His glory on behalf of humanity.

A Testimony Of The Supernatural Rains

This one day while one of our members was busy with her household chores at home, she heard the sound of the splashing of water and then saw water cascading down at the doorway. She thought someone was playing with a water hose but when she took a step to check, she found that no one was there but the water was still cascading off the top of the entrance way. She also told other experiences of how oil would appear on her fingers, and water on her palms. She would wipe away the water but it would come again. This is how the supernatural rains manifests in these end time days, to provide refreshing to those going through the dry seasons in their lives.

CHAPTER ELEVEN

THE REALM OF CREATIVE MIRACLES OF GOD'S GLORY

It is worth exploring the divine truth that heavens are pregnant with the possibilities of God and the womb of the spirit is ready to unleash the supernatural realities of God. There is a stirring and brewing taking place in the spirit realm as the spirit of God is hovering over the masses to prepare the world for the second coming of Jesus Christ. This is therefore a season of glory, a time of creative miracles where the glory of God is unreservedly unveiled to the masses. In this next move of God we will begin to see extreme demonstrations of God's power and glory that will suspend the very laws of gravity. There have been many miracles recorded in the Bible that seem to defy the laws of nature and gravity. For instance, Samson lifted the gates of an entire city, killed thousands of men with the jawbone of a donkey as well as many other amazing feats. Elijah outran a chariot, and Philip was transported faster than a blink to another town to preach. Jesus demonstrated the first invisible cloaking device when He disappeared from the midst of a crowd ready to stone Him! They had rocks in their hands and were looking right at Jesus— the next moment, He was gone. (Judges 16: 3; 1 Kings 18: 44-46; Acts 8: 39-40; John 8: 59; 10: 39.) It is evident in the above mentioned scenarios that superhuman strength and power come from a supernatural God. The kind of things that happened from Genesis through Revelation will happen again in this end time season as humanity in all extreme quarters of the world operate in the glory realm.

As the church delves into this arena of the glory invasion, I believe we will see an unusual dimension of miracles in our day that are not even recorded in the Bible. In other words, God is exploding in the demonstration of signs and wonders such that you will be catapulted into an unusual *realm of unrecorded miracles* as God is not limited to the pages of the Bible. To the sceptics who presume that every miracle that takes place in our present time should have been recorded in the Bible, I have good news for you! Have you not read that *there were many other miracles which Jesus performed that were not recorded in the Bible?* In fact, John puts it this way, *"And there are also many other things which Jesus did, which, if they should be written, I suppose that even the world itself could not contain the books that should be written"* (John 21:25). This is to tell you that there are tremendous manifestations of God's glory that are birthing forth new creative miracles that will ruffle the feathers of the sceptics and those comfortable with the status quo.

Consider what God had to say concerning the realm of the unrecorded miracles in this season:

> *"I'm bigger than the Book,"* sayeth the Lord. *"For the world that I created cannot contain all that I have said and done. I'm still creating, inventing and unfolding new things from My Throne Room. Although these are natural to me, they are new to the inhabitants of the natural realm. Therefore, think beyond what is written, for I will do the unrecorded, the uncharted and the unknown. I will do that which no one ever heard of imagined — a third wave of Signs and wonders that will ruffle the feathers of those comfortable with the status quo and dumbfound the sceptics. Therefore, look beyond the natural and make room for the supernatural, for I will amaze you with an endless stream flow of spectacular signs and wonders that are normal to me."*

In view of the above, as you step into the arena of glory in this end time season, you will experience a torrential downpour of unrecorded miracles, fresh from the *Throne Room of Heaven* which humanity has never been seen before. However, in order to see a greater demonstration of these creative miracles, we must see God as a creator so that we can tap into that dimension of creativity. We must know God more as the Creator in order to abound in the realm of creative miracles. This is because God manifests the way you perceive him, hence you must widen your perception by seeing Him in unlimited aspects and you will see unlimited manifestations of Him. Unfortunately, those who are still worshiping the invisible God will be left behind because God is no longer a secret. His glory is being transmuted into the physical realm in a tangible and visible way. God is revealing Himself right where you are in your leaving room, office, streets, market place and every sphere of humanity to demonstrate His sovereignty in the light of His creation. As He unveiled this revelation into the depths of my spirit, God said,

The Realm of Glory

"Tell my people that the dimension of miracles that I'm about to unleash from the reservoir of My Glory, right across the body of Christ is so deep such that believers should be cautioned to relook into their theology and be established in faith so that they might not be sceptical or critical of this new move of the glory of My Spirit"

In what He described as the third wave of signs and wonders, God said,

"I'm unveiling the fullness of My glory, grace and love for My children in this very hour which marks the final chapter of human history in order to conclude my eternal plan for the planet earth".

This is to tell you how expedient it is to tap into the glory zone and harness the power for creative miracles in this final chapter of human history. We must therefore be circumspect in our approach to the supernatural and not to immediately discard anything of a supernatural nature just because we don't understand it. Believers are therefore advised not to be too sceptical because those who do that will be left behind in this new move of God. There is a spiritual awakening shaking the body of Christ as the fullness of the might and strength of God is unleashed on earth. Many of the creative miracles that shall take place in this season are a brand new grace straight from the hand of God. Tapping into the scriptures as a point of reference, God said, *"Behold I'm doing a new thing. Something which you did not know yesterday. Can't you perceive it as it spring forth"* The reason why it is called a *"new thing"* is because it's something fresh from the breath of God. It doesn't have a name as yet but a brand new substance unfolding from God's Throne. The question you are probably asking yourself is: When these creative miracles happen, where does the material that generates them come from? It comes from the invisible part of God. The Bible attests to the divine truth that *the things which were seen were not made of things which do appear.* This implies that the matter or material used to make the things which were not seen were invisible. If God is creating out of Himself, then the material or matter He uses to produce creative miracles comes out of that invisible part of Himself. He predesigns and produces a manifestation which is a reflection of something already existing in the eternal past, and yet it is visible now. The following are some of the major creative miracles of God's glory which shall become a common occurrence in the Body of Christ in this season as humanity launches into greater depths of God's glory: Presented below is a catalogue of the amazing acts of God which He showcases in the glory realm to bring multitudes in faith to Him.

Supernatural Gold Teeth fillings

This speaks of a phenomenon whereby people's teeth are supernaturally filled with gold, silver or any other supernatural substance from heaven. This shall be beneficial especially for those who have lost self-esteem and confidence in life by virtue of having lost teeth. The teeth are the most important part of a human being because people tend to be judged by the presentation of physical appearance of our teeth. Hence, in these end times where God is nearer to humanity than ever before, He demonstrates His love in a remarkable way, by altering people's teeth. This is a height-ened degree of God's love, to prove that He is concerned about even the smallest things that affect His children. So, if you require a tooth filling, don't you dare loose your self-esteem. The time for shame and reproach is over. Papa God has one for you, a gold one for that matter. I'm not taking about a temporary gold feeling but a permanent mark which can confound the wisdom of those who seek to undermine you. In our ministry, we have seen people's missing teeth, as well as hair, cartilage, and thyroids reappear, even after they have been surgically removed.

Supernatural Increase or decrease in height

In the atmosphere of God's glory, it is possible for a person's height to be com-manded either to increase or decrease. For example, a short person *(dwarf)* can be commanded to instantly grow in height under the power of God. On the other side of the coin, a person who happens to be extremely tall and is not comfortable with that kind of height can be commanded to decrease in height. In the dimensions of God there are neither tall nor short people. Everybody is of an appropriate height ac-cording to the original blue print God designed us to be. When God looks at you, no matter how tiny or short you might be, He doesn't see a short or skinny guy. That is why He looked at the tiny, little and fearful Gideon and said to him, *"Gideon mighty man of valour"*. It happens in the natural realm that some people might not be comfortable with their heights, hence God changes them as they wish. Note that God doesn't not change your heart because He made a mistake during creation and He is now trying to rectify it. No! He changes your height for your sake, so that you can believe and have your faith strengthened in Him. The body is part of the natural realm and if God could change things in eternity while should it be impossible for Him to change a body whose life span is limited? That is why even raising people from the dead is not a big deal to God because everything can be changed in the realm of glory.

Supernatural germination of hair on bold heads

This is a spiritual phenomenon whereby those who are not comfortable with their bald hair and have lost their self-esteem can be commanded to grow hair instantly. Change in the colour of natural hair can also be effected depending on the desire of a recipient. Others will go to the extent of having different hair styles cut buy angels themselves in the invisible realm. Rather than spending a lot of money going to a hair salon, one would just bask in the glory of God and have their hair done. This is a supernatural reality and angels are behind the manifestations of such experiences. In the Old Testament days, the dignity of a person was always connected to the presentation of his hair and so does in these end time days. Everything created cannot be destroyed but can only be converted into another form. So, if you have lost your hair, it still exist somewhere- it has just been converted to another form, but it still exist. Therefore in the glory realm, wherever your hair is, it can still recommended to come back and it will respond. Your hair has sound waves and can hear and respond when you call out, "Hair, come back". And it can return to its original state and respond to your words spoken under the direction of the Holy Spirit. In our ministry, we have seen more bald people receive instant hair growth. A certain man received hair growth while we were all watching in amazement. We actually saw his bald spots filling in with hair. On another meeting, hair appeared instantly on top of a man's bald head where he was totally bald, such that the colour of his new hair was its original dark colour. We have also seen people with white hair have their hair turned to its original colour. This is what we call *transformation in the glory*.

Supernatural Change in human complexion

While in the natural realm a complexion is something permanent, in the realm of God's glory, it can be altered. There is virtually nothing that cannot be changed in the glory. For example, a person who is extremely dark in complexion and doesn't like it because others are ridiculing him, or has lost his self esteem can have his complexion changed into a lighter one, vice versa. Although it boggles the mind, others can even receive a supernatural make up so that they look very beautiful. If God says a darker complexion can be changed into a lighter one and a lighter complexion be changed into a darker one, who am I to contradict him? Anything is possible to God. He asked Abraham a rhetoric question, *"Is anything too hard for the Lord to do"*. In this season, it is not necessary for people to go for surgery in order to have part of their body parts cut to conform to a specific shape. Instead, the Holy Ghost is actively involved in terms of shaping body parts. God wants to show you that He is concerned even by the very things that bother you a lot.

Supernatural change in bodily structure

In the realm of God's glory, the people who have certain body parts or organs which they don't like or are not comfortable with, can have them instantly changed by the glory. For example, a long nose can be commanded to be shorter, big ears can be commanded to be of an appropriate size, even the so-called private parts can be commanded either to lengthen or decrease size depending on the desire of the recipient. Note that case the devil's tool to mislead people though penis enlargement can be thwarted because in the atmosphere of God's glory, a person's male organ can be commanded to be longer for those who would want that kind of spiritual therapy to be performed on them. God is a creator and If He used His wisdom to create the whole human being, why should it be difficult to change or modify certain features. Nothing is too hard for the Lord, glory to Jesus!.

Supernatural age increase and age reduction

It might happen that some people grow older easily, yet they want to look younger so that they can fulfil God's purpose in their lives. The glory can affect their bodies to such an extent that a 50 year old can look like a 16 year old. Since we are living in a day and age whereby everybody wants to stay fresh and look young, the secret is in the nourishment of the glory of God. These miracles are possible in the glory of God. Did you know that Adam and Eve were never infants and they were created as adults but they never grew old because of the life of Glory. Even after a death sentence was adjudicated upon them, their mortal bodies still carried them for over 800 years before they eventually died. This is to tell you how impactful the glory of God is on a human body. There is neither decay, aging nor death in the life of glory. If you wanted to stay for ever young, energetic and fresh, the solution is to stay in the presence of God and cultivate an atmosphere of glory in your life. If a dry rod left in the presence of God's glory produced buds and almond fruits within 24 hours, how much more would it not be possible that God can transform an older, aging skin texture into a softer and younger looking one? Do you know that Sarah carried a baby at an old age? How possible is it that an old lady can carry a baby for nine months? This is scientifically impossible. However, in the life of glory anything is possible. Anything that contacts or comes into contact with God's glory receives newness of life. Her body had been so much mingled and infused by God's glory such that she looked like a sixteen year old. The glory had so much quickened, activated and vitalised her mortal body, specifically her dead reproductive cells such that her body looked ten times younger. This is what the glory can do for you in this season as you dive deeper into the pool of creative miracles in this very hour.

Supernatural Increase in life span

In a similar fashion in which God extended Hezekiah's life by fifteen years, in the atmosphere of glory, people can be commanded to live longer than expected. There- fore, anybody who wishes to live longer especially those who are approaching old age, can have their life spans extended as per God's will. It must be expressly understood that God doesn't want people to die prematurely, especially if they have not fulfilled their destiny in Him. Instead, He wants His children to live abundantly. God's will to have our lives extended is reflected in Jesus declaration that, *"I have come that you might have life and have it abundantly"*. Therefore, if you feel you have wasted a lot of time and would want God to extent your life so that you can fulfil His will on earth, your life span can be extended according to your desire.

Supernatural pregnancy.

Do you know that in the atmosphere of God's glory, it is possible for someone to get pregnant supernaturally? Jesus demonstrated this reality by being born without the natural processes of intimacy or fertilization. Mary received a prophecy form the Angel of the Lord that she would be pregnant with Jesus. (Luke 1:26-28). How long do you think it took for that prophecy to come to pass? Instantly! She was already pregnant afterwards because in the next verse she is hastily walking over to visit Elizabeth and the baby John the Baptist leaped in his mother's womb at the presence of Jesus in Mary (Luke 1:39-45). This event took place *at the most three days* later (or however long it took to walk to Elizabeth's house). It is possible in the realm of Glory for a pregnancy to be commanded on a lady and within any stipulated time, even three days, a person can give birth. This is called *supernatural pregnancy*. Did you know that in the glory, not only do you have the grace to command a creative miracle, but you also have the exclusive right to declare the specific time you want that miracle to take place. For example, by saying to a lay who desperately need a baby, *"I decree that within 7 days from now, you shall have a son"* and it shall he established for you exactly according to your word. How is this possible? Because we have dominion over time, hence when operating in the glory realm, the law of time is broken so that you will not have to go or wait through all the natural phases and processes of time to deliver a baby. In this season of invasion or explosion of glory, it is even possible for a woman to be pregnant and even deliver the baby on the same day. Such babies are released directly from the hand of God, hence they might be dedicated unto the lord throughout the days of their lives in a like manner in which Samuel was conceived and born.

These children are called *supernatural babies* because they are not born following the natural processes. Does this sound quizzical to you? Don't you know that in this critical era, we have stepped into Amos 3:9 whereby *a ploughman shall overtake the reaper and the treader of grapes him that sows seed?* In other words, in this season, immediately after we sow a seed, we see a harvest. In the context of this revelation, immediately after a seed is planted in a womb, the baby is supernaturally delivered as birth is overtaking pregnancy? How possible is it that one can give birth within 3 days? Because God lives outside our time dimension, hence in the glory realm, time is not of essence because the normal stages of conception, incubation and gestation are cut short such that immediately after one conceives, she delivers a baby. Once something is declared in that atmosphere of glory, it matures instantly. The greater truth is that we are living in a season in which the eternal realm is overtaking time in the natural realm, culminating in untold acceleration of events in the natural realm. The realm of glory is a realm of acceleration and speed hence, taking into account the nature of the dispensation into which we have been ushered, it is no longer necessary to wait for ever in order to have things delivered to you.

The other reason behind the possibility of giving birth within 3 or 7 days is because in the glory realm, time can be altered in line with the will of God. The fact that women usually take 9 months to deliver the baby does not necessarily mean that everybody is bound by that time frame. That time was stipulated by God for those who live in the league of the ordinary, hence it can be easily altered in the atmosphere of glory when deemed necessary. Do you remember that when Joshua was at war and needed more time, God allowed him to command the sun to stop so that he would finish his business? This is to tell you that time is not an issue at all when operating in the glory zone; it can either be shortened or lengthened depending on what needs to be accomplished in the realm of the spirit. Therefore, if it takes nine months in the natural realm for a baby to be born, in the glory realm, it can take just few days. By the same token, if it takes five years for a baby to grow to a certain height, in the atmosphere of God's glory, it can take just take few days for that process to be effected.

Supernatural weight loss and weight gain

In the realm of glory, people who are overweight can have their weight supernaturally reduced to an appropriate size. On the other side of the coin, those who are underweight can be supernaturally commanded to increase in weight. It is disheartening to note that many children of God tend to spend a lot of money buying certain chemicals that are meant to keep their weight down. In a world dominated by a lot of pressure for slimming, others go to the extent of spending a considerable length of time that they should have used for prayer, in the gym subjecting their bodies to the extreme in order to burn fat. However, in this season, God is unreservedly unleashing His love and grace, to command supernatural weight loss to boost the self-esteem and confidence of His children since many are not able to confront the world with boldness to preach the gospel due to lack of confidence resulting from their physical appearance. This realization is why we are witnessing instant weight loss in most of our meetings as we command fat cells to depart. Imagine if you commanded your fat cells to be stretched out as far as the east is from the west: you would no longer be able to see the fat. This is how a lot of creative miracles happen.

Supernatural growth and development of new organs or body parts in areas where they previously did not exist

The greater truth is that God is a creator and the one who comes up with the original prototype of the design of humanity, hence in the atmosphere of glory, people who do not have any body parts can be commanded to have them. This is because there is an original blue print of every body part in heaven. Therefore, if it happens that you loose any part of your body due to either accident, misfortune or any other calamity such as an eye, leg, hand or teeth, you can have them replaced within a flip of a moment in the glory realm. While in the glory zone, you can command a mangled leg that has been traumatically torn off from the body to be restored back to its original position and it shall be established. Creative miracles of this nature have already begun sweeping right across the Body of Christ and in these end times, their manifestation shall be a widespread global sensation. In our ministry, we have seen people's missing teeth as well as hair, cartilage, and thyroids reappear, even after they have been surgically removed.

It is of paramount importance in this regard to establish the fact that everything was created by the glory of God and the sound of the spoken word So, when the heaviness of God's glory is present in a meeting, for example, we know that everybody part and creative miracle needed is available. But how do you extract those creative miracles from the glory in the meeting? By realizing that all the miracles and body parts are in the glory— but in an expanded form. Similarly, your body parts are in the meeting and the glory of God is present. You were created from His glory, so body parts are present but are suspended in the glory in an expanded form. The power is there for a miracle and the body parts are there; now we need to extract a particular body part from the glory realm that is in the room. You do so by declaring the body part to be made manifest and the parts to come together so you can see the miracle visibly in the natural realm. We must understand that this creative realm is valid. It is not a faith realm where we have to stir it up to get it. If you get in the glory of God, your eardrums are there. Your new eyes are there. Your bones are there. If you really get in the Glory of God and stay there, your missing body part will form of its own accord. To substantiate this divine truth with reference to experiential evidence, Apostle Renny McLean testifies that while he ministered in Kenya, there was a man sitting in the congregation with an extremely short leg. When he looked at the man in the natural, the leg was very short but when he looked at him in the spirit, the leg was normal. Then God said to him, *"This is how I see the leg. He's been sitting on his leg all his life. His leg is still there, it's just that he can't see it"*. God didn't say that the leg wasn't there. He said the man couldn't see it. This is to tell you that there is an original blue print of every body part such that although you can't see it in the natural realm, it is present in the spirit although in another form.

The second ingredient for a creative miracle is the sound waves or a spoken word, commanding an object to form out of the raw material of the glory. The divine truth is that everything created can listen and obey, as it too is made of sound. We also know that nothing created can ever be destroyed but only changes form. Knowing this, you can command your hair or your cartilage to return and be reformed or recreated from the glory that is present. The body part has the capacity to obey. Accepting this revelation helps us pray with much greater faith and authority for creative miracles and body parts.

Supernatural restoration of malfunctioning electric gargets, cars, cell phones, instruments, tools or any other equipment.

It is a divine truth that in the glory realm, there is neither death, decay nor any infirmity. As the glory of God raises the dead, it can also supernaturally cause the dead, malfunctioning or broken electric gargets, equipment or tools such as cars, refrigerators, laptops and computers to function instantaneously. In this season of the effulgence of glory, it might not be necessary every time to run around looking for a mechanic to fix your car or other electric gadgets. Just by being catapulted into the realm of glory, which is a super plane or higher realm, all the natural laws are broken as God's sovereignty takes precedence. Therefore, all the old, fractured and broken tools are supernaturally repaired, polished and strengthened in the glory zone. This is because any object whether living or non-living, that comes into contact with God's glory, receives an impartation of the life of God, which causes it to function normally. That is why in the glory realm, healing is not only for human bodies, for even the land itself can also be healed. God does this so that your faith in Him can be strengthened.

Manifestation of Miracle Money in the natural realm

Taking into account that we have dominion over all substances in the natural realm, in the atmosphere of glory, money can be commanded to supernaturally appear in people's wallets, bank accounts, cars, houses and even pockets. Some people receive airtime supernaturally loaded in their phones as a manifestation of miracle money. This is made possible by angels of finances that operate in the invisible spirit realm to cause a transmutation of the substance of money from the spirit realm into the natural. This is similar to the miracle money which Jesus demonstrated in Mathew 17:27 when he commanded Peter to go fishing and take money from the mouth of a fish. In the same way a father pays fees for his child, God is supernaturally releasing miracle money in the natural realm to cover for school fees, grocery, transport and virtually every need in every sphere of human endeavour. You can also use this money to pay for your debts or advance the gospel of Jesus Christ. While others have experienced creative miracles whereby they have been able to make calls from their cell phones without loading airtime, in this end time season, the glory of God shall intensify to such an extent that others will even be able to make phone calls even without cell phones. They will make actions of faith by placing their hands on their ears and instantly they will start decoding messages from the spirit realm and be attuned to the frequency of the Holy Ghost such that they will start communicating with those whom they intend to talk to. The life of gory is that of impossibilities, hence believers are cautioned to move from impossibility thinking to possibility thinking where everything is possible with God. In one of our meetings while the glory of God was moving, people ran down the aisles to give and by the time they got back to their seats, the exact amounts they had given in the offering baskets was back in their pockets! Although it boggles the mind, this is how the miracle money grace operates. For a Deeper revelation of the phenomenon of miracle money, I would kindly refer you to one of my books titled, *"Unveiling The Mystery Of Miracle Money"*.

Supernatural Debt Cancellation

It is a fact that God does not like His children to be enslaved by debt. In a world dominated by a myriad of economic challenges, even the children of God at times get caught up in a situation whereby they borrow money and property from banks and then find it difficult to repay it. When this happens, some find themselves concentrating on the payment of their debts instead of focusing on worshiping God. Therefore, in the atmosphere of glory, God can supernaturally cancel the debt to alleviate their burden so that they can focus on worshiping Him and fulfilling their destiny in Christ. Elijah performed a debt cancelation for a widow who was on the verge of losing her sons by commanding her to gather empty jars and then filling them with water. As she demonstrated her actions of faith by pouring water into the jars, oil supernaturally appeared in the jars, hence she was commanded to sell it and paid her debt in full. This is what God is about to do to you in this season if you relentlessly pursue His glory.

Supernatural change of weather patterns or conditions over geographical territories of the world: Power to command rain, wind, sun, stars, moon, light or darkness in a specific direction.

It is worth exploring the divine truth that every creation whether its trees, rocks, wind, water or buildings responds to sound waves spoken while in the glory realm. Therefore, in these end times, believers shall be catapulted into a higher realm of glory whereby they shall command natural phenomenon such as wind, sun or rain to either prevail or stop operating in certain geographical territories. In the same way Elijah commanded rain to fall, and Joshua commanded the sun to retreat backwards by six degrees and Jesus walked on water, believers shall function so much in the glory such that even nature shall obey them. Jesus said, *"Greater things than these shall you do"*. Therefore, as part of demonstration of greater works, rain shall be commanded to fall especially in those regions characterized by aridity and dryness and in some cases it can be commanded to stop as part of a supernatural demonstration, to show people that God is near to them. For instance, while operating in the glory, a believer will just take the congregation to a nearby pool and make a practical demonstration by walking in water; another will command rain to fall in the church and the congregates shall be drenched in the glory rain; one will command wind to blow and move everybody in the congregation in a specific direction; and another will command the glory cloud to descend and envelop the congregation such that the prevailing temperatures will be changed.

Supernatural manifestations of fire in the natural realm

In the atmosphere of glory, supernatural fire can be commanded to appear visibly to burn demons and other tools of darkness. I'm not talking about the fire of God in the spirit but a dimension in the glory whereby fire is transmuted into a visible and tangible form that shall be seen consuming substances in the natural realm. In the same way Elijah commanded fire to come down from heaven and consumed the wood and the offering, believers in these end times shall command fire to appear physically to perform certain ministerial tasks. It must be expressly understood that the glory of God is no longer a secret. The fire of God is no longer hidden, but shall be seen visibly in the same way the children of Israel saw it as a pillar of fire by night. As God performs mass revival, restoration and deliverance, as witch doctors and magicians surrender their occult tools, fire shall supernaturally appear and physically burn these into ashes.

Driving a car without petrol

Do you know that in the atmosphere of glory, it is possible form one to drove a car for a long distance even without a single drop of fuel in it? In the glory realm, as much as a body can leave for some time without food and water, a car can also move on the road without petrol. This is a divine revelation of what's going to happen in these end times as the glory of God invades the natural realm. In cases where believers desire to preach the gospel in certain places but do not have money for petrol, by tapping into the realm of glory, they shall command their cars to move and drive on even without petrol. If God commanded a donkey to speak, why should it be impossible for Him to command a car to move without petrol? If God commanded water to appear supernaturally in a desert to the extent that the ditches and rivers were full of waters, why would it not be possible for the same God to command fuel to fill your tank? In this end time season, believers shall be catapulted into a higher realm of glory where they shall drive their cars with fuel gauges increasing as they drive and their groceries resurfacing as the month goes by. Remember that when Elijah commanded the widow of Zeraphath to pour water into the jars, that oil appeared supernaturally. This is exactly what will happen to many believers in this end time season.

Commanding crops to grow instantaneously

As aforementioned, in the glory realm anything can be transformed and responds to sound waves spoken under the glory. This is one of the key principles of operating in the glory. In this end time season, believers shall command crops to grow instantly immediately after planting a seed in an atmosphere of glory. While in the natural realm crops require nutrition, water and soil to grow, in this season of glory, as natural laws and processes are altered, the glory is the number one nutrition required for crops to instantaneously flourish. Hence, immediately after sowing a seed, there shall be a harvest. Did you know that seed time and harvest time came after Adam lost the glory? In the life of glory Adam and Eve did not have to wait for a harvest after sowing. Sowing and harvesting took place at the same time. In this season, believers shall be catapulted into a realm whereby immediately after they sow, they shall see a harvest. The natural laws of time and waiting shall are altered to accentuate an avenue for the overruling, overarching law of Glory to prevail.

Therefore, in this season of glory, multitudes of believers shall literally step into Amos 3:9 whereby *the ploughman shall overtake the reaper and the treader of grapes him who sows a seed.* Put this in your Spirit. The Reaper is harvesting as fast as he can. On his heels comes the Ploughman. He is already preparing another harvest in the soil that the reaper has just harvested. When the two of them meet in the field there is celebration. Instant seeding is reaping instant harvesting! There is no separation on their seasons. They are no longer in the gestation of time, they are in the now. The seeding and the harvesting is no longer in relayed time. It happens suddenly and simultaneously. Can you not see this miracle? The more you plant, the more you harvest. The faster you seed, the faster you drive the reaper? Can you not see the miracle of this law of multiplication. Even before the reaper has touched the harvest, the sower has once again planted seed in the ground. There is no end to the seeding and reaping. And in both cases, neither one is actually working. The Lord of the Harvest is at work. You may say to yourself that is not so. Well, what about the following passage. John 4:35-38 (KJV), *"Say not ye, There are yet four months, and then cometh harvest? behold, I say unto you, Lift up your eyes, and look on the fields; for they are white already to harvest.* Do you notice that the Bible says there are still 4 months left yet the crops are already ripe and ready for harvest. In other words, the crops are commanded to be ripe way before their time. This is the realm that I'm talking about which shall become a common occurrence to God's children in these end times.

A heightened degree of divine visitations to the Throne Room (In and out of body experiences).

This is a spiritual phenomenon of being caught up to the third heaven. In these end times, believers shall be translated into the throne room, to behold the beauty of the heavenly realm as God wills. A heightened degree of *inside-the-body* and *outside-the-body* experiences shall be encountered in this season as the masses are catapulted into a higher realm of glory, right into the throne room. of heaven. The mystery of Heaven is now unveiled to all humanity. Heaven is no longer a secret, fantasy or an imaginary plane but a realm which anybody can be catapulted into any time. Multitudes of believers shall experience visions of either heaven or hell as they unreservedly yield to the atmosphere of glory. Such divine experiences shall leave a non-erasable mark in your life and strengthen your faith to believe God for the impossible. I remember the day I was catapulted into the third heaven and saw Jesus. Since that day, my confidence in Christ drastically changed.

Divine Transportation and disappearance into the spirit dimension.

A spiritual phenomenon that shall become a common occurrence in the Body of Christ is disappearance in the Spirit dimension. Do you know that it is possible for you to disappear like Elijah such that your body becomes invisible in the natural realm? God can easily expand the molecules in your body in such a glory that you become invisible. The reality is that when you are in the glory zone, the molecular structure of your own body starts to change. Your body, which is made of glory, comes in contact with a greater glory when worshiping or praying, and it changes your body's cellular structure. You start to feel lighter in the presence of God, as gravity seems to have less hold. For instance, you may arrive at a meeting very tired, but as you worship God, you become energized physically, and even sickness departs. To an extreme degree, at times, you may feel so light that you will fly away, because your body is changing into an expanded form. Smith Wigglesworth, known for unusual miracles, has been quoted as saying, *"The life that is in me is a thousand times bigger than I am outside."*

As your spirit starts to expand, it affects your body. In fact, a person can get so light when the spirit expands in the glory that someone can be transported from one place to another! Ezekiel was in the Spirit when he was transported to a valley of dry bones (Ezekiel 37: 1) Philip was transported after sharing the Scriptures with and baptizing the Ethiopian eunuch (Acts 8: 39-40). Elijah was often transported and would disappear for days and be found on a mountain somewhere far away from the masses. How is this possible? When you are in the glory zone you feel light, and the very cells and molecules of your body change as your spirit begins to expand.

As the glory of God is manifested to a heightened degree on earth in this season, divine transportation shall become a common occurrence in the Body of Christ. In the same way Philip was divinely transported into the spirit dimensions and was later found in Azotus, believers who yield themselves to the directorship of the Spirit shall be transported to different parts of the world to undertake certain ministerial tasks of which upon completion, they will be transported back. Taking into account the nature of the end time season into which we have been ushered, God cannot rely on the natural processes and means of transportation in order to have His work done. Therefore, rather than relying on cars and planes, God will supernaturally transport believers to different parts of the world. To an extreme degree, others will just disappear in the natural realm and re-appear as God wills. This phenomenon though it boggles the mind, shall become a common occurrence right across the Body of Christ as God intensifies the glory of the last days on earth.

Physical appearance and visible manifestation of angels in a contracted human form and appearance of Jesus in a glorified body

---

The reality is that when you are in the glory zone, angels are there too, but in an expanded form. Sometimes they will contract and you will be able to see them in solid form. In this season of later glory, angels shall be visibly seen operating in the natural realm, to help believers execute certain heavenly tasks with speed. While in the past, angels had been restricted to operate visibly in the natural realm, in this end time season, where there is a spiritual invasion of God's glory on earth, angels shall manifests visibly and shall be seen parading on the earthly territories – streets, market place and places of worship and the public arena. The time has come in the realm of glory whereby the unseen will no longer remain unseen. The spirit world will start to walk amongst men. Now is the hour when angels will begin to come into your churches and sit down with you. You are going to have services where angelic beings will walk into the services and escort Jesus into the worship service. Some will be seen dancing with us during worship, others will be seen carrying internal body organs and external body parts and implanting them on human bodies of those who would have lost them, others will be seen casting a mantle upon believers for ministration purposes.

Prophetically speaking, to an extreme degree, angels shall be visibly seen driving cars of believers, operating more during worship sessions, imparting the glory and other spiritual substances on believers to enhance their spiritual capacity. In some cases, angels shall be seen shopping and dispatching grocery, clothes and other properties to believers who are in urgent need. Angels of finances shall also be visibly seen raining down miracle money during worship sessions. The only thing that angels are restricted to do is to preach the gospel. However, they will awaken man into a revival, to spread the gospel with a sense of urgency. Abraham saw angels live not in vision or dream and he ran and welcomed them and even prepared dinner for them. This is the extent to which many believers shall interact with angels in these end times. That is why Paul warned us not to forget to entertain strangers for some entertained them unaware. Angels shall manifest visibly in an unusual manner in this season of glory. For example, a student shall talk to an angel thinking that he is talking to a teacher; a parent shall talk to an angel thinking that she is talking to her own child; a driver shall give a lift to a group of hiking angels thinking that it's pedestrians; a manager shall interview an angel thinking that he is interviewing a candidate for a job; a sports fanatic shall watch a game with an angel at the stadium thinking that it's a another fan. Angels shall physically manifest in every sphere of human endeavour and shall not be confined only in the church. For example, they shall appear in the streets, in the market place, in offices, in people's houses, in malls, in stadiums, in the parliament and literally in every sphere of human existence to accomplish divine tasks with speed.

Besides the physical appearance of angels during worship sessions in our meetings, Jesus shall physically appear in our meetings to strengthen the faith of believers around the world. I have personally seen a recent footage of Jesus captured on video while He appeared on stage during a Crusade against cancer in America. The footage could be visibly seen showing Jesus descending on stage in His glorified body, covered with a dazzling while garment with His arms spread wide open. Imagine the Master of the Universe himself marching on the stage. These are indeed the most exciting and spectacular moments to be alive and witness!

Walking Through Walls

One of the mind blowing miracles that shall become a common occurrence in these end times is the phenomenon of believers walking through walls in the same way Jesus entered the room where His disciples stayed, although in a glorified form. Jesus came to earth as a man from an extreme glory zone— the throne of God. He was crucified, resurrected, glorified, took the keys of death, hell, and the grave, appeared to many witnesses, and ascended to the Father. Before He ascended, His body was still in its expanded form to such a degree that He could travel through walls after His resurrection, such as when He appeared to the disciples in the house without going through the front door (Mark 16: 1-7.)What explanation can you give to this divine phenomenon? You see, when you are experiencing extreme glory you are, in essence, in an expanded glory where the cellular structure of your body may expand. The molecules in your body are stretched out when in expanded form and will have no trouble going through walls at a certain level of high glory. Your spirit body basically dominates your physical body. Just as sounds can travel through walls, you can travel through walls too, because you are made of sound and glory. When you are in an extreme state of glory, the sound waves of your body can penetrate walls as they expand. Even though you are a physical being made of sound and solid matter, you can still experience this phenomenon. Just as a television picture, which can travel thousands of miles from a satellite in space into your home and deliver sounds and light in the form of a picture, you are created from the same stuff— sound waves and light. Once the glory hits a certain level, it affects the sound waves inside your body and the entire molecular structure of your being.

Albert Einstein theorized that a *fourth dimension* exists where time is absent and eternity reigns. The fourth dimension that is beyond time and space can only be pierced by an object traveling at twice the speed of light. I believe Einstein was alluding to something he did not realize— the invisible Kingdom of Heaven that is all around us. As we are in the glory zone, we pierce through our current three-dimensional realm into another realm— the Kingdom of Heaven that is more real than what we see. If a scientist basing all his information on facts can realize there is another realm, how much easier should it be for us to believe? After all, there are examples of this other realm throughout the Scriptures.

Walking on water

One of the miracles which shall be publicly demonstrated by believers in these end times is walking on water just like what Jesus did (Matthew 14: 22-33). How did Jesus and Peter walk on water? This miracle is possible while in the glory zone. Jesus, who came in the form of a human like you and me, knew how to get into the glory realm, just as you and I can. The gravity and molecular structure of His body changed and He became light enough in the glory to walk across the surface of the water. It is possible that in His presence the molecular structure of the water could have changed and contracted tighter under each step He took, just as water can change into ice, a more solid form of the same substance. Jesus and Peter defied this world's three-dimensional law of gravity and operated out of Heaven's fourth or unlimited dimension as they both experienced the glory zone. By faith, Peter asked for permission to join Jesus as He walked on the water. Peter lunged into the glory realm where his body weight did not make him sink, but the water actually became solid enough for him to walk on. In a similar vein, Israel walked through the Red Sea, as God defied the laws of gravity by suspending the massive amounts of water in the air until His people travelled safely to the other side. The secret to taping into these dimension is to walk by the spirit, not the flesh (Galatians 5: 16). The flesh is your natural, carnal, worldly, and three-dimensional limited way of thinking. As soon as Peter began to analyse and revert to past experience and acquired knowledge, he began to sink. Although he did not understand how he was walking on water, he simply did it by faith. Faith with action will get you into the glory realm of creative miracles faster than anything else— even if you don't understand it. I hope that this insight will give you some understanding of miracles and add to your faith and confidence about what goes on behind the scenes when these things occur.

Prophetically speaking, in the atmosphere of glory, walking on water shall become a common occurrence right across the Body of Christ. While in the current times such performances boggles the mind, a time is coming shortly whereby their manifestation shall become a common place to God's children. If ever you thought that walking on water is an implausible act of impossibility, wait until you see a believers walking comfortably over a pool of water in this season. In the dimension of glory, a believer will just take others to a nearby pool or water reservoir and publicly demonstrate by strolling on the surface of its waters as if he is walking on his own yard. Jesus demonstrated a practical example of the power that we have over nature. In the natural realm, according to the law of gravity, if a man attempts to walk on water he sinks and if he attempts to walk on air, the law of gravity will bring him down to the ground. However, the law of glory works contrary to the law of gravity. In the law of glory, the natural laws of gravity, density, weight and distance are broken such that the body attains a certain level of weight or quality whereby it is enabled to walk on water or though air without sinking. This is God's marvellous work which is only possible in the life of Glory.

Therefore, in this season of glory, don't be shocked when you see a believer comfortably walking on water as if he is marching on top of his own yard. Although it's mind blowing, believers shall function in these realms mightily as natural laws are defied to allow God's work to be accomplished with speed. In the same way a gate keeper lifts the entrance of the gate to allow cars to pass though, God has lifted some natural laws that inhibits believers from accomplishing certain divine tasks with speed so that His work is not delayed. In the same way a customs officer at a border post stamps a passport to grant either an entry or an exit, God has put a stamp of His approval, authenticated by the inscription of His own hand writing upon every believer in this end time season , to grant them access to deeper realities of His glory. Believers will have the power to change weather conditions and decide what type of weather should prevail in their locality. In the realm of glory, believers will not spend a lot of money buying fans and umbrellas to protect themselves from certain weather conditions. For example, a believer will just walk through the rain and not get wet. Another will jump into a pool of water and come out as dry as a rock.

Levitation: Walking in the air

It is worth exploring the truth that gravity-defying miracles such as believers levitating or walking in the air shall become a common occurrence in the church. I have heard of Saint Luke the Younger, a Greek believer who was one of the first saints recorded to have been seen levitating during prayer. Another quintessential example is that of Saint Joseph of Cupertino was also known for levitating— he was often referred to as the *"flying friar."* His experiences are some of the best documented in church history. He was always in the Spirit and seemed oblivious and unshaken by anything in the natural world. It is recorded that Saint Joseph of Cupertino had extensive visions and heavenly trances triggered by simple things like music and hearing the name of Jesus. There are more than 70 recorded instances of Joseph levitating, along with numerous miraculous healings that were not paralleled in the reasonably authenticated life of any other saint. Joseph's most radical instance of flight was when a group of monks were trying to place a large cross on the top of a church building. The cross was 36 feet high, taking the efforts of ten men to lift; when suddenly, Joseph flew 70 yards, picked it up "as if it were straw," and put it in place. Although it boggles the mind, in this season of glory, don't be shocked when you are driving your car at 100 km/hour and all of a sudden you see a believer walking past you in the air.

In some of our meetings, we have experienced instances whereby the glory came so strong such that people were suddenly lifted about five inches off the ground and then flipped over in the air for a few more seconds, and then slowly came down. Souls were saved in each and every meeting, along with miracles, signs, and wonders displayed; and believers repented of sin in their lives. The Scriptures say that Jesus' disciples watched as He ascended to Heaven (Acts 1: 9). Elijah was taken up in a chariot of fire (2 Kings 2: 11). Today, there have been reports from various countries about people levitating while preaching. If people involved in magic and sorcery can levitate and can draw a crowd in broad daylight, as has been known to happen around the world by modern-day magicians and those using demonic power, how much more can the true children of God, blood-bought believers, move in even greater demonstrations of His power? These examples from the Bible and recent history are foreshadows and glimpses of what the last day church will look like and do for His glory and to display His power. Even powerful sorcerers in the Bible like Simon and Bar-Jesus were totally stunned and defeated by the superiority of the power of God demonstrated by the apostles and believers. Today, though, most Christians shy away from believing God's power and label it all as strange or dangerous.

Rising or floating under the power.

As much as believers across the Body of Christ have been acclimatized to the divine phenomenon of people falling under the power for decades, during ministration sessions, a new spiritual phenomenon or divine experience called *rising or floating under the power* is being unleashed from heaven as a key characteristic feature of the last wave of signs and wonders that shall see the Body of Christ launched into greater depths of the miraculous. Under this new divine experience of glory, rather than having people falling either backwards or forward under the power as is the norm in the modern day charismatic church, the people being ministered to just spring up and float hysterically in the air.

This divine phenomenon is already surfacing in the Body of Christ in some parts of the world as the glory of God is manifested intensely. I have read a testimony of a man names David Hogan, in Mexico, who is so anointed to such an extent that he can shake a handkerchief towards the congregation and all those being ministered to start floating about in the air. This is not something mysterious or spooky because after Jesus was raised from the dead, he walked in the air and was soon taken up by a cloud and since we have the same divine nature as Him, we have the ability to manifest that grace in these times.

Such a divine phenomenon shall usher multitudes of believers into the realm of raising the dead, whereby the death victims spread on beds or lying in coffins shall through this demonstration, be commanded to spring forth and stand. This is a similar fashion in which Smith Wigglesworth would command a dead body lying in a coffin to spring forth and walk. The difference is that through this divine experience, there won't be a physical dragging of the dead but a spiritual magnetic force or resurrection power shall be released that shall cause the dead to rise, even without any body contact. In some instances, believers shall walk right through the air without the law of gravity affecting or touching them. The spirit of believers shall take on a distinct level of quality that would enable their bodies to float. This will depend on the extent to which their spirit and body is synchronized or harmonised. There is state of equilibrium between the spirit and body that can enable a person to float in the air. If the weight of the spirit is greater than the weight of the body, then the person will be enabled to float in the air or rise under the power. Believers must therefore focus more on developing their spirit man than focusing on meeting the needs of their bodies since according to 1 Timothy 4:18, bodily exercise profits a little.

The same spiritual force or power that is at work when people fall under the power is the same that works when they rise or float under the power. The only difference is in the direction of the falling or rising. In the case of falling under the power, the spiritual force is exerted downwards, causing a spiritual "*push*" of gravity on the ground while in the case of floating under the power, the spiritual force is exerted upwards casing a spiritual "*pull*" into the air. Different demonstrations of people falling under the power have been done in some cases people falling either backwards or forward but in this end time season, people will neither fall backwards nor forward but upwards. The phenomenon of people rising or floating under the power shall also serve as a prophetic action, gesture or dramatic prophecy that shall depict the rise of a distinct breed of believers in this season.

Raising the dead: Manifestation of Resurrection Glory

In this season of latter glory, there shall be widespread reports of mass resurrection taking place right across the globe as the flood of God's glory sweeps right across the nations. Those who would have died way before their time and not in line with God's will shall be commanded to rise back to life. Resurrection centres shall be established right across the Body of Christ whereby people who would have died shall be brought forth and laid in coffins so that they are commanded to arise. In a healing revival, the Bible says many *people brought the sick and laid them on streets on beds and couches so that at least the shadow of Peter passing by shall fall on them* (Acts 5:15). This time, it shall not only be a healing revival but a *Resurrection movement*. There is a transition from healing school or healing centres to resurrection centres as the gravity of God's glory is intensified in these end times. A time is coming shortly, whereby raising people from the dead shall become a common experience to God's children just like healing a headache. God said that He is raising a distinct breed of believers who shall move in the dimensions of resurrection glory just like Smith Wigglesworth. This shall provoke an unprecedented avalanche of billions of souls across the globe into the Kingdom. For a deeper revelation on the subject of raising the dead, I would kindly like to refer you to one of my books titled, *"The Realm Of Power To raise The Dead"*.

Demonstrating the power of God in judgment through commanding agents of the Devil (Satanists, devil worshipers, magicians or witches) and those who resist the move of God to die physically as was the case of Saphirah and Ananias).

It is worth noting that while the glory of God shall give birth to unusual manifestations of the Spirit in this end time season, believers shall be catapulted to a dimension of authority whereby they shall command those who stand in the way of the move of God to die instantly. As much as we raise the dead, those who work against the kingdom of God can also be commanded to die or rather be removed permanently from the face of the earth. It must be expressly understood that the power of God works in both *the positive and negative direction* It's just like electricity; if you use it properly it will bless you with heat and light but if you mess up with it, it will electrocute you. By the same token, if you use the power of God to benefit the masses, the dead are raised. However, if you stand on the way of the move of God like Saphirah and Ananias, then you can be removed from the scene. Have you ever wondered why Saphirah and Ananias died? Was it because they lied? No! They were definitely not the first to lie in the New Testament. However, judgment was instantly and harshly declared against them because they stood on the way of the move of God's glory. They made a bad example at such a time when the Holy Spirit was moving and ushering a new dimension of glory. Remember that God said *suffer not a witch to live* (Exodus 22:18). While this might be a portion of the Old Testament dispensation, however it reveals God's original master plan concerning Satan and his cohorts. Some of them make efforts to hinder the work of God by keeping people bound in poverty and witchcraft just like the Sorcerer who was trying to turn the Proconsul away from faith but Paul had to execute instant judgement against him by making him blind for days. Therefore, in this season of glory invasion, those who would stand on the way of God can be commanded to die instantly, depending on the nature or gravity of the situation. Others can be commanded to be blind, Just like Elymas who attempted to draw the right hand man of the King away from faith and Paul commanded blindness upon him and he fumbled his way and the proconsul was saved (Acts 13:6-17). This is what we call *judgemental anointing* at work.

Elijah demonstrated a measure of this *judgemental anointing* when he called down fire from heaven (2 Kings 1). Peter exercised a measure of the *judgemental anointing* when he commanded Ananias and Sapphirah to die instantly (Acts 5). Paul pronounced judgement on Elymas the sorcerer (Acts 13:8-10). This would definitely be a special and unique manifestation of the anointing, which our Lord Jesus Christ did not manifest while on earth because it was reserved by God to be demonstrated at His second coming. Note how He stopped before vengeance in His reading of Isaiah, in the middle of a sentence (Luke 4:19, 20; Isaiah 61.2). However, there is some measure of the manifestation of this peculiar anointing in the church age as demonstrated in Acts 5 and Acts 13. In the last days, as the church confronts the evil in the age, this particular anointing will be demonstrated more as a sign of things to come.

Supernatural earthquakes: Visible shakings of geographical territories in the natural realm

In the realm of end time glory, there is going to be physical shakings of geographical areas as God, in His sovereignty marches across the nations to expedite His work. The Bible records that when the disciples of the early church gathered for prayer the place where they were meetings was visibly shaken. The early church walked at a higher level of *resurrection power* such that at one point when they gathered for prayer, they sparked off an explosion in the realm of the spirit to the extent that the place where they met was visibly shaken by the *resurrection power* of God (Acts 4:31). Immediately after praying, the building was shaken to its core as they experienced a dawn of greater glory. That dynamic prayer opened a door into the supernatural which allowed for an explosion of God's *resurrection power* as the hand of God manoeuvred its way down to touch the sphere of the earth. This is the same degree of power that had earlier caused a supernatural earthquake that split the rocks and ripped the graves apart such that many bodies of saints who had died were raised and came out of their graves at Jesus Christ's resurrection (Mathew 27:50-53).Therefore, when the disciples prayed, they tapped into this realm of *resurrection power* and transmuted it into a tangible substance manifesting in the natural realm.

Imagine if there was a dead person lying in that prayer room! He would have arose and started running. But what was their secret? How did they tap into such an extreme degree of power? It was through *faith* and *revelation* that they unlocked the power of resurrection from the *Heavens' Power House* and precipitated it over geographical territories in the natural realm in such a way that the power of God had crystallised into a solid form that could be visibly seen and tangibly felt as a vibration on the surface of the earth. There are instances whereby the power of God is highly concentrated in a particular territory such that it changes or transmutes itself from a vaporised state into a liquid form in what we call a *liquidisation of God's power*. But in this instance, the power of God had changed or graduated from a liquid state in the spirit realm into a solid form that shook geographical territories in the natural realm. This is what we described as *the condensation of God's power* in one of my books titled, *"How To Operate in the Realm of The Miraculous"*. This was a manifestation of the glory of the latter days. In this end time season, not only shall things be shaken spiritually or in the spirit but the shaking shall even be transmuted into the physical realm. Such signs shall company the preaching of the word in these days especially where there is a resistance to the gospel. As the power of God visibly shakes some territories, millions of souls shall stream into the Kingdom, glory to God!

Converting natural substances into another form in the natural realm.

It is important to highlight that the glory of God brings trasfomation. In the atmosphere of glory, it is possible to redirect an object to be another created thing through *sound waves*. If the raw materials needed to create a certain object are present (*Holy Spirit, faith and revelation*), then sound can redirect the same object into another form. – if you are in the glory realm, where the spirit is hovering. Nothing created can be uncreated- things created only change form. According to the first law of *thermodynamics,* burned wood turns to ash but does not disappear. Although she seem to dissolve, it is reduced to smaller molecules that still contains imbedded sound particles. By the same token, one created thing can turn into another created thing if directed by sound waves or commanded under the direction of the Holy Spirit. For example, Moses threw his rod down and it turned into a serpent, Jesus changed water into wine and so did Elijah change water into oil. Prophetically speaking, we will start to see the renewal of these types of miracles taking place again in these days ahead because we have authority over all creation.

It is worth exploring the divine truth that nothing created by God can be destroyed. It can only be converted into another form from the natural realm into the spirit realm. So, if everything created cannot be destroyed but can only be converted into another form, then your lost hair, leg or arm still exists somewhere- it has just been converted into another form. But still exists. There is no distance in the glory so whenever your lost hair is, it can still respond. And because your hair has sound waves, and can hear and respond, when in the glory zone, you can call, "*Hair come back*" and it can turn to its original state and respond to your words spoken under the direction of the Holy Spirit.

Multiplication of natural substances.

This is a direct multiplication or recreation of the substance of money by either speaking it into existence or converting a spiritual substance into a natural substance. Concerning the power of multiplication of natural substances, Jesus said, *"... If ye had faith as a grain of mustard seed, ye might say unto this sycamore tree, Be thou plucked up by the root, and be thou planted in the sea; and it should obey you."* It must be expressly understood that in the context of this revelation, Jesus was not talking just about a sycamore tree. He was giving a physical illustration using objects that were probably in the vicinity of where He was at the time. What was Jesus referring to in regard to the sycamore tree?. He was talking about faith's ability. He said that when you speak to something in faith, whatever you speak to must obey you.

The truth is that if you have faith to see an object turn into another object, how much easier is it to see things created multiply themselves? Everything generally produces after its own kind. The fish and the loaves easily multiplied at Jesus's command. In some instances believers shall be catapulted into God's creative power to speak money into existence for example by converting any tangible or visible substances into miracle or taking a twenty rand note and multiplying it into a twenty thousand rand note. To bring the above- mentioned scripture into clarity of explanation, Luke 17:6 could easily read as, *'If you say to money, 'Be plucked up and come over to my house,' it should obey you.* This is the same dimension of power which God operate in when He spoke to the darkness and said *let there be light* and light came.

It must be understood that as believers we have the same creative power of God in our spirit such that we are able to speak anything we want to see into manifestation in the physical realm and it shall be so. It must be understood that during the creation, God did not use one method to create the world and creators. In some cases, He spoke the word and material substances supernaturally appeared, in some cases He took material substances and converted them into another form. For example, He took dust and converted into a person. In the same way believers have the power to create money from any substances which they might wish to. I know that I'm stepping on some religious toes because in some cases people's level of faith is not so much developed that they are not aware that we can operate like God on earth and follow the exact pattern which he followed to create substances.

Conclusively, as you start to meditate on this revelation and on how big God really is. You will begin to believe and then you will see these same streams of gravity-defying miracles happen in your own life. You will begin to function and operate in a realm which the multitudes only dream of.

CHAPTER TWELVE

THE SEVEN-FOLD END TIME DIMENSIONS

OF THE NEW WAVES OF GLORY.

Unveiling The Mystery of The End Time Glory

THE GOLDEN GLORY:

The manifestation of the wealth of heaven, evidenced by Gold dust, Diamonds, Silver stones, Gem stones and other precious stones.

It is of paramount importance to highlight right from the onset the divine truth that contrary to what multitudes of believers presume, the manifestation of *gold dust* and other precious stones is not a new phenomenon in the realm of God. Taking centre stage recently in packed churches is a new phenomenon that really is not that new. It is the appearance of *"gold dust"* and the transformation of fillings or crowns into *"gold."* These transformations have been hailed as a new move of God that is sweeping the charismatic churches worldwide. Throughout ages, the wealth of heaven and God's supernatural provision has been manifested in divergent ways, whether it be, gold dust, gold fakes or gold teeth. However, the gravity and intensity of its manifestation is heightened in these last days in what I call *"a new wave of gold manifestations"*. The truth of the matter is that the unparalleled degree of manifestation of gold dust in this end time season is not intended to be just a *Church phenomenon*, but a *Church revelation*. It is of paramount significance in this regard to unveil the divine truth that in every new move of God, there are different people who play different roles. There are those who *reveal it*, others will *teach about* it while others will *write about it*. Documentation of divine phenomenon is essential in terms of reinforcing a significant level of understanding so that multitudes of people across the globe can abundantly partake of the grace which God is currently unleashing upon the church.

The Bible foretold that signs and wonders of such a great magnitude would be seen in the last days, and the manifestation of gold dust, diamonds, silver as well as other precious stones is one of them. Over the last few years, there has been a lot of reports of gold and silver dust appearing upon people, mainly in charismatic Christian meetings. Some have also received gold coins, gems, as well as oil dripping from hands of individuals in their homes and yards. Others are receiving angelic manifestations seen above them as flowing beautiful transparent figures and circles of faint light referred to as *angel orbs*. Moreover, angels' feathers, gemstones, coloured sparkle and gold dust are accelerating. Many are attaching prophetic significance to this current wave of gold manifestations, heralding a new phase in the church, being prophetic of the establishment of God's Kingdom on earth, or being symbolic of the transference of wealth from the wicked into the Church. Angels of precious stones which works in conjunction with angels of prosperity shall be seen on the rise, dominating the scene where God is worshiped in truth and in spirit.

To cement the revelation of this divine phenomenon with reference to practical evidence, manifestations of *gold dust"* on hands and other parts of the body has been reported occasionally in some meetings. These are what appears to be tiny specks of gold appearing in the hands, where wiping the hands has the effect of depositing the gold specks on clothing. This manifestation appears to be transferrable, either by prayer or by simple contact, others do exhibit this manifestation. The *law of contagious experience* seem to have taken its course in this new move of God. For example, during one of our meetings, gold dust started appearing in the hands of one lady. Upon wiping her hands on her clothing, the gold dust appeared to have been deposited upon her clothing and yet the amount of the dust on her hands seem to remain constant as if the gold dust spontaneously reappeared after wiping on clothing. This woman then started laying her hands on anyone around her lining up to receive the blessing and many others reported the appearance of gold dust on their own hands.

Moreover, Gold dust was reportedly appearing not only in hands, but also on the face and in the hair of the congregants. There were even reports of *gold fakes* appearing in the pages of people's bibles, cars, bags and houses. Not only gold, but manifestations of silver and even diamonds and other precious stones such as onyx, pearl, jasper and emerald has also been reported. Others found the gold dust in the prayer rooms and on worship instruments and it was constantly appearing further and further back along the walls until it finally met at the back doors of the sanctuary. Moreover, people reported gold appearing spontaneously in their teeth. In some cases, the dark amalgam fillings in the teeth appears to have transmuted itself into gold fillings. In other cases, gold in the shape of crosses appeared in teeth, and also gold crowns covering the teeth. Along with the *"gold teeth"* manifestations, occurrences of gold dust, gold fakes are increasing worldwide. Shiny sparkles of diamond dust and silver dust were received during services as people received the gold inlays and silver fillings, some in the form of a cross and the actuality of gemstones falling from the atmosphere, inside churches. Accompanying this divine manifestation, it has been further reported that a *"Glory Cloud"* appeared during worship services. In short, a cloud of gold-like dust was hovering up by the roof. It caused some hysteria during worship as multitudes of people were crowding together in exhilaration and gathering underneath it.

To substantiate this supernatural manifestation with reference to scriptural evidence, God declared in His word that *behold I'm doing a new thing. Can't you perceive it as it springs forth?* (Isaiah 43:19). Gold dust is one of the new manifestations which are encapsulated in this revelation. The reason why God calls this manifestation a *"new things"* is because it is fresh from the throne room of God and do not have a name as yet in the natural realm. Moreover, God declared in Jeremiah 33:3 that *"Call unto me, and I will answer thee, and show thee great and mighty things, which thou knowest not."* This implies that there are newer, deeper and higher things in God which the world has not discovered yet but God unfolds them to His children through the power of the Holy Spirit. Therefore, in this end time season, we have been catapulted into a *realm of new things.* The greater truth is that in every generation, God unleashes or reveals His hidden wisdom through the revelation of new things. These are divine substances which are released for heaven to earth, which unveils the reality of God's presence. It seems that the Lord is now doing very unusual things which simply don't have any physical explanation. Since God is still a Creator, He is still in the business of creating new things and each new move of His Spirit has its own mark upon it. The Bible declares in Isaiah 40:5, that,

The Realm of Glory

The glory of God shall be revealed and all flesh shall see it.

This implies that this is the season of visitation of the glory of God. It further says in Habakkuk 2:14 that *the earth shall be filled with the knowledge of the glory of God.* In this last wave of signs and wonders, God is therefore raining down gold dust as a new spiritual substance in the same way He rained manna down in the wilderness for the children of Israel to eat. When God rained down manna, it was a completely brand new spiritual substance to the children of Israel just like the gold dust appearing these last days. Through these new things or supernatural appearance, God is proving Himself as a visible and tangible God who is not far away from His people but is practically involved in the affairs of humanity of on a daily basis. In this end time season, God is therefore doing a new thing, and sharing with His people the glory of His face, and a little of His splendour is rubbing off in the form of dust, so that the individual may be edified, as with tongues, the Church strengthened, and the lost brought into the Kingdom of God.

The greater truth is that God will do whatever it takes to get our attention and gold dust manifestations are a wakeup call that is only going to intensify in this end time season. He is shocking His Body, and at the same time testing the waters as to who will be open to His workings of supernatural provision. *"Why did Jesus Christ walk on water when he could use the available boats? "Why turn fish and bread into thousands while the disciple could go and buy food?"* These are not miracles, they are signs and wonders. God does them to prove a point. Therefore, gold dust is a sign that God is present. God said we should expect signs that would point to Himself. He declared *"I will show wonders in the heaven above and signs on the earth below, blood and fire and billows of smoke"* (Acts 2:19). The manifestation of gold is a sign and wonder that points to His internal and external qualities, part of a visible representation of an invisible God.

In its original form, gold dust represents the wealth of heaven which God is unreservedly manifesting on the earth in the last days. God declared that, *"Silver is Mine, and the gold is Mine. The glory of this latter temple shall be greater than the former,"* (Haggai 2:8-9). Moreover, the Bible says that wealth belongs to God and He has given it to the son. The Bible further says in Job 22:24 that,

Then shalt thou lay up gold as dust, and the gold of Ophir as the stones of the brooks. If you lay gold in the dust, and gold of Ophir among the stones of the torrent-bed, then the Almighty will be your gold and your precious silver.

This is where the divine revelation of gold dust stems from. This implies that God owns everything and does not owe anything hence, He has freely given or lavished such humongous wealth to His children. This wealth is manifested in the form of gold dust and other precious stones. This means that a global revival which shall by far exceed any other revivals ever manifested in the history of humanity shall be accompanied by gold dust and other precious stones in these last days. However, it is of paramount importance to note that the gold dust is not an end in itself but a means to an end. It is only a sign of what is to come. The end is that an avalanche of billions of souls will be saved across the globe. When the gold appears, it is an indication that the spiritual climate is ripe and the atmosphere in a meeting is charged for miracles, hence anything can happen that can lead to a stream flow of multitudes of souls into the kingdom. This is the same anointing in which Jesus operated when he raised the dead and moved in signs and wonders and practically demonstrated miraculous provision. By sending this unusual manifestation into our midst, God is saying to us that we can expect to see even greater things than these in this end time season.

The question is: Why does God rain gold dust and other precious stones on earth in this time?

Spiritually speaking, Gold is the *colour of harvest* hence, the heightened degree of manifestation of gold dust represents the fact that the harvest of billions of souls across the globe in this end time season is ripe. As God pours out His Spirit in this unusual and unprecedented way, the golden glory is attracting, magnetising and drawing multitudes into the kingdom in record numbers. As a matter of fact, the manifestation of gold dust has proven to be a most powerful tool for evangelism and reach out campaigns in these last days. This is because the nature of this generation is such that people are generally curious, and would want to see something tangible and visible for their faith to be strengthened in God and this manifestation is the exact kind of recipe that draws the curious into the kingdom. The gold is therefore a visible sign that the glory of God has returned to His people, and that glory is no longer a mysterious, invisible or distant phenomenon but a reality of this age. Men who have *"sinned and come short of the glory of God"* are drawn to it when they hear that it has appeared. When they see it manifested, they are drawn to repentance and are saved. The prophet foretold: *Arise, shine; For your light has come! And the glory of the LORD is risen upon you* (Isaiah 60:1). When the glory of God is seen upon us, people are attracted to it like metal to a magnet. This makes it easy for us to bring in the harvest. It is just as God showed Isaiah it would be:

The manifestation of gold dust signifies the revelation of the visible and tangible latter glory of God.

It is a product of God's glory. Whenever the glory of God manifests in a tangible and visible way, gold dust usually appears as an evidence of its manifestation. Whenever the glory of God used to appear or manifest in the Old Testament, thunder, clouds, smoke and lightning would accompany its manifestations. These were not the glory but the symptoms or signs which show that the glory is present. While God has million ways of manifesting His glory, in this end time season, He chooses to rain down gold dust and other precious stones as evidence or signs of the presence of His glory. I recall vividly the day when I preached on (Isaiah 60:2), and suddenly gold dust, supernatural oil and other precious stones began to fall and appear in the hands of many present and since then it has continued to happed in all our meetings till today.

The greater truth is that Gold dust is meant to attract or draw multitudes of people to God.

This is what the Bible means when it says *that the Gentiles shall come to your light, And kings to the brightness of your rising.* This means that as the *light* which represents the glory of God is displayed through gold dust, millions of souls shall stream to the kingdom to worship God. The *brightness of your rising* speaks of the glorious gold dust anointing which is elevating you to a higher realm of dominion and son-ship in Christ. When it says *"Lift up your eyes all around, and see; They all gather together, they come to you; Your sons shall come from afar, And your daughters shall be nursed at your side* (Isaiah 60:3-4)." It is actually talking about an unprecedented avalanche of billions of souls from every sphere of human existence into the Kingdom as the glory of God is manifested through gold dust and draws every creation to the father. Therefore, the manifestation of the glory of God through gold dust leads to a harvest of souls as the *rain of the Spirit* produces a bumper harvest.

Prophetically speaking, the glory of God shall even extend outside the church doors and bars into the streets, market place and public arena, and drug addicts shall be drawn to the glory and be saved. In some cases, golden rain shall come down so thick like snow and gold fakes shall appear everywhere, all over the carpets, bibles, on the chairs, on the floor, and on the hands and faces of people during worship sessions or even at home to the extent that such manifestations shall inevitably culminate in many finding Christ as their Saviour.

Our aim therefore through the gold dust manifestations is to make God more real and being born again a fashionable experience right across the whole world. The message we are sending across is that no one should be left behind when God is visibly and tangibly moving on behalf of all humanity.

However, it is worth mentioning that the gold dust phenomenon has suffered severe criticism by sceptics who lack revelation and an understanding of spiritual things. I too was a bit sceptical about it when it first occurred and that the Lord led me to (Haggai 2:8-9) where the Lord states, *"The silver is Mine and the gold is Mine. The glory of the latter house will be greater than the former."* The Lord then told me that the latter house is the present church and that His glory is associated with God's presence intensely manifested in every believer which shall invade every sphere of life in this end times. Therefore, I strongly believe the manifestation is a sign of the imminence of Christ's second coming. Prophetically speaking, in these end times, the shekinah glory dust is manifesting like rain, showers of gold and is available for those who are receptive to it. That is why it says,

"Arise, shine, for your light has come, and the glory of the Lord rises upon you. See, darkness covers the earth and thick darkness is over the peoples, but the Lord rises upon you."

In other words, although darkness covers the sceptics and critics and those who reject the glory of God, gold dust shall fall upon you like rain. In another scripture in Zechariah 10:1, it says,

"Ask rain from the Lord in the season of the spring rain, from the Lord who makes the storm clouds, and he will give them showers of rain, to everyone the vegetation in the field."

This implies that anybody who shall open up to this new wave of signs and wonders shall qualify to be a recipient of this glorious phenomenon. However, those who shall resist, criticise and condemn it shall close a door against themselves hence, shall only see but not partake of it. However, in a view to reinforce the veracity and authenticity of evidence of this supernatural manifestation, the following are *"tests"* to determine if a manifestation such as gold dust is a genuine work of the Holy Spirit: No. 1. *Does it honour the person of Jesus Christ?* No. 2. *Does it produce a greater hatred of sin and a greater love for righteousness?* No. 3. *Does it produce a greater regard for Scripture?* No. 4. *Does it lead people into truth?* No. 5. *Does it produce a greater love for God and man?* If the answer to all the above questions is yes, then the gold dust manifestation is directly from God.

Sometimes as I stand in the glory, my hands and feet will begin to drip with supernatural oil, representing the miracle anointing of God. Many times I will use this supernatural oil to pray for the sick and have seen tremendous healing miracles take place. The supernatural oil that flows from my hands often carries a heavenly aroma – the fragrance of Jesus (Song of Songs 2:1). In Psalm 23:5 David says, *"You have anointed my head with [fresh] oil."* God is anointing us with a fresh new impartation from his Spirit! Other times in the glory of God, I have seen tiny sparkles appear in the air or on people. Sometimes the glory will come as a shower of golden rain; sometimes this golden substance will come out from the pores of my skin. I have seen this happen in many churches on many different people.

This supernatural golden substance is a sign of the glory of God coming upon his people. Gold represents the glory of God. In the Old Testament the children of Israel brought their riches of gold, silver, and jewels into the wilderness tabernacle. The tabernacle was filled with these symbols of the glory of God. When the Lord gave instruction for Solomon's temple, He told them to overlay everything with gold, including the walls and ceiling. Even the veil that separated the manifest glory of God from the rest of the temple had golden thread woven into it. God has always chosen to represent His glory with a golden substance. Isn't it amazing to realize that as New Testament believers, we are now the carriers of God's glory? We carry His presence here on Earth; we are His temples. If the glory of the Old Testament was just a fading glory (2 Corinthians 3:7-11), then how much more does the Lord want to cover us in the presence of His glory today! I believe that these things we are experiencing are simply prophetic signs of the glory of God being released upon the earth. God wants us to display His glory in the earth in these days of His outpouring!

A supernatural phenomenon in the realm of God's glory that has been happening for quite some time now is gold dust appearing on people as a sign of the manifestation of the wealth of heaven on earth and the unveiling of higher realms of God's glory. This wealth of heaven has been manifested supernaturally in divergent ways evidenced by the appearance of gold dust, silver and diamond stones and supernatural oil soaked on people's bodies, on the ground or on buildings where saints gather for worship. Naturally there have been strong speculations as to the sources of these phenomena in Christian circles and it seems that the main questions arising about these miracles are firstly what is the source? And secondly what is the purpose? However, it must be fully understood that these are end time manifestations of God's glory. The supernatural manifestation of Gold dust, silver and diamond stones is this most recent wave of glory and prosperity that is sweeping the world. We have been ushered right into the very special divine moments in the calendar of God where we are feeling the first sprinkles of the greatest revival of miracles, signs and wonders ever recorded since the Book of Acts. This is the result of the highest level of concentration of the glory of God being manifested upon the Earth. This wave of revival shall be greater than any other because we are entering the culmination of time, when we will experience the former rains and the latter rains of revival glory combined. Some of the things we are experiencing are familiar, but many things are brand- new. This, too, was foretold in God's Word concerning the last days. A season of exploration and discovery has been ushered as great mysteries are being rediscovered that will unleash the greatest outpouring of God's glory and harvest since the early Church, even since the beginning of time. Therefore God's golden glory shall bring forth a golden harvest.The Prophet Isaiah prophesied the following words:

" *For behold, darkness will cover the earth and deep darkness the peoples; But the LORD will rise upon you and His glory will appear upon you.* " (Isaiah 60:2).

Today, this scripture is being fulfilled as the tangibility and visibility of God's glory is grossly manifested upon people. It must be known therefore that God can and will use whatever He pleases to show himself real to people. Moreover, God dust represents the wealth of heaven. The Bible declares in Ephesians 1:3 that *we are blessed with all spiritual blessings in the heavenly places* and gold dust is a visible and tangible evidence of manifestation of these blessings. Therefore the miraculous appearance of gold dust and other precious stones most frequently during times of worship or prayer when hearts are focused on God's splendour and majesty is a reflection of the spiritual truth that God is majestic and rich in spiritual blessings. Moreover, God declared in Deuteronomy 31:6-8 that, "*I will never leave you nor forsake you*" and these supernatural manifestations are an incontestable or undeniable evidence that God is with us and when the gold dust manifests itself, this truth is confirmed and our hearts soar in praise of our Royal King who created the universe and can create gold dust, gems, oil, or any other substance. He wishes to give us a glimpse of His power and greatness.

Speaking about the Greater Gory in the end time dispensation, God declared in Hagai 2:8. 7, that,

'I will shake all the nations; and they will come with the wealth of all nations, and I will fill this house with glory,' Says the LORD of hosts. The silver is mine and the gold is mine,' declares the LORD of hosts. *The latter glory of this house will be greater than the former,'*

Note that in the context of the above-stated scripture God talks about Gold dust and silver after emphasizing the shaking. In actual fact there are three things which God unveils in this scripture, firstly the *spiritual shaking,* then the *silver and gold manifestation* and lastly *the appearance of the glory.* This implies that the manifestation of gold dust is a sign of a great shaking, spiritual awakening and the supernatural move of God. It is a visible and tangible manifestation of God's glory in these end times. When heaven is shaken off, it releases an uninterrupted flow of wealth of heaven such as gold dust and silver. In the scripture, God mentions that glory will be greater. That means there is a connection between gold dust and the glory. This implies that gold dust is a manifestation of the latter glory. In actual fact it is the Glory of God that rains gold dust and diamonds in church. When God said, *"The glory of the latter house shall exceed the former",* He actually spoke of these new waves of signs and wonders which shall invade the natural realm in this last dispensation as the masses witness unusual signs and wonders.

However, God shall continue to orchestrate, manifest and release these new waves of miracles at ever increasing glory. As these precious stones shall continue to fall and oil oozes out supernaturally from the atmosphere, it is as if God is revealing a glimpse of His glory to this church. He is revealing Himself as a supernatural God on behalf of His children while worldly people shall see but not partake of this grace. As ministers across the globe preach on Isaiah 60:2, gold dust, oil and precious stones shall begin to fall and appear in the hands of many present and since then it has continued to manifest in greater intensity. It is of paramount significance to emphatically reiterate the divine truth that Gold dust is a sign of God's majesty, wealth and glory present in our lives. It is a spontaneous manifestation of the wealth of heaven on earth. However, some people think it is strange that God would reveal His majesty in this way, but we should try to let God out of the box since He has every right to display His glory and reveal Himself in whatever way He sees fit! The Bible tells us that gold pave the streets of heaven. We think this is amazing, but if God wants to use gold to pave the streets who are we to tell him that he should use asphalt? When Moses and the elders of Israel went up Mount Sinai they came into the glorious presence of God and the pavement under their feet was made of sapphire. Therefore, we should not insist that God does things our way. Philosophically speaking, God doesn't have to use cement and asphalt on His heavenly roads. He can use sapphire, gold, silver or whatever precious stones He chooses. He doesn't have to use human means of communication. We like words. We like pictures. But if God wants to use gold and diamonds and gems to communicate with His children, then who are we to tell Him that He is doing it wrong? Nothing is too difficult for God. We should not be surprised that He is making gold dust and gems appear out of thin air. All he has to do is speak and it is done. But we should praise Him and love Him for choosing extravagant and creative ways to reveal Himself to us. The Bible declares in Job 22:21-25 that,

> *Acquaint now thyself with him, and be at peace: thereby good shall come unto thee. Receive, I pray thee, the law from his mouth, and lay up his words in thine heart. If thou return to the Almighty, thou shalt be built up, thou shalt put away iniquity far from thy tabernacles. Then shalt thou lay up gold as dust, and the gold of Ophir as the stones of the brooks. Yea, the Almighty shall be thy defence, and thou shalt have plenty of silver.*

This implies that there are also many beautiful and useful elements underground such as gold, silver, gems, coal, and oil which He has created. I don't see it as contrary to His nature throughout the centuries for Him to bestow the actual physical elements of gold, silver, gems, oil or other gifts supernaturally whenever He might choose. The Bible makes it clear that God created everything, God sustains everything and God owns everything. In Psalm 104:24, David declares: *"The earth is full of Your possessions."* In 1 Chronicles 29:11, it reads, *"Yours, O LORD, is the greatness, the power and the glory, the victory and the majesty; for all that is in heaven and in earth is Yours."* Everything in the ground, above the ground, everything in the air, everything that passes through the air ultimately belongs to God. He owns the cattle on a thousand hills and the wealth in every mine. But the truth is it's not ours; it's God's. Wealth is a stewardship from God. So, whether it's money, land or possessions, we will never be rightly related to what we have until we recognize that it is not ours. In an endeavour to ascertain the credibility and authenticity of this supernatural phenomenon, some diamonds were taken to experts who analysed and examined them and accordingly declared that the cutting of these stones was so perfect, that they couldn't give them value for the percentage of the diamond stones for there were none like that on earth.

Prophetically speaking, in this end time dispensation, there shall be a wide spread global manifestations of gold, silver dust and gemstones appearing upon people mainly during church meetings. Supernatural oil shall be seen visibly dripping from hands and figures of people, some of which shall receive gold coins, jewels, gems, diamond or silver. It must be expressly understood that these precious stones are not limited to Gold dust and silver stones only but to other supernatural experiences of other precious stones such as sapphires, topaz, emerald and rubies. In this season, God has sent the *angel of precious stones* for His people to experience manifestations of diamonds, topaz, emerald, rubies as well as gemstones falling from the atmosphere, inside churches by the hands of angels. The scriptural reference to this supernatural phenomenon is found in Exodus 13:30 where it is recorded that *the High Priest wore breastplates adorned with twelve precious stones*. Therefore, gold dust, silver and diamond stones are just exactly like the twelve stones of the Ephod, the twelve stones of the twelve tribes of Israel.

Moreover, a heightened degree of angelic activity, visitation and manifestation shall be experienced as believers shall visibly see these beautiful transparent figures or spiritual beings. However, the degree, intensity and magnitude of manifestation of these spiritual experiences shall all depend on the degree of adoration, level of sensitivity and openness to this spiritual phenomena as well as the depth of worship by believers. However, this phenomenon shall spill over to people's houses, homes and yards, businesses, schools, in the streets, market place where God manifest the visibility and tangibility of His glory to all creation in fullness. In the face of a darkening global economic outlook, God renders a supernatural bail out from poverty, lack and debt and believers shall sell the gems and diamond stones they are receiving supernaturally for money to pay off debts. In the Old Testament, the Israelites needed food miraculously. They couldn't have used money at that time as there was no food to buy. So, God provided the manna for that time and that need was met. By the same token, God shall provide gems or gold coins (*as some have received*) to be sold to buy food or meet our material needs and give us enough to help others whenever He chooses to. Strange as it may sound, we may personally need these items someday soon hence, it is best not to limit God in any way. Some of these precious stones shall be sold for a value worth of millions of rands and this shall create a platform for many believers across the world to be elevated into the realm of Kingdom Millionaires.

A heightened degree of angelic manifestation and visitation evidenced by Angel feathers falling on people during worship sessions.

Angels spend time in the glory hence have been entrusted with the propagation of glory to mankind. They have ability and capacity to contain glory, move in the glory, propagate it and impart it to mankind according to God's will. It must be understood that angles play a key and integral role in the manifestation of miracle money. Without the direct, active involvement and work of angles, miracle money would not manifest. Angles are the ones whom God has entrusted with the responsibility to despatch or propagate miracle money to earth so as to fulfil His end time purpose and divinely orchestrated kingdom plans. Believers are therefore advised to be vigilant and sensitive to the work of angels. It is for this reason that Paul cautioned the believers in Ephesus not to forget to entertain strangers for some entertained angels unaware. Sensitivity to angelic operations means acknowledging the work of angels, cooperating with their presence as well as provoking their manifestation just like How Abraham behaved when he saw two angels purporting to be passing by. Therefore, if ever you want to abundantly partake of this sacred grace, it is of paramount importance that you actively engage angels.

In the realm of God's prosperity, angels regulates the economy of the kingdom of God and are actively involved in the invisible realm by supernaturally depositing money in the bank accounts of believers. Hence, there is in the realm of prosperity such a thing as *angelic deposits*. In the light of this revelation, believers must therefore be awakened to the reality that money is spiritual and as much as it is widely used in the natural realm, the original blue print of it is in heaven hence angels have control and access to create, distribute and deposit money supernaturally. Angelic deposits is therefore one of the ways through which God distributes millions of wealth in this end time dispensation. One of the key functions or roles played by angels in God's financial prosperity plan is through impartation of spiritual substances. In some instances, besides impartation of the power, anointing and the glory, some of these spiritual substances which angels impart upon people is real *money*.As much as angels do impart the anointing and the glory upon human vessels, they can also impart money into your spirit and your duty is to learn how to tap into the realm of prosperity to practically apply God's spiritual laws and principles to draw the millions of wealth from your spirit. *Your spirit is the first point of contact with either angels or the Holy Spirit.* Even during ministerial sessions, God touches your spirit first before touching the people that you are ministering to. Therefore, you need to understand that the blessings of God are first imparted in to your spirit before they could manifest in the physical. Contrary to what many people think, the blessings of God don't just fall like apples falling from an apple tree. In most cases your blessings are not located in the realm of the spirit but they are in you. So many people are ignorant of the system of God's provision such that they always cry out to God for blessings, yet their blessings were long released from His hands and imparted into their spirits but just because they operate so much in the realm of the flesh they are oblivious or unconscious of the presence of those blessings in them. That is why from this minute forth, you should change the content and direction of your prayer. Rather than saying, *"Lord Give me a blessing"*, let your prayer be, *"Lord open my eyes to see the blessing that you have imparted in me and give me the revelation and wisdom to withdraw from the blessings that are in my spirit"*. It is a greater truth that God touches your spirit first before He could touch your soul and body. Even whenever someone gets healed in the body, it is because healing would have started first in the spirit and then assimilated into the soul and ultimately filtered into the body to bring forth a manifestation. Although you see the results of manifestation of healing in the body, it would have actually started in the spirit. Spiritual manifestations like shaking and falling under the power are a visible sign of the out flow of blessings of God from the spirit of a man into his body. Knowing how to convert the blessings of God from your spirit to visible manifestation is therefore highly imperative. When the Bible declares in Ephesian 1:3, that *we are blessed with all spiritual blessings in the heavenly places*, it is talking about *the blessings of God in their raw, crude, undiluted or original state* but the refined and processed blessings of God are in your spirit. There is a paradigm shift and migration of blessings from their location or disposition in the heavenly places into your spirit and then from your spirit into the physical world through confession. This is what I call *a chain of manifestation of blessings*. For your blessings to manifest in the physical realm, they need to pass first through your spirit and mingle with faith in your spirit and then be released forth from your spirit into the physical realm through prophetic utterance. There is a spiritual reaction that takes place in your spirit as the imparted blessings of God mingle with your faith and word of God in your spirit to produce the results of what it talks about. This is a pattern or model of how blessing or millions are created or given birth to in the realm of the spirit. That is why faith is such a vital element in the creation of our blessings because without faith, our blessings would not manifest in the physical because faith is that force that would command the blessings of God in your spirit and draw or propel them to manifest in the physical realm.

In the realm of God's prosperity, there is what is called *God's wealth transfer plan*. This is a major characteristic feature of the end time dispensation that involves transferring wealth, resources, property and financial assets from the hands of unbelievers to believers for kingdom financial purposes. The Bible says in Proverb 13:22, that *God shall take the wealth from the wicked to the righteous*. That season of restructuring, reformation and *redistribution of wealth* has come and God accomplishes this programme through the work of angels. It is angels who are sent to initiate, implement and monitor the smooth flow of transaction and transfer of wealth between the two parties. By reason of this spiritual law, there are a lot of economic and financial transactions that are taking place in the invisible realm in favour of believers although the process cannot be instantaneous but a smooth transition. This is the reason why God said in Judges 1:1-2:5, that *He would not drive out the Hivites and Ammonites from the land of Canaan in one day because their wickedness was not yet complete.* In some extreme cases, God might not directly snatch the wealth out of the hands of the wicked but will cause unbelievers to give or finance the visions, ministries and programme of the kingdom.

Prophetically speaking, this end time dispensation shall witness a wave of millions of wealth being blown over the body of Christ by the south wind and this shall result in the rise of a multitude of kingdom millionaires across the globe. The people, who shall own the best places of the world, control its economic and political systems, regulate its monetary and wealthy structures are Christians. There are angels that sit in the invisible realm in the committees of EU, World Bank, Reserve Bank to enforce decisions to transfer the funds in the realm of spirit in favour of believers. Angels have an influence over how money is created, circulated and used, hence they play such a key and strategic role in this end time wealth transfer process. While for ages, the wealth of the world has been in the hands of unbelievers, evidenced by the multitude of unbelieving millionaires, God is initiating a wealth transfer process that will see a drastic transition, change and migration in wealth from the hands of unbelievers to the children of God. Imagine the impact that such change will have on the body of Christ. However, it is quite important that believers live within the context of God's will through a life of consecration so that they could qualify for this programme because God will not take the wealth from unbelievers and give it to disobedient, sinful and lukewarm believers. He is not prepared to defeat the ends of justice by violating His spiritual laws and principles in the face of His creation. In the first place the reason why He is transferring wealth from unbelievers is because of their sins of disobedience hence it would not make any spiritual sense for Him to take wealth from sinners and give it to another bunch of believing sinners. This is the reason why Israelites did not qualify to enter Canaan although God had initially promised to give it to them. On that note, believers must therefore, learn to live in total consecration, righteousness, humility and obedience to the word at all times in order to qualify to amass alarming wealth of heaven.

It must be understood that not only do angels worship in heaven as what some folks might think. On the contrary there are a myriad of duties, assignments, and financial projects entrusted or committed into the hands of angels by God one of which is to handle the aspects of Kingdom prosperity. At a high level, high ranking angels hold occasional spiritual gatherings to decide on the fate of humanity and how heaven's wealth will be distributed amongst unbelievers on earth. Ministering angels gather in heavenly meetings to decide, handle or deliberate on key financial matters of kingdom. It is through such occasional gatherings and deliberations that finances are released in the spirit and the angels are sent to cause them to manifest in the physical. In accordance with the will of God, the names of people who are meant to be entrusted with the wealth of the kingdom are short listed, picked up, called and brought forth as in the case of boardroom nominations. New Visions and spiritual programmes and ministries are then given birth to in the spirit during such angelic discussions, conferences and meetings. This is largely the work of *ministering or financial angels* who serve in heaven's finance department and are chiefly responsible for processing financial transactions, financial requisitions, making angelic deposits and transfers, and making sure that every godly vision is financed.

When God gave me this revelation, my spirit was carried through the waves of the air and I saw in the spirit a book being opened with the names of people that the *board of heaven* had chosen to finance the kingdom's end time plans, visions, ministries and spiritual programmes. As I peeped into the book, I was ecstatic to realise that my name was also written in the book amongst a thousand other names. Millions of wealth measurable in money, gold, platinum and the top world currencies were allocated for each name for the accomplishment of God's divine plans and purpose. I also noticed the inscription of three words popping up and inscribed by God's own handwriting and these are Grace, Mercy and Destiny. And I heard the voice of the angel saying the work has to be completed for the time is now.

The manifestation of SEVEN supernatural dimensions of financial prosperity one of which is the unusual manifestation of Miracle money in people's accounts, bags and houses.

The **SEVEN** dimensions of supernatural financial prosperity such as the Supernatural *Wealth transfer, Supernatural Miracle money, Gold & silver dust, Supernatural Debt cancellation, Supernatural Translation and Recreation of natural substances, Supernatural multiplication of wealth and Supernatural Reclamation of property* are not based on the law of sowing and reaping but on the higher laws of financial prosperity because you have full access to partake of them even without sowing anything. They are accessed based on the availability of God's grace, glory and degree of manifestation of His presence. It is highly imperative in your road to becoming a Kingdom Millionaire that you secure an in-depth understanding of *the* **SEVEN** *Supernatural dimensions of financial prosperity.* In a biblical context, David was one of the richest people in the world in gold, silver, money, property and wealth because he understood how to operate and tap into the supernatural dimensions of financial prosperity. He describes these dimensions in Psalm 78:23-29 when he says,

God commanded the skies to open; He opened the doors of heaven. He rained down manna for them to eat; he gave them bread from heaven. They ate the food of angels! God gave them all they could hold. He released the east wind in the heavens and guided the south wind by his mighty power. He rained down meat as thick as dust—birds as plentiful as the sand on the seashore! He caused the birds to fall within their camp and all around their tents. The people ate their fill. He gave them what they craved.

These are the supernatural dimensions of financial prosperity which are a major characteristic feature of this end time dispensation whereby God is launching believers into the depths of His supernatural provision.

The unveiling of these supernatural dimensions of financial prosperity is therefore centred on this revelation. The greatest challenge that we have in the Body of Christ is that multitudes of believers have relied so much on the natural world for provision to such an extent that they have become oblivious of the dimensions of God' supernatural provision. However, the creative force of your faith and revelation is what will cause you to move away from impossibility thinking and its limitations into the open heaven of possibility thinking whereby you can freely operate, function and access ALL these dimensions of supernatural financial provision in this present hour.

In this new wave of signs and wonders, many people around the world are beginning to experience money supernaturally appearing in purses, pockets, and bank accounts. Also, instant debt reduction and debt cancellation are commonplace as this wave of generosity swells with kingdom wealth. The glory of God is being released in this day with a flow of financial blessing! Paul declared,

"I pray that you may prosper in every way and that your body may keep well, even as I know your soul keeps well and prospers."

This is to tell you that God has end-time transference of wealth available for you as He is releasing Miracle Money. The greater truth is that this is the season for Miracle Money. The Bible speaks of the Sons of Issachar who had an acute understanding of times and seasons of God hence they knew what Israel ought to do at a time. Specifically it says in 1 Chronicles 12:32 *"from Issachar, men who understood the times and knew what Israel should do—200 chiefs, with all their relatives under their command.* Moreover, the Bible says in Ecclesiastes 3:1 that *"There is a time for everything, and a season for every activity under the heavens."* You may know your season but if you don't know your time, you might act after God has passed by. And it is dangerous for a believer to be standing at a bus stop waiting for God yet God had long passed by. In this season both the times (*Cairos*) and seasons (*Cronos*) have come together marking the climax of highest concentration of God's power. Miracle money is a key characteristics of feature of the last wave of prosperity. In (Habakkuk 2:2-3) God said,

"Write down the revelation and make it plain on tablets so that a herald[a] may run with it. For the revelation awaits an appointed time; it speaks of the end and will not prove false. Though it linger, wait for it; it will certainly come and will not delay."

This speaks of the end time season whereby believers shall be catapulted into the depths of the miraculous to practically demonstrate the revelation of Miracles Money. We may want to do things in our timing, but we need to work in accordance with God. A vision waits for an appointed time, but at the end, it shall speak. Likewise, miracle money speaks and cries out for a man or woman of faith to tap into the spirit dimension to command it into manifestation. Psalm 102:13 reads,

"Thou shall arise and have compassion on Zion, for it is time to show favour to her; the appointed time has come."

This is indeed the set time to walk in the fullness of the son-ship by practically demonstrating the miracle money grace which God has unreservedly poured upon the Body of Christ in this end time season.

Increased visitations to the Throne Room in Heaven.

In these last days, translation shall become a common experience as believers are caught up in the spirit dimension to the third heaven. Philip experienced it. Many shall be caught up in the spirit dimension to minister in other countries and back. There shall be intense manifestation of God's glory where people will function under an open heaven such that they will go to public places and supernaturally know specific conditions of certain people, cities or nations.

This is a realm that we can tap into when we have walked, fellowshipped and communed with God so much such that by His grace He grants us permission to temporarily visit His throne in heaven in order to get a foretaste or glimpse of how this are like in His throne. Prophetically speaking, this is a characteristic feature of the end time dispensation and in *this season of visitation*, many believers will be catapulted right into the throne room on a study tour to explore the glory of God. This is the realm that Paul tapped into in 2 Corinthians 12:2, when *he was caught up to the third heavens*. We also have testimonies of some believers around the world who are still entering that realm as God pleases like the seven Columbian youths whom Jesus took to both heaven and hell to see what is happening there.

A heightened degree of signs and wonders manifested through creative miracles.

All creative miracles are given birth to in the glory of God and these shall become a common experience in these end times. Hair germination on bald heads, growing teeth, increase in heights, development of body parts, charging electric gadgets, phoning without airtime are just but a few examples of creative miracles of the end times as the glory of God manifests intensely in this very hour *Anything that comes into contact with the glory of God whether living or non-living, comes to life*, whether it be a dead body, malfunctioning car, broken cell phone or refrigerators, people being translated from one place to other out of danger, disappearance and reappearance in the spirit, being caught up in the spirit dimension, people falling under power in streets and markets places without ushers, song or congregation as the glory of God invades streets and public arena is one such characteristic feature of the end times.

By definition, a creative miracle *is an impartation of a completely brand new organ or body part upon an individual who previously did not have it in existence*. It is a creative miracle in the very sense of the word; to create means to bring forth into manifestation or existence something that was previously not there. It is a creative miracle in the sense that an organ did not exist at all in the body but now a brand new one has been imparted.

For example, the creation of flesh and bones where there was previously nothing, the infilling of new gold teeth, appearance of hair on bold heads, supernatural appearance of miracle money in people's accounts, wallets or bags, instantaneous supernatural loss of weight as well as the appearance of eyes, hands, legs and other body parts in areas where there was completely nothing, a short person getting tall instantly, instant development of a pregnancy evidenced by a growth of a big tummy, giving birth to a baby within three days of pregnancy are all creative miracles.

The rationale behind creative miracles is that there is an original blue print of every body part in heaven's power house such that in the event that someone loses one of his body parts due to accident, misfortune or complications at conception or birth or any calamity of life, their parts can be instantly reinstated, imparted or restored to their original position of normal perfection. It should therefore be understood that in heaven there is a power house that consists of an original blue print of all body parts where one can tap into the realm of power to command that specific body part to be imparted upon an individual who has a missing organ in his body. I'm not talking about a situation whereby God restores a body organ to its proper function but a case where God creates something that was completely not there. In a practical sense, one could command a person's left hand to shorten and be pushed back in Jesus' Name to conform to the person's original blueprint found in heaven. For example, if God has created you to be 5 feet 10 inches, and you are slightly deformed and are only 5 feet 7 inches, then under the anointing of the Holy Spirit, one can command your backbone to be straightened up and reach your ideal height according to the blueprint God made you to be. However, one cannot pray that you grow to be 8 feet because that is not your original blueprint in heaven. Prophetically speaking, taking into account the nature of this end time dispensation, God wants us to migrate or graduate from the realm of ordinary miracles to the realm of creative miracles.

Greater manifestations of open heaven, open visions and translation to the throne room.

It is worth unveiling the divine truth that in these end times, believers shall walk in an incredible realm of the supernatural, where prayers shall be answered even before finishing them, believers will walk into buildings and places and supernaturally know who is there and the lives which people live, see into the lives of people, read their minds and understand their lives even without talking to them as well as writing volumes of books within a short time period.

This is the highest level of operation or life in God. The Bible says in Genesis 5:24 *that Enoch walked with God and was caught up to heaven.* In other words, you start with walking with God and when you have matured in that realm, God can translate you straight to heaven. *Why was Enoch translated?* Because when he reached that realm his whole physical body transformed. He found he was no more breathing in the natural. He was breathing in the spiritual just like angels. He lived like a spirit being on earth and that was when the translation took place. Elijah was another man who walked close with God and there was no one who moved in the spirit dimension like he did. Elijah walked with God, performed miracles, closed and opened heavens at his own discretion and reached a certain quality of the spirit which qualified him to be catapulted into this realm and chariots of fire came and took him.

Elijah walked so close with God that angelic visitations were like contact with human beings. You see him at the end of his life, in 2 Kings 1 and 2; he seemed to be always with God. He made this statement: *"I am Elijah who stands in the presence of God."* And he stood in such presence that earthy mortals could not reach. When he was lonely, God sent His angels because there were not many saints in the Old Testament who had entered that realm. There was a level he reached, he walked so close with God that when he was about to complete his ministry, the Lord said: *"Come straight home"*. Jesus was translated to heaven after His resurrection and the Bible records that as they looked up the saw Him enter a cloud until He was no more. *This is the highest realm that a man will ever enter in God.* In this realm, you don't taste death nor decay but you are taken to heaven straight away. It is possible not to taste death or the grave. If Old Testament folks walked with God without the regenerate spirit, how much more us the new creation could tap into that realm? If only you could catch this revelation, you can be the next wonder in this world. The difference between the realm of visitation and translation is that visitation is temporary but translation is permanent. In both realms, the will of God is paramount for one to encounter such an experience. Paul spoke about the abundance of revelations in the *6th dimension* which is the realm of visitation but in this last dispensation, we will talk about the abundance of revelations of the *7th dimension* which is the realm of translation.

Deepening of the realm of the miraculous evidenced by the raising of the dead.

It is a divine truth that the dead are raised when the glory of God comes into contact with dead bodies. In the life of glory, there is no dead or sickness hence as the glory of God comes into contact with anything dead, it is quickened back to life. In essence, the anointing heals the sick, sets free those who are bound, opens the eyes of blind but the glory is what elevates us to the level where we raise the dead. The reason why many people have tapped into the realm of the miraculous but failed to tap into the realm of raising the dead is because they are functioning on the realm of the anointing and not in the glory. Although resurrections have taken place in isolated incidents around the world, we shall enter a time when this dimension of glory will seem normal to every believer just like healing and deliverance. This shall culminate into a season of mass salvation of millions of souls across the globe as humanity witnesses the resurrection power and glory of God.

It is of paramount significance to unveil the divine truth that we are now living on the verge of the most momentous days in the history of the church. This implies that we have been catapulted right into the very special divine moments in the calendar of God whereby the earth shall be pregnant with the glory of God and the womb of the spirit is ready to unleash the realities of the glory to food even the extreme quarters of the world. In essence, we are living in the days of the latter glory, a season whereby we shall witness a heightened degree of miracles, signs and wonder ever recorded in the history of the bible. Mass resurrection of people from the dead is one of the notable miracles, which shall become a common experience to God's children in these end times and an order of the day as God unleashes the fullness of His power to conclude His eternal plan on earth. The Bible speaks of *the sons of Issachar who had an acute understanding of the times and seasons and knew exactly what Israel ought to do in a particular time* (1 Chronicles 12:32) and in terms of the current times and seasons as stipulated in God's calendar, all scriptural evidence seem to align with the fact that this is indeed the most ripe season and opportune time to raise the dead as God is calling and launching men and women into a deeper walk with Him to a sacred and special ministry to display the fullness of His majesty and glory.

Therefore, a new apostolic and prophetic generation is arising, coupled with the manifestation of the sons of God who are taking centre stage on the global scene to manifest the intensity, gravity and magnitude of God's *resurrection power* in this season which marks the conclusion of God's eternal plan on earth. This is a new and distinct breed of believers who are ready to move forward, overcome, and occupy their full inheritance in Christ by steeping up to their positions of son-ship in Christ, to raise the standard of power which God has set for the church. This also entails the rise of a unique breed of believers who shall step out of the crowds and convictions of ordinary life into spiritual maturity as they encounter new realms of Glory to unreservedly showcase, exhibit and manifest the glorious expression of the Heavenly Father from within the *third dimension*. The trumpets of heaven are therefore sounding forth the call to assemble for conquest men and women of distinct, noble and rare calibre who shall come together to break through that which has been holding the church in bondage. Get ready for in this end time season, you shall raise the dead as if you are waking up people from their slumber.

THE PROPHETIC GLORY

Unleashing God's Prophetic Revelation Concerning The
Propagation of The End Time Glory.

In the presence of God the Father, Jesus Christ the Lord, the Holy Ghost and all hosts of Heaven, I stand in the Apostolic and Prophetic office (*Position of Sonship in Christ*) and with all the *power and authority* invested in me from above, I proclaim and pronounce the dictates and directives of Heaven as I stand on the Grand stand to report on the Heavens Broadcasting Commission. By the mandate of Heaven, I prophetically declare and decree that I hear a sound of the abundance of rain. There are Heavenly waves of glory approaching the earth that have never been seen before and their current is changing as these waves are breaking forth on the surface of the earth, causing explosive tides of glory streaming to the furthest extremes of the world. Prophetically speaking, the end time church is now nearer to the *Throne Room of Heaven* than ever before as these waves of the eternal realm are invading time in the realm of the natural. And as a custodian of God's glory on earth, I therefore adjudicate and broadcast though the Heavenly frequency, the provocative and executive news that the global rain of resurrection glory is precipitating upon the earth as the glory of God has gone beyond the church walls to engulf the masses in the streets, market place, the public arena and every facet of human existence. As I connect myself through the Heavenly airwaves and attune my spirit to the frequency of the Holy Ghost in the realm of the spirit, I hear God say:

"Son, blow the trumpet, sound the horn and declare in the hearing of all nations that a season of the invasion of End time glory to the extreme ends of the world has just begun. There is coming upon the earth, an unprecedented End time supernatural invasion of My glory, as I release a flood of My resurrection power to sweep right across the nations like never before. Just as My people were in the Upper room on the day of Pentecost when suddenly there came a sound like a violent rushing wind, there will come once again a noise that I will release from Heaven and this sound will reverberate through the Heavens and infiltrate every corridor of the realm of the spirit, right to the ends of the earth. This sound I'm about to unleash from My throne will spark off the greatest glory revival ever witnessed in the generations gone by. While I'm not calling any of my people to sit in an upper room and wait for what I have already given them, I'm calling My people to a place where their spirit is in an upper room position, rightly positioned and spiritually aligned to receive what I'm about to release in this very hour. Therefore, in this critical *kairos moment*, ask yourself this rhetoric question: In what direction is the Wind of the Spirit blowing and are we navigating the high seas of adventure by setting our sails to catch the Wind? God says, "For too long have my people been clinging on the shoreline and existing on the shores of tradition and religion but the time has come for you to sail through the deeper realms of My glory. The current is changing, waves are shifting, and the clouds are raging, heralding the time to sail into the great adventure of this unknown dimension. For too long have my servants been standing on the side-lines watching the parade go by but the time has come for you to rise beyond the confines and dictates of the realm of time into the glory realm to experience the life transforming glory of My presence. For I desire worshippers and not just a crowd that seek to be blessed by My presence. For in the greater depths of worship, is the purest and deepest flavour of My glory revealed, sayeth the Lord.

In what He described as a voyage of exploration, God says, "There are realms of My Glory that have not been revealed yet. I have created higher realms of glory in the Heavens that have not yet been known. There is a reservoir of the effulgence of My glory that has remained largely untapped in the Heavens and have yet to be manifested on the earth. There are deeper, higher and unexplored territories of the Glory Realm that have remained a mystery to My people for ages. The angels have not seen all the Glory in Me. The living creatures, the Cherubim and Seraphim have not seen all the Glory in Me. Even angels have to keep parading around My Throne in order to catch a glimpse of the higher realms of My glory. As the angelic hosts have to constantly migrate from one dimension of glory to the next, so must you also move from Glory to Glory so as to align yourself with the blueprints of Heaven and capture the revelation of the ever-transitioning spectacle of My glory. Therefore, step out from the *first dimension* of faith into the *second dimension* of the anointing, so that you may enter the *third dimension* of My glory. Step higher and come up hither, sayeth the Lord. While My people keep asking Me to go down there and fix things, I'm making an open invitation for anybody to step up and come to My Throne. For when you step up to the glory realm, the door of Heaven opens, and you will see another side of My Glory that has never been seen in the days gone by." I'm therefore broadcasting through the Heavenly airways, at the loudest sound of My voice, as it penetrates the vastness of the spirit realm, declaring the end from the beginning, and from ancient times the things that are about to unfold in this final chapter of human history.

As I have declared in My Word saying, "*Once more and in a little while, I will shake the heavens, I will shake the earth, I will shake the seas and all flesh shall come to the desires of nations (Jesus)*", in this *kairos* moment, I'm therefore shaking all the three realms of existence with the substance of My glory, a spectacular move that will usher a supernatural acceleration of My divine plans and purpose in this very hour. The movement of the glory will culminate in a mighty stir brewing, agitating and shaking in the Heavens, as the very essence of the manifested Christ in throne ship, dominion and executive power is pouring out the abundance of glory to all humanity, bringing a powerful release from the futility, captivity and brutality of death, sickness, poverty and disease. Artistically, the glory cloud will blast off on the surface of the earth, skyrocket back to the Heavens, bounce back to splash on the sea and spread like veld fire to engulf the extreme territories in every continent on the face of the earth and unprecedented tidal waves of resurrection power will cover the earth as the waters cover the sea. Just like a cloud as small as a man's hand which Elijah build up in prayer, the movement of the glory shall begin as small as a current of water; the current will increase until it becomes a stream; the stream will grow into a great river, which will overflow and become a sea and that sea will transform into a powerful ocean. Then the resurrection power of God will cover the earth as the waters cover the sea.

In what Elijah described in prophetic language as, "*the sound of the abundance of rain*", on the horizon, there is a rumbling of an approaching storm as the river of My glory is gushing forth from the Throne Room, heralding an outpouring of the Spirit over the extreme quarters of the earth, of such dramatic proportions that will culminate in the greatest ingathering of souls this word has never seen. There is a rumbling, thundering and reverberating sound that is echoing through the Heavens as the third wave of My glory is shaking geographical territories across the world. I'm releasing a sound from Heaven to connect you with this season and cause you to move with the credence of Heaven. Can't you hear the sound of the thundering hosts of Heaven? Can't you hear the sound of the flapping wings of angels marching across the earth? Can't you hear the sound of the Spirit as of the gushing down of mighty waters? Can't you hear the sound of the shuttering of every stronghold? Can't you hear the sound of the walls crashing to the ground before you? That's the sound of the glory explosion; the shackles are broken, the waves are shifting and the skies are changing. I will cause lids to be lifted off the pots, doors to fall like dominoes and gates to be blown off the hinges. I'm therefore realigning, re-shaping and re-positioning My people to be riders of destiny, to mount on the holy steeds and ride me into the battle, for the battle is not yours, it is My battle, sayeth the Lord. In tandem with this move, I'm therefore birthing forth a distinct breed of believers who are uncomfortable with the status quo but have developed a perennial hunger, insatiable appetite and unquenchable thirst for the global demonstration of My glory in this season. A distinct breed of believers who shall rise on this epic transition to curtail the mass rampage instigated by the enemy through alarming deaths around the world by de-programming his operations, while installing the agenda of Heaven. I'm therefore calling out men and women to step out of the mundane world of religion and tradition, to spearhead a radical soul winning campaign directed at propagating the effulgence of My glory to the furthest extremes of the world. For this reason have I created you, to awaken you to an arena of divine exploits so that you can be an embodiment of My glory, a quintessence of My very being and the ultimate extression of My glory of on earth. For in the glory, is the very original atmosphere in which I birthed you into being," sayeth the Lord. "Before I planted you in your mother's womb, I formed and fashioned you according to a unique and resplendent design. In your unformed substance, I communed with you and brought you forth into the earth at a time and hour appointed, for you to be a live demonstration of My glory. Therefore, exude My glory, live in the atmosphere of My glory and showcase My glory, for in the inner recesses of your earthen vessel, have I placed the treasure of My glory," sayeth the Lord.

God says, "I'm ushering My people into a dimension of My glory that is to become common place to the church and walking in the supernatural, a normal mode of operation. My glory will be multiplied exponentially across the Body of Christ and will be seen and felt experientially right across the globe. And I will increase the heavy weight of My glory on earth such that it will surge through you in demonstrably real, tangible and visible ways. The days have come whereby the thickness and viscosity of My glory shall manifest tangibly on earth such that an average believer will walk into a hospital and on account of his presence, all the patients shall be instantaneously healed and an ordinary Christian shall step into a mortuary and command the dead to rise back to life and it shall be established. This shall culminate in mass resurrection of people from the dead, an epic transition in which mortuaries shall be vacated as the liquid power of My glory liquidates their businesses. When this happens, funeral processions shall be turned into revival sessions, Burial societies into Church committees and mortuaries into Worship centres, as the cloud of My resurrection glory invades the earthly realm. As I have planned beforehand, in my own time and purpose, the most remarkable manifestations of My glory through unusual miracles, signs and wonders will take place before millions around the world in an instant and this shall culminate in an exodus of an avalanche of billions of souls from the kingdom of darkness into My Kingdom," sayeth the Lord.

There is a new dimension of glory that is surfacing on the horizon and the Lord is echoing the same words which He spoke through the voice of Isaiah thousands of years ago and He is saying:*"Behold, I'm doing a new thing! They are created now, and not so long ago, you have not heard of them before today, so you cannot say, "Yes, I knew them"* There is a rebirth of new manifestations in these end times such that you will not be able to look at it or recognise it because it will be completely fresh and brand new just like when manna, the food of angels was rained down on earth for the first time from my Throne. God says, "Down through the ages, I have given every man and woman a foretaste of My glory but what is coming now, it's never been seen". There are glories coming into meetings worldwide such that you won't know how to contain it. If ever there is an hour when I'm going to unreservedly pour out a new wave of My glory, it is now. God says, "I'm about to explode in the demonstration of signs and wonders by doing something so brand new that you won't have the language to describe it, neither would you have any vocabulary to speak about it. It would be like what Paul described as, *"Something inexpressible for man to tell"* because there won't be any vernacular, jargon or vocabulary good enough to define it. The reason why I call it a *"new thing"* it's because it doesn't have a name as yet. It's a brand new phenomenon unfolding from My Throne Room in Heaven such that even the angels are still trying to comprehend it. It doesn't exist in your dictionary nor does it have a reference point. Hence, you will not call it by the name you used in the past because then, you would need a new vocabulary to describe it. Therefore, aligh your spirit with the blueprint of Heaven and be ready to shift with My movements in order to flow in the fullness of what I'm about to do in this final chapter of human history," sayeth the Lord

In what appeared to be a stern warning, God says, "Tell My people that the dimension of the miraculous that I'm about to unleash from the reservoir of My Glory in the *Heavens' Power House*, right across the Body of Christ is so deep such that believers should be cautioned to relook into their theology and be established in faith so that they might not be sceptical or critical of this new move of the glory of My Spirit".

In what He described as a worldwide thrust of glory, God says, "I'm unveiling the fullness of My glory, grace and love to My children in this very hour which marks the final chapter of human history, in order to conclude my eternal plan for the planet earth with speed. Therefore, in this season of the *glory invasion,* you need to break loose from the old and step into the new and deeper realms of glory, so that you can impact the nations with the fresh spark of My glory.

God says, "For many years, has the church prayed and anxiously awaited another wave of Heavenly glory that would catapult My people out of spiritual lethargy into the greater depths of the miraculous never demonstrated in past revivals. Therefore, in this season, their prayers are being answered as tremendous manifestations of new realms of glory are surfacing on the horizon and the Body of Christ is catapulted right to the ultimate climax of My glory. The clouds of My glory are constantly changing, and new glory cloud formations are surfacing on the horizon. You are about to enter an eternal zone where time is losing its grip on earth as eternity is invading time. Heaven is coming closer to the earth as you are adjourning quickly towards the second coming of Christ. You are at the consummation of time, early in the morning on the third day when Heaven's atmosphere is invading the earth. This Heavenly atmosphere brings with it the eternal realm of glory. Therefore, My glory is going to manifest so intensely such that you will not have to pray with your eyes closed anymore because the glory will be manifesting visibly in the natural realm so much that it becomes naturally supernatural to live in the natural realm, as I bring down the golden rain and litter every one of your meetings with My precious stones. I'm therefore awakening your spirit to an arena of divine consciousness in which living in the Glory Realm is a norm and visitations to My Throne Room is a common occurrence.

God says, "In this prophetic era in which I have preordained you to live, events are quickly unfolding as nations are being positioned both spiritually and politically to enact the final scenes of history. Within this dynamic, the Body of Christ is being prepared and aligned by the Heavens to fulfil its destiny by positioning My people in the extreme quarters of the earth to move in the *resurrection power* in unimaginable ways to the extent of literally bringing Heaven to earth. I'm amplifying My glory and power such that you will now enter the season of the amplified. I'm amplifying my voice on the earth to shake the strongholds of the enemy. I'm amplifying miracles, signs and wonders to expedite My work. My angels are working to amplify the efforts of My kingdom. Therefore, the world will see an amplified version of My kingdom for there will now come a flow and an overflow of glory from Heavens that is expansive, explosive and expedient. If you can think of the speed of a jet plane flying overhead, that is how fast things are going to happen in the Body of Christ at this very hour. As the *overtaking anointing* is unreservedly unleashed from My Throne upon humanity in every sphere of life in this season, things that would normally take ten years to happen on earth will only take ten weeks—even ten days. This is a critical hour in which the degree of manifestation of My glory is so heightened that it is on the verge of breaking forth from the womb of the Spirit, to precipitate over the extreme quarters of the world.

Heaven is therefore waiting for a distinct breed of believers who have an unstoppable passion for My glory to step into the pool of *resurrection power*. I am setting the stage right now for this distinct breed of believers to step out from the crowd, out of the convictions of ordinary life of mediocrity, complacency and passivity to parade on territories in the glory realm which have remained a mystery for ages. Therefore, allow me to officially announce the expiry date of mediocrity in your life and adjudicate by the power of the Holy Ghost that the stage has been set for a global demonstration of *resurrection power* in this season. For too long have my servants been operating in the realm of gifts and anointing but I'm endorsing a paradigm shift, drastic transition and revolutionary leap in the realm of the spirit from the realm of the *anointing* to the realm of *resurrection glory*. Therefore, stir yourself up and get consummated in My glory because you are the *Heavens' Power House* on earth. The central headquarters of Heaven are in you; in the extreme quarters of your spirit. You are an *operational centre* from which I administer the affairs of Heaven on earth. You are a point of contact with divinity, which is why all Heavens' attention is directed towards you in this season. You are a conveyer and dispenser of divine verities on earth hence; all forces of divinity are compelled to partner with you in executing My plans and purpose.

The secret of success in any ministerial endeavour in this time is learning the art of how to flow in the river of My glory. Your breakthrough is in the river, your prosperity is in the river, your healing is in the river and virtually your future is in the river of My glory. Therefore, delay no longer but step into the pool of the ever coursing torrential flow of My glory. Let My glory incubate and intubate you and get so infused and mingled in the glory such that you literally become the glory. Marinate yourself into the greater depths of the river of My glory, that you may be a live demonstration of what My Word talks about. For too long have My people been clinging on the shoreline but the time has come that you take a huge splash into the river of My glory as it gushes forth from the Throne room to precipitate over territories in the natural realm.

While I invariably marks creation changes with My prophets as they are the time-pieces that set the tempo and pace of My momentum, paradigms are shifting as now is the time for Me to showcase the integrity of My prophetic glory to the nations with such a mighty demonstration of signs and wonders, never seen in the history of humanity.. This is an hour I'm beginning to change the prophetic language of my people. The way that you release and understand prophecy and how I'm working in the atmosphere is now changing. I'm opening your eyes in a new way and bringing you up to an aerial veiw so you can shift from *futuristic prophecy* to a dimension of *prophetic glory* in this season. There is therefore a drastic shift and revolutionary leap from *forth telling* to *telling* as I'm ushering in a new prophetic dimension in which things happen the instant they are declared. For too many of My prophets today are putting into the future what I have already done and is available now. Many have been preconditioned to wait on things My Word say they are now. But the time has come that prophecy will no longer be about a future event waiting to come to pass. Instead, as the prophetic words are coming out of your mouth, that which you say will already be created and in motion before you finish speaking. When you step into the dimension of prophetic glory and speak from the glory realm, you are actually allowing Me to create that which you are speaking. Therefore, declare My word in the glory realm against any debilitating situation facing My people and My angels will swiftly set in motion whatever you have decreed. The secret is therefore to call it from the realm in which it already exists into the realm in which it will manifest.

The time has come in the realm of My glory that the unseen will no longer remain unseen anymore as the spirit world will start to walk amongst men. In this season of the latter glory, angels shall be visibly seen operating in the natural realm, to help you execute My plans with speed. While in the past, I have restricted My angels from operating liberally and visibly in the natural realm, in this season of the *glory invasion*, angels shall manifest visibly to the extent that they shall be seen parading on the earthly territories – in the streets, market place, places of worship and the public arena, to accomplish My purpose. New angels are being assigned to you to get things done without having to work too hard. Now, is the hour when angels will begin to come into your churches and sit down with you. My angel armies have mounted on war horses to reinforce and battle alongside you. You are going to have meetings where angelic beings will walk into the services and escort Jesus into the worship service. *"Are they not ministering spirits sent out for your salvation?",* Sayeth the Lord. Therefore, take advantage of My grace and collaborate with every provision that I have made available for you in this very hour, for the time is short. As I have commanded, Arise, shine, for the glory is risen upon thee. Stop clingimg on the shoreline and step into the river of My glory. Wake up from your slumber, dust your feet and delve into the refreshing waters of My presence. Tighten up and fasten your seat belt for the time has come for you to sail through an expedition into the vastness of the glory realm.

The Lord of Hosts has spoken, Glory to Jesus!

PRAYER FOR IMPARTATION OF THE SUBSTANCE OF GLORY

Heavenly Father, in the Name of Jesus Christ, I thank you for the depth of revelations of your Word encapsulated into this writing. I believe your Word and embrace these revelations for my season. My whole being is saturated with the power of your Word, such that thoughts of success, possibilities and glory are inspired within me! And as I speak accordingly, my life is transformed, adversities are quelled; and negative situations are altered to conform with God's perfect will for me, in Jesus' Name. By faith, I receive an imparta-tion of the glory into my spirit and believe that I'm catapulted into the higher realms of glory. I therefore receive the grace to radiate the effulgence of God's glory upon humanity in the furthest extremes of the world. By faith, I believe I'm illuminated by the effulgence of God's glory and now I'm rightly positioned and ready to propagate the world with the glory of God. I therefore declare and decree that I'm the ark of God's glory on earth. I'm loaded with high voltage of God's glory, marinated to the depths of His presence and filled to the brick of full spiritual capacity with the electrifying power of God's glory. I proclaim and pronounce that I live, operate and function in the realm of glory, where sickness, disease, infirmity or death is not permitted to reign.

I'm the effulgence of God's glory, beauty and grace. I'm conscious of the supernatural life of Glory in me; therefore greatness, excellence and success are in my spirit! And through my words and actions to-day, I'm unveiling the glory, virtues and perfections of divinity de-posited in my spirit to my world! I'm a peculiar treasure unto God, born anew with the supernatural life of glory, excellence and power in my spirit! In my words and actions today, I'm showing forth the wonderful deeds, and displaying the excellences of my heavenly Fa-ther, who has called me unto glory, honour and excellence. Therefore, I declare that my life is for your glory, and I show forth your virtues, excellence, perfections, and beauty, in Jesus' Name. I carry in my heart the divine attributes of divinity, and I bless my world today, with your glory that I carry, in Jesus' Name. My life is the expression of the glory of Christ; He's unveiled in me to my world today! The divine life is manifested through me, and I bring others into this life through the Gospel. I live in the consciousness of my divine life and origin in Christ, knowing that His wisdom, ability, and power are working in, and through me, in Jesus' Name. I have the life and nature—a life of glory, dominion and excellence; free of sickness, disease and infirmities. I walk in the reality of this truth today.

Thank you for making me such a wonder in this world and a miracle worker to launch the world into greater depths of the miraculous. Thank you for making me a peculiar treasure unto you, and for making me the custodian of eternal verities. I recognize myself as one charged with the divine responsibility of influencing my world with the glory of God and I diligently carry out this glorious ministry in Jesus' Name. I extol your majesty for making me an expression of divine personality. As Jesus is now, so am I in this world. Therefore, at every opportunity, I express the character of Christ; His love and impeccable nature of righteousness in me, to the world, in Jesus' Name. Amen. I ascribe unto thee all the glory, Honour and Power due your name.

PROPHETIC ACTION:

Begin to pray in the Holy Ghost right now, to activate the glory that has already been imparted into your spirit, Glory to Jesus!

Congratulations!
And Welcome to the Glory Realm!

PRAYER FOR SALVATION

If you have never received Jesus Christ as your Lord and Personal saviour, loudly recite the following prayer, now:

> *Dear Heavenly Father! I present my life before you today. I confess with my mouth that Jesus Christ is Lord and believe in my heart that He died on the cross and was raised from the dead after 3 days, for the remission of my sins. I acknowledge that I'm a sinner and ask you to forgive me for all the sins I have ever committed. Wash me with the precious blood of Jesus Christ and write my name in the Book of life. I therefore receive eternal life into my spirit right now. I declare that from henceforth, Jesus Christ is my Lord and Saviour and I proclaim His Lorship over every area of my life. Thank you Lord Jesus Christ for saving my soul. I'm now a child of God, born again, born of the Spirit of the living God.*

Congratulations and Welcome to the family of God. You are now a brand new creation that belongs to the lineage of the blessed, the Royal priesthood, the Chosen generation and the highly favoured! Most importantly, you have now received the divine legitimate right, authority and power to operate in higher realms of glory, glory to Jesus!

ABOUT THE AUTHOR

Frequency Revelator is an apostle, called by God through His grace to minister the Gospel of the Lord Jesus Christ to all the nations of the world. He is a television minister, lecturer and gifted author, whose writings are Holy Ghost breathings that unveil consistent streams of fresh revelations straight from the Throne Room of Heaven. He is the president, founder and vision bearer of Frequency Revelator Ministries (FRM), a worldwide multiracial ministry that encompasses a myriad of movements with divine visions such as Resurrection Embassy (*The Global Church*), Christ Resurrection Movement (CRM) (*a Global movement for raising the dead*), the Global Apostolic & Prophetic Network (GAP) (*a Network of apostles, prophets and fivefold ministers across the globe*), Revival For Southern Africa (REFOSA) (*a Regional power-packed vision for Southern Africa*) and the Global Destiny Publishing House (GDP) (*the Ministry's publishing company*). The primary vision of this global ministry is to propagate the resurrection power of Christ from the Throne Room of Heaven to the extreme ends of the world and to launch the world into the greater depths of the miraculous. It is for this reason that Frequency Revelator Ministries (FRM) drives divergent apostolic and prophetic ministry visions and spiritual programmes such as the Global School of Resurrection (GSR), Global Resurrection Centre (GRC), the Global Healing Centre (GHC), Global School of Miracles, Signs and Wonders (SMSW), Global School of Kingdom Millionaires (SKM), Global Campus Ministry as well as Resurrection Conferences, Seminars and Training Centres. To fulfil its global mandate of soul winning, the ministry spearheads the Heavens' Broadcasting Commission (HBC) on television, a strategic ministerial initiative that broadcasts ministry programmes via the Dead Raising Channel *(a.k.a Resurrection TV)* and other Christian Television networks around the world.

Presiding over a global network of apostolic and prophetic visions, Apostle Frequency Revelator considers universities, colleges, high schools and other centres of learning as critical in fulfilling God's purpose and reaching the world for Christ, especially in this end-time season. As a Signs and Wonders Movement, the ministry hosts training sessions at the Global School of Resurrection (GSR) which includes but not limited to, impartation and activation of the gifts of the Spirit, prophetic declaration and ministration, invocations of open visions, angelic encounters and Throne Room visitations, revelational teachings, coaching and mentorship as well as Holy Ghost ministerial training sessions on how to practically raise the dead. This global ministry is therefore characterised by a deep revelation of God's word accompanied by a practical demonstration of God's power through miracles, signs and wonders manifested in raising cripples from wheel chairs, opening the eyes of the blind, unlocking the speech of the dumb, blasting off the ears of the deaf and raising the dead, as a manifestation of the finished works of the cross by the Lord Jesus Christ. The ministry is also punctuated with a plethora of manifestations of the wealth of Heaven through miracle money, coupled with the golden rain of gold dust, silver stones, diamonds, supernatural oil and a torrent of creative miracles such as the development of the original blue print of body parts on bodily territories where they previously did not exist, germination of hair on bald heads, weight loss and gain, as well as instantaneous healings from HIV/AIDS, cancer, diabetes and every manner of sickness and disease which doctors have declared as incurable.

The author has written a collection of 21 anointed books, which include *The Realm of Power to Raise the Dead, How to become a Kingdom Millionaire, Deeper Revelations of The Anointing, Practical Demonstrations of The Anointing, How to Operate in the Realm of the Miraculous, The Realm of Glory, Unveiling the Mystery of Miracle Money, New Revelations of Faith, A Divine Revelation of the Supernatural Realm, The Prophetic Move of the Holy Spirit in the Contemporary Global Arena, The Ministry of Angels in the World Today, Kingdom Spiritual Laws and Principles, Divine Rights and Privileges of a Believer, Keys to Unlocking the Supernatural, The Prophetic Dimension, The Dynamics of God's Word, The Practice of God's Presence, Times of Refreshing and Restoration, The Power of Praying in the Throne Room, The End Time Revelations of Jesus Christ and Rain of Revelations,* which is a daily devotional concordance comprising a yearly record of 365 fresh revelations straight from the Throne Room of God.

Apostle Frequency Revelator resides in South Africa and he is a graduate of Fort Hare University, where his ministry took off. However, as a global minister, his ministry incorporates prophecy, deliverance and miracle healing crusades in the United Kingdom (UK), Southern Africa, India, Australia, USA, Canada and a dense network of ministry visions that covers the rest of the world. As a custodian of God's resurrection power, the apostle has been given a divine mandate from Heaven to raise a new breed of Apostles, Prophets, Pastors, Evangelists, Teachers, Kingdom Millionaires and Miracle Workers (*Dead raisers*) who shall propagate the world with the gospel of the Lord Jesus Christ and practically demonstrate His resurrection power through miracles, signs and wonders manifested in raising people from the dead, thereby launching the world in to the greater depths of the miraculous. To that effect, a conducive platform is therefore enacted for global impartation, mentorship, training and equipping ministers of the gospel for the work of ministry. Notable is the realisation that the ministry ushers a new wave of signs and wonders that catapults the Body of Christ into higher realms of glory in which raising the dead is a common occurrence and demonstrating the viscocity of the glory of God in a visible and tangible manner is the order of the day. Hence, in this book, Apostle Frequency Revelator presents a practical model of how one can tap into deeper territories of the Glory Realm to harnesss God's glory, impact the nations of the world and usher an unprecedented avalanche of billions of souls into the Kingdom, Glory to Jesus! May His Name be gloried, praised and honoured forever more!

AUTHOR'S CONTACT INFORMATION:

To know more about the ministry of Apostle Frequency Revelator, his publications, revelational teachings, global seminars, ministry schools, ministry products and Global missions, contact:

Apostle Frequency Revelator

@ Resurrection Embassy

(The Global Church)

Powered by Christ Resurrection Movement (CRM)

(Contact us in the United Kingdom, South Africa, USA, Canada, Australia, India, Holland & Other nations of the world).

As a Global Vision, The Ministry of Apostle Frequency Revelator is present in all the continents of the World. You may contact us from any part of the world so that we can refer you to the Resident Ministry Pastors and Associates in respective nations. Our offices and those of the ministry's publishing company (Global Destiny Publishing House (GDP House), are ready to dispatch any books requested from any part of the world.

Email:

frequency.revelator@gmail.com

Cell phone:

+27622436745

+27797921646/ +27785416006

Website:

www.globaldestinypublishers.co.za

Social Media Contacts:

The Author is also accessible on Social media via Facebook, twitter, instagram, YouTube, and other latest forms of social networks, as Apostle Frequency Revelator. For direct communication with the Apostle, you may invite him on facebook and read his daily posts. You may also watch Apostle Frequency Revelator on the Dead Raising Channel a.k.a Resurrection TV and other Christian Television channels in your area.

Christian products:

You may also purchase DVDs, CDs, MP3s and possibly order all of the 21 anointed books published by Apostle Frequency Revelator, either as hard cover books or e-books. E-books are available on amazon.com, Baines & Nobles, create space, Kalahari.net and other e-book sites. You may also buy them directly from the author@ www.gdphouse.co.za. You may also request a collection of all powerful, revelational teachings by Apostle Frequency Revelator and we will promptly deliver them to you.

Ministry Networks & Partnerships:

If you want to partner with Apostle Frequency Revelator in executing this Global vision, partnership is available through divergent apostolic and prophetic ministry visions and spiritual programmes such as the Global School of Resurrection (GSR), Christ Resurrection Movement (CRM), Resurrection TV (a.k.a The Dead Raising Channel), the Global Apostolic & Prophetic Network (GAP), Global Resurrection Centre (GRC), the Global Healing Centre (GHC), Global School of Miracles, Signs and Wonders (SMSW), School of Kingdom Millionaires (SKM), Global Campus Ministry and other avenues. By partnering with Apostle Frequency Revelator, you are in a way joining hands with God's vision and thus setting yourself up for a life of increase, acceleration and superabundance.

GLOBAL MISSIONS, PARTNERSHIPS & Collaborations:

Should you be impacted and catapulted to the higher realms of glory following the reading of this book, please share your testimony with Apostle Frequency Revelator at the contacts above, so that you can strengthen other believers' faith in God all around the world. Your testimony will also be included in the next edition of this book.

If you want to invite Apostle Frequency Revelator to your church, city or community to come and spearhead Resurrection Seminars, Conferences, Dead Raising Training Sessions or conduct a Global School of Resurrection (GSR), whether in (Europe, Australia, Canada, USA, South America, Asia or Africa), you are welcome to do so.

If you want to start a Resurrection Centre or establish the Global School of Resurrection (GSR) in your church, city or community under this movement, you are also welcome to do so. We will be more than willing to send Copies of this book to whichever continent you live.

If you want your church or ministry to be part of the Christ Resurrection Movement (CRM) and join the bandwagon of raising the dead all around the world, you are welcome to be part of this Heaven-ordained commission.

If you want more copies of this book so that you can use them in your church for seminars, teachings, conferences, cell groups and global distribution, please don't hesitate to contact Apostle Frequency Revelator so that he can send the copies to whichever continent you are. Upon completion of this book, you may also visit www.amazon.com and under the "Book Review Section," write a brief review, commenting on how this book has impacted your life. This is meant to encourage readership by other believers all around the world.

If you want to donate or give freely to advance this global vision, you may also do so via our ministry website (wwww.resurrectionembassy.org) or contact us at the details provided above. If you need a spiritual covering, impartation or mentorship for your Church or ministry as led by the Holy Spirit, you are welcome to contact us and join the league of dead-raising pastors that we are already mentoring in all continents of the world.

If you have a burning message that you would like to share with the whole world and you would want Apostle Frequency Revelator to help you turn your divine ideas and revelations into script and publish your first book, don't hesitate to contact us and submit a draft of your manuscript at the Global Destiny Publishing House (www.gdphouse.co.za). We will thoroughly polish your script and turn it into an amazing book filled with Throne Room revelations that will impact millions across the globe, glory to Jesus!

The Lord Jesus Christ is coming back soon!